PPP DESIGN, IMPLEMENTATION, and DEBUGGING

SECOND EDITION

PPP DESIGN, IMPLEMENTATION, and DEBUGGING

SECOND EDITION

James Carlson

 ADDISON–WESLEY

Boston • San Francisco • New York • Toronto • Montreal
London • Munich • Paris • Madrid
Capetown • Sydney • Tokyo • Singapore • Mexico City

Many of the designations used by manufacturers and sellers to distinguish their products are claimed as trademarks. Where those designations appear in this book and we were aware of a trademark claim, the designations have been printed with initial capital letters.

The publisher offers discounts on this book when ordered in quantity for special sales.

The author and publisher have taken care in preparation of this book, but make no expressed or implied warranty of any kind and assume no responsibility for errors or omissions. No liability is assumed for incidental or consequential damages in connection with or arising out of the use of the information or programs contained herein.

For more information, please contact:

Pearson Education Corporate Sales Division
One Lake Street
Upper Saddle River, NJ 07458
(800) 382-3419
corpsales@pearsontechgroup.com

Visit AW on the Web: www.awl.com/cseng/

Library of Congress Cataloging-in-Publication Data
Carlson, James.
    PPP design, implementation, and debugging / James Carlson.—2nd ed.
      p. cm.
    Includes bibliographical references and index.
    ISBN 0-201-70053-0
    1. PPP (Computer network protocol) I. Title.
    TK5105.582. C37 2000
    004.6'2—dc21   00-040627

ISBN 0–201–70053–0
Text printed on recycled paper
1 2 3 4 5 6 7 8 9 10—CRS—0403020100

First printing July 2000

For Beth, Madeline, and
our second addition, Ben

Contents

Acknowledgments

Although this book has only one name on the cover, many people have contributed time, effort, and material toward its publication. First and foremost, I thank my wife Beth, our daughter Madeline, and our son Benjamin for their patience and understanding during the months this project has taken and for the lost hours every night and weekend.

Many reviewers and contributors made this book more readable, more complete, and more accurate than I ever expected. Thanks are due to Fred Baker, Paolo Bevilacqua, John Bray, Miguel Cruz, Craig Estey, Craig Fox, Gary Greenberg, Terrance Hodgins, Michael Hunter, Marco S. Hyman, J. S. Jensen, Frank Kastenholz, Patrick Klos, Al Longyear, John P. Matias, Art Mellor, Bill Melohn, John Nagle, Bill Palter, Marc C. Poulin, Paul Raison, Scott Reeve, Craig Richards, William Allen Simpson, Mike Taillon, William Mark Townsley, Andrew Valencia, and Rohit Verma. A special thank you goes to Vernon Schryver, who has gone above and beyond the call of duty as a reviewer to take the time to explain patiently many of the more esoteric ideas.

Special thanks are also due to the good folks at Addison-Wesley who have seen this project through: my editor, Mary Hart; Executive Editor Karen Gettman; and all of the artists, publicists, marketers, and other people behind the scenes who get the job done.

Finally, thanks to Richard Stallman for all the tools.

This book was written on AIX 4.1.5 using emacs-19.30 and xfig-3.1 for drawings, then composed in Quark Version 3.32. No Wintel PCs were harmed during the production of this work.

Preface to the Second Edition

When I say writing, O, believe me, it is rewriting that I have chiefly in mind.
—ROBERT LOUIS STEVENSON

Since the first edition of *PPP Design and Debugging* went to press a little over two years ago, PPP itself has matured greatly. Just two years ago it was common to see proposals for additions to PPP on the IETF mailing lists and rare to find designers with direct experience in the protocol itself. Now the situation is reversed. The working group is now focusing on advancing the existing extensions through the standards process rather than creating new extensions, and many people are now familiar with the protocol.

In the past two years, I have collected hundreds of notes on various implementation particulars, new developments, and other issues. These update nearly every page of this book. Also in this edition I have expanded the information about PPP's links to the outside world, including details on various physical layer technologies such as SONET/SDH, security services such as RADIUS, and other protocols such as L2TP. I also describe in detail one particular implementation—Paul Mackerras' freely available ppp-2.3.

Introduction

I hate quotations. Tell me what you know.
—RALPH WALDO EMERSON

Today, when most users think of Point-to-Point Protocol (PPP), they probably think of personal computers (PCs), modems, and surfing the Internet. PPP, however, is a much broader protocol that is used to transfer data between diverse kinds of computers and computing systems, such as routers, satellites, and mainframes. This one protocol has the ability to span from the lowest to the highest data rates in use and is compatible with almost every networking technology ever developed.

This book covers PPP from the bits and bytes transmitted through the connections to other networking software. Along the way, it gives guidance in the often confusing array of standards documents and tips for debugging PPP connections and implementations.

It does not give many specific details on particular interfaces, such as modem drivers, since these interfaces are quite numerous and are well covered in other books. Nor does it pretend to replace the Request for Comments documents (RFCs), because these documents are both easily available and very detailed. Instead, this book works as a companion alongside the operating system reference works of your choosing and the aforementioned public documents.

There have been several waves of advancement in computing techniques, although these advances have hardly been linear. In fact, the pattern for most of these advances is quite regular and repeats often. The first advances were often made by researchers and mainframe computer users and then were either rediscovered or borrowed by minicomputer and workstation users and finally by microcomputer users. Each generation, of course, leaves its own mark on the technology, but the pattern remains the same.

Packet Switching Networks

The history of machine-to-machine communication is similar to the development of computing in general. Leonard Kleinrock's 1961 Ph.D. Thesis, "Information Flow in Large Communication Nets,"[1] is regarded as the first published paper on packet switching theory. This paper influenced the initial research done by the U.S. Defense Department's Advanced Research Projects Agency, or ARPA, in the 1960s. From this effort came the ARPANET research network.

In the commercial world, mainframe and public network communications developed many of the concepts important to networking in general, such as routing and layering, in the 1960s. This work led to numerous incompatible protocols, which were somewhat simplified by standardization efforts in 1974 by the Comité Consultatif International de Télégraphique et Téléphonique's (CCITT's) X.25 suite and International Business Machine's (IBM's) Systems Network Architecture (SNA).

In the research world, Robert Kahn began work on a successor to the ARPANET's Network Control Protocol (NCP) in 1973. He and Vint Cerf designed what eventually became TCP/IP (Transmission Control Protocol/Internet Protocol). DARPA, the former ARPA, issued contracts to implement TCP/IP on various systems. One of those implementations, by Bolt, Beranek, and Newman (BBN), was ported into the Unix variant under development at the University of California at Berkeley (UCB) and then widely disseminated. This implementation became the reference standard for TCP/IP. By 1983, the old NCP was shut down on all ARPANET nodes simultaneously, and TCP/IP became the only Internet protocol.

Commercial efforts toward proprietary networking included Xerox's XNS (Xerox Network Systems) in the late 1970s, Novell's later IPX (Internet Packet Exchange; actually just a direct copy of XNS), and Apple's AppleTalk. The International Organization for Standardization (ISO), which continued the CCITT's work, created the CLNP-based Open Systems Interconnect (OSI) protocols for public networking.

Few of these protocols are in use today. The IP-based protocols developed by the DARPA researchers have proven more scalable, interoperable, and practical than any of the protocols developed previously or since. This is due in part to the way in which IP makes delegation of authority possible and, to a great degree, the foresight of the people who built the organizations that allocate addresses and names.

1. Available from his Web site at http://www.lk.cs.ucla.edu/LK/Bib/.

Dial-Up File Transfer Protocols

For most Unix users, machine communication began in the 1970s with a series of protocols called UUCP (Unix-to-Unix Copy Protocol), which eventually developed into a robust and widespread automatic file and electronic mail (e-mail) transfer protocol built out of an ad hoc network of machines. Many of the services that people now refer to as parts of "the Internet," including the bulletin-board-like news groups known as "usenet" and e-mail, were actually developed using this automated file transfer protocol.

For small computers, communication began with file transfer protocols, such as Ward Christiansen's X Modem. This simple protocol allowed two computers to exchange a single file at a time using a simplex protocol. Later innovations, such as Chuck Forsberg's Z Modem, extended this idea to higher speeds by omitting the positive acknowledgments used in a traditional simplex protocol and reporting only negative acknowledgments, at the expense of protocol resilience in the face of congestion and buffering. These protocols led to an explosion of interest among PC users in Bulletin Board Systems (BBSs).

At the same time, others were developing protocols for both the new PCs and larger computers, such as Kermit and BLAST (Blocked Asynchronous Transmission), that borrowed the networking concept of *windowing*. Windowing permits a set number of acknowledgments to remain outstanding at a given time, thus mitigating the effects of transmission buffering, latency, and occasional data corruption. Notably among these, Columbia University's Kermit also permitted remote execution of commands via extensions to the file transfer protocol.

All of these special-purpose file transfer protocols are asymmetric. One side, usually called a *client,* requests actions such as the transferring of a file, and the other side, called a *server,* performs the requested actions. This design is therefore known as a *client/server* design.

Dial-Up Networking

In the Unix world, TCP/IP began gaining ground against the file transfer protocols faster than the supporting telecommunications technologies could be developed. Although 3MB and then 10MB Ethernets and many proprietary schemes were available for local networks, the only means of communicating over distance was either leased lines or primitive dial-up modems. These connections were either single-user and terminal-oriented or were expensive and used for bulk file transfer.

Leased lines are synchronous digital links, which means that they operate as a continuous stream of raw data bits, and are usually quite expensive. Thus, they were usually connected to equally expensive dedicated routers. The standards for data networking were first set by a babel of incompatible proprietary synchronous protocols, summarized in RFC 1547 Section 4.3, which include Cisco, Proteon, Ungermann-Bass, and Wellfleet variations on High-level Data Link Control (HDLC).

Unlike a leased line, a modem generally provides an asynchronous (start/ stop, or character-at-a-time) interface. To make use of dial-up modems for packet-oriented networking, a simple protocol called SLIP (Serial Line Internet Protocol) was developed at UCB. This protocol is easily described and implemented. To transmit a raw IP datagram, it is first expanded by replacing any byte equal to hexadecimal C0 with the sequence DB DC, and any byte equal to DB with DB DD; then the modified IP datagram is transmitted, preceded and followed by C0 as framing. This process is easily reversed at the other end of the link to produce an IP datagram. If the data are ever corrupted, synchronization can always be achieved by looking for the next C0, since this marks the beginning of a packet and will never occur in the user's data. RFC 1055, which documents SLIP, is only six pages long. Note that this protocol requires a hardware link that can transmit arbitrary 8-bit bytes without modification.

The data networking protocols, such as SLIP and the proprietary HDLC variations, are fundamentally different from the file transfer protocols. Notice that it is not at all obvious from the description given how one would send e-mail over these protocols, or even transfer a file between two computers reliably, even though the description above is complete. With these protocols, all that you are given is an unreliable means of transmitting packets from one computer to another over a serial line.

In the networking world, this difference is called *layering*. In the old file transfer programs, the definitions of the protocols included such things as detecting the start of the data, recovering from errors, and signaling the file name to the receiver, all in the same protocol. With networking, there are instead application programs (such as file transfer) that use the services of transport protocols (such as TCP) that, in turn, run on network protocols (such as IP), and finally on top of link-level protocols (such as SLIP). Each of these protocols is separately implemented, performs a separate function, and is described in a separate document.

There are many advantages to this technique, including the ability to use old applications on the latest network devices and to develop and migrate between networking protocols and applications without disturbing the link layer. This means that design and development of each part of the system can continue independently, unlike the more primitive file transfer protocols, which usually required a complete rewrite to support enhanced error-control algorithms or new media types.

Notice also that, unlike the client/server file transfer protocols, the data networking protocols are inherently symmetric. Neither side is defined to be the client or the server. Such protocols are termed *peer-to-peer*, since both sides of the link are equal parties to the conversation and both may request and perform actions.

PPP owes much to SLIP and the proprietary HDLC protocols. The marketplace for dial-up Internet connectivity, which has driven much of the developmental work on PPP, would not exist if it were not for SLIP; many of the important algorithms in use with PPP were first developed for the other protocols; and most of the important design mistakes were learned by using all of these links. When the groups that were working separately on the next generation of SLIP and on a common router-to-router synchronous protocol were merged, this history was recorded in a document that was eventually published as RFC 1547.

Unlike many of the other so-called standards of the microcomputer and minicomputer world, including SLIP, PPP was developed by a standards body. The Internet Engineering Task Force (IETF), which has guided PPP development, is made up of representatives from industry, telecommunications, academia, and user groups. It is an open group; anyone with an interest in setting the standards is free to participate.

The rules of the IETF are a little different from those of other standards bodies, such as the International Telecommunications Union (ITU) and the ISO. Unlike these bodies, the IETF is not a membership organization and has no political standing. The IETF has instead fostered a culture in which it is far more important to produce a working protocol than it is to produce documents with which all participants agree. Unlike the other standards bodies, it is common for IETF participants to discuss their prototype implementations and experimental results at the same time the protocols are being written.

This environment produces specifications that are usually rather brief and very dense in subject matter, and documentation that is scattered among a large number of documents that do not necessarily refer to each other. It also occasionally produces experiments that turn out to be dead ends. One of the aims of this book is to tie all of these documents together for PPP and illustrate some of the important but unwritten concepts.

PPP, like all other network protocols, exists as a layer between two other layers of the protocol stack. Below it is the hardware interface, which must be some kind of bidirectional data stream, and above it are the network-layer protocols, such as IP, IPX, and DDP (Datagram Delivery Protocol, for AppleTalk). These connections are illustrated diagrammatically in Figure 1.1. Support of multiple simultaneous network protocols in this way was a goal of the PPP working group because it was once believed that future networks would support many protocols at once rather than just IP.

PPP, the bulk of which is described in RFCs 1661 and 1662, borrows part of High-level Data Link Control (HDLC) from the telecommunications world for its low-level interface, although it restricts the feature set that is usable in a conforming implementation and extends many features of the protocol through the use of negotiable options. By using HDLC, it can run on hardware that cannot properly deal with certain byte sequences. It does not, however, go so far as to allow the use of the HDLC-defined mechanism for running on hardware that cannot transfer full 8-bit bytes, as do Kermit and Z Modem.

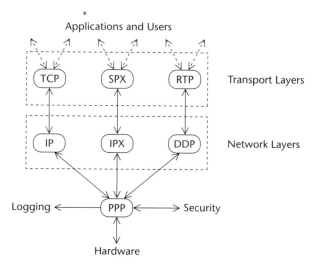

FIGURE 1.1 Networking Layers with PPP

Thus, PPP has the following basic set of features and limitations for synchronous lines.

- It can be used with standard HDLC controllers.
- It is defined only for point-to-point links; any kind of multidrop usage is a proprietary extension due to address restrictions.
- It can coexist with other HDLC-based protocols on the same link only if the other protocols are restricted in address usage. (In practice, it does not coexist well with other HDLC protocols and is usually run atop or in place of those protocols.)

For asynchronous lines, PPP has a different set of features and limitations, as follows:

- It can be run on lines that use software flow control and are unable to transfer some binary values.
- It cannot be run on lines that do not support full 8-bit bytes without nonstandard extensions.
- Defines error-detection mechanisms and multiprotocol support that were missing from SLIP.

For the network-layer protocols, PPP presents a packet-oriented interface, and it can provide sequencing and reliability if needed (although it typically does not), as well as data encryption and compression.

PPP also has relationships with certain applications that provide services for PPP in an implementation-dependent manner. For instance, a dial-up communications server may need to use RADIUS (Remote Authentication Dial-In User Service), TACACS (Terminal Access Controller Access Control System), or ACP (Access Control Protocol) to verify the dial-up peer's identity or to obtain network addresses for negotiation. It may also have implementation-dependent relationships with protocols such as Dynamic Host Configuration Protocol (DHCP) and Domain Name Service (DNS) for address allocation and name resolution, syslog and other logging devices for tracking of errors, and encryption key servers for secure communications.

Throughout this book, data values are given in hexadecimal unless otherwise noted. Equivalences for these values in decimal and octal are given in Appendix B.

PPP Communication Basics

IN THIS CHAPTER

This chapter provides all of the background necessary to understand the rest of this book. In it, we cover the link-level details of transmission and reception of PPP data and how PPP connects to the rest of a networking stack. Subsequent chapters go into detail on the PPP internals—the overall PPP state machines, each protocol within PPP, and variant forms of transmission. Remember that all values are in hexadecimal unless otherwise noted.

How PPP Fits In

Figure 2.1 shows how a PPP implementation might be connected in a system using TCP/IP. PPP is a network interface and is similar to Ethernet in capabilities. Note that since PPP is not a broadcast interface, Address Resolution Protocol (ARP) does not run over PPP. Some implementations, however, emulate an Ethernet via PPP and require special tests to generate fake ARP replies.

The components that make up PPP—the Link Control Protocol (LCP), the authentication protocols, and the Network Control Protocols (NCPs)[1]—will be covered in detail in later chapters.

---

1. PPP's NCPs are not related to the obsolete ARPANET protocol also called NCP.

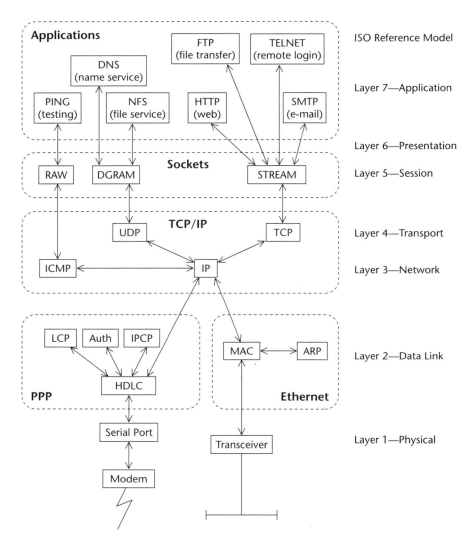

FIGURE 2.1 PPP in a complete system

Media

PPP runs on virtually all media that are full-duplex in nature and can be modified to run on some that are half-duplex.

The two principal means of communication on serial lines are *synchronous* and *asynchronous*. Asynchronous line hardware, usually called a UART (Universal

Asynchronous Receiver/Transmitter), can send and receive one character at a time. Synchronous line hardware, sometimes called a USART (Universal Synchronous/Asynchronous Receiver/Transmitter) or framer, can send or receive a variable-length block of bytes at one time. These two techniques are used over a wide variety of electrical interfaces. A few of these interfaces (all full-duplex) are as follows.

- EIA RS-232, an electrical and cabling standard that has little to say about the bit-level protocols used. It uses the familiar "D"-shaped 25-pin connectors (or sometimes the nine-pin variant found on PCs). Traditionally, however, RS-232 is used to carry asynchronous serial traffic, like the connection from a PC to a modem. On some equipment, RS-232 is used for synchronous data. The standard allows for data rates through 9,600bps, but common implementations run as fast as 230.4Kbps for short cable lengths.
- RS-422, a lower-voltage and higher-speed cabling standard similar in many respects to RS-232.
- RS-485, a multidrop version of RS-422. PPP requires proprietary, although obvious and simple, modifications to run point-to-point in a multidrop system.
- V.35, a common interface used for synchronous lines over short distances from 9,600bps (DS0-B) up through 2Mbps (E1).
- HSSI (High Speed Serial Interface), a less-common serial interface defined by EIA-613 that uses a 50-pin connector and runs at data rates through 52Mbps, but is usually run at 34.368Mbps (E3), 44.736Mbps (T3), or 51.84Mbps (OC-1). The connector is similar in appearance to a SCSI-2 connector.
- BRI S/T, one of the ISDN (Integrated Services Digital Network) interfaces (BRI stands for Basic Rate ISDN). It is a four-wire interface that is usually used with RJ-45 connectors (which are similar to but wider than the RJ-11 modular jacks used with standard household telephone wiring) and runs two synchronous channels at 64Kbps each plus a third at 16Kbps. The other common interface (or *reference point* in telecommunications jargon) for BRI is the U interface, which connects the Network Termination (NT1) to the Central Office (CO).
- T1/E1, standard electrical (or *metallic*) telecommunications interfaces. Both are synchronous and carry a data rate called DS1. T1 (used in the United States, Canada, Japan, Hong Kong, and Taiwan) is usually wired with four wire circuits and RJ-48 connectors and runs at 1.544Mbps with at most

1.536Mbps available for user data. E1 (used in most of the rest of the world) is sometimes wired with coaxial cable and runs at 2.048Mbps with 1.984Mbps available. Besides T1 and E1, the DS1 format can also be carried on optical (or *photonic*) interfaces. PPP is also used on PRI (Primary Rate ISDN) lines. PRI runs over DS1, and therefore on T1 and E1 lines.

- OC-3, an optical telecommunications interface. In a common configuration, the data stream is called STS-3c and runs at 155.52Mbps with 149.76Mbps available to PPP. This interface can be channelized in a large number of ways. For instance, it can carry three STS-1 (OC-1) streams or 84 DS1s.

In addition to the physical interfaces listed above, PPP is also used on several interfaces provided by other protocols. In general, these encapsulations of PPP are similar in operation and use hex CF as a frame type [Network Layer Protocol ID (NLPID)] to identify PPP. These interfaces are as follows.

- PPP in Frame Relay, described in RFC 1973, requires little more than a modification of the standard PPP address and control fields.
- PPP in X.25, described in RFC 1598, is a bit more complex since X.25 includes a fragmentation/reassembly function and message sequencing.
- PPP over FUNI (Frame User Network Interface), described in RFC 2363, is similar to Frame Relay but provides direct access to Asynchronous Transfer Mode (ATM) networks.
- PPP over AAL-5 (ATM Adaptation Layer 5), described in RFC 2364, puts PPP directly over the AAL-5 Common Part Convergence Sublayer (CPCS).

A wide variety of other standards may come into play when working with PPP, depending on the hardware in use. For instance, modern modems implement V.42bis for data compression, V.42 for error correction, V.90 for the actual modulation, and V.8 for negotiation. On some hosts, there are also interface standards that must be followed. For instance, on PCs running Microsoft software, a standard known as *plug and play* is used for communicating with hardware, such as modems. (See Chapter 11 for references to other books that may be helpful in understanding these other standards.)

On ISDN, Frame Relay, X.25, and ATM, many other standard signaling protocols are used in addition to PPP. These include Q.931 for ISDN, FRF.4 for Frame Relay, and Q.2931 for ATM. These standards are far more complex for software to support and essentially represent separate networking protocol implementations run in parallel with PPP and TCP/IP.

HDLC

PPP is built atop a restricted subset of the standard HDLC protocol, so a description of that protocol's features first will be helpful. HDLC operates conceptually in two stages—frame formation followed by medium-dependent frame transmission—although typical implementations mix these two together for efficiency.

Taking frame formation first, an HDLC frame consists of three variable-length fields and one fixed-length field (Figure 2.2). The fixed-length check value is usually a standard Cyclic Redundancy Check (CRC) over the preceding three fields and occupies the last two or four octets. Putting this value last allows optimized generation of the CRC in most implementations, as we will see later. This number is transmitted least significant octet first, also known as *little-endian,* even though all other networking values are normally *big-endian.* This is done because the CRC is defined to be calculated bitwise on the data transmitted, and all common media, with the notable exception of Synchronous Optical Network/Synchronous Digital Hierarchy (SONET/SDH), transmit data least significant bit (LSB) first. By preserving this ordering in the transmission of the CRC itself, the residue calculated over any intact packet is always equal to a constant.

In the basic HDLC frame, address and control are each single octets. They may alternatively be used in an extended mode, where the address and control fields are each single integers of variable length. In extended mode addressing, the HDLC protocol reserves the LSB as a flag (often called *Poll/Final*) to indicate whether or not more octets follow; a 0 bit means that more octets follow while a 1 bit indicates the last octet. For example, the decimal value 533 (hex 215) would be sent as an HDLC-encoded integer as the sequence 08 2B, formed as shown in Figure 2.3. Of course, all sequences of the form 00 . . . 00 08 2B would logically be equivalent, since leading zeros would not change the value of the number. By definition, however, ISO/IEC 3309 reserves the use of a single 0 octet address as the "no stations" address, so padding with zeros in this manner is not legal.

The address field is intended for multidrop links, so the devices on the link need examine only the first N octets, up to the first octet with an LSB of 1, in

FIGURE 2.2 HDLC frame

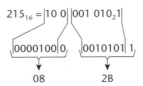

FIGURE 2.3 HDLC integer encoding

order to identify frames intended for that device. Decimal address 127 (encoded as FF including the Poll/Final bit) is reserved to mean "all-stations" or "broadcast." (Note that this is often, and incorrectly, assumed by many sources to be address 255.) The control field specifies a type of message. Its primary purpose is to distinguish frames used for error and flow control when using higher-level protocols such as Link Access Procedure–Balanced (LAP-B).

The variable-length HDLC information field consists simply of those bits following the control field and preceding the check value. Its contents depend on the application used but are generally filled with user data.

Since PPP uses standard HDLC medium-dependent frame transmission, this will be discussed after the following section on PPP's use of HDLC. (For more information on HDLC itself, see ISO 3309 and 4335.)

HDLC and PPP

PPP restricts its use of the general HDLC protocol in the following ways, as described in RFC 1662.

- The HDLC address field is fixed to the octet FF (all stations).
- The HDLC control field is fixed to the octet 03 (unnumbered information).
- The receiver must be prepared to accept an HDLC information field of 1,502 octets.
- The HDLC information field is constrained to an integer multiple of 8 bits in length.
- Seven Bit Data Path Transparency (SBDPT) defined in ISO/IEC 3309 is not used.

A device using PPP may accept the variable-length HDLC integer fields, but any interoperable implementation must default to transmitting only the fields as described above. Note that variable-length fields are used when PPP over Frame Relay is used and when RFC 1663 "reliable transmission" ("Numbered Mode") operation is selected. See Chapter 3 for more information on Numbered Mode.

PPP also adds a third variable-length HDLC-like extended mode integer at the start of the HDLC information field (immediately following the control value). However, to cause all values that follow to fall on four-octet (32-bit) boundaries, this value is constrained to a two-octet representation by default, including a zero-octet pad if necessary. (Most modern system architectures permit faster operation if data are kept on even boundaries. This is why alignment should always be considered when protocol headers are designed.)

Although the PPP protocol field very much resembles the other HDLC integer values, the PPP specification avoids describing the encoding and decoding process by simply declaring and using all values in their encoded forms. Thus, for example, you will read about protocol 00 21 (IP) for PPP, instead of protocol (decimal) 16 as you might for other HDLC-based protocols. The lack of this encoding description is a hazard for the unwary designer who does not read Section 2 of RFC 1661 very carefully when assigning new protocol numbers. [In fact, such an error was made during the design of the Shiva Password Authentication Protocol (SPAP) security protocol, and the protocol number had to be reassigned after the implementation was in the field. Such errors are very difficult to correct.]

PPP's information field, as defined in RFC 1661, follows this PPP protocol field. From now on we will refer only to PPP's information field, and not the HDLC information field that also includes the PPP protocol field. The final structure is shown in Figure 2.4.

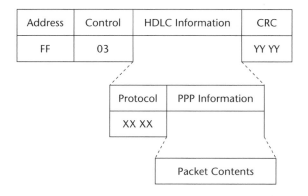

FIGURE 2.4 PPP frame format

PPP Framing

PPP declares three framing techniques for use with various media. These are all documented in RFC 1662 and are referred to as asynchronous HDLC (or AHDLC), bit-synchronous HDLC, and octet-synchronous HDLC.

AHDLC

AHDLC is used for all asynchronous lines, such as modems used on ordinary PCs. PPP's AHDLC, which is taken directly from ISO/IEC 3309, makes use of two special octet values, which are 7E and 7D in hexadecimal. These values serve the same function in PPP as the C0 and DB values used in SLIP and are never found in any of the transmitted user data. The 7E value is a frame delimiter, which marks the end of one frame and the beginning of another. The 7D value is an escape character, to be interpreted by the receiver as a signal to form the next actual decoded octet value in the HDLC frame as an exclusive-OR between the next transmitted octet and the fixed value 20. For example, the value 7E in the user data would be sent as 7D 5E.

In addition to this escape mechanism, ISO/IEC 3309 Section 4.5.2.1 defines a complex mechanism, called SBDPT, to deal with links that support only 7-bit characters. This mechanism groups octets into segments of seven octets each and moves the bits around to create eight 7-bit characters. Escaping for control characters must then be applied to the result. See the accompanying CD-ROM for an implementation of this mechanism as an optional part of the AHDLC implementation.

PPP does not use SBDPT. The only defined character-escape mechanism for PPP is exclusive-OR with the value 20, which can never transform a value below 80 into a value over 80. Thus, asynchronous PPP cannot run on any link that does not transfer 8-bit values. For instance, an asynchronous line that is set to 7 bits with even parity (a typical setting on old Unix systems) will destroy the value of the most significant bit. PPP cannot recover from this kind of configuration error, although many implementations can detect the problem and report it to an administrator.

By default, all values between 00 and 1F (inclusive) plus the values 7D and 7E are escaped by the transmitter when sending the PPP frame. The transmitter may also escape 7F, FF, and 80 through 9F at its option, and often does. The reason the values 00 through 1F are escaped by default is that PPP is designed to work over the widest possible array of serial links. These values correspond to special control characters on some links. For instance, many older (pre-V.42) modems require in-band XON/XOFF flow control using values 11 and 13. Even worse, X.3 PADs (Packet Assembler/Disassembler) interpret most of the control characters as local commands. Another reason is that a front-end device may use control characters for text input editing, and the default escapes will get the PPP data past the input editor to a process that can handle them.

As transmitted, an example PPP frame that looks like Figure 2.5 (ignore the information field contents for the moment) will look like this on the serial link:

```
7E FF 7D 23 C0 21 7D 21 7D 21 7D 20 7D 2E 7D 22 7D 26 7D 20 7D
20 7D 20 7D 20 7D 27 7D 22 7D 28 7D 22 70 34 7E
```

Several things should be noted here. First, the data transmitted waste a significant amount of time sending escape codes. Second, the CRC is performed on the original data, not the escape codes, and the CRC is itself escaped if necessary.

The initial 7E is optional here, but decent implementations will send it if the previous frame is not immediately back-to-back with this frame. This technique improves reliability with naturally bursty network traffic on links with random errors by discarding what is likely to be just interframe noise, rather than treating it as part of the next transmitted packet.

A possible output routine for PPP frames could do the two octet-oriented operations, escaping and CRC generation, at once in a procedure such as the following. (This example, as well as the other coding examples in this book, is intended only to illustrate the main ideas. It is not written in any particular machine-readable language. There are C code examples of these same routines on the CD-ROM.)

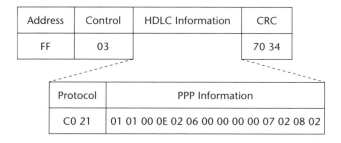

FIGURE 2.5 Example PPP frame

```
send initial 7E                                    (mark frame start)
while (frames in output queue) do

    get next frame to send from queue

    set CRCvalue to FFFF
    while (octets left in current frame) do      (send frame)
        get next octet as "value"
        recalculate CRCvalue based on value
        if value less than 20 or value is 7D or value is 7E then
            send 7D
            set value to value XOR 20
        endif
        send value
    enddo ; go do next octet

    set value to low-order octet of CRCvalue XOR FF    (send CRC)
    if value less than 20 or value is 7D or value is 7E then
        send 7D
        set value to value XOR 20
    endif
    send value

    set value to high-order octet of CRCvalue XOR FF  (send CRC)
    if value less than 20 or value is 7D or value is 7E then
        send 7D
        set value to value XOR 20
    endif
    send value

    send 7E                                        (mark frame end)

enddo ; go do next frame
```

See RFC 1661 for the standard CRC-16 and optional CRC-32 procedures used in PPP.

This description of AHDLC escaping is incomplete. See Chapter 3 for the Asynchronous Control Character Map (ACCM) parameter, which allows this

escaping to be mostly disabled on links that can safely handle some or all of the
values in the range 00 to 1F.

On input, this data stream can be decoded as follows.

```
set escaped to FALSE
set datapointer to start of receive buffer
set CRCvalue to FFFF
set octetcount to 0
while (link is attached) do
    get next input octet as "value"              (get input)
    if value less than 20 then
        discard value
        continue while loop for next octet
    endif
    if escaped then                              (handle escaping)
        set escaped to FALSE
        if value is 7E then
            ; silently discard (RFC 1134)
            set datapointer to start of receive buffer
            set CRCvalue to FFFF
            set octetcount to 0
            continue while loop for next octet
        endif
        set value to value XOR 20
    else if value is 7E then                     (handle frame end)
        if CRCvalue is F0B8 then
            remove last two octets in buffer (CRC)
            deliver HDLC frame in buffer
        else if octetcount greater than 3 then
            signal receive CRC error
        endif
        set datapointer to start of receive buffer
        set CRCvalue to FFFF
        set octetcount to 0
        continue while loop for next octet
    else if value is 7D then
        set escaped to TRUE
        continue while loop for next octet
```

```
        endif
        if octetcount greater than or equal to buffer size then
            signal receive error
            set datapointer to start of receive buffer
            set CRCvalue to FFFF
            set octetcount to 0
        else                                            (store received data)
            recalculate CRCvalue based on value
            store value at datapointer
            advance datapointer
            increment octetcount
        endif
    enddo
```

Again, this description is somewhat incomplete. See the Asynchronous Control Character Map (ACCM) discussion for modifications of this procedure for different transparency modes, and see the CD-ROM for a C language implementation.

The magic number F0B8 that appears above is the result of running CRC-16 on a message of "00 00." It represents a message concatenated with a CRC remainder of zero.

Although the PPP specification and the examples above describe escaping only the ASCII control characters 00 to 1F, and the framing characters 7D and 7E, any source character may be escaped other than 5E and any other character already being escaped XOR 20, since the result of escaping these characters would be 7D followed by an illegal value. For example, escaping 5E would give 7D 7E, which should be interpreted as a "discard-frame" signal, and escaping 21 would give 7D 01, which is itself normally escaped before transmission.

For another example, to run PPP over rlogin, which cannot pass 8-bit data cleanly because of the "window size change" sequence,[2] an implementation of PPP may legally elect to escape FF as 7D DF. All conforming PPP clients must be able to decode correctly any escaped characters received at any time, regard-

---

2. BSD rlogin protocol defines a special character sequence (FF FF 73 73) indicating that the terminal window size is being changed by the user and that the new size in binary follows in the data stream. This sequence was chosen as "unlikely" to be typed by a human user. Of course, PPP is not a human user and may accidentally trigger this feature, causing packet loss or even connection failure. Escaping FF when running PPP over rlogin avoids this problem.

less of the negotiated ACCM. The sender need not inform the recipient which values will be escaped and may elect to escape values that the receiver hasn't requested.

Escaping of characters outside the range 00 to 1F is not negotiated by the PPP protocol options in RFC 1662. Doing this typically requires administrator controls to set the list of escaped characters, such as with the "escape" keyword in the freely available ppp-2.3 implementation.

AHDLC users should be aware that at least one version of Livingston's Port-Master, a well-known and widely used dial-in server system, has a longstanding bug in which it will insert spurious 00 octets once every 128 bytes or so and also corrupt the data sent. This occurs when this implementation attempts to transmit a packet with too many bytes needing to be escaped. There is no known work-around. If this problem affects your implementation, you may need to upgrade the firmware or find alternative dial-in servers.

AHDLC and Flow Control

AHDLC links often employ flow control, either in-band [XON/XOFF, typically 11 (ASCII DC1) and 13 (ASCII DC3)] or out-of-band (RTS/CTS or, in rare cases, DTR/DSR). For in-band flow control, the flow control characters appear at arbitrary locations in the data stream. The receiver must discard these characters after modifying the flow control state (stopping or starting its own transmit process) and must not include them in any part of the received data or CRC calculation, and the transmitter must always escape the characters also used for flow control if they appear in the transmitted HDLC frame.

Often, the removal of these characters from the input data stream and the handling of flow control happen automatically in a low-level serial driver. PPP's handling of escaping integrates well with almost any in-band flow control implementation, since removal or insertion of these escaped characters is ignored by PPP.

For a user monitoring the data, this situation adds the complication that the user must ignore these values when present in the data stream. They are not part of the PPP data. Negotiation of the ACCM, though, will alter this situation, and the user must follow these negotiations to know which characters are ignored and which are data.

Out-of-band flow control uses separate hardware signals, such as Request to Send (RTS) and Clear to Send (CTS) in RS-232, to signal when transmit and receive are possible. For most systems, this action is transparent for PPP and presents no additional complications, although it requires two more wires than in-band flow control and some hardware support logic.

AHDLC and Other Protocols

Since PCs usually have inexpensive asynchronous hardware but rarely have synchronous adapters, AHDLC is used over a wide variety of ITU-T (Telephony) protocols to adapt PPP to synchronous channels. These protocols are needed because most telecommunications facilities, such as modems and ISDN, are inherently synchronous. Among these protocols are

- V.14, an older modem protocol that directly adapts asynchronous data in a bitwise manner and does not do error correction.
- V.42, a newer modem protocol that packs groups of characters received on an asynchronous port into HDLC frames. V.42 can do error correction.
- V.110, an ISDN terminal adapter protocol popular in Europe that adapts asynchronous data in a bitwise manner similar to V.14 and also cannot do error correction.
- V.120, an ISDN terminal adapter protocol that uses LAP-F (Framed) over HDLC for error correction.

These encapsulations are very common and generally must be used for compatibility with dial-up devices, but none is compatible with PPP over synchronous HDLC as described by RFC 1662.

Bit-Synchronous HDLC

Bit-synchronous HDLC is used on most telecommunications interfaces for PPP, such as "switched 56," T1, and most ISDN links. Unlike AHDLC, it is commonly implemented in hardware devices that do the framing and CRC work, no escape characters are used, and there is no flow control. Instead, all of the work is done at the bit level. Using the same PPP message as in the AHDLC example (Figure 2.5), we have the following data in binary format (note that HDLC transmits LSB first, so all of the octets appear to be written backwards).

```
11111111 11000000 00000011 10000100 10000000 10000000 00000000
  (FF)     (03)     (C0)     (21)     (01)     (01)     (00)
```

```
01110000 01000000 01100000 00000000 00000000 00000000 00000000
  (0E)     (02)     (06)     (00)     (00)     (00)     (00)
11100000 01000000 00010000 01000000 00001110 00101100
  (07)     (02)     (08)     (02)     (70)     (34)
```

HDLC will frame these bits for transmission by inserting a 0 bit after any run of five consecutive data bits set to 1. This distinguishes the user data from the HDLC end-of-frame mark, which is 01111110 in binary, or a run of six 1's, which cannot by definition be part of the encoded user data. After framing and this "bit stuffing," the data above become:

```
0111111011111S11111S00000000000011100001001000000100000
0000000000011100000100000001100000000000000000000000000000
0000000000011100000010000000001000001000000000001110001011
0001111110
```

where the "S" bits are the 0 bits "stuffed" into the user data. Of course, the octet boundaries are now meaningless, and this is just a stream of bits.

The receiver can easily decode this stream by counting consecutive 1's. If this counter reaches 5 and the next bit is a 0, then that 0 is an S bit and should be deleted. If this bit is 1, the frame is complete.

An additional complication for the user who is decoding synchronous traffic is that many interfaces use only a subset of the bits on the wire. For instance, in an ISDN data-over-speech-bearer-service (DOSBS) application in the United States, the bits are presented from the hardware as 8 bits per sample at 8,000 samples per second, but with the last bit in each octet possibly destroyed as a result of old equipment using bit-robbed signaling or Alternate Mark Inversion (AMI) coded lines. For voice applications, this limitation destroys only the LSB in some samples and adds some noise to the audio, since pulse code modulated (PCM) audio data are sent most significant bit (MSB) first.

For PPP, however, this means that the data must be sent in 7-bit chunks with a dummy bit inserted after each chunk, which restricts the usable data rate from $8 \cdot 8,000 = 64,000$ down to $7 \cdot 8,000 = 56,000$ bits per second. Continuing with the example above, this same frame might, depending on the sender's initial bit alignment, be sent as

```
0111111X 011111SX 11111S0X 0000000X 0000111X 0000100X
1000000X 0100000X 0000000X 0000111X 0000010X 0000001X
```

```
1000000X 0000000X 0000000X 0000000X 0000000X 0001110X
0000010X 0000000X 0100000X 1000000X 0000111X 0001011X
0001111X 110. . . .
```

or, reversing the bits and converting back to hex to show what a DS0 or B channel raw data capture device might display, as

```
7E 3E 1F 00 70 10 01 02 00 70 20 40 01 00 00 00 00 38 20 00 02
01 70 68 78 03
```

Operating over fractional T1 is still more complex, since each DS1 frame of
193 bits will contain some number of possibly noncontiguous 7- or 8-bit samples
that must be extracted and concatenated to reconstruct the transmitted HDLC
bit stream. Hardware designed for operation with these data formats (such as
the Motorola MPC860) usually has complex but flexible and programmable bit-
steering features.

Octet-Synchronous HDLC

The third RFC 1662 encapsulation technique, octet-synchronous HDLC, is relatively rare. Octet-synchronous framing is essentially identical to AHDLC, with
the same escape and framing codes. The only significant difference is that the
ASCII control characters need not be escaped.

RFC 1662 simply describes this technique as an option, and RFC 1618 goes
so far as to describe this as the "recommended" way of communicating over
ISDN links, although not the default. This is not the case, and in fact all ISDN
equipment in existence that uses PPP does bit-synchronous framing since this is
far more efficient when implemented in low-speed hardware and reduces the system overhead to simply per-packet handling rather than per-octet processing for
escape characters.

Octet-synchronous HDLC is used on special media with a default hardware
interface that presents individual octets at very high speed. On these devices,
processing individual bits is prohibitively complex. RFC 2615 (PPP over
SONET/SDH) describes the only current such interface, which is the SONET
and SDH family of media. These interfaces run at very high speeds, generally
multiples of 51.84Mbps, with the highest-speed interface defined for PPP, OC-192,
running at 9.95328Gbps.

SONET and SDH interfaces are telecommunications standards defined by ANSI T1.105 and ITU-T G.708. They are based on a synchronous frame structure that can be multiplexed and demultiplexed easily to combine traffic over expensive long-distance links. The basic frame structure for SONET is represented as a block of bytes organized as 90 columns by 9 rows; 8,000 such blocks are sent per second to give a 51.84Mbps STS-1 data stream. The basic frame structure for SDH uses a 270-by-9 block and a different framing mechanism, but is otherwise similar. Unlike nearly all other communications protocols, SONET/SDH bytes are transmitted MSB first. Because of this, the PPP FCS, which must be calculated bytewise on SONET/SDH, is not equal to the FCS that would be calculated bitwise.

Within the rows of an STS-1 stream, the first three columns are overhead information and contain two management network communications channels called the Data Communications Channel (DCC; bytes D1–D3 and D4–D12), a signaling mechanism to handle fail-over called Automatic Protection Switching (APS; bytes K1 and K2), and several other features. One of the overhead features is a pointer value (bytes H1–H3) that gives the start of the next *path frame*, which contains the user data. The path frame, in turn, contains a single column of overhead that includes the Path Signal Label (C2 byte), which tells the type of user data transported. As shown in Figure 2.6, the remaining 86 octets of path data (shaded) provide a 49.536Mbps stream usable by PPP.

The separation between the SONET/SDH framing and the path framing allows SONET/SDH links to handle slight differences in clocking between the path data and the SONET/SDH network, the latter of which is typically referenced to a Stratum-1 atomic clock. [These clock sources should not be confused with the reference clocks used by Network Time Protocol (NTP), which are also designated by the term "stratum" to indicate accuracy.]

There are two Path Signal Label values allocated for PPP. The first value is CF. This is reserved for unscrambled PPP over SONET/SDH. The second value is 16 and is allocated for scrambled PPP. The PPP scrambling operation is identical to the self-synchronous payload scrambling used for ATM. The transmitted PPP data stream is XORed with the output of a 43-bit shift register that is fed with the output data stream. Recovery at the receiver takes place by a similar operation, with the received data XORed with a 43-bit delayed version of the received data. See Figure 2.7.

Proper SONET/SDH clock recovery and framing depend on the relative density of 1's and 0's in the data stream. It is possible for a SONET/SDH network to

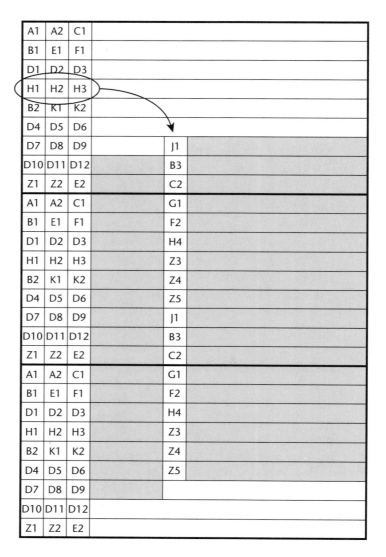

FIGURE 2.6 STS-1 SONET frame

be disrupted by malicious attack if unscrambled PPP is used on high-capacity circuits. Therefore, unscrambled PPP should be implemented for compatibility
with older equipment, but should be avoided in use wherever possible. Implementors should note that U.S. Patent 5,835,602 (PMC-Sierra) covers at least this
method of scrambling packetized data for use on SONET/SDH.

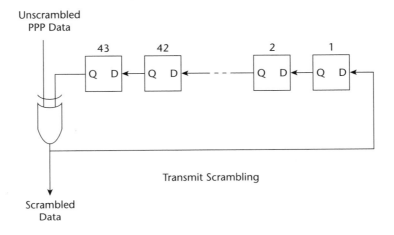

Transmit Scrambling

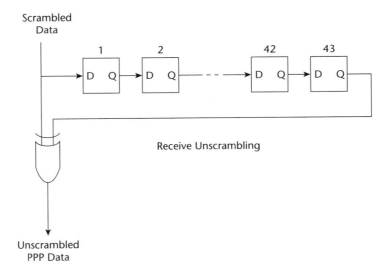

Receive Unscrambling

FIGURE 2.7 SONET/SDH payload scrambling

Owing to some confusion between the ITU-T, which uses hexadecimal in most documents, and the IETF, which uses decimal, some implementations may erroneously use hex 10 for scrambled PPP.

To get higher-rate data streams, these basic STS-1 streams are concatenated to form STS-Nc streams. This is done by performing the pointer processing to locate the path data in only one of the STS-1 channels, setting the pointer values to a special concatenation marker in the other channels and interleaving the streams. This concatenation process results in duplicate section and line overhead bytes called *fixed stuff* that must be ignored. An STS-3c stream has 270-by-9 blocks of raw data, with 260 columns available for user data or 149.76Mbps of usable bandwidth.

In addition to the more common optical interface, the lower-data-rate forms of SONET and SDH can run over cable-television-grade coaxial cable.

Other Framing Techniques

Other, nonstandard framing techniques are also defined for PPP. These techniques include Lucent's Simple Data Link (SDL) in RFC 2823 and Consistent Overhead Byte Stuffing (COBS). These two techniques allow more predictable throughput and better integration with other services. SDL also provides very rapid detection of link failure.

Translation

It is possible to translate between any two of the several forms of HDLC framing and, at network boundaries, between most of the encapsulated forms. Of course, translating between octet-synchronous HDLC and AHDLC, which are nearly identical, is rather trivial. The only serious concern is the need for the octet-synchronous system to respect the additional transparency rules for AHDLC. Unfortunately, this simple translation is never required in practice.

Translating between bit-synchronous HDLC and AHDLC is more interesting. Such a device needs to eavesdrop on the negotiation to discover which characters the remote system wishes to remove from the transparency rules (see ACCM in Chapter 3) and needs to perform the necessary octet escaping. In order to make this work, any system that supports bit-synchronous HDLC must accept the asynchronous ACCM option and acknowledge any value, but it must not escape any characters.

This kind of translation is popular for ISDN interfaces to PCs. PCs usually are not equipped with the necessary synchronous hardware, and the software implementations of PPP found on PCs generally do not support such hardware, but these machines usually have high-speed asynchronous ports. An ISDN Terminal Adapter (TA) can attach to the asynchronous port on a PC and place an ISDN call to a system running bit-synchronous PPP without user intervention. Examples of such TAs are the Motorola BitSurfr and the 3Com Courier I-Modem. These

devices often go far beyond simple translation and offer additional PPP protocols such as MP (Multilink PPP) and CCP (Compression Control Protocol).
Doing this requires extensive processing of the PPP data during negotiation, such
as adding an MRRU (Maximum Reconstructed Receive Unit) option to the LCP
Configure-Request message as it passes by, and requires special effort to make
things such as security on multiple links for MP work transparently.

PPP with Framing Conversion (William Simpson, `draft-ietf-pppext-
conversion-01.txt`) was an attempt to describe some of the processing done in
these devices but did not adequately explain the more complex options. In particular, it stated that translating between MP and single-link PPP requires routing functions when in fact common devices are able to do the conversion
without routing.

Standard Encapsulations

Several PPP-related RFCs provide mechanisms for running PPP over non-IETF
standard networks, such as Frame Relay (RFC 1973), X.25 (RFC 1598), and
ATM (RFC 2364). These encapsulations are mostly enhancements of the transmission methods described above. For instance, Frame Relay uses the HDLC
Address field to direct traffic in a packet-switched environment, but it uses the
same bit-synchronous HDLC format already described.

These encapsulations impose additional restrictions on the PPP options that
may be negotiated in order to coexist with signaling protocols and to interoperate with internetwork gateways. In particular, the Address and Control fields
must not be negotiated away, because they are defined by the standard HDLC
format used with these networks.

For Frame Relay, the HDLC Address and Control fields are handled by the
Frame Relay interface, and an NLPID byte signals the presence of PPP. Figure
2.8 shows an example PPP packet on Frame Relay using DLCI 16.

When PPP is run over an ATM interface using AAL-5, two options are available: PPP may be either LLC encapsulated or VC multiplexed. In both cases, the
PPP CRC is omitted because the AAL-5 CPCS contains a CRC-32 covering the
frame contents. With LLC encapsulation, shown in Figure 2.9, a fixed header of
FE FE 03 CF is inserted before the PPP Protocol field. If FRF.8 interworking is
used, a packet sent over an ATM VC in this manner arrives at the Frame Relay
peer in the format shown in Figure 2.8.

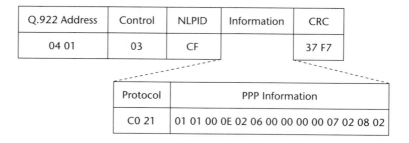

FIGURE 2.8 PPP on Frame Relay

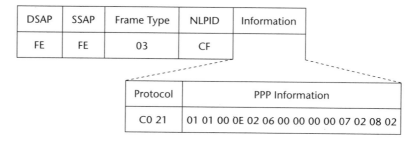

FIGURE 2.9 LLC-encapsulated PPP on ATM

With VC-multiplexed PPP, shown in Figure 2.10 and sometimes referred to as "null encapsulation," the AAL-5 CPCS frame begins with the PPP Protocol field. This form is incompatible with FRF.8 interworking devices because it does not include the LLC/SNAP header. Implementors should be aware that some routers are reported to insert HDLC Address/Control (FF 03) before the PPP Protocol field on these frames.

An ATM-related service called FUNI can also be used with PPP, as described in RFC 2363. FUNI specifies a mechanism for translating HDLC-framed data directly into ATM VCs. This mechanism is simpler and more efficient than regular ATM for packet-oriented interfaces and allows ordinary HDLC controllers on T1 lines to interface directly with ATM signaled networks. When this service is used, PPP may use either LLC-encapsulated or VC-multiplexed forms, as with regular ATM, and the service interoperates directly with ATM-attached peers and, if LLC encapsulation is used, with Frame Relay peers. An example VC-multiplexed FUNI frame is shown in Figure 2.11.

Protocol	PPP Information
C0 21	01 01 00 0E 02 06 00 00 00 00 07 02 08 02

FIGURE 2.10 VC-multiplexed PPP on ATM

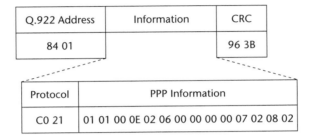

Q.922 Address	Information	CRC
84 01		96 3B

Protocol	PPP Information
C0 21	01 01 00 0E 02 06 00 00 00 00 07 02 08 02

FIGURE 2.11 VC-multiplexed PPP on FUNI

All PPP operation over ATM uses AAL-5 to map packets into cells. ATM AAL-5 first appends padding and a trailer to the end of transmitted packets. The padding and trailer are eight to 55 octets in length and pad out the final cell transmitted to the required 48-octet size, as shown in Figure 2.12. "H" in this diagram is the five-octet ATM header, which includes the connection identification (*Virtual Path Index*, or VPI, and *Virtual Circuit Index*, or VCI), error control, and flags. One flag in the header is used to indicate the last cell in an AAL-5 frame. This final cell is padded to 40 octets, and the eight-octet CPCS trailer is inserted at the end of the cell. The CPCS contains two unused octets (*User-to-User*, or UU, and *Common Part Indicator*, or CPI) both set to 00, two octets giving the frame length in network byte order, and four octets of CRC over all of the data bytes including the pad, UU, CPI, and length fields, but not including the cell headers.

PPP over X.25, described in RFC 1598, is a bit different. X.25 includes error control and segmentation/reassembly, so the PPP MRU is actually the X.25 software layer's maximum reassembled frame rather than the physical medium's MRU. This is typically 1,600 octets. Unlike Frame Relay, an X.25 link running PPP must run only PPP. The NLPID is placed in the Call User Data byte during call set-up, rather than in each frame.

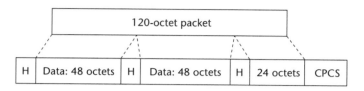

FIGURE 2.12 AAL-5 segmentation

The frame diagram given in the RFC is somewhat misleading. Only the first X.25 frame of a fragmented sequence contains the PPP Protocol field. Subsequent frames, up to and including the next frame with the M bit set to 0, are simply continuations of the current PPP packet.

As with the other encapsulations described here, no Address and Control Field Compression or FCS Alternatives can be negotiated, and the frame integrity is guaranteed by the HDLC CRC used by X.25. The PPP Protocol field immediately follows the X.25 frame sequence number byte.

PPP, SONET/SDH, and ATM

On SONET/SDH media, ATM is often a competitor to PPP. A great deal of effort has been spent developing specialized implementations of some of the ATM layers in hardware, while initial PPP implementations have depended on general-purpose processor (CPU) speed and have only recently been found in commercial SONET/SDH hardware.

Currently, the following three typical configurations are possible for these media.

- PPP may be run directly over SONET/SDH with octet-synchronous framing. This is also known as Packet Over SONET (POS).
- Networking protocols may be run over ATM AAL-5 on SONET/SDH without PPP using Multiprotocol over ATM (MPOA), Local Area Network Emulation (LANE), or Classical IP over ATM (CLIP).
- PPP may be run over ATM virtual circuits using AAL-5.

Each solution may make sense in some particular set of circumstances. One reason for using IP over ATM is to be able to reroute links in the core of a network in order to implement traffic engineering (load balancing at the network level). MPLS can also be used for this on Packet over SONET (POS) links and has lower overhead and less complexity than ATM. Another reason to run over ATM is to take advantage of ATM's Traffic Management and Quality of Service features.

One proposed but not yet widespread use of PPP over ATM is with ADSL (Asymmetric Digital Subscriber Line) services. While not technically necessary for ADSL, ATM is one way to add telephone company features to the network, such as the ability to select an ISP in the same manner as choosing a long-distance carrier. In these cases, PPP is carried over ATM over the telephone company's network to connect the user to the ISP of his or her choice.

ITU-T V.110

V.110 is used chiefly in European mobile data communication, as part of a system called GSM (Global System for Mobile Communication). V.110 is a technique that allows asynchronous data, such as AHDLC-encoded PPP, to be carried over a synchronous data channel. It was intended as an easy mechanism to implement in hardware but is often coded in software with some difficulty.

V.110 uses an 80-bit frame structure that repeats continuously in the data channel regardless of whether or not there are user data to be sent. This frame contains room for 48 user data bits plus 32 overhead bits to carry flow control and framing information. The user bits are encoded using asynchronous character framing, so a V.110 implementation must scan the received data bits for a start bit (0), extract the single byte of data in LSB bit ordering, check for the stop bit (1), and repeat for every byte of data transferred before performing AHDLC processing. Because asynchronous communication for PPP is normally done with 1 start bit, 8 data bits, no parity, and 1 stop bit—10 bits per character—characters do not fit evenly into the frames, and an implementation must be able to span frames while decoding characters.

V.110 also defines the method by which 56K synchronous data are inserted into a 64K channel. This involves using the first 7 bits of each octet and fixing the last bit in each octet to 1. The 80-bit framing structure described above is not used at all. Because this mode of operation is documented in the standard, some manufacturers confusingly refer to ordinary synchronous operation as V.110 56K or V.110 64K mode.

ITU-T V.120

V.120 is not an essential part of PPP, nor is it defined by the IETF. It is used in ISDN Terminal Adapters (TAs) to provide a modem-like asynchronous interface for regular PCs. It is also used as part of PPP Serial Data Transport Protocol (SDTP) (see Chapter 5 for details).

V.120 is built atop LAP-F (Q.922), which is a reliable protocol similar in operation to LAP-B. (LAP-F is not used with SDTP; only the H and CS bytes, as described below, are used.)

Following the HDLC Address and Control bytes, the V.120 packets have a one- or two-octet header. The first octet, called H, is mandatory, and its format is as follows:

E	BR	0	0	C2	C1	B	F

The BR bit is set to 1 to indicate a break (serial line held in MARK state for longer than a valid character interval) on an asynchronous line. The B and F bits are used only when encapsulating synchronous HDLC data, and these bits mark the Beginning and Final frames. If a user frame is too large to fit in the MTU, then the B and F bits are used to fragment the frame into multiple consecutive V.120 frames in exactly the same manner in which the B and E bits are used in Multilink PPP. For transport of asynchronous data, the B and F bits must always be set to 1, because fragmentation is not required.

The C2 and C1 bits are used to signal errors end-to-end. For asynchronous data, C1 signals a stop-bit error and C2 signals a parity error.

For synchronous HDLC data, these bits are defined as follows.

```
00 No error
01 CRC error
10 HDLC abort (flag with seven or more consecutive ones)
11 Overrun error
```

The E (extension) bit is 1 if the user data immediately follow the H octet, or 0 if the CS (control state) octet, shown below, follows next.

E	DR	SR	RR	0	0	0	0

The E (extension) bit is as above, but no extensions are defined beyond the CS octet, so this bit must always be set to 1. The DR bit is set to 1 to indicate that the system is ready. SR is set to indicate that the system is ready to send data. RR is set to indicate that the system is ready to receive data.

When transmitting a V.120 CS octet, DR is equivalent to DTR on a modem, and RR is equivalent to RTS. When receiving a V.120 CS octet, DR is equivalent to DCD, and RR is equivalent to CTS.

The send ready (SR) bit has no equivalent in any modern modem signal. (However, it is equivalent to the old usage of RTS on half-duplex modems. Because such modems are extremely uncommon, this usage is rarely encountered in practice.) Many systems simply set SR to 1 at all times. The receiver should logically AND the SR bit received from the peer with the local flow control state to produce the RR bit to transmit.

Until the first CS octet is seen, V.120 will assume that DR, SR, and RR from the peer are all set to 1.

Flow control in V.120 is generally accomplished at two levels. First, the LAP-F RNR (Receiver Not Ready) and RR (Receiver Ready) frames are used to signal between the two V.120 speakers. Second, the RR bits in the CS octet are used between the two users of the V.120 channel (the asynchronous serial port users) to signal RTS/CTS readiness.

Statistics and Management

In addition to the SNMP MIB-2 objects for serial lines, the various physical interfaces and telecommunications protocols, a PPP implementation may include RFCs 1471 (LCP and LQM), 1472 (PAP and CHAP security), 1473 (IPCP), and 1474 (bridging). These MIBs both provide statistics on the operation of PPP and can, in some implementations, control configuration.

Because PPP is often connected to external databases for authentication and user profile management, the configuration control options of these MIBs are not always able to set PPP variables.

Few PPP implementations provide SNMP management interfaces. Those that do also generally include extensive enterprise (proprietary) MIBs.

Auto-Detecting

When a fixed set of protocols is expected to be used over a point-to-point link (for example, in a dial-up access device), it is sometimes convenient to identify automatically the protocol in use by the peer. This process is variously known as *auto-detecting* and *sniffing*.

Of course, the expected protocols depend both on the link-level medium and on the population of devices at the other end of the link. In this section, we will consider two scenarios, one in an asynchronous environment and one in a synchronous environment, that will illustrate the important ideas. None of these techniques is perfectly reliable in all situations, since they rely on finding patterns in expected data and on timing. Systems that implement these detection algorithms should also have a means of disabling their use.

Configuring Common Implementations

One common implementation of PPP auto-detect is called "mgetty." This is a replacement for the common Unix "getty" login dæmon that can automatically recognize PPP, voice, facsimile, and other connections and direct each type of connection to a different service. Below is one possible configuration.

```
/etc/inittab:


    p1:2345:respawn:/usr/sbin/mgetty ttyS1 -i /etc/issue.mgetty


/usr/local/etc/mgetty+sendfax/mgetty.config:


    port ttyS1
    debug 6
    data-only y
    init-chat "" AT&F OK ATS0=0&B1&C1E0 OK


/usr/local/etc/mgetty+sendfax/login.config


    /AutoPPP/ - - /usr/local/bin/pppd debug -detach +chap auth
```

Another common implementation is in use in Nortel's Annex communications servers. For plain serial ports, auto-detect is enabled by the following single NA/admin command.

```
set port=all mode auto_detect
```

For synchronous ports (on the RA8000, 5399, and other products), the more complex Session Parameter Blocks (SPBs) in the config.annex file must be used. One possible use is

```
%wan
begin_session dodetect
call_action detect
end_session
begin_session accept
detected any
end_session
```

In contrast, the Lucent PortMaster series of communications servers always automatically detect PPP at login time and this feature cannot be disabled.

Asynchronous Auto-Detect

In an asynchronous implementation, two forms of information are available: data patterns and timing. We will first consider the data patterns. Let us assume that we are implementing a device that can handle PPP, AppleTalk Remote Access Protocol (ARAP) versions 1 and 2, and SLIP, and that it is possible to read raw input data without alteration.

The initial packet from PPP is always an LCP frame (see the next chapter for details). This frame has one of the following forms, depending on the escaping configuration.

```
7E FF 03 C0 21 ...
7E FF 7D 23 C0 21 ...
7E 7D DF 7D 23 C0 21 ...
7E 7D DF 03 C0 21 ...
```

It is possible that an auto-detect routine could use the next octet as well, which must be 01 for Configure-Request, although practice suggests that this is unnecessary.

SLIP and ARAP do not negotiate like PPP but do have known formats that allow their detection. These formats are

```
SLIP:       C0 45 ...
ARAPv1:     16 10 02 ...
ARAPv2:     01 1B 02 ...
```

One possible way to build a detection routine would be to build a table containing each of these sequences and to run a state machine to recognize any of the given forms. At this point, however, it is a good idea to take a step back to consider the available timing information.

Reasonable implementations of either SLIP or PPP may have a delay between the initial 7E or C0 and the rest of the data, since this may actually be the trailing framing character from a previous (unrecognized) frame. However, no reasonable implementation should have a significant delay between characters mid-packet. ARAP is even simpler, since the frame start and frame end characters are distinct.

Given this information, the following procedure suggests itself.

```
array of forms = list
    { FF 03 C0 21 }
    { FF 7D 23 C0 21 }
    { 7D DF 7D 23 C0 21 }
    { 7D DF 03 C0 21 }
    { 45 }
    { 16 10 02 }
    { 01 1B 02 }
listend

while (still in detect mode) do
    set inter-character time-out
    read until time-out keeping only first seven octets
    if fewer than seven octets received then
        discard data read
        begin reading again
    endif
```

```
        set flag[0] through flag[6] to TRUE
        if first octet read is 7E then
            set flag[4] through flag[6] to FALSE
            discard first octet
        else if first octet is C0 then
            set flag[0] through flag[3] to FALSE
            set flag[5] through flag[6] to FALSE
            discard first octet
        endif
        compare remaining received data against list of forms
        if matched one and flag[index of match] is TRUE then
            exit ; detected protocol
        endif
    enddo
```

This process can be altered to detect terminal-mode users by watching the received buffers for isolated characters or pairs of characters, since humans cannot type as fast as a computer. It is also worthwhile first to emit a text message saying, "Please start your network software now or press any key to bring up a menu." Peers that are already in PPP, ARAP, or SLIP mode will simply discard this text as a badly formed packet.

Synchronous Auto-Detect

Auto-detecting on a bit-synchronous link, such as an ISDN dial-up, is more complicated than on an asynchronous link but also more reliable. For this example, let us assume that we will be accepting both PPP and V.120 (a terminal adapter protocol for ISDN) at either 56K or 64K data rates on a single bearer channel of an ISDN interface. Unlike AHDLC, there is only one PPP frame to consider, since no escape codes are used. This frame is

```
FF 03 C0 21 ...
```

For V.120, either of two possible frames might be received first, either a LAP-D SABME (Set Asynchronous Balanced Mode Extended) or a control frame. These two frames are

```
08 01 7F
08 01 03
```

(Unlike normal HDLC, V.120 uses one bit, called *command versus response* or *C/R,* from the first octet of the Address field to signal the direction of the data. The Address field, termed *Logical Link Identifier* or *LLI* in V.120, has a default value of 256 decimal, which would be 04 01 in normal HDLC encoding but is instead 08 01 because the C/R bit has the value zero and is inserted as bit 1 of the octet, to the left of the Poll/Final bit. V.120's reply to these messages would then start with the C/R bit set, or 0A 01.)

Note that the first transmitted bit of the PPP frame (the LSB of FF) is 1 while the first bit of the V.120 frame (the LSB of 08) is 0. This means that only one bit of the message must be seen to identify which sequence to expect.

Now we will encode these values in bit-synchronous HDLC form without the initial flag sequence. The bit-encoded forms are

```
PPP:                 1111101111100000000000001110000100
V.120 SABME:         0001000010000000111110110
V.120 control:       00010000100000011000000
```

Since this is a bit-oriented protocol, the first task of the auto-detect routine will be to discover the bit offset of the initial flag sequence, or *sync marker.* Consider Table 2.1, which shows the data patterns to be expected for the sync marker with the first two octets of a valid frame, assuming either 64K "clear channel" or 56K restricted data path. The "v" bits in the table are valid data bits from the frame itself, "x" is arbitrary data, and "." is the mangled bit in each sample when 56K service is used. (The bits here are again given in reverse order, as they

TABLE 2.1.	Sync Marker Patterns		
64K Clear Channel		56K Restricted	
First	Second	First	Second
01111110	vvvvvvvv	0111111.	0vvvvvv.
x0111111	0vvvvvvv	x011111.	10vvvvv.
xx011111	10vvvvvv	xx01111.	110vvvv.
xxx01111	110vvvvv	xxx0111.	1110vvv.
xxxx0111	1110vvvv	xxxx011.	11110vv.
xxxxx011	11110vvv	xxxxx01.	111110v.
xxxxxx01	111110vv	xxxxxx0.	1111110.
xxxxxxx0	1111110v		

would appear on the wire. HDLC devices transmit and receive the LSB first, so these values usually must be reversed to construct properly the software tables needed for decoding.)

Now it is a simple matter to build a pair of tables of bit masks with 256 entries each for the first and second octet values in Table 2.1 (filling in the "v" bits with bits from each of the protocol sequences in turn) and then to use these bit masks to detect the start of the data. If a sync marker is found, then the auto-detect routine must test the next two to four octets, depending on the protocol assumed and the bit offset. In fact, using just these two protocols causes the table to be unambiguous in determining the protocol to test in all but one case: the last 56K restricted case has no "v" bits in it, and thus all possible protocols (with just one alignment and encoding, however) must be tested. This means that after testing the bit mask indexed by each octet, a single two-to-four-octet string comparison will uniquely identify both the protocol and the type of connection.

For example, seeing the octets FC BE should make the auto-detect routine expect to see 64K PPP data of 0F 00 0E after that sequence, since this pattern matches only the second row of the 64K encoding table with PPP data filled in for the "v" positions, and the one "x" value set to 0 (this choice is arbitrary, and the "x" value could have been set to 1, so FD BE also leads to the same state and the same string comparison). The pattern substitution is shown in Figure 2.13.

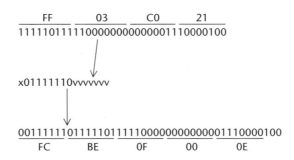

FIGURE 2.13 Synchronous PPP detection

Note that the initial FC could also be the start of a 56K sequence (second row of the 56K table), but that would be eliminated as a possibility by BE, which could not be the second octet of either a PPP or a V.120 sequence with 56K encoding.

The construction of a suitable auto-detect procedure and complete tables is left as an exercise for the reader. (My reference implementation required 93 lines of assembly code.)

AHDLC Start-Up Issues

The receiver of a PPP call over an asynchronous line generally has an easy task to perform, since the caller is usually expected to initiate the switch into PPP mode. At most, a simple auto-detect procedure may need to be run. Sometimes these devices are even configured to run PPP at all times.

The initiator has a more difficult task. Most consumer-grade modems use an in-band command channel (the familiar "AT" command set). Unfortunately, this same channel is also used for the user data, and no reliable synchronization mechanism is defined for switching from command to data mode and back. Worse, neither the commands the modem may accept nor the possible responses are well defined or even consistent among models of modems made by a single maufacturer.

In addition, some serial hardware is notoriously deficient. For instance, the DIN connector serial port on old Apple Macintosh computers does not carry the Data Carrier Detect (DCD) signal. This means that PPP implementations on these machines must go to great lengths to detect lost connections by other means, such as using Link Control Protocol (LCP) Echo-Requests. This book describes these mechanisms but does not give a comprehensive list of all such broken hardware or all possible work-arounds.

This book is far too short to provide a comprehensive treatment of communications using modems, but here are a few suggestions.

- If you use hard reset on the modem, wait several seconds before attempting communication with it. Most modems have a relatively lengthy self-test and initialization sequence during which they will not accept new commands.
- Attempt to synchronize with the modem's autobaud mechanism first. This requires the sending of at least CR+"AT"+CR (0D 41 54 0D). Beware: some common brands of modems will lock up if the first CR is too close in time to the "A." I recommend at least a 250-millisecond delay between these characters.

- Send an initialization string. "ATZ" or "AT&F" will usually do as a start. Some modems may glitch Data Carrier Detect (DCD) or Data Set Ready (DSR) when this is done, which may cause serial driver errors on some systems. Most modems then require a delay of 300 to 500 milliseconds after an "ATZ" is sent. This should then be followed by the parameter set-up string. This should include settings to disable the in-band command mode break ("TIES"), to disable any software flow control, and to set any other special configuration necessary. Do not include "&w" because this unnecessarily stresses the modem's finite EEROM life span.
- Dial the line. A timer is very important here, since some modem firmware flaws can actually cause the modem to crash during negotiation.
- Wait for both DCD and a connect string. These may arrive in either order. Once both have been received, wait a short period (perhaps 250 milliseconds) before sending data. Sending data too early on some modems will cause connection drops.
- If a log-on script (sometimes known as a *chat script*) is required, run it.
- Sending a short, intentionally invalid PPP frame before starting the real PPP process can shorten the delays caused by the use of auto-detect by the peer. I suggest sending 7E FF 7D 23 C0 21 7E.
- Start PPP. For several seconds after connecting (especially if a chat script was required), the remote system might not be running PPP. To detect this, one possible trick is to look for reception of frames where the CRC matches the last CRC sent. A slightly more complex but more common technique is to use the magic number negotiation procedure from RFC 1661. Note that you may have to extend the counter limit for Configure-Request failures if you use this technique for detecting temporary loopbacks, since several requests may be sent before the peer even starts to run PPP.

It is also possible that either the serial ports or the modems themselves are misconfigured such that each character has fewer than 8 valid bits. PPP cannot run at all under these conditions. To detect this misconfiguration, use two variables, one set to 00 and the other set to FF. Logically OR all received data into the former and AND into the latter. If LCP fails, check these variables. If the OR variable is not set to FF or if the AND variable has bit 6 or 7 set (hex C0), then it is likely that either the serial port or the modem is configured for 7-bit operation. An operator should be notified that the line is not 8-bit clean.

See the CD-ROM for a C language example that handles these two cases and even/odd parity detection as well as part of the AHDLC implementation.

Switched Circuit Integration

When used on a switched circuit, such as a modem on a telephone line, the up/down messages from the switching system may be translated into Up/Down events into LCP, although they need not be. A system that automatically maintains the link, such as a dial-on-demand system, or one that experiences frequent short outages, such as a radio modem, might opt to wait for a short period before sending the Down event to LCP while a redial or wait for carrier is attempted. The implementor of such a system should be cautioned that the price of faster reconnection is lowered security. Any such technique used must, of course, be configurable, since it is not the default.

I must caution any implementor considering such a scheme that doing this greatly weakens security. Before considering any such "short hold" option, especially for ISDN or regular dial-up, a cautious implementor would first exhaust all possible ways to speed up normal PPP authentication. On most media, this can be made to be much faster than any circuit-switched set-up time. In particular, ISDN, which is about 100 times faster in call set-up than common analog modems, still has a call set-up time in the hundreds of milliseconds, while PPP negotiation can be an order of magnitude faster when well implemented. Thus, the security cost of implementing a short hold option is much higher than the supposed reduction in negotiation time.

It is highly recommended that the system that initiated the link should also be the system that tears down the link to save toll charges when the link is idle. This rule avoids thrashing when demand dialing is used. Of course, in some unusual circumstances, such as "toll-reversing" lines, a separate negotiation of either callback or Bandwidth Allocation Control Protocol (BACP, page 228) might be needed.

Note that the distinction between caller and callee should be made available to the PPP authentication layer. See Authentication Protocols and About Security in Chapter 4.

Null-Modem Connection to Windows NT

Windows NT requires a small handshake before it will begin running PPP on a dedicated serial port connected to a device speaking PPP. (Such a cable often needs to be wired with the modem control signals reversed on each end. This configuration is known as a "null-modem," since it makes the link look as though modems were in place. For this reason, the driver used with NT RAS in this case is called the "null-modem driver," and many users refer to this configuration as a "null-modem connection.")

Although oddly nonstandard, this handshake is very simple. Windows will send the text string "CLIENT" and wait for a response. The peer device should answer with "CLIENTSERVER" and a CR/LF sequence in order to start PPP running on the NT side.

General Implementation Issues

Specific PPP implementation techniques vary widely, but good PPP implementations each have the following common attributes.

- **The Robustness Principle.** In RFC 791 (the Internet Protocol), Jon Postel wrote:

  > In general, an implementation must be conservative in its sending behavior, and liberal in its receiving behavior. That is, it must be careful to send well-formed datagrams, but must accept any datagram that it can interpret (e.g., not object to technical errors where the meaning is still clear).

  This has been paraphrased as, "Be liberal in what you expect and conservative in what you send." This is the golden rule of network software design, and good implementations follow it. In particular, it is worthwhile to study the various obsolete versions of a particular protocol before implementing it, including the Internet Drafts and obsoleted RFCs. Products often will be released that conform to these obsolete versions, and interoperability occasionally depends on behavior that is not documented in later versions. Even more important, following the protocol rule will allow your implementation to interoperate with flawed peers. There are, sadly, many PPP implementations in the world today that have glaring bugs. It is better for your reputation if your implementation logs the error but continues to operate in a reasonable manner, if possible, rather than giving up.

- **Resilience.** PPP negotiation protocols have a variety of different field length values and restrictions on the values of certain other fields. Good implementations will carefully check that these values are consistent with the type of data received and the overall packet length before acting on the data. It is quite common for errant PPP packages to send incorrect field lengths, and it is unfortunately more common for bad implementations to crash when presented with such data.

- **Renegotiation.** Any layer of the PPP protocol may be separately renegotiated at any time. Good implementations handle this gracefully and do not treat it as an error. In particular, options that require storage, such as data compression, will need to free the storage and reallocate it on successful renegotiation, and all options must be reset to default values.
- **Loop Avoidance.** The standard PPP negotiation model can easily fall into nonconverging patterns, also called *loops*. Good implementations detect these loops by means of timers and counters.
- **Configurability.** Good implementations permit each supported protocol to be disabled separately and any variables to be modified. A good implementation should not rest simply on the PPP negotiation mechanism, since it is occasionally true that another implementation will properly negotiate an option but will not properly implement that option itself. Allowing the user to modify or eliminate an offending protocol or configuration option from negotiation is an effective work-around.
- **Event Logging.** Good implementations can log events at varying levels of detail to aid in debugging of failed connections. It is especially helpful to log the state of each layer that is not in "Initial" state and to have the ability at least to log the raw data sent over the wire. It's also helpful to log in a consistent format to allow for later parsing and searching of the messages and to use common mechanisms, such as syslog.
- **Legibility.** Good implementations provide error messages that are meaningful to both experienced and inexperienced users and may also suggest fixes. For instance, "could not negotiate a compatible set of protocols" is a particularly useless message. A better message might be, "IPCP failure—local IP address is not set and peer refuses to provide one."
- **Peer-to-Peer Design.** PPP is inherently a peer-to-peer protocol and most emphatically not a client/server protocol. A good implementation will not make arbitrary distinctions based on the system on which it is executing. In particular, all implementations should both offer authentication to their peers and demand authentication when so configured, and all should be able to configure desired values for all negotiable parameters rather than always conforming to the peer's demands.

As you read the following chapters, keep these issues in mind and compare them with the information presented. Where possible, I will provide hints and details from actual implementations to illuminate these concepts.

LCP and the PPP State Machines

IN THIS CHAPTER

This chapter covers the general PPP state machines, the first protocol always negotiated, called the Link Control Protocol (LCP), and the basic methods of parameter negotiation for all of the PPP protocols.

Variations on the techniques described in this chapter are used for the rest of the protocols in this book.

PPP Outline

RFC 1661 describes a set of link phases for PPP, as shown in Figure 3.1. These states are not always fully or directly implemented in a PPP daemon. For instance, the common ppp-2.3 implementation has nine link phases but uses them only sparingly in control of the protocol. In particular, the initiation of the Network Control Protocols (NCPs) is done by the authentication module itself rather than the main link phase state machine.

Another way to implement the three basic phases of negotiation—Establish (LCP negotiation), Authenticate [Authentication Protocol and Link Quality Management (LQM)], and Network (NCP negotiation)—is to consider them to be layers in the protocol design sense. In this model, each layer sends Up and Down events to the adjacent layers (with a hypothetical additional "physical"

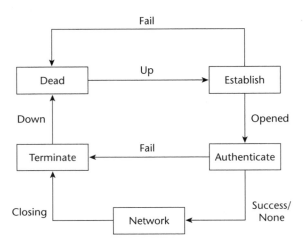

FIGURE 3.1 RFC 1661 link phases

layer below LCP and the network interfaces above the individual NCPs), as shown in Figure 3.2. These layers, however, are not layered in the protocol sense using nested PDUs, but instead are run sequentially. They have more in common with each other than protocol layers normally do, so we will discuss them together.

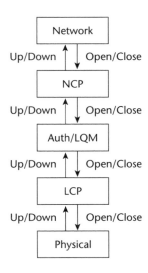

FIGURE 3.2 PPP phases as layers

Bringing a layer "up" is the result of three things: an Open request from a higher layer, an Up event from the next lower layer, and the successful negotiation of parameters at that particular layer. When these conditions are met, the layer sends an Up event to the next higher layer.

Typically, either a user requests that the link be established through some sort of interface, or a network interface requests the establishment through a demand-dialing mechanism when packets are enqueued for transmission on an idle interface. This causes an Open event to be sent through the NCP to the Authentication and LCP layers of the PPP stack, as shown in Figure 3.3.

When LCP starts, depending on the implementation, the physical link is established. This may involve dialing a modem and waiting for carrier, creating a Permanent Virtual Circuit (PVC) over an ATM interface, or, for hard-wired links, no action at all. Once this procedure is complete, this interface sends an Up event into LCP.

LCP then begins negotiation by sending out Configure-Request messages to the peer. Once the peers settle on a set of configuration values, LCP then sends an Up event into the Authentication layer. If authentication is desired, this layer runs until the link is authenticated. Otherwise, it just sends an Up event to the NCP layer.

Once authentication is complete, the link is generally considered to be "up." No user data yet flows across the link, however. In order to bring up network interfaces that will pass user data on the link, the NCP for each network interface must be negotiated. The NCPs are independent and may join or leave the

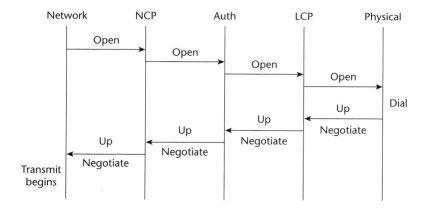

FIGURE 3.3 Example demand dial

link as needed while the link is up. Often, the link is torn down by sending a Close event to LCP when the last NCP closes, but this is not strictly necessary. If system resources and user configuration permit, the link could be left up but idle until needed again by another network layer interface.

On tear-down, each NCP should separately terminate itself from the link, then LCP should terminate, and finally the physical layer should terminate in an implementation-dependent manner (hanging up the telephone, for example). It is necessary for PPP implementations to handle termination of LCP without the termination of the NCPs and to handle termination of the physical link with no notification at all. These are very common operational cases that generally require implementation-dependent handling to tear down all link services at once.

The Negotiation State Machine

Each layer can be in any of ten different states. This leads to a rather difficult-to-interpret state table in RFC 1661. To simplify this, I will describe the establishment and tear-down sequences separately before putting everything together into a complete state machine.

As a layer is brought up, there are two stages of the process. First, the state machine must make certain that the lower layer is already up and that the current layer should be started. This is done with states 0, 1, and 2, with 1 representing open requested, and 2 representing lower layer up. Then it is necessary to negotiate with the peer and to converge on a set of parameters to use for the layer. This is done with Request, Acknowledge, Negative-Acknowledge (Nak), and Reject messages in states 6, 7, and 8, which synchronize the bidirectional negotiation so that both sides can finish. Finally, the layer is up when in state 9, and the next higher layer is then signaled. Refer to Figure 3.4. (This diagram is greatly simplified and does not show error handling or the various timers in use.)

Bringing a layer down (Figure 3.5) is simpler and requires only sending a Terminate-Request message and listening for a Terminate-Acknowledge message. The only complication in this process is that the peer may initiate the termination sequence rather than the local system; thus the need for states 3 and 5, where the peer has brought the layer down, but locally both the next higher and next lower layers are still up. Again, this diagram is greatly simplified to illustrate the important parts of the state machine related to termination.

In the combined state machine shown in Figure 3.6, I am including notations from RFC 1661 that indicate the events that cause the transition as well as the resulting actions. This diagram is for illustrative purposes; implementors are

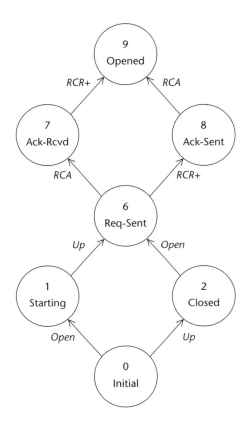

FIGURE 3.4 Simplified layer establishment

encouraged to read the state transition table on pages 12 and 13 of the RFC as it is suitable for translation into source code.

Not shown in this diagram are the facts that RXR is ignored by the state machine in all states and that event RUC causes action SCJ in all states except 0 and 1. The events and actions shown are as follows.

- Up   Lower layer reaches Opened state.
- Down   Lower layer leaves Opened state (except in order to implement a graceful close, in which case "Down" is signaled to a higher layer only when going from Closing to Closed or Initial, or from Opened to any state other than Closing).
- Open   Request from higher layer to begin negotiation.

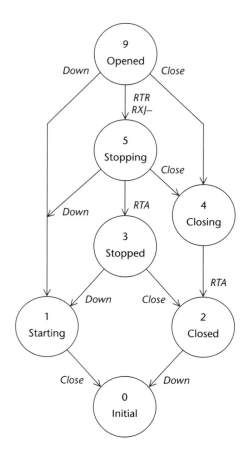

FIGURE 3.5 Simplified layer tear-down

- Close   Request from higher layer to terminate (except when not in Opened state, in which case termination of the state machine is preferred in order to produce LCP Protocol-Reject).
- TO+   Time-out and retransmit.
- TO−   Time-out; too many retransmissions.
- RCR+   Receive acceptable Configure-Request message.
- RCR−   Receive unacceptable Configure-Request message.
- RCA   Receive Configure-Ack message.
- RCN   Receive Configure-Nak or Configure-Reject message.
- RCX   Any of RCR+, RCR−, RCA, or RCN events.
- RTR   Receive Terminate-Request message.

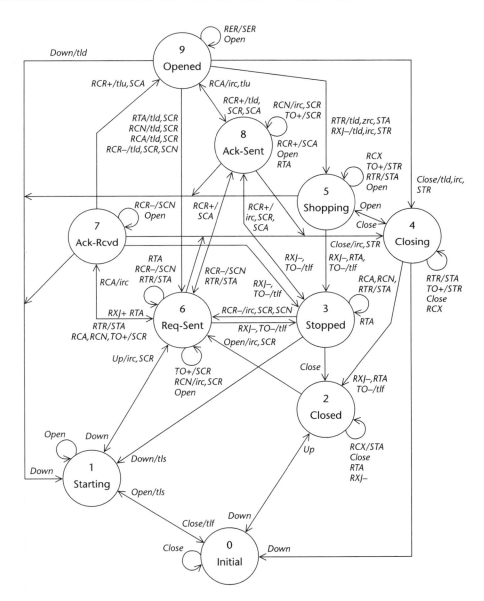

FIGURE 3.6 Complete state machine

- RTA   Receive Terminate-Ack message.
- RUC   Receive unknown code number in message.
- RXJ+   Receive Code-Reject message where code number can be disabled. (RFC 1661 states that this event is also for use with Protocol-Reject in allowing for termination of NCPs. I disagree because I believe that implementing as nested state machines, where Protocol-Reject terminates the affected NCP but leaves the other protocols running, results in a more natural implementation. Worse, the RFC 1661 view causes the state machine to send more messages with the rejected protocol number after the next time-out interval. This is clearly illegal.)
- RXJ–   Receive Code-Reject where the code number cannot be disabled—for example, codes 01 through 04. (RFC 1661 states that this should be used for Protocol-Reject of LCP itself. I disagree for the same reasons as those given above for RXJ+. Terminating the state machine for the affected NCP on Protocol-Reject leads to a clearer implementation and better behavior.)
- RER   Receive Echo-Request. (RFC 1661 lumps this together with Echo-Reply and Discard-Request. Of course, one does not send an Echo-Reply in response to an Echo-Reply.)
- RXR   Receive Echo-Reply or Discard-Request.
- SCR   Send new Configure-Request message.
- SCA   Send Configure-Ack to last received Configure-Request.
- SCN   Send Configure-Nak or Configure-Reject, as appropriate.
- STR   Send Terminate-Request message.
- STA   Send Terminate-Ack message.
- SCJ   Send Code-Reject message.
- SER   Send Echo-Reply message.
- tls   This layer started—the next lower layer should be sent an Open event.
- tlf   This layer finished—the next lower layer should be sent a Close event (where appropriate).
- tlu   This layer up—the next higher layer should be sent an Up event.
- tld   This layer down—the next higher layer should be sent a Down event.
- irc   Initialize-restart-count—set the counter back to the proper value (max retransmit) and set the timer interval back to the default.

- zrc   Zero-restart-count—set the counter to zero. This is used when Terminate-Request is received in Opened state, and it causes the state machine to pause quietly in Stopping state for one time-out period before proceeding to tear down the next lower layer.

Do not be intimidated by the complexity of the diagram in Figure 3.6 and the long list of events and actions above. It is rarely necessary to debug a PPP implementation through this state machine. Instead, most of the work involved in an implementation and most of the problems that occur are related to the negotiation exchange itself, which is covered in detail in a later section.

Note in this state machine that a Terminate-Request received (RTR event) during negotiation (Req-Sent, Ack-Sent, and Ack-Rcvd states) puts the state machine back into Req-Sent state and does not terminate the NCP. For this reason, the Close event should not be delivered to an NCP that is failing to negotiate. It is better simply to disable that NCP entirely so that Protocol-Reject will be sent.

Although this state machine is described only in the LCP document, RFC 1661, the same state machine and messages are also used for all of the NCPs.

The Negotiation Messages

PPP is a symmetric peer-to-peer protocol. There is no such thing as a "client" version or, for that matter, a "server." All of the protocol negotiation that follows reflects this fact.

PPP uses four messages to negotiate parameters for almost all protocols. These messages, documented with the LCP in RFC 1661, are called Configure-Request, Configure-Ack, Configure-Nak, and Configure-Reject, which are often abbreviated as Conf-Req, Conf-Ack, Conf-Nak, and Conf-Rej, respectively. Each of these messages contains within it a list of options and parameters, and all options in a given layer are thus negotiated simultaneously.

The system sending Configure-Request is telling the peer system that it is willing to receive data sent with the enclosed options enabled. If the peer does not recognize (or administratively prohibits) one or more of the options in the Configure-Request message, it must return just these options in a Configure-Reject message and the original sender must then remove the options from subsequent Configure-Request messages.

If some of the options were recognized but unacceptable with the supplied parameters, the peer would then respond with a Configure-Nak containing only the offending options and a suggested modified value for the parameters (called a *hint*). The receiver of the Configure-Nak then should decide if the hinted value is acceptable and, if so, send a new Configure-Request reflecting the requested changes plus the original values for the unchanged options. The sender of the Configure-Request may not send back any message other than Configure-Request in response to Configure-Nak, so the only recourses available if the hint is unreasonable are to drop the option from subsequent Configure-Request messages, use Protocol-Reject to disable the protocol, or disconnect the link entirely.

Finally, if all of the options are acceptable, the peer then responds with Configure-Ack with exactly the same option list as given in the Configure-Request to indicate that all of the enclosed options were acceptable and that all are now enabled.

Note that both systems will issue Configure-Request messages. The negotiation procedure outlined above is repeated in the opposite direction in order to negotiate the options in use in each direction on the link. Normally, there is no need for the options negotiated in each direction to match, although some particular options do have usage restrictions.

In some situations, one peer will absolutely require the use of a particular option. If that option is not presented in the Configure-Request message from the peer, and no Configure-Reject is needed, then that peer may reply with a Configure-Nak hinting that this additional option (or options) is needed. This is often referred to as an *unsolicited Configure-Nak*. Of course, this is rarely successful in actually prodding the Configure-Request sender to include the option. Instead, it usually causes the link to fail to come up since it gets stuck in a Configure-Request/Configure-Nak loop. However, it is useful in that a well-written peer will log that the other system was sending Configure-Nak for an unknown option, which can allow an administrator at least to diagnose the problem. (A good implementation should not make undue restrictions on which options must be used, since such restrictions usually make the implementation prone to interoperability problems. In particular, some peers refuse to negotiate IPCP addresses for no good reason. If the necessary addresses are known from some other information—perhaps a database look-up on the authenticated peer name—then it is safe and reasonable to proceed with negotiation without this option.)

Note that if the unsolicited Configure-Nak does not cause the peer to change its Configure-Request, it is impossible to tell if the peer failed to receive the Configure-Nak or simply cannot honor it, since behavior when retransmitting

Configure-Request due to a time-out after the loss of the response is identical to having the peer simply ignore the Configure-Nak. For this reason, most systems that send an unsolicited Configure-Nak in order to request an option will do so during the initial negotiation of a given protocol and not during any subsequent renegotiation. Some implementations will even send the Configure-Nak message exactly once and then give up.

Some options do not have associated data values but instead are *Boolean* (on/off) switches. These options are generally not modified with Configure-Nak, except with possible unsolicited Configure-Naks as in the paragraph above, but instead are negotiated "on" with Configure-Ack and "off" with Configure-Reject. Some other options represent general statements of fact, such as the name of the manufacturer, and likewise should not be in a Configure-Nak.

Example Negotiations

This example uses a hypothetical situation with two peers, A and B, attempting to negotiate the use of several options in each direction. Following are the logs of the negotiation (the sender's name is given on each line).

```
1. A: Configure-Request   ID:1  [ 1 4:01010101 5:80 9 ]
2. B: Configure-Reject    ID:1  [ 1 5:80 ]
3. A: Configure-Request   ID:2  [ 4:01010101 9 ]
4. B: Configure-Nak       ID:2  [ 4:01010102 ]
5. A: Configure-Request   ID:3  [ 4:01010102 9 ]
6. B: Configure-Ack       ID:3  [ 4:01010102 9 ]
7. B: Configure-Request   ID:1  [ 2 9 ]
8. A: Configure-Ack       ID:1  [ 2 9 ]
```

Here they are rendered as English dialog.

1. A: "Please send me data with options 1 and 9 enabled, and with option 4 set to 01010101 and option 5 set to 80."
2. B: "I don't understand options 1 and 5 at all."
3. A: "OK, then, please send me data with option 4 set to 01010101 and option 9 enabled."
4. B: "I'd rather have option 4 set to 01010102."
5. A: "OK, how about sending me data with option 4 set to 01010102 and option 9 enabled."

6. B: "I agree. I will now send you data with option 4 set to 01010102 and
       option 9 enabled."
7. B: "I want you to send me data with options 2 and 9 enabled."
8. A: "I will now send you data with options 2 and 9 enabled."

There are actually two independent conversations here, with one represented by
the sequence 1 through 6 and the other represented by messages 7 and 8. These
two could also be intermixed, with messages 7 and 8 appearing between any of
the other messages, depending on timing. In messages 1 through 6, the options
for data flowing from B to A are negotiated, while messages 7 and 8 negotiate
the options for data flowing from A to B.

Assuming that the peers have gotten both the Up indication from the next
lower layer and the Open indication from the next higher layer at the start of this
conversation, and that peer B sent a Configure-Request that was dropped by
peer A before the first message shown, the corresponding state transitions are as
follows.

```
Peer A                             Peer B
0.                                 (->Req-Sent) (state 6)
1. ->Req-Sent (state 6)
2.
3.
4.
5.
6. Req-Sent->Ack-Rcvd (7)          Req-Sent->Ack-Sent (8)
7.
8. Ack-Rcvd->Opened (9)            Ack-Sent->Opened (9)
```

Note that the state transitions are usually triggered by the events that cause
an implementation to transmit a Configure-Ack message or the reception of
Configure-Ack.

Packet Loss Scenarios in Negotiation

When packets are lost during negotiation, there are rare cases in which user data
can be lost. Here are four scenarios, illustrated in Figures 3.7 through 3.10,
showing how negotiation proceeds with packet loss. Each line shows what is
sent by that peer, and the numbers in parentheses show the state transitions.

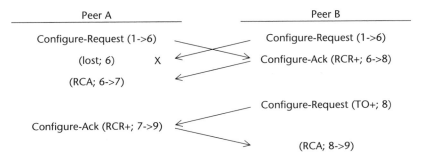

FIGURE 3.7 Lost Configure-Request

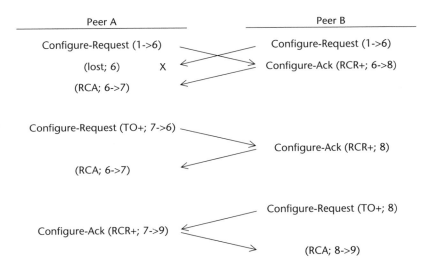

FIGURE 3.8 Lost Configure-Request with peer time-out

(Decimal state numbers are given here; refer to Figure 3.6 or RFC 1661 for the names of these states.)

In the simple case shown in Figure 3.7, one of the initial Configure-Request messages was lost. The sender times out first (event TO+) and the negotiation then completes. In the example in Figure 3.8, one of the initial Configure-Request messages was again lost. However, in this case, peer A has a shorter time-out configured than peer B. The negotiation completes only after peer B has timed out. In the example in Figure 3.9, one of the Configure-Ack messages has been lost. Note that peer A goes to Opened state (9) until peer B's timer expires.

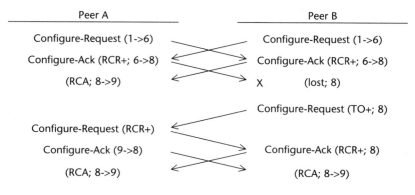

FIGURE 3.9 Lost Configure-Ack

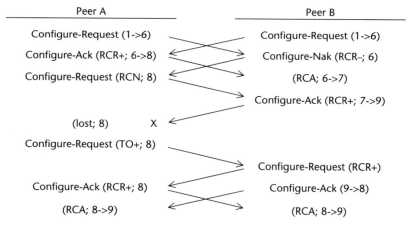

FIGURE 3.10 Another lost Configure-Ack

If this is an NCP, then any user data that might be sent by peer A will be lost. If it is the LCP, then initial negotiation messages from the next higher layer (either Authentication or the NCPs) will probably be sent by A but discarded by B, and this will trigger additional time-outs in those negotiations due to the loss of those Configure-Requests.

The last example (Figure 3.10) shows another Configure-Ack message being lost in a slightly different case. Again, however, one of the peers (B) briefly proceeds to Opened state before the other, and data may be lost.

Notice that the data loss occurs only with dropped Configure-Ack messages. This is fortunately a rare event, since the mechanisms that cause packet loss usually tend to act on the first few messages sent rather than on packets that come later in the data stream.

Negotiation Packet Formats

Each of these four messages (Configure-Request, Ack, Nak, and Reject) follows the same basic packet format, shown below.

Code	ID	Length	Options

Codes 01, 02, 03, and 04

The Code field is a single octet with value 01 for *Configure-Request*, 02 for *Configure-Ack*, 03 for *Configure-Nak*, and 04 for *Configure-Reject*. The ID field is also a single octet and is an arbitrary number for the message that helps to pair requests and subsequent replies. The Length field is two octets long and represents the length of the message, including all of the options that follow and the four-octet header (composed of Code, ID, and Length). The ID field is changed for each new Configure-Request sent. Since timers are used by the PPP state machine, it is possible to receive a message in reply that refers to an "old" Configure-Request and that must be discarded. Thus, it is necessary for the system generating the other three messages in response to a Configure-Request to insert the ID number from the Configure-Request message that is being interpreted into the response message, and the receiver of these responses must compare the ID number received against the ID of the last Configure-Request message sent. This prevents accidentally delayed messages from confusing the system.

Some common PPP packages do not bother to check the received ID fields and will happily accept and act on stale responses. This can cause trouble with authentication since a delayed response (common when external databases are used) can be misinterpreted as the reply to a later retransmitted request. When the retransmitted request is handled, the now-unexpected reply may cause the peer to disconnect.

Most PPP implementations start each layer's ID field at zero and increment when a new ID is needed. RFC 1661 does not specify this behavior, and neither a strictly linear increment nor any particular starting value should be relied on. In fact, it is generally a good practice to choose the first ID number randomly if possible, since doing so tends to avoid problems when layer renegotiation is necessary. PPP analyzers (human and otherwise) should make no assumptions about the ID field, but rather treat it as a randomly generated number.

Also note that a system generating a Configure-Request message identical to the last Configure-Request message sent (when triggered by a time-out) may send the same ID number. Except for security protocols, doing this is legal and can help a link with long latency times establish itself correctly, although not quite in a foolproof manner. Consider the example in Figure 3.11, with the time-out configured to be less than the latency across the link. Either changing the ID on time-out or using an increasing time-out will prevent the endless looping behavior shown in this diagram. Changing the ID value will cause this link to fail due to the sending of an excessive number of Configure-Request messages. Using an increasing time-out value is not required by RFC 1661 but will allow this link to settle and correctly establish itself.

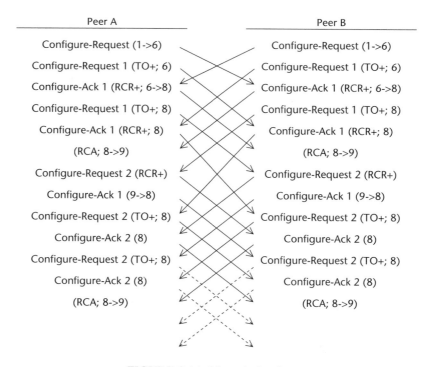

FIGURE 3.11 Negotiation loop

If the peer ignores the ID field, as some nonstandard implementations do, then only an increasing or adjustable time-out can fix the negotiation loop problem above. No good implementation should ignore this field.

Both Configure-Request and Configure-Ack may be sent without options (length field set to 0004), which means that the defaults for any optional parameters should be assumed. However, it is meaningless to send Configure-Nak or Configure-Reject with zero options. This should not be done by any good implementation. There are, however, common implementations that send these nonsensical messages. Replying with LCP Protocol-Reject is perhaps the best response.

Option Encoding

The Options field in each of the four negotiation messages contains a list of variable-length blocks in the following format.

Type	Len	Data

The Type field is a single octet and represents a single option for the protocol being negotiated. The Len field is also a single octet and is the length of the option block, including the two-octet header (composed of Type and Len). The Data field, if present, is information for the option being negotiated.

Returning to the example message used when describing HDLC encoding (Figure 2.5 on page 17), we can now begin to examine the components that make up the following message.

```
FF 03 C0 21 01 01 00 0E 02 06 00 00 00 00 07 02 08 02 70 34
```

This frame consists of the following elements.

```
FF 03            - Standard PPP HDLC address and control fields
C0 21            - Protocol number C021 (LCP)
01               - Code field; 01 is Configure-Request
01               - ID field (number 1)
00 0E            - Length field (14 octets)
02               - Type field; option 02 for protocol C021
06               - Len field (6 octets)
00 00 00 00
                 - Data for this option
```

```
07              - Type field; option 07 for protocol C021
02              - Len field (2 octets)
08              - Type field; option 08 for protocol C021
02              - Len field (2 octets)
70 34           - CRC
```

These structures are shown graphically in Figure 3.12. Notice that the length fields are redundant in many ways. The HDLC frame itself gives an indication of length by the framing marks. The Length field in the Configure-Request message header must be less than or equal to the total length of the frame minus the HDLC overhead (normally four octets; Address, Control, and CRC) and the PPP Protocol number overhead (two octets), so for this 20-octet message, the Configure-Request message length must be 14.

Each of the Option fields has a Len field, and the sum of all Len fields plus four (for the Code, ID, and Length fields) must be equal to the Length field. And, of course, most options have fixed lengths due to their definitions.

This redundancy helps an implementation do a number of sanity checks on the data before attempting to act on them. The PPP standard says that any mal-

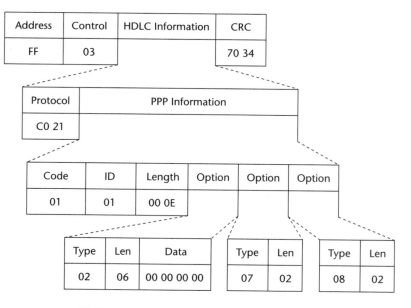

FIGURE 3.12 Configure-Request structure

formed packets must be silently dropped. Thus, if any but the last test in the previous paragraph fails, the frame is just ignored. If, however, an option has an improper Len field for that type of option but all of the lengths otherwise add up correctly, then the option should, according to RFC 1661, be included in a Configure-Nak message with the Len field changed to the proper length. (Dealing with a Len field set to 00 or 01 is a gray area in the standard. I recommend treating this as though it had been 02 for the sake of verifying the packet integrity when doing the length checks; if these checks succeed, a Configure-Nak should be returned with the correct Len field for those options. Other implementors reasonably argue that Configure-Reject is appropriate since the peer could not possibly implement an option correctly if it cannot even get the length right. Still others argue that such errors should result in Protocol-Reject, since the peer is obviously confused, and attempting to continue negotiation of a broken protocol may be unwise.)

Other Code Numbers

Besides the four main negotiation messages, several other message code numbers can appear on the link. These additional messages all have the following basic format, which is very similar to the negotiation messages.

Code	ID	Length	Data

Codes 05 and 06

Terminate-Request (Term-Req; code 05) and *Terminate-Ack* (Term-Ack; code 06) are used to tear down a running link or network protocol in a graceful manner. These messages have the following format.

Code	ID	Length	Text

For LCP, these codes are most often useful on links that have no external control signals, such as the DCD signal on a modem, to shut down operation. They are also useful in Multilink PPP (MP) systems when tearing down an unneeded link since they can prevent packet loss. For the other protocols, they allow individual network protocols to be shut down to conserve resources or for security reasons.

The length of these messages is usually 4, but some implementations put termination reason text into the data field that follows the length field. Any such message is implementation dependent but should be a printable text string.

RFC 1661 specifically indicates that a system sending Terminate-Request must begin discarding network-layer data received since it must leave Opened state. However, as long as the link is not being torn down due to authentication failure, I recommend instead that network-layer data should still be properly handled in Closing state after having sent Terminate-Request until Closing state is exited. Although this is a violation of the RFC, it is well supported by many members of the IETF working group and follows the "liberal in what you accept" design rule.

An exchange of messages for termination of the IPX protocol could look like this:

```
FF 03 80 2B 05 14 00 0D 49 27 6D 20 64 6F 6E 65 2E 0C 4F
FF 03 80 2B 06 14 00 04 A1 10
```

where the first message decodes as

```
FF 03              - Standard PPP HDLC address and control
                     fields
80 2B              - Protocol number 802B (IPXCP)
05                 - Code field; 05 is Term-Req
14                 - ID field (number 20)
00 0D              - Length field (13 octets)
49 27 6D 20 64 6F 6E 65 2E
                   - Text string saying "I'm done."
0C 4F              - CRC
```

and the second as

```
FF 03              - Standard PPP HDLC address and control
                     fields
80 2B              - Protocol number 802B (IPXCP)
06                 - Code field; 06 is Term-Ack
14                 - ID field (number 20)
00 04              - Length field (4 octets)
A1 10              - CRC
```

Codes 07 and 08

Code-Reject (Code-Rej; code 07) and *Protocol-Reject* (Proto-Rej; code 08) are used to indicate that the sender's code number or PPP protocol number is unknown and have the formats shown below.

07	ID	Length	Bad Code	Rcvd ID	Received Length	Rcvd Data

08	ID	Length	Bad Protocol	Received Data

In these cases, the entire offending message is sent back to the sender in the Data fields of these two messages starting with the beginning of the PPP information field for Code-Reject, which is sent from any protocol level, and with a two-octet PPP protocol field for Protocol-Reject, which is sent only from LCP, and only when LCP is Opened. Note that if the Protocol Field Compression option (see page 79) is in use, this protocol number must be uncompressed before insertion into this message. Generally, Code-Reject should not occur in normal usage, and it means that the sender is running a much newer version of the protocol, or that it is confused and sending corrupted packets. The Protocol-Reject message is relatively common while protocols are being negotiated, and it means that the sender does not know the given protocol at all. Protocol-Reject, however, must be ignored when LCP is not in Opened state. For example, a system may offer to handle AppleTalk (ATCP), IPX (IPXCP), and IP (IPCP) by sending Configure-Request for each of these NCP protocols after entering the Network phase. The receiver may elect to run just IP by sending Protocol-Reject for the other two Configure-Request messages.

In either case, the system that receives one of these messages must stop sending the indicated code number or protocol. The notes in the state machine section of RFC 1661 (Section 4.3, "Events") are somewhat unclear on this. Instead, the comments in Sections 5.6 and 5.7 are better references.

The following points should be noted about these messages.

- Seeing LCP Protocol-Reject for an unfamiliar protocol in a packet trace is not an indication of an error. This is normal operation of PPP.
- Sending Protocol-Reject is quite different from simply sending a Configure-Reject for all requested options. Configure-Reject leaves the protocol enabled while Protocol-Reject disables it.

- Section 5.7 of RFC 1661, which describes the usage of Protocol-Reject, is sometimes misunderstood by developers. An implementation must reject a protocol that it does not understand. It must not, however, reject a protocol that it does implement but has not yet negotiated or initialized, unless it intends never to negotiate that protocol during the life of the link. In other words, you should send Protocol-Reject for any protocol not in your table of known protocols and for any protocol explicitly disabled by an operator, but send nothing at all for protocols that you are simply not yet ready to receive.

There is at least one very common implementation in use in central sites that occasionally gets confused and sends a Protocol-Reject for LCP itself. RFC 1661 states that this should cause event RXJ– in LCP, which generally tears down the link. However, I recommend that these messages should instead be ignored from a state machine standpoint but logged where an administrator can see them, since they represent obvious nonsense. This same implementation occasionally generates erroneous configuration messages with the PPP Protocol field set to 0000, which usually leads to interesting exchanges with properly implemented peers.

Codes 09, 0A, and 0B

Echo-Request (Echo-Req; code 09), *Echo-Reply* (Echo-Rep; code 0A), and *Discard-Request* (Disc-Req; code 0B) are generally used for monitoring link integrity and during debugging of an implementation. Each of these messages has the same data format: four octets of the locally assigned magic number (see "Magic Number" on page 78) followed by arbitrary text, as shown below.

Code	ID	Length	Magic Number	Text

Usually, these messages are sent and received only from LCP. Echo-Request and Echo-Reply are used commonly, but use of Discard-Request is fairly rare.

Many implementations send periodic Echo-Request messages on idle links in order to check the viability and integrity of the link. This is done by setting one timer at, say, a 10-second interval to generate Echo-Request messages when the receive side is idle. A second, longer timer at, say, a 30-second interval is also set on the receive side and restarted when any traffic is received. If this second timer expires, the link is probably not operational and should be dropped.

In general, timers used for dead link detection must be gauged to the speed of the link. For some links, such as SONET/SDH links, fast error detection is very important. On some other media, such as analog modems, the timers may need to be set much longer due to such phenomena as V.42 error correction and data pump retraining. On still other media, such as wireless links, LCP echoes on an idle link may be too expensive to use at all. Timing of Echo-Request messages tends to be application and usage dependent.

One important implementation note is that it is necessary to place Echo-Requests at the front of the transmit queue, if possible, when they are used for dead link detection. If the queue is full, it is preferable to drop user data rather than to lose the link due to a lack of echo replies. This detail may vary depending on the system architecture.

Another important implementation note is that the magic number included in the Echo-Reply message is not copied from the corresponding Echo-Request message. Instead, this field must always be written with the sender's magic number value. (Some implementations, however, have gotten this aspect wrong and may misbehave under test.)

On MP links, an LCP Echo-Request should be sent without MP encapsulation as a normal LCP message, and the reply should be sent on the same link over which the request was received. An implementation must not attempt to pass these replies through the normal MP output routine, which load-balances across the available links.

Code 0C

Identification (Ident; code 0C) is described in RFC 1570, "PPP LCP Extensions," and has the following format.

Code	ID	Length	Magic Number	Text

There is no negotiation for this message, and no response is defined. This message has the same format as the messages above: four octets for the magic number followed by an arbitrary text string. The Identification option allows an implementation to identify itself to the peer using a simple unauthenticated string. This string may include version numbers, manufacturer information, or any other data. It can be used for debug logs, enabling proprietary options, or licensing restrictions. This message can be sent before LCP is in Opened state and generally should be sent as early as possible in order to be most useful. (RFC 1570 recommends sending it when a Configure-Reject is sent, before disconnecting due to negotiation failure, and when LCP goes to Opened state. I recommend also sending it earlier as well—either before or after the first Configure-Request during LCP negotiation.)

This message is unfortunately somewhat rare, but is worthwhile to implement. Newer Windows NT systems send "MSRASV4.00" in an LCP Identification string twice after LCP goes to Opened state and before any other protocols are negotiated. These systems do not handle LCP Code-Reject, however, so this message cannot be disabled.

Code 0D

Time-Remaining (Time; code 0D) is also described in RFC 1570 and has the following format.

0D	ID	Length	Magic Number	Time-Remaining

There is no negotiation for this message, and no response is defined. The Time-Remaining message has a format similar to the messages above: four octets for the magic number plus four octets for an integer representing the number of seconds remaining for the link, followed by an optional variable-length text string. The Time-Remaining message allows a PPP system to notify its peer that the connection is subject to some kind of administrative control that will terminate the connection in a known amount of time. This message is handled by the peer in an implementation-dependent manner. If the peer has a user interface, then it should present this message to the user. If not, then it might generate an SNMP trap or log a message for use by an operator. Unlike Identification messages, Time-Remaining may be sent only after LCP has reached Opened state.

This message is quite rare. It is likely limited to a few Apple-related implementations.

Codes 0E and 0F

The *Reset-Request* (Reset-Req; code 0E) and *Reset-Ack* (code 0F) messages are used with data compression. See Architecture and Error Recovery for the CCP protocol in Chapter 6 for details.

Code 00

The *Vendor-Extension* (code 00) message can be used for any proprietary purpose that requires sending a packet from one peer to the other. These messages may be sent at any time. The message format is shown below.

00	ID	Length	Magic Number	OUI	Data

It includes a four-octet magic number, three octets of vendor identification [which should contain the first three octets of an Ethernet address assigned to the vendor or, alternatively, a number assigned by the Internet Assigned Numbers Authority (IANA), which always begins with the value CF], and a variable-length data field for the proprietary message. This extension is described in RFC 2153.

The Vendor-Extension codes—except for unintentional coding flaws—are rarely seen. Most vendors either allocate code numbers from the IANA or, in some cases, expropriate unused codes without bothering with the formal procedure.

Notes on Message Code Numbers

The Identification and Vendor-Extension messages can cause negotiation problems if they are unsupported by the peer. If either is sent immediately after Configure-Request, the peer may respond with Code-Reject after sending its Configure-Ack. Receiving the Configure-Ack will put LCP in Ack-Rcvd state, but the Code-Reject will push it back to Req-Sent state. RFC 1661 requires disabling of these extensions if Code-Reject is received, but many implementations, including ppp-2.3, fail to do this.

Peers based on the current RFC 1661 will not change state on receiving an unknown code number. Unfortunately, this is not true of peers based on RFC 1661's predecessors. Implementations based on RFC 1331 will tolerate unknown codes during negotiation but will restart negotiation if an unknown code is received while the layer is in Opened state. Older implementations based on RFC 1171 or the original RFC 1134 will shut down completely on receipt of an unknown code in any state.

In July 1999, it was reported on comp.protocols.ppp that some versions of NT DUN will send LCP Identification messages but will shut down if LCP Code-Reject is received in response.

Since interoperability is an important goal, it should be possible on a good implementation to bar the transmission of potentially troublesome code numbers, such as Identification and Vendor-Extension, and it should be possible to configure specific code numbers to be silently ignored.

Codes 00 (Vendor-Extension), 0B (Discard-Request), 0C (Identification), and 0D (Time-Remaining) are rarely used. The others are fairly common.

LCP Negotiation Options

There are quite a few LCP options—more than for any other protocol within PPP. This is true for several reasons. First, several of these options change framing-level details and are thus convenient to settle as soon as possible. Second, some of these options imply changes in authentication methods or parameters and thus must take place before the authentication phase of the PPP session. And some are here for no good reason at all, except that LCP tends to be a catch-all for other options.

Conspicuously absent from the typical LCP negotiation is any type of peer identification and authentication. This means that LCP option settings must be selected either on a global basis or, where available, on the basis of external peer identification, such as call parameters or external prompting. Future LCP options may include authentication. (See LCP Authentication Option on page 90 for one possibility.)

Options 01 (MRU), 02 (ACCM), 03 (Authentication Protocol), 05 (Magic Number), 07 (PFC), and 08 (ACFC) are nearly universal. Options 11 (MRRU), 12 (Short Sequence), and 13 (Endpoint Discriminator) are common in MP implementations. A few implementations use option 09 (FCS Alternatives). The others are rarely used.

LCP Option 00   Vendor Extensions   Rare

This option is described in RFC 2153. It allows vendors to exchange proprietary options between devices of like kind. This option follows the format shown below.

00	Len	OUI	Kind	Values

where OUI is a three-octet Ethernet address prefix for the vendor or an identifier assigned by the IANA, Kind is a single octet with implementation-specific meaning, and Values are vendor defined.

See also option 14 (Proprietary) on page 88, which does not require the use of an OUI, and also option 16 (Multi-Link-Plus Procedure) on page 89, which has a variant implementation that conflicts with the Vendor-Extension option.

LCP Option 01	Maximum Receive Unit (MRU)	Common

This option, described in RFC 1661, has a two-octet data value associated with it, as shown below.

This value in a Configure-Request message is the maximum size of a PPP Information field that the implementation can receive. (This count does not include the HDLC Address, Control, and Check fields or the PPP Protocol field, so typical implementations will need room for at least another six octets.)

The negotiated MRU is used both for subsequent NCP negotiation messages and for the actual user data. This means that the actual MRU negotiated must be at least as large as the largest negotiation message or user datagram sent. In particular, if the user-configured MRU is too small, it may need to be altered by the LCP implementation to allow authentication to proceed.

It may seem at first glance rather illogical ever to send a Configure-Nak for this option unless the message itself is corrupted. If the peer sends a Configure-Request with a small MRU, then any reasonable implementation should be able to limit its messages to the requested size. If the peer indicates a larger-than-expected MRU, there is no harm in sending Configure-Ack for this value but then sending only the largest messages possible, even though these messages may be less than the requested MRU. In other words, reasonable implementations should reply with Configure-Ack if the offered value is any value greater than some small lower bound (say, 64 octets).

There is, however, at least one case where Configure-Nak is useful for MRU. Since the MRU requested by the peer often maps locally into the interface MTU as long as MP is not in use, this means that systems with preconfigured and unchangeable interfaces, such as most systems doing dial-on-demand, may need to use Configure-Nak to inform the peer that a particular MRU is required if the offered MRU is too small. In practice, if this value is over 1500, this tactic often fails, but it does prevent unusable links from being established.

Note also that all implementations are required to accept a PPP Information field of at least 1,500 octets at all times, regardless of the negotiated value. If the peer requests an MRU that is too small for any reason, and the MRU you want to have is 1,500 octets or fewer, then it is reasonable simply to send Configure-Reject for the peer's MRU option. This forces the peer to use the default of 1500.

Some implementations calculate an MRU to offer based on connection speed. This is generally not worthwhile at or above 14.4Kbps for TCP/IP connections.

Choosing a good MRU turns out to be quite complicated due to compression protocols, which may inflate rather than compress some types of data, because of link layers that have intrinsic MTUs, and because of optional network layers that cannot handle fragmentation. Regardless of any automatic MRU selection implemented, user controls that allow tuning of both the advertised (via Configure-Request) and required (via Configure-Nak) MRUs should be provided in any good implementation. Choosing good defaults based on possible protocol overhead, such as with MP, CCP, and ECP, is a good practice, since it reduces the administrative burden. Headers for these protocols can add as many as 20 octets to the messages. Other protocols, such as bridging, can add more.

In order to be as compatible as possible with existing implementations, it is reasonable to allow for a maximum MRU of 1600 [unless Fiber Distributed Data Interface (FDDI) bridging is in use; see Chapter 5]. Do not trim the input data to the negotiated MRU since some broken peers may go slightly over this amount in some cases. Trimming of output data is also not necessary, but cases where the output message is too large for the peer's MRU should be detected and should be logged since this is indicative of internal errors.

Some implementations, such as SGI's PPP for IRIX, change the MRU requested when other options are changed. For example, if it is configured to run RFC 1990 Multilink PPP (MP), it will send an MRU of 1505. If the MRRU is rejected by the peer during LCP negotiation, disabling MP, it will drop back to a default MRU of 1500, which, of course, is not included in the LCP Configure-Request message at all since it is the default. Note that this means that implementations must be prepared to receive an MRU in one Configure-Request but then to have it absent in a subsequent Configure-Request. When this happens, the implementation must drop back to the default. Some systems fail to implement this correctly. Good implementations set all option values to the default on reception of a Configure-Request before processing the request itself.

Implementation errors that I have seen with the MRU option include attempting to force a larger-than-default MRU without special configuration (I have seen 1524, 1576, and 1600 as common values), failing to abide by LCP Configure-Reject, negotiating the default value (this is never necessary), sending Configure-Nak with the hint set to the default value (this is never necessary either), and failing to return to the default MRU when LCP is renegotiated.

| LCP Option 02 | Asynchronous Control Character Map (ACCM) | Common |

This option is described in RFC 1662 and has the following format.

| 02 | 06 | Async Control Character Map |

Its value is a four-octet bit map that enables (bit set) or disables (bit clear) character escapes (the AHDLC 7D code) for the 32 ASCII control characters in the range 00 to 1F. The first octet of the value has the bits for control characters 18 through 1F, with the MSB representing 1F and the LSB representing 18, the second octet has bits for characters 10 through 17, and so on. The default is FFFFFFFF, or all control characters escaped. Values typically negotiated are 00000000 for links that can handle arbitrary data and 000A0000 for links with standard XON/XOFF software flow control.

Unlike the pseudocode in the preceding chapter, the implementations on the CD-ROM properly handle ACCM.

The ACCM negotiation handler should combine the value received in a Configure-Nak via a logical bitwise OR operation with the last Configure-Request value it sent. This result should then be sent in the next Configure-Request message. If a Configure-Request is received whose bit mask includes cleared bits for characters that the local implementation knows to be problematic (perhaps by way of an administrative option or some kind of hardware information), then it should send a Configure-Nak with the prior value modified to have these bits set.

When negotiating LCP, caution must be used to set the ACCM at the proper point in time. The RFC indicates that this is to be done as LCP transitions to Opened state. In order to be as compatible as possible with poorly written implementations, I recommend that the receive ACCM be set immediately on reception of Configure-Ack or Configure-Nak from the peer. The transmit ACCM should be set only after LCP has transitioned to Opened state and all pending output has been sent. (Waiting to set the transmit ACCM until the peer begins negotiation of the next layer is even better because it eliminates the possibility of confusion due to a lost Configure-Ack message but is impractical in some implementations.)

When renegotiating LCP, the transmit ACCM should first be set to the default. The receive ACCM, however, should be left at its previous value since the peer may miss the first LCP Configure-Request or simply fail to reset its transmit ACCM. Instead, the receive ACCM should be set on the basis of the received Configure-Ack or Configure-Nak from the peer.

An implementation may instead choose to detect the use of LCP within the AHDLC output code, perhaps by testing the PPP Protocol field, and temporarily force the transmit ACCM to FFFFFFFF while performing the AHDLC framing. This may be simpler than dealing with the timing issues above but does mean that the AHDLC driver must "know" a little bit about the protocol running above it. It would be a slight layering violation.

Synchronous implementations should not negotiate this parameter by default but must accept any parameter sent by the peer without actually acting on the value. This requirement allows interoperability between synchronous devices and asynchronous devices through translators, as mentioned in Chapter 2. The tests for escape characters are implemented by the translating device, not by the synchronous device.

Developers and testers should be aware that there are some modern synchronous systems that still violate this requirement. These systems are not compliant with the current RFC 1662, the prior RFC 1331, or even the original RFC 1172 for PPP.

Developers and users should also be aware that many asynchronous implementations have terrible bugs in their handling of the ACCM option. It is often necessary to be able to configure an explicit ACCM of 00000000 or 000A0000 without negotiating or to use such an explicit ACCM value regardless of the result of negotiation in order to interoperate with these badly designed products.

LCP Option 03   Authentication Protocol   Common

This option is described in RFC 1661 and has the following format.

| 03 | Len | Authentication Protocol | Data |

The Authentication Protocol field is the assigned PPP protocol ID of the desired authentication protocol, and any additional octets in the Data field are described by the particular RFC for that authentication protocol.

Receiving a Configure-Request for this option means that the peer wants the receiving system to identify itself using the indicated protocol. The receiver of Configure-Request may reply with Configure-Nak to request use of a different protocol, but the sender of Configure-Request may simply reply by terminating the link. Once a system sends Configure-Ack, it must then identify itself using the chosen protocol. The receiver of Configure-Ack should verify that the peer does indeed do this and should not allow network protocols to be negotiated until this identification is complete.

Note that some authentication protocol documents erroneously state that LCP Configure-Reject should be used to select different protocols, and that this has led to some implementation errors. The proper response for an implementation that can identify itself using some protocol but not the one requested by the peer is Configure-Nak with the contents altered to be a preferred protocol. Of course, an implementation that has no authentication protocols at all, or that cannot identify itself using any of the protocols it has (which happens if the user has not configured the right secrets or passwords), should send LCP Configure-Reject to ask to remain anonymous.

Current common values are C0 23 for PAP (RFC 1334), C2 23 05 for standard MD5 CHAP (RFC 1994), C2 23 80 for Microsoft CHAPv1 (RFC 2433), C2 23 81 for Microsoft CHAPv2, C2 27 for EAP (RFC 2284), C0 27 for SPAP, and C1 23 for the old version of SPAP. See Chapter 4 for more information on these authentication protocols.

LCP Option 04   **Quality Protocol**   Uncommon

This option is described in RFC 1661 and has the following format.

| 04 | Len | Quality Protocol | Data |

It is negotiated in exactly the same manner as the authentication protocol above, where the first two octets are the desired link quality monitoring protocol to use. Currently, only protocol C025 (Link-Quality-Report), specified in RFC 1989, is defined. The negotiation for this particular protocol includes an additional four octets after the protocol number that specify the requested

FF	03	C0	25
Magic Number			
Last Out LRQs			
Last Out Packets			
Last Out Octets			
Peer In LRQs			
Peer In Packets			
Peer In Discards			
Peer In Errors			
Peer In Octets			
Peer Out LRQs			
Peer Out Packets			
Peer Out Octets			

FIGURE 3.13 An LQR packet

maximum time between quality reports from the peer in hundredths of a second, as shown below.

04	08	C0 25	Report Interval

RFC 1989 describes the reports, called LQRs, which are packets with PPP protocol C025 and an Information field with 12 4-byte integers (48 octets), as shown in Figure 3.13. These integers give information on the numbers of octets and packets lost in both directions. The RFC specifies the meanings of these numbers and directions on handling them (a process called LQM), but analysis and policy decisions (i.e., what constitutes a "bad" link and what action to take) are left to the implementor.

Some implementations send LQR messages without negotiating LQM in LCP. These implementations depend on LCP Protocol-Reject to disable LQM if necessary.

LCP Option 05   Magic Number   Common

This option is described in RFC 1661. It contains a four-octet Data field, called the *magic number,* as shown below.

05	06	Magic Number

The magic number is a random number chosen to distinguish the two peers and detect error conditions, such as looped-back lines and inadvertently echoed-back data. The negotiation of this option is a little different from negotiation of other options. In particular, each peer must compare the magic number received in a Configure-Request message with the last magic number sent in a Configure-Request message, and likewise for the corresponding Configure-Nak messages. If either pair is equal, then a new magic number must be chosen and sent by Configure-Request. Also, Configure-Reject is taken to mean the same thing as Configure-Ack for this option, since the sender of Configure-Request for this option must never reject it.

If the line is looped back, this will result in an endless loop of Configure-Request and Configure-Nak messages. Implementations should detect this with counters and should log this specific error. (Generally, looped-back lines occur most often on asynchronous dial-up when one side of the connection is in PPP mode but the other side is still in some kind of command-line mode, since command lines usually echo user input. This is usually due to the failure of the preceding chat script rather than a problem with PPP itself.)

An implementation that does not include this option should send 0 in all cases where a magic number is required (such as with the Echo-Request message). This is a generally useful and easy-to-implement option, however, so all implementations should support it.

LCP Option 06	Reserved	Do not use

This was originally the link-quality-monitoring proposal. LQM has since been renumbered.

LCP Option 07	Protocol Field Compression (PFC)	Common

This Boolean option is described in RFC 1661 and has the following format.

07	02

When this option is negotiated, the sender of the Configure-Request indicates that it can receive "compressed" PPP Protocol fields. To compress a PPP Protocol field, the protocol number must have a most significant octet of zero; that is, it must be in the range 0000 to 00FF (remembering, of course, that neither 0000 nor 00FF is a legal PPP protocol number). The compressed protocol is sent as a single octet containing just the least significant portion of the protocol number.

After sending Configure-Ack, the sender is not obligated to compress the PPP Protocol field, although it is expected to do so. Uncompressed PPP Protocol fields must always be accepted.

The receiver of compressed PPP Protocol field messages can detect the compressed protocol since the least significant octet of a protocol is always odd (has its least significant bit set) and the most significant octet is always even (has its LSB clear).

A robust implementation may decide to handle arbitrary-length PPP Protocol fields by using the standard HDLC integer-reading procedure (read an octet, append to prior octets read, stop when LSB is nonzero). If so, beware that all protocol numbers specified in the RFCs are in HDLC-encoded form. Using the regular HDLC procedure is plainly not required by RFC 1661 and may result in an unnecessarily complex implementation but allows for some elegant solutions to alignment restrictions. In particular, encryption might have benefited from such an implementation to meet the 8-byte alignment restriction, had the protocol designers made use of it.

A suggested procedure for handling compression is

```
if protocol <= 00FF and peer allows PFC then
    write protocol as one octet
else
    write protocol as two octets
        (most-significant first)
endif
```

A suggested decompression procedure is

```
if LSB of octet is set then
    if peer agreed to do PFC then
        protocol = value of first octet
    else
        discard frame
        record receive error
    endif
```

```
else
    protocol = value of first two octets
endif
```

The CD-ROM presents C language examples.

These procedures may need to be modified if CCP-STAC compression using extended mode is negotiated. See Chapter 6 for details.

LCP Option 08   Address and Control Field Compression (ACFC)   Common

This Boolean option is described in RFC 1661 and has the following format.

Negotiating this option indicates that the sender of the Configure-Request wishes to receive messages without the leading HDLC Address and Control fields (normally set to FF 03). The system sending Configure-Ack for this option may send subsequent non-LCP frames without these octets (beginning each frame with the PPP Protocol field) but is not required to do so.

This option cannot be used with RFC 1663 numbered mode or with any of the encapsulations that use the HDLC header, such as RFC 1973 PPP in Frame Relay and RFC 1598 PPP in X.25.

The Address and Control fields must always be included on LCP messages, regardless of the negotiation of this option. Receivers must always be prepared to receive and handle these octets, again regardless of the negotiation.

A suggested procedure for handling compression is

```
if ACFC allowed by peer and protocol not C021 then
    do nothing
else
    write FF 03 as first two octets of frame
endif
```

A suggested decompression procedure is

```
if first two octets of frame are not FF 03 then
    if peer agreed to do ACFC then
```

```
            continue with PPP protocol field
        else
            drop frame
            record receive error
        endif
    else
        remove first two octets
        continue with PPP protocol field
    endif
```

LCP Option 09	FCS Alternatives	Uncommon

This option is described in the "extensions" RFC 1570 and has the format shown below

09	03	Options

where the Options octet is the logical OR of any of the following values.

01 Null FCS (no CRC at all)
02 CCITT 16-bit CRC
04 CCITT 32-bit CRC

It allows the default 16-bit CRC to be either negotiated into a 32-bit CRC or disabled entirely. At one point, a 48-bit CRC was also considered, but it was dropped from consideration due to a patent held by Digital Equipment Corporation.

This is a tricky option to implement correctly. First, there are several documents that mandate the use of particular FCS types on particular media. For instance, RFC 1662 gives the default as CRC-16 for most media. However, RFC 2364 mandates the omission of the FCS on AAL-5, since AAL-5 has its own built-in CRC-32 in the CPCS trailer. RFC 2615 mandates the use of CRC-32 on SONET/SDH and prohibits the use of CRC-16 on all but STS-3c. Both of these RFCs completely prohibit the use of this option for FCS negotiation in clear violation of basic PPP principles, even though such negotiation would be safe and perhaps even advantageous for SONET/SDH. Also, this option is typically not used with RFC 1973 PPP over Frame Relay, although that document does not specifically prohibit it.

More importantly, switching between the FCS modes can be difficult. In general, LCP is negotiated in the default FCS mode (usually CRC-16), and the new FCS mode takes effect when LCP goes to Opened state. In order to renegotiate LCP or terminate the link, it is necessary to send the message at least twice—once in the previously negotiated mode and once with the default. The RFC describes this as necessary only for Down events in the Ack-Sent and Opened states, but it is wise to do this continuously until LCP using the default FCS is heard from the peer, and wiser still to use each of the supported FCS types, rather than just two.

If "null FCS" is negotiated, the PPP negotiation frames must still include a CRC-16 by default. This is usually implemented by allowing CRC checking in the HDLC driver but retaining failed packets and the CRC field itself. If the packet is a data packet, then the CRC result is ignored and the entire message is passed to the network layer. If the packet is a negotiation packet (detected by checking the PPP Protocol field), then the CRC result is checked. The packet is discarded if the CRC failed or has the trailing CRC removed if it is intact. (Note that the length field in the negotiation messages will cause a properly implemented receiver to ignore the FCS bytes in any case.)

It is also possible, although not strictly necessary, to implement the HDLC receiver such that it runs CRC-16 and CRC-32 in parallel at all times and can give positive indication to LCP when the peer switches modes unexpectedly.

LCP Option 0A	Self-Describing Pad (SDP)	Very rare

This option, described in the "extensions" RFC 1570, provides a simple method for placing unambiguous padding octets at the end of the PPP Information field in order to cause messages to fall on "natural" boundaries (typically, powers of 2). When this option is enabled, packets are padded by adding the octet sequence 01 02 03, and so on, until the boundary is reached. If the packet falls on the boundary and the final octet is not in the range 01 through the boundary number, nothing is done. If it ends in such an octet, it is padded out to the next possible boundary.

The option negotiation contains a single octet of data that specifies the boundary, called the Maximum Pad Value, as shown below. Typically, this value ranges from 01 to 07, and is 1 less than the alignment modulus.

0A	03	Max

The receiver checks the final octet of the Information field (located before the CRC) on reception. If this octet is in the range 01 through the boundary number (inclusive), then octets are stripped and checked until 01 is removed, or until an out-of-order octet is found, which is an error that results in dropping of the frame.

A PPP implementation may pad frames as necessary without using this option, but only if the network protocols in use can tolerate padding. Such padding is generally not part of the standard itself, but is rather a local implementation issue. Implementors should be aware that Cisco routers do not calculate IP transport layer (UDP and TCP) checksums properly, and thus any needed padding must therefore be done with 00 octets only.

There are currently three possible uses for this procedure. One is to allow network protocols that do not tolerate padding to run over physical layers that require padding. I know of no such implementations. Another is with the rarely used Compound-Frames option. The third is with encryption via the Encryption Control Protocol (ECP). Many encryption algorithms require the source data to fall on some kind of natural boundaries, such as the U.S. Data Encryption Standard (DES), which requires 8-byte boundaries.

Note that this boundary requirement is placed on the network-layer data presented to the DES algorithm but that SDP negotiated by LCP pads only the link-level data. Negotiating the SDP option by LCP is therefore not useful for ECP. (Indeed, since the output of DES is always aligned, SDP is counterproductive in this case.)

LCP Option 0B	Numbered Mode	Uncommon

This option is described in RFC 1663 and is shown below.

0B	Len	Window	Address

This option enables the ISO 7776 (LAP-B) standard for reliable data transport, which the RFC calls *Numbered Mode* operation in contrast to RFC 1661 PPP *Unnumbered Mode*. In order to do this, the implementation must maintain a queue of messages for retransmission and must implement several special timers.

The negotiated Window parameter indicates how many frames may be outstanding at one time. If this number is less than 8, then basic mode (modulo-8 counters) is selected. If it is greater than or equal to 8, then extended mode (modulo-128 counters) is selected. (LAP-B super mode is not used.) The Address field in the Configure-Request message contains the HDLC address at which the implementation will receive LAP-B packets. This field is present because PPP does not make the DTE/DCE distinction that ISO LAP-B requires. Also, by selecting address 07 or 0F instead of 01 or 03, it is possible to enable the ISO 7776 Multi-link Procedure if desired.

Once this option has been negotiated and LCP goes to Opened state, an extra PPP link phase is inserted between LCP and Authentication. During this new phase, the side with the numerically lower Magic Number sends SABM (Set Asynchronous Balanced Mode; for basic mode operation with modulo-8 counters) or SABME (for extended mode operation with modulo-128 counters) using the current LCP Configure-Request timer until the peer responds with UA. At this point, Numbered Mode operation is enabled and authentication can proceed. The PPP Address and Control fields are switched to ISO LAP-B usage. For this reason, ACFC must not be negotiated with this option. The rest of the packet, the PPP Protocol and Information fields, remain the same as with Unnumbered Mode.

Numbered Mode has one oddity with respect to LCP. If the link is renegotiated, the RFC requires leaving Numbered Mode enabled, rather than resetting to the default as is customarily the case. The RFC, however, has a mechanism for recovering from the reset of the peer: it sends DM and then falls back to Unnumbered Mode if it receives an unnumbered packet.

Using this option means that the upper-level protocols will not see frame loss if errors occur, unless, of course, the link itself goes down. It also means that the upper-level protocols will experience relatively large variances in latency times over the link, which can have a severe impact on the performance of reliable transport protocols, such as TCP.

I recommend limiting implementation of this option to rare circumstances, such as PPP over spread-spectrum radio [although Forward Error Correction (FEC) would likely be a better choice in this case]. In particular, it is not worthwhile over typical modem connections, which usually already have error-correcting features, such as V.42, or over common synchronous connections, which are usually highly reliable. It cannot be used if reordering of packets can occur, as on tunneled connections.

One of the main uses of this option is to support CCP (see Compression Negotiation on page 177 in Chapter 6), which can exacerbate packet loss.

An example implementation of LAP-B for PPP is included on the CD-ROM.

LCP Option 0C   Multilink Procedure   Do not use

This option apparently was assigned in error for the ISO 7776 Multi-link Procedure but never described in any document. With the advent of PPP Multilink
(MP) in RFC 1990, it is no longer necessary to support this option or the ISO
7776 Multi-link Procedure. MP is functionally similar to the ISO protocol but
allows fragmentation and reassembly, which reduces latency for large packets
and overall burstiness due to reordering. See Chapter 7 for details on MP.

LCP Option 0D   Callback   Common

This option is described in RFC 1570 and has the following format.

| 0D | Len | Operation | Message |

The Operation values and Message field are described in detail in Chapter 7.

Callback allows a way for a peer to indicate that it wishes to have the link terminated after authentication and to have the other system call it back in an
implementation-dependent manner, either for security reasons or as a toll-saving
feature.

Unfortunately, this option is somewhat flawed. It is negotiated at LCP time
when the peer has not yet been authenticated. In most cases, this means that it is
not possible to determine whether the callback will be authorized at the time this
option is acknowledged. The only realistic options available in the cases where
callback is available but the peer is not authorized to use the service are either to
terminate the link after going through authentication, possibly with a meaningful error message in the LCP terminate request, or to renegotiate LCP and send
Configure-Reject for the Callback option when the peer next requests callback.
LCP renegotiation, although a mandatory part of the PPP standard, is not well
tolerated by many implementations. In particular, according to engineers from
Shiva, both ShivaRemote and Windows 95 will hang up the telephone if LCP
renegotiation is attempted.

A proposed solution to this problem, which involves the use of an NCP-
like protocol called Callback Control Protocol (CBCP), is documented in
`draft-ietf-pppext-callback-cp-02.txt`. This proposal, discussed in more
detail in Chapter 7, is strongly tied to machines with a CP/M lineage and to

analog modems with Hayes-compatible command sets. This draft has expired, and no replacement has been proposed as of 2000. It should not be implemented in new systems, because no general consensus exists on how its features should be supported.

LCP Option 0E	Connect Time	Do not use

This option was originally part of the PPP AppleTalk Control Protocol, and was briefly changed into a configuration option and then into a separate code number to become the LCP Time-Remaining message. This option is obsolete.

LCP Option 0F	Compound Frames	Do not use

This Boolean option is described in RFC 1570 and has the format shown below.

0F	02

This option enables a method to encapsulate multiple PPP frames within a single link-layer frame. It could be used, for instance, to save on per-packet charges incurred on some kinds of packet-switched networks by sending fewer, larger packets. Its use was shaped by the IP over Large Public Data Networks (IPLPDN) working group. This option is obsolete, but see PPP Muxing on page 92 for an alternative.

LCP Option 10	Nominal-Data-Encapsulation	Do not use

This option was described in the expired Internet Draft named `draft-ietf-pppext-dataencap-03.txt`. It specified a way for data frames that would normally travel within PPP to use some other encapsulation technique (called *nominal encapsulation* by this draft) instead. The goal of the draft was to introduce the use of PPP parameter negotiation to existing systems that exchange network data. The exchange of the data would not be altered and would stay in its possibly proprietary format, but PPP would also be negotiated over the link in order to establish security and other parameters. This option is obsolete.

LCP Option 11	Multilink-Maximum-Reconstructed-Receive-Unit MRRU	Common
LCP Option 12	Multilink-Short-Sequence-Number-Header-Format SSN	Common
LCP Option 13	Multilink-Endpoint-Discriminator (ED)	Common

These three options together are described in RFC 1990. These options form the basis of Multilink PPP (MP). In particular, negotiation of an MRRU means that this link is one of possibly several links to be aggregated together into a single bundle. The other options modify MP operation, but do not enable it.

Frames are sent in MP by breaking them into small fragments, which are sent in parallel over all participating links and then reassembled at the remote end. Like IP fragmentation, there is no retransmission if a fragment is dropped. Instead, the entire frame is simply lost. See Chapter 7 for a detailed description of this protocol and of these LCP options.

| LCP Option 14 | Proprietary | Very rare |

This option is proprietary to Funk Software. Its format was discussed by Funk on the IETF PPP mailing list in June 1996. The option contains the fields shown below.

| 14 | Len | ID Type | ID Len | Vendor ID | Data |

The ID Type is a single octet with the value 00 if the Vendor ID is an Organizationally Unique Identifier (OUI; the first three octets of an Ethernet address) or 01 if the Vendor ID is a unique arbitrary-length string, generally containing a company name or trademark. The ID Len is a single octet with the length of the Vendor ID string in octets. Its value should be 03 if ID Type is 00, since an OUI is three octets long.

All information in the Data field is in a proprietary format defined by the indicated vendor and need not be interoperable with any other system or publicly documented.

Funk uses the following format for its Data field.

| Suboption Type | Suboption Length | Suboption Data |

The Suboption Type field is a single octet with the values 65 (Node Type), 66 (Authentication), 67 (NodeID™), 68 (Name), 69 (Container Control), and 6A (Proprietary Flags). The Suboption Length field is also a single octet representing the length of the entire option.

For the Node Type suboption, the Data field is a single octet set to 01 for WanderLink Server, 02 for WanderLink Free Client, and 04 for WanderLink Paid Client. The Name suboption allows the name to be used for authentication to be queried before starting authentication. The other suboptions are not documented.

LCP Option 15   **DCE-Identifier**   **Rare**

This option is described in the Informational (non-standards-track) RFC 1976. It specifies a way to distinguish communications devices, such as CSU/DSUs, from regular PPP bridges and routers. The intent of this option proposed by engineers at Adtran, a manufacturer of telecommunications equipment, is to have devices such as CSU/DSUs communicate using a stripped-down version of PPP. This would provide a standard means of negotiating desirable features, such as data compression and encryption. It is intended to be used with RFC 1963, which specifies a way to transport ordinary serial data over PPP using a form of V.120.

LCP Option 16   **Multi-Link-Plus Procedure (MP+)**   **Rare**

This option negotiates the use of Ascend's proprietary MP+ protocol, which is documented in Informational RFC 1934. The option currently has two octets of data, which are unused, as shown below.

16	04	00 00

This is essentially a Boolean option, despite the Data field. See Chapter 7 for details on MP+.

Note: some MP+ speakers use option 00 instead of option 16 with this same data. This usage is not compatible with RFC 2153 but can be detected because of the short option length.

LCP Option 17   Link Discriminator   Uncommon

This option negotiates a two-octet integer that is used by RFC 2125 Bandwidth Allocation Protocol (BAP) to distinguish links in a multilink bundle. The option format is shown below.

| 17 | 04 | Link-ID |

See Chapter 7 for details on BAP.

LCP Option 18   LCP Authentication   Do not use

This option was proposed in September 1996 by Funk Software as Internet Draft `draft-ietf-pppext-link-negot-00.txt`. This is an elegant scheme to incorporate security within LCP negotiation itself using a challenge/response model based on Configure-Nak as a challenge mechanism. Implementation of this option would make the separate authentication stage unnecessary and simplify the implementation of callback and multilink.

LCP Option 19   Consistent Overhead Byte Stuffing (COBS)   Very rare

This option, described in `draft-ietf-pppext-cobs-01.txt`, uses a framing technique invented by Stuart Cheshire and Mary Baker at the Stanford University Computer Science Department. The format of this option is shown below.

| 19 | 03 | Flags |

COBS framing works by picking an arbitrary framing byte value and removing it from the data stream by transforming the data into small counted blocks representing the data that occur between the bytes that happen to have the framing byte value in the original source. Unlike the simple escape mechanism in RFC 1662, which has a worst-case expansion ratio of 100%, COBS never expands the data transmitted by more than 0.5%.

The Flags octet contains the following bits.

0	0	0	0	0	0	Pre	Zxe

The Pre bit is set to 1 if the receiver supports packet preemption and resumption, which are used to minimize latency for support of multiple classes of service on a line. The Zxe bit is set to 1 if the receiver supports Zero Pair Elimination (ZPE) and Zero Run Elimination (ZRE) extensions to the basic COBS format.

Because these values simply inform the transmitter of the receiver's capabilities, they should not be subject to Configure-Nak. A transmitter that does not implement these options can safely ignore the bits. A receiver that does not implement these options will not receive the unexpected encodings, since the transmitter is obligated to omit any extensions the receiver does not support.

LCP Option 1A	Prefix Elision	Rare
LCP Option 1B	Multilink Header Format	Rare

These two options are described in RFCs 2686 and 2687. RFC 2686, "The Multi-Class Extension to Multi-Link PPP," describes the basic option format for Prefix Elision as follows.

1A	Len	Class	Prefix Length	Prefix . . .	Prefix Length	Prefix . . .

Class is one of the traffic classes created by the Multilink Header Format option, Prefix Length is the length in octets of the prefix to be elided from the transmitted data, and the Prefix Length/Prefix sequence runs to the end of the option defined by Len. It describes the Multilink Header Format option as

1B	04	Code	Classes

where Code is 02 for MP long sequence number format with classes and 06 for MP short sequence number format with classes, and Classes is the number of suspension classes supported.

RFC 2687, "PPP in a real-time oriented HDLC-like framing," describes two additional Code numbers for the Multilink Header Format option to enable Fragment Suspend Escape (FSE)—0B for an extended compact format and 0F for a real-time format.

LCP Option 1C   Internationalization   Uncommon

This option is described in RFC 2484. It allows an implementation to request that any PPP negotiation packets containing human-readable text strings be given in a preferred character set and language. The option format is

| 1C | Len | MIBenum | Language-Tag |

The MIBenum value is an integer representing the character set from RFC 2277. The Language-Tag is an ASCII string with the name of the desired language from RFC 1766.

LCP Option 1D   Simple Data Link (SDL)   Very rare

This Boolean option switches from RFC 1662 octet-synchronous framing to Lucent's Simple Data Link (SDL) framing on a SONET/SDH link, as described in RFC 2823. The option format is

SDL framing works by prepending a four-octet header to each PPP packet. Unlike octet-synchronous framing, the PPP data inside the packet are not escaped or altered in any way. Instead, the header has the length of the packet and an error-correction code. The length of the packet gives the distance in octets to the next SDL header. This allows an SDL framer to detect synchronization using an ATM-like alpha-delta framer. Once the framer is in sync, small errors can be corrected by the built-in header CRC.

SDL has many advantages, including predicable and low overhead, rapid link-loss detection, and simple scaling to very high speeds.

LCP Option 1E   PPP Muxing   Very rare

This Boolean option, described in `draft-ietf-pppext-pppmux-00.txt`, is geared toward the use of voice over RTP and RFC 2508 compression. The option format is

1E	02

The multiplexing operation is similar to the earlier compound frames proposal and is useful for eliminating small amounts of overhead on very-low-speed links. It allows multiple small packets to be packed into a single PPP frame.

When this option is negotiated, multiple packets of 127 octets or less each can be concatenated into a single PPP frame using PPP Protocol 0059. The encapsulation for these subframes prefixes each with a single octet containing a flag bit and 7 bits of length. If the flag is set, a PPP Protocol field follows this octet. Otherwise, the upper-level data follow and the PPP protocol is the same as the previous subframe. The flag bit on the first octet must always be set so that the decoded protocol is known. Any two or more frames may be combined in this manner except LCP frames.

The two possible subframe formats are shown below.

1	Length	Protocol	Information Field . . .

0	Length	Information Field . . .

Authentication and Security

IN THIS CHAPTER

This chapter covers the PPP link authentication protocols and the general topic of system security. Data encryption (ECP), however, is described in Chapter 6, since it shares many architectural features with data compression.

Authentication Protocols

The authentication protocols generally do not follow the negotiation model laid out in the preceding chapter. They are in a sense special protocols because portions are non-negotiable by design and because they do not have many optional parameters but rather consist of an exchange that leads to either confirmation of identity or failure.

The base RFC for PPP authentication is 1334. This RFC covers Password Authentication Protocol (PAP) and the original version of Challenge-Handshake Authentication Protocol (CHAP). The current RFC for CHAP, however, is number 1994 and does not include PAP. The Extensible Authentication Protocol (EAP) is covered by RFC 2284. The three other protocols in common use are proprietary—Shiva's SPAP and two variations of Microsoft's MS-CHAP.

The protocol to use for authentication is negotiated during LCP option negotiation. A PPP implementation should be prepared to request its strongest option first and to be able to accept hints from the peer for only those options that have been configured as acceptably secure by a system administrator. Authentication is often computationally expensive, requiring database look-ups, communication with external servers, and occasionally long calculations. For this reason, good implementations should relax retransmit timers and counters for these protocols.

Despite notes to the contrary in some drafts and RFCs (such as RFC 2433), LCP Configure-Nak must be used to suggest a different authentication protocol if the peer's offered authentication protocol is not available. Using LCP Configure-Reject will cause all authentication to be disabled and usually will result in the link being dropped.

These protocols provide only identification and authentication of the peer. They do not provide confidentiality. This fact is significant when considering security measures for tunneled PPP connections, such as those used with L2TP. See also About Security on page 120.

Password Authentication Protocol (PAP)

PAP is protocol number C023, and its packets have the following format

Code	ID	Length	Data

where Code is 01 for *Authenticate-Request* (Auth-Req), 02 for *Authenticate-Ack* (Auth-Ack), and 03 for *Authenticate-Nak* (Auth-Nak), the Data field format depends on the code number, and ID and Length are as previously described.

In the Authenticate-Request message, the Data field has two counted strings, which are arbitrary sequences of octets with a single octet prepended that indicates the length of the sequence. The first string is the Peer-ID, which is commonly, although incorrectly, referred to as a user name, and the second is the password. An example PAP Authenticate-Request looks like this before HDLC framing:

```
FF 03 C0 23 01 01 00 0F 03 6A 6F 65 06 53 65 63 52 65 74 85 6B
```

which decodes as

```
FF 03          - Standard address and control field
C0 23          - PPP Protocol field for PAP
01             - Authenticate-Request
```

```
01                  - ID number
00 0F               - Length
03                  - Peer-ID length--three octets
6A 6F 65            - The letters "joe"; the peer's name
06                  - Password length--six octets
53 65 63 52 65 74
                    - The letters "SecRet"; Joe's password (He's
                      apparently not too concerned about security!)
85 6B               - CRC
```

The possible replies to this message are the Authenticate-Ack or Authenticate-Nak messages, where the Data field contains a single octet message length plus an optional message for the human user (if any exists). If authentication fails, the system sending Authenticate-Nak should also attempt to terminate the link to frustrate a would-be system cracker, although a small number of attempts are often permitted, since some peers will have an interface to a human user and will permit retries. Systems that do not expect to have peers with users actively typing in passwords during the establishment of the link need not support any retries. Most dial-up systems should support a small number of retries, but most stand-alone routers should not.

An example PAP Authenticate-Ack message looks like this:

```
FF 03 C0 23 02 01 00 05 00 8B 3B
```

which decodes as

```
FF 03               - Standard address and control field
C0 23               - PPP Protocol field for PAP
02                  - Authenticate-Ack
01                  - ID number
00 05               - Length
00                  - Message length zero--no message
8B 3B               - CRC
```

An example PAP Authenticate-Nak message looks like this:

```
FF 03 C0 23 03 01 00 21 1C 55 6E 6B 6E 6F 77 6E 20 70 65 65 72
2D 49 44 20 6F 72 20 70 61 73 73 77 6F 72 64 2E 99 85
```

which decodes as

```
FF 03              - Standard address and control field
C0 23              - PPP Protocol field for PAP
03                 - Authenticate-Nak
01                 - ID number
00 21              - Length
1C                 - Message length--28 octets
55 6E ...
                   - ASCII text "Unknown peer-ID or password."
99 85              - CRC
```

One known, but rare, implementation error with PAP attributed to some Windows NT systems is to send an Authenticate-Ack message that contains only the data through the Length field and omit the required message length octet. A work-around for this problem, which is included in the latest versions of ppp-2.3, is to accept Authenticate-Ack messages even if they are one octet shy of the correct length. Doing so does not harm system security.

The examples above used ASCII characters in the Peer-ID, Password, and Message fields. This is commonly the case in practice, but nothing in the protocol requires this particular usage. Since authentication by PAP necessarily requires the prior agreement of two peers in order to coordinate the peer-ID and password in use, any use of those fields desired may be made, and good implementations should allow such use. In particular, strcmp() and strcpy() functions should not be used to manipulate data in these fields, because they may contain NUL characters in some configurations.

Note that the authentication session is controlled by the authenticatee sending requests, rather than by the authenticator, and that PAP authentication, if used, can usually be used only once during the lifetime of a link. To reauthenticate using PAP on a live link, it is necessary to renegotiate LCP in order to trigger PAP authentication again.

Figure 4.1 shows the standard state machine marked for use with PAP authentication. The notations in this figure are the events and actions to be performed. These notations are as follows.

- Up-1   Event Up (LCP goes to Opened state) on a system doing bidirectional PAP.
- Open-1   Event Open on a system doing bidirectional PAP.

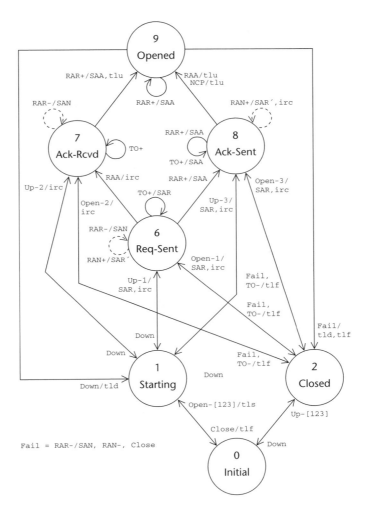

FIGURE 4.1 State machine marked up for PAP

- Up-2   Event Up on a system demanding PAP from its peer (sent LCP Configure-Request with PAP) but not providing its identity to its peer. Sometimes referred to as a "server."
- Open-2   Event Open on a "server" doing PAP.
- Up-3   Event Up on a system supplying its identity to its peer (sent LCP Configure-Ack with PAP) but not demanding identification from the peer. Sometimes referred to as a "client."
- Open-3   Event Open on a "client" doing PAP.

- Close   Upper layers requesting shutdown.
- Down   Lower layer down (LCP leaves Opened state).
- RAR+   Receive a good Authenticate-Request (validation succeeds).
- RAR–   Receive a bad Authenticate-Request (validation fails).
- RAA   Receive Authenticate-Ack.
- RAN+   Receive Authenticate-Nak on a system with the ability to query a user for a new peer-ID and password.
- RAN–   Receive Authenticate-Nak without the ability to query a user.
- TO+   Nonfatal time-out (retransmit).
- TO–   Fatal time-out (retransmit limit reached).
- NCP   Receive any NCP negotiation message (optional feature; allows negotiation to proceed quickly if Authenticate-Ack is lost).
- SAR   Send Authenticate-Request.
- SAR′   Send a modified Authenticate-Request on a system with the ability to query a user for a new peer-ID and password.
- SAA   Send Authenticate-Ack.
- SAN   Send Authenticate-Nak.
- tls   This Layer Started—LCP should be sent an Open event.
- tlf   This Layer Finished—LCP should be sent a Close event.
- tlu   This Layer Up—the next higher layer (the NCPs) should be sent an Up event.
- tld   This Layer Down—the next higher layer (the NCPs) should be sent a Down event.
- irc   Initialize-Restart-Count—set the counter back to the proper value (max retransmit) and set the timer interval back to the default.

States 3, 4, and 5 are not used with PAP because this protocol does not use the Terminate-Request and Terminate-Ack mechanism.

The transitions shown with dotted lines in Figure 4.1 are optional. They represent the actions necessary for support of retries. Event RAN+ is a received Authenticate-Nak that causes the implementation to prompt the user for a new peer-ID and password. Action SAR′ is the new Authenticate-Request generated after the user enters the new data. Implementors should be aware that allowing retries reduces security by allowing the peer to probe for valid peer-ID and password combinations, but no more so than allowing multiple login attempts through a regular text "login:" prompt.

PAP sends a Close message to LCP to tear down the link if it transitions from any state greater than 2 to a state less than or equal to 2 (Closed), and sends Down messages to the NCPs if it transitions from state 9 (Opened) to any other state.

With PAP, you are necessarily giving away a peer name and password to any peer that requests it. It should be immediately obvious that the peer name and password sent out by an implementation should not be a valid peer name and password accepted by that implementation. This implies that for each connection, a separate peer name and password must be configured at each peer or that PAP should be used in only one direction. A separate pair of passwords, one for each call direction, should also be used for each pair of peers if the link may be initiated by either peer, as in symmetric demand-dialing. This means that the hardware must keep track of which peer dialed in order to select the password to use. If this is not done, a third party may trivially break security by calling both parties and relaying the messages between them. This problem does not occur if only one peer answers the call and the other ignores incoming calls.

Challenge-Handshake Authentication Protocol (CHAP)

CHAP is protocol number C223 and uses two basic packet formats. For the *Challenge* (code 01) and *Response* (code 02) messages, the format is

Code	ID	Length	Value-Size	Value	Name

where the Value-Size field is a single octet representing the length of the Value field in octets, the Value field is the randomly generated challenge or the encoded response, and, unlike PAP, the Name field follows without a Length octet.

The Name field in the Challenge message identifies the system performing the authentication, and in the Response message it supplies the name of the system proving its identity. Unlike PAP, this allows a system to use different CHAP secrets for different peers automatically and without relying on external information, since the peers identify themselves by name. For this reason, two names are used when one peer authenticates the other, and four names when each authenticates the other. Of the four names, two are simple identifications used in Challenge messages and two are authenticated identities used in the Response messages. There is no requirement that any of these four possible names match.

An example CHAP Challenge looks like this:

```
FF 03 C2 23 01 01 00 23 10 F7 11 7A E8 5A EE A7 05 83 33 F0 34
60 CB 49 44 44 69 61 6C 2D 75 70 20 53 65 72 76 65 72 78 E7
```

which decodes as

```
FF 03                - Standard Address and Control Field
C2 23                - PPP Protocol field for CHAP
01                   - Challenge
01                   - ID number
00 23                - Length (35 octets)
10                   - Value-Size (16 octets)
F7 11 7A E8 5A EE A7 05 83 33 F0 34 60 CB 49 44
                     - Randomly generated value
44 69 61 6C 2D 75 70 20 53 65 72 76 65 72
                     - Name "Dial-up Server"
78 E7                - CRC
```

The Name field in the Challenge is not authenticated and must not be used for any purpose that requires an authenticated peer name, such as identifying new links in a bundle in Multilink PPP (MP). (See Chapter 7.) Only the Name field in the Response is authenticated.

The Response message is generated by computing a one-way hash over the ID field in the Challenge, the locally stored secret, followed by the Value field from the Challenge. The one-way hash algorithm is negotiated at LCP time, and the Message Digest 5 (MD5; see RFC 1321) algorithm must be supported for any RFC 1994-compliant system. (In order to preserve the security of the secret, I recommend that an implementation receiving a Challenge message with a too-short Value field terminate the link. Also, if possible, it is worthwhile to include proprietary identifying marks, such as a local IP address, in the Challenge Value and detect received Challenges that have these marks. This can be used to lessen the chance of compromising security if an administrator misconfigures dial-in and dial-out secrets to be identical.)

The computed hash value is placed in the Value field of the Response message, and the ID field is copied from the Challenge. An example response, using MD5 and based on the Challenge above and a shared secret of "SecRet" and peer-ID "joe," looks like this:

```
FF 03 C2 23 02 01 00 18 10 AA D1 55 6B 62 0A 0C 18 44 53 FF 9C
3B A0 FF E8 6A 6F 65 AE C8
```

which decodes as

```
FF 03              - Standard address and control field
C2 23              - PPP Protocol field for CHAP
02                 - Response
01                 - ID number (copied from Challenge)
00 18              - Length (24 octets)
10                 - Value-Size (16 octets)
AA D1 55 6B 62 0A 0C 18 44 53 FF 9C 3B A0 FF E8
                   - MD5 hash over ID, secret, and Challenge Value
6A 6F 65
                   - Name "joe"
AE C8              - CRC
```

For the *Success* (code 03) and *Failure* (code 04) messages, the packet format is similar to the PAP response codes but does not include a message-length octet:

Code	ID	Length	Message

The Success and Failure messages are formed by copying the ID field from the Response and including an optional message.

An example CHAP Success message is

```
FF 03 C2 23 03 01 00 04 79 92
```

which decodes as

```
FF 03              - Standard Address and Control Field
C2 23              - PPP Protocol field for CHAP
03                 - Success
01                 - ID number (copied from Response)
00 04              - Length (4 octets)
79 92              - CRC
```

An example CHAP Failure message is

```
FF 03 C2 23 04 01 00 29 49 20 64 6F 6E 27 74 20 6B 6E 6F 77 20
79 6F 75 20 61 6E 64 20 49 20 64 6F 6E 27 74 20 77 61 6E 74 20
74 6F 2E C2 B3
```

which decodes as

```
FF 03              - Standard Address and Control field
C2 23              - PPP Protocol field for CHAP
04                 - Failure
01                 - ID number (copied from Response)
00 29              - Length (41 octets)
49 20 64 ...
                   - ASCII Text "I don't know you and I don't
                     want to."
C2 B3              - CRC
```

As in PAP, the message supplied, if any, should be a human-readable string. Usually, systems supporting CHAP do not permit retries, so a failure message should be followed immediately by link termination.

Unlike PAP, the conversation is controlled by the authenticator sending a Challenge message, and CHAP may also be renegotiated at random during the life of a link without renegotiating LCP or disrupting data in order to lessen the chance that an eavesdropper could successfully "hijack" a connection.

The operation of CHAP is quite a bit more complex than PAP. First, the system that wants to identify its peer using CHAP must generate a random sequence of octets (called the *challenge*) and send this along with an identifying name (which may not necessarily be the same as a user or peer name at that site). Only then may the recipient of this message respond. The recipient uses the name supplied in the Challenge message to look up a clear-text secret to use with this peer (perhaps in a local database or by asking a human user), then uses the hash algorithm negotiated at LCP time to generate a response from the secret and the challenge value, and then transmits this value back as the Value field in a Response message, along with its name. Figure 4.2 shows the processing of these messages in more detail.

The system that sent the Challenge message then performs the same hash algorithm. If the result matches the received Response value, it sends a Success message. Otherwise, it sends a Failure message.

Here is an example configuration that shows mutual CHAP authentication between two peers named A and B. It includes the separated databases and Challenge/Response names.

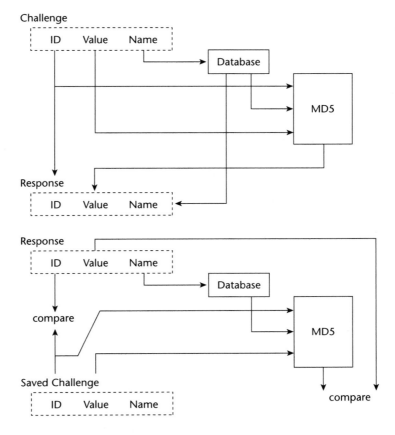

FIGURE 4.2 CHAP message processing

Preconfigured data on each system:

System A: Identify self as "sys A" in CHAP Challenge
System B: Identify self as "sys B" in CHAP Challenge

Databases on each system:

System A:
    Response-generate:
        "sys B" has secret "prove me to B" and name "System-A"

Response-validate:
    "System-B" has secret "prove me to A"
System B:
    Response-generate:
        "sys A" has secret "prove me to A" and name "System-B"
    Response-validate:
        "System-A" has secret "prove me to B"

The exchange might then proceed as follows.

```
System A                              System B
Send Challenge:
   name="sys A"
   value=random1
(Save for later.)


                                      Look up "sys A" in Response-
                                      generate database, retrieve
                                      name and secret "prove me to
                                      A", then send Response:
                                         name="System-B"
                                         value=MD5(id,secret,value)


Look up "System-B" in
Response-validate database
to get "prove me to A"
and check that received value
is MD5(id,secret,random1)


                                      Send Challenge:
                                         name="sys B"
                                         value=random2
                                      (Save for later.)


Look up "sys B" in Response-
generate database, retrieve
name and secret "prove me to
B", then send Response:
```

```
name="System-A"
value=MD5(id,secret,value)
```

```
                              Look up "System-A" in
                              Response-validate database
                              to get "prove me to B"
                              and check that received value
                              is MD5(id,secret,random2)
```

It is essential that this validation of the peer's Response be done using a database of secrets separate from that used to generate CHAP Response messages on a system. If a CHAP implementation both generates and validates Responses using a single secret, then it has effectively no security at all. An attacker could just echo back each message to gain access, since the Responses generated would be exactly the ones accepted as authentic. As with PAP, symmetric demand-dialing systems should use separate secrets depending on which system originates the call.

Figure 4.3 shows the standard state machine marked up for use with CHAP authentication. The notations are the events and actions to be performed:

- Up-1   Event Up (LCP goes to Opened state) on a system doing bidirectional CHAP.
- Open-1   Event Open on a system doing bidirectional CHAP.
- Up-2   Event Up on a system demanding CHAP from its peer (sent LCP Configure-Request with CHAP) but not providing its identity to its peer. Sometimes referred to as a "server." Such a machine should not respond to CHAP Challenge, Success, and Failure messages, and should log the event if these messages are received.
- Open-2   Event Open on a "server."
- Up-3   Event Up on a system supplying its identity to its peer (sent LCP Configure-Ack with CHAP) but not demanding identification from the peer. Sometimes referred to as a "client." Such a system should ignore CHAP Response messages and should log the event if these messages are received.
- Open-3   Event Open on a "client."
- Close   Upper layers requesting shutdown.
- Down   Lower layer down (LCP leaves Opened state).

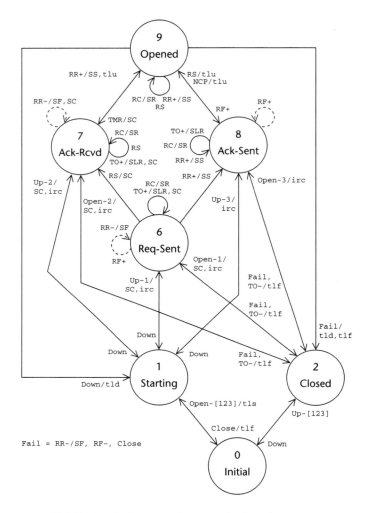

FIGURE 4.3 State machine marked up for CHAP

- RC   Receive a Challenge message.
- RR+   Receive a good Response message (validation succeeds).
- RR–   Receive a bad Response message (validation fails).
- RS   Receive a Success message.
- RF+   Receive a Failure message on a system with the ability to requery
            a user for a new shared secret value. (Nonstandard implementa-
            tion option—see text below.)

- RF–   Receive a Failure message.
- NCP   Receive any NCP negotiation message (implementation option).
- TO+   Nonfatal time-out (retransmit).
- TO–   Fatal time-out (retransmit limit reached).
- SC   Send a Challenge message.
- SR   Send a Response message.
- SS   Send a Success message.
- SF   Send a Failure message.
- SLR   Send last generated Response message (if any; this is a nonstandard implementation option—see text below).
- TMR   Rechallenge timer event. Unlike most state machines, CHAP should not signal a Down event to the NCPs when leaving the Opened state on a TMR event.
- tls   This Layer Started—the next lower layer should be sent an Open event.
- tlf   This Layer Finished—the next lower layer should be sent a Close event (where appropriate).
- tlu   This Layer Up—the next higher layer should be sent an Up event.
- tld   This Layer Down—the next higher layer should be sent a Down event.
- irc   Initialize-Restart-Count—set the counter back to the proper value (max retransmit) and set the timer interval back to the default.

There are two important, nonstandard implementation options shown in the marked-up state machine. First, the RF+ event allows for retries on authentication failure. Most systems using CHAP do not permit retries, but this option is useful with human users who may not get the secret right on the first try, especially since most implementations do not echo the secret as it is typed and editing is therefore difficult. Forcing the link to disconnect and reconnect will result in a lengthy restart while the modems retrain. Implementors should be cautioned, however, that adopting this option allows the peer to probe for valid peer-IDs and secrets more easily.

The second nonstandard option shown in the state machine is the ability to resend the last generated response on a TO+ event. This need not be implemented at all, but it can sometimes speed up negotiation if the local timer is shorter than the peer timer and a Response message has been lost.

Four important implementation errors I have seen with RFC 1994 CHAP are as follows.

- One large router vendor shares the CHAP secret between the Response generation and checking code. This means that breaking into these routers is as simple as echoing back all of the packets received.
- One dial-up system was noted in January 1998 on comp.protocols.ppp to send CHAP Challenges without having negotiated CHAP at all. It is very important not to respond to Challenges unless CHAP is at least properly configured by the user, but I suggest that a robust implementation should respond to these Challenges normally if configured to identify itself with CHAP and, of course, log the fact that CHAP was used by the peer without having used normal LCP negotiation.
- Another dial-up system was noted in February 1998 on comp.protocols. ppp to send an extra 00 octet in the LCP Authentication-Protocol option for CHAP. In other words, it sends 03 06 C2 23 05 00 instead of the correct 03 05 C2 23 05. In order to accommodate poorly implemented peers gracefully, I recommend that a CHAP implementation should send Configure-Ack for a slightly malformed option containing extra octets and just log the event.
- One Unix vendor PPP implementation sends LCP Configure-Reject instead of LCP Configure-Nak when presented with unexpected authentication options. There is no work-around for this bug.

Note that NT RAS uses information in the local registry to do RFC 1994 CHAP authentication. It does not use the NT domain services, so the peer name presented by the peer can be arbitrary. It does not have to follow the "domain\ username" format used for MS-CHAP (described below).

PAP Versus CHAP

Good implementations should support both CHAP and PAP authentication methods, even though the PAP protocol has been officially deprecated by RFC 1994. Many users believe that CHAP is always "better" than PAP. This is not the case. Each of these two protocols has its own advantages and failings. In CHAP, the secret never appears on the wire in any form, but the failing is that both sides must keep a clear-text version of the password in order to calculate the response value, and this password could be compromised. In PAP, this particular problem can be avoided by the use of one-way hashing to validate passwords, a technique that cannot be used with CHAP, but using PAP means that the clear-text password must be sent over the wire and that a rogue peer could be used to extract a user's password.

The RFC does not state that the PAP password must be a fixed value or even that it must come from a user. One way to use the password, which makes PAP more secure than CHAP, is to use it with a token card, such as Enigma's Safe-Word or Security Dynamics' SecurID. These hardware devices (which resemble credit cards with LCD numeric displays) give one-time passwords that are useless to an attacker if intercepted. Since the validation routines for these cards can check a given value but will not reveal the current password for use with other calculations, these cards usually cannot be used with CHAP at all but can be used with PAP by placing the one-time key value in the password field. [Limited use with CHAP can be made if the one-time key is appended to the peer name and used in addition to a shared secret. Cisco uses an asterisk (*) to separate the actual peer name from the one-time key in the peer name field.]

Such a one-time password system will usually need prior arrangement to signal the use of this validation scheme, often based on the peer name. Because of the time-sensitive nature of the one-time passwords, this system also requires the implementation to refrain from prompting the user until LCP goes to Opened state. Because common PC-based PPP implementations prompt the user for credentials before even attempting to establish the modem link, these implementations often do not work well with one-time passwords.

Of course, such a scheme is also impractical if periodic reverification is desired. For these applications, specialized hardware with interfaces to smart cards might be employed to generate secure responses. Some newer devices on the market have USB ports and can be queried without human intervention. These devices are quite appropriate for use with rechallenges.

MS-CHAPv1

MS-CHAPv1, described in Informational RFC 2433, uses a protocol similar to RFC 1994 CHAP but with algorithm 80 negotiated at LCP time instead of 05 for MD5. When this option is accepted, the MS-CHAP documentation gives a complex set of possible ways to form a response from an eight-octet challenge value. The two main options are LAN Manager– and Windows NT–type responses. When using the obsolete LAN Manager form, the user's password is hashed by using it as a key to encrypt a well-known string with DES. For the

Windows NT form, the user's password is hashed by running it through the public MD4 (RFC 1320) algorithm.

In either case, the response to the challenge is generated by using DES to encrypt the random challenge value from the peer using the hashed password from the last step as a key. Note that for this step of the operation, standard CHAP does a similar operation but uses MD5 instead. The Response Value field for MS-CHAPv1 always contains 49 octets. The first 24 are reserved for the LAN Manager response, if any, and are expected to be filled with zeros on all new implementations. The second 24 octets are filled with the Windows NT response. The last octet is a flag value and should be 01 to indicate the use of the Windows NT response.

When using MS-CHAP with non-Microsoft software, be aware that the user name and Windows network domain strings must be concatenated to form the peer name passed to an NT host if a domain is configured, since NT RAS authenticates this information using the NT domain services. For example, if the domain is "office" and the user name is "mary," then the peer name passed to NT should be "office\mary." In a pppd configuration file on Unix, the backslash in this string will need to be escaped, so the peer name for this case appears in the file as "office\\mary." Also note that NT systems do not identify themselves to their peers. The peer name in the Challenge message from an NT system will be zero length.

MS-CHAPv1, unlike regular CHAP, requires a baroque text format for the Failure message and insists on the use of a particular international character set known as "UNICODE" for the Peer-ID. The common error codes are listed below.

```
646 Restricted log-on hours
647 Account disabled
648 Password expired
649 No dial-in permission
691 Authentication failure
709 Changing password
```

These codes also occasionally appear as four-octet integers in network byte order in the text field of LCP Terminate-Request messages.

MS-CHAPv1 also defines two new message types that can be used after a particular Failure message is given. The code numbers are 05 for *Change-Password-1* and 06 for *Change-Password-2*. The Change-Password-1 message allows the authenticator's stored hash value to be altered by an intruder without requiring knowledge of the unhashed password. The Change-Password-2 message shares this flaw and adds the capability for an attacker to recover passively the new password in unhashed form by the inclusion of a data block containing the new password reversibly encrypted with the old hash as a key. This mechanism is also useful for *Trojan horse* programs that gather user passwords, since a dial-up Windows95 or 98 system never demands authentication from its peer.

MS-CHAPv2

MS-CHAPv2, described in Informational RFC 2759, is a new variation on the MS-CHAPv1 protocol described above. This version uses a new algorithm number (81) at LCP negotiation time and thus does not interoperate with MS-CHAPv1 implementations and removes backward compatibility with obsolete LAN Manager password databases.

As in MS-CHAPv1, the user's password is hashed using MD4 to give the actual secret key. Unlike MS-CHAPv1, the new version uses Secure Hash Algorithm (SHA-1; US NIST FIPS Publication 180-1) on the original challenge value, a locally chosen random value, and the user name (but not the domain) to produce a new challenge value that is then DES encrypted as in MS-CHAPv1. This additional step is effectively moot, however, since all of the SHA-1 inputs appear on the wire where they can be intercepted by any attacker. MS-CHAPv2 also adds a few extra checks for validity of the Success message, but these are also dependent entirely on the visible data transferred on the wire and are therefore no more secure.

MS-CHAPv2 introduces a new variation of the password-changing security flaw using code 07 for *Change-Password-3*. As in the previous version, the new password is included in the message reversibly encrypted using the old password hash value.

RFC 1994 Versus MS-CHAP

Of course, there's no way for a system identifying its peer using either of the two MS-CHAP protocols to "know" whether the peer system did as the RFC states, starting with the user's typed password and doing the initial DES or MD4 hash, as specified for both versions of MS-CHAP, or just used a stored copy of the hash value and perhaps has no knowledge of the user's password at all. Indeed, the Windows NT dial-in system ("RAS") doing the MS-CHAP validation stores the hashed password value as the key for the user, in exactly the same way a CHAP system must store the shared secret. In truth, this system does not differ much from regular CHAP in that both use a shared secret, which is a configured string for regular CHAP and the output of a hash routine for the MS-CHAP system. If one were to obtain the MD4 hashed user passwords, either by breaking into a Windows NT password registry using the readily available "PWDUMP" utility or by snooping on any network running Server Message Block (SMB), where the MD4 hash is sent in the clear, one could then successfully authenticate PPP connections into that system using a modified PPP client that does not implement the hash function, and thus have complete access to the target network, including all SMB file- and resource-sharing operations.

The claimed advantage for this variant of CHAP, other than the incorrect claim of stronger, C2-compliant security, is one of simplicity. The user can reuse his dial-in password as his simple password for other applications (such as logging into the NT system itself for file access), since the system is not storing this password in the clear and any compromise of that hash value does not reveal this "upper-level" password. However, since using the same password for PPP link authentication as is used for access to other systems is generally a bad idea, this is a dubious advantage at best.

Worst of all, MS-CHAP provides a way to change the stored password from within PPP. After having broken into the system using the technique given above, a trespasser can use this flaw to set the user's real password to any convenient value in order to gain complete access. This flaw can also be used to gather passwords passively over time by recording Change-Password messages; all of the data necessary to recover the actual passwords pass over the wire.

What should have been done instead to implement these features would have been to simply use the hashed password as the shared secret for RFC 1994 CHAP. The implementation could be made slightly easier to use, if desired, by appending to the Challenge Value field, which has arbitrary length, a distinguished string such as "WindowsNT" to indicate that the authenticator will be validating against an MD4 hash rather than against the raw user-specified password. The implementation could then select at authentication time which procedure to perform, and similarly modify its Name field in the Response message to indicate that the hash was done.

Implementations that performed RFC 1994 CHAP as an authenticatee would not include the distinguishing mark in the Response message, and the authenticator could then either disconnect or find a standard CHAP secret in the local registry. Implementations using RFC 1994 CHAP as an authenticator would not provide the distinguished string in the Challenge message, and the enhanced client would skip the MD4 stage and therefore be backward-compatible.

Such a design would be compatible in situations where MS-CHAP is not, such as an RFC 1994 CHAP speaker authenticating a Microsoft client, and would be no less secure.

Extensible Authentication Protocol (EAP)

EAP (protocol C227) is a new authentication scheme for PPP described in RFC 2284, and is not yet in widespread use. The packets have code numbers and formats similar to those of CHAP. The first two valid message codes are 01 (*Request*) and 02 (*Response*), which have the packet format

where Type is one octet indicating the contents of the Type-Data field that follows. Type is one of the following.

```
01 Identity (RFC 2284)
02 Notification (RFC 2284)
03 Nak (RFC 2284)
04 MD5-Challenge (RFC 2284)
05 One-Time Password (RFC 2289)
06 Generic Token Card (RFC 2284)
09 RSA Public Key Authentication
   (draft-ietf-pppext-eaprsa-04.txt)
0A DSS Unilateral (draft-ietf-pppext-eapdss-01.txt)
0B KEA (draft-ietf-pppext-eapkea-01.txt)
0C KEA-VALIDATE (draft-ietf-pppext-eapkea-01.txt)
0D EAP-TLS (RFC 2716)
0E Defender Token (AXENT)
0F Windows 2000 EAP
```

The other two valid message codes are 03 (*Success*) and 04 (*Failure*), which have the packet format

Code	ID	Length

Unlike PAP and CHAP, no text string can be sent with these messages. Although not intended for this purpose, the Notification message could be used to convey a success or failure text string before sending the final Success or Failure message if desired.

The operation of this protocol is quite different from that of PAP or CHAP. The peers hold a conversation consisting of the exchange of several Request and Response messages, with Requests coming from the system performing the authentication and Responses coming from the system being authenticated, until the authenticator is satisfied that the peer has been identified or has failed identification, at which point it sends either the Success or Failure message instead of the Request message.

An example EAP initial request message is

```
FF 03 C2 27 01 01 00 14 01 45 6E 74 65 72 20 75 73 65 72 20 6E
61 6D 65 25 C0
```

which decodes as

```
FF 03              - Standard Address and Control field
C2 27              - PPP Protocol field for EAP
01                 - Request
01                 - ID number
00 14              - Length (20 octets)
01                 - Type Identity
45 6E 74 ...
                   - ASCII Text "Enter user name"
25 C0              - CRC
```

The reply from the peer might be

```
FF 03 C2 27 02 01 00 08 01 6A 6F 65 E9 12
```

which decodes as

```
FF 03              - Standard Address and Control field
C2 27              - PPP Protocol field for EAP
02                 - Response
01                 - ID number (copied from Request)
```

```
00 08              - Length (8 octets)
01                 - Type Identity
6A 6F 65
                   - ASCII Text "joe"
E9 12              - CRC
```

The next message could be another Identity message, with a prompt for a PAP-style password, or it could be an MD5 Challenge message to do a CHAP-style handshake. The sequence of Requests should be configurable to allow for flexible, administrator-controlled authentication procedures.

This flexibility creates a complication for implementors. If the observable behavior of the system is different for successful authentications than for unsuccessful ones, an attacker has a much easier time of breaking security by attacking one layer at a time. For instance, if the Response to an Identity Request message gives an unknown user name, a good implementation should still go through the motion of requesting (and discarding) other identification data before sending the Failure message. Failing to do this weakens security by allowing an attacker to guess a valid user name first, then a password, and so on until access is gained.

Shiva Password Authentication Protocol (SPAP)

SPAP is protocol number C027 or the illegal protocol number C123 for the older version. On the IETF PPP mailing list, Shiva engineers discussed a few of the features of this protocol, such as support for token cards. However, no documentation for this protocol exists in any of the standard public sources, and it appears that Shiva intends to license this protocol to selected companies rather than documenting it publicly.

As documented by the Klos sniffer (see Chapter 11), the LCP option to request SPAP is C027 plus four octets of unknown data set to 01000002. The LCP option for the old SPAP is C123 plus two octets of unknown data set to 0000.

Old SPAP appears to use a message format that is identical to regular PAP, except for the protocol number. The Password field contains an obscured (although not quite encrypted) version of the text password.

Regular SPAP uses a message format modeled after the option format used for the NCPs. Codes 02 (*Ack*), 03 (*Nak*), and 06 (*Request*) are used. The option numbers are 01 (*Peer-ID*), 02 (*Password*), plus several unknown options. The Peer-ID contains just the name of the peer as text. The Password contains two octets that form a "secret" value, perhaps similar in function to the Unix password "salt," plus the obscured password.

Other Authentication Protocols

Several other authentication protocols are defined for PPP, including

- C225   `draft-ietf-pppext-public-key-00.txt`
          This is a protocol developed by Novell that apparently has been abandoned.
- C229   Mitsubishi's Security Information Exchange Protocol
- C26F   Stampede's Bridging Authorization Protocol

as well as several proprietary protocols, such as C281, C481, and C283. These protocols are generally not seen in the field.

PPP also includes a privacy protocol called Encryption Control Protocol (ECP). Because its implementation shares many features with data compression, ECP is described along with the data compression protocols in Chapter 6.

External Security Servers

External security servers are systems used to provide centralized administration of dial-up accounts. These servers generally support user identification and authentication, authorization control, and accounting, which are abbreviated as AAA. For authentication, the PPP system must send parts of the user's authentication packets to the server, and the server must perform part of the PPP-defined validation. For authorization, the server may inform the PPP system of network layer addresses to allow for the user, or filters to apply to the link, or any other restrictions. For accounting, most servers allow event logging to databases that can be used to develop user billing and tracing.

Historically, external security servers have been proprietary systems. Two of the oldest are Encore's ACP (now Nortel) and Cisco's TACACS. These systems were designed for terminal servers and adapted over time to fit the needs of PPP. Livingston (now Lucent) developed its own proprietary security server protocol, but because the company released the source code for free use and because of much enlightened effort on the company's part, it was eventually adopted as a standards-track IETF protocol.

TACACS/TACACS+

Terminal Access Controller Access Control System (TACACS) is generally associated with Cisco Systems but is based on a much older protocol developed by BBN for MILNET. TACACS was first publicly described in Informational RFC 1492.

RFC 1492 TACACS is a simple User Datagram Protocol (UDP)-based protocol that allows a central system to control text-mode login and use of SLIP. Two Cisco extensions not included in that RFC are ARAP (AppleTalk Remote Access Protocol) and CHAP authentication code numbers. For CHAP, request type 13 is used, and the Password field has the one-octet Challenge ID and variable-length Value fields. For PAP, TACACS users simply duplicate the SLIP login procedure.

TACACS+ is a TCP-based protocol described in expired `draft-grant-tacacs-02.txt`. TACACS+ uses the same port number over TCP (49) as TACACS does over UDP. The similarities end there, however, because TACACS+ is a completely different protocol.

ACP/RACP

Access Control Protocol (ACP) was based on Encore Computer Corporation's ERPC (Expedited Remote Procedure Call) and SRPC (Secure Remote Procedure Call) mechanisms. It runs over UDP port 121 using a simple ack/nak retransmit mechanism and provides encryption of the data using a 256-cam, single-rotor Enigma machine.

Reliable ACP (RACP) is a much newer version of this protocol that runs on TCP. It is designed to work more reliably over WAN links and with large dial-up servers.

One of the distinguishing features of ACP is that it uses remote procedure calls for all functions. Both the PPP system authenticating a user and the security system itself may perform RPCs. This means that the protocol is extremely flexible—for example, the security system may prompt the user at any time for new data, or may invoke arbitrary functions on the dial-in system or on any other system.

Unfortunately, ACP is not publicly documented.

RADIUS

Remote Authentication Dial-In User Service (RADIUS) is described in RFC 2138, a Proposed Standard protocol. This protocol was originally a Livingston

Enterprises (now Lucent) proprietary system, but is now on IETF standards track and is implemented by all major vendors.

RADIUS runs on UDP port 1812. The authorization portion of the protocol consists of four simple messages (Request, Accept, Reject, and Challenge) plus a list of 43 different attributes that can be used in each message through a type-length-value mechanism. These attributes carry the CHAP Challenge value, peer name (referred to as "user name" in the RFC), and other information.

For example, an access system using RADIUS would first negotiate LCP with the dial-up user and then, if the user agreed to use CHAP, send a CHAP Challenge to the user. When the access system gets the CHAP Response from the user, it sends an Access-Request message including both the original CHAP Challenge value and the user's Response value to the RADIUS server. The RADIUS server then validates the Response and returns Access-Accept or Access-Reject. The access system translates these into CHAP Success or Failure messages and sends the result to the user.

RADIUS does not support authentication to a peer. It cannot be used to generate CHAP Response or PAP Authenticate-Request messages to send to a peer.

Because RADIUS is easily extensible, most manufacturers have extended it to support proprietary features (such as VPNs), and these extensions can make interoperability troublesome. Worse yet, most of the current implementations are either clearly inadequate for large-scale ISP use or distributed under strict licensing terms. However, since RADIUS is publicly documented and supported, open and flexible implementations may one day exist.

About Security

There are two primary facets of security in PPP, authentication and confidentiality, and these are intimately related. Measures that provide for one facet usually depend on the other, and both must be considered together during system design. Successfully decrypting valid data, for instance, often implies something about the peer's identity, and, conversely, verifying the identity of the peer prevents the accidental release of private information.

Security is hard. Replacing your front door with a solid steel version with electronic locks will encourage burglars to try the windows. Barring the windows might encourage a more enterprising one to take a chainsaw to an exterior wall. Similarly, employing complex security measures in your telecommunications system may cause an intruder intent on gaining access to employ what is sometimes known as *social engineering*—a simple telephone call to a cooperative administrator or other legitimate system user can reveal the secrets necessary for access.

Security is therefore a system issue. Employing the most cryptographically secure authentication and encryption methods is a wasted effort if the building doors are not locked or an administrator is willing to change a password based on a telephone conversation. One security expert colorfully describes this common error as "putting a dead-bolt lock on a grass hut." Worse yet, some seemingly good methods are actually counterproductive. In order to use more secure methods, longer keys and frequent changes are usually necessary. Users, however, have limited memories, and forcing the use of these supposedly more secure methods often causes them either to write down their passwords in a convenient location or to choose easy-to-remember, and therefore easy to break, passwords.

It is therefore far too easy for implementors to expend great effort on minutiae. Worrying, for instance, about the predictability of the plaintext padding used with a DES encryption system might not be worthwhile if a VLSI device that can crack DES is available to the attacker. The effort should be commensurate with the value of the data and the likelihood of attack and should avoid mechanisms with known weaknesses.

PPP Security Pitfalls

A comprehensive list of the ways security in PPP can fail is probably impossible to produce. The following precautions relate to common implementation and usage errors. For switched-circuit access systems, such as dial-up servers and PCs with modems:

- **Do not use a PAP peer name and password combination on more than one system.**
  Doing so means that a caller requesting authentication will receive information that is also valid on that system.
- **Do not use the same PAP password or CHAP secret for both dial-in and dial-out when offering credentials to the peer.**
  Doing this means that an attacker can call one peer to get the other's PAP password or can relay the Challenge from one called system to another to get authenticated.
- **Pay close attention to switched-access features and interactions among them.**

For instance, *glare,* which occurs when a line being used for dial-out receives a call at the same time it attempts to dial, can be exploited in several ways. Consider a PC-based system that uses a modem to call a central system. Many PCs automatically redial the central system if the connection is lost. Unfortunately, many telephone lines in use with modems also have a "call-waiting" feature that can cause a modem to disconnect in a predictable way. A viable and difficult-to-detect attack would be to call the PC's modem once briefly to cause the connection to drop, then to redial as the PC starts its automatic redial attempt and thus force an intentional glare. At this point, the PC modem will "think" it is reconnected to the host system when in fact it is attached to the attacker's system. Using authentication in both directions generally alleviates this problem but unfortunately is not common in dial-up PPP implementations. Special telephone lines, such as ground-start, can also help by eliminating glare, as can use of features to disable call-waiting (usually "*70" in the United States) and randomly delaying automatic redial or requiring user intervention instead.

- **Do not log peer names from failed attempts in any accessible location.**
  Users often accidentally type their passwords in place of their user names. Logging these mistakes in an open place will compromise security.

Following is a similar precaution for unswitched (leased-line) systems:

- **Bidirectional authentication and random challenges are still important.**
  Good authentication prevents simple problems, such as wiring errors, as well as more complex problems, such as attackers who have access to the telephone company routing tables, which establish leased-line connections.

The following precautions are for any kind of system:

- **Do not indicate whether the peer name or password is wrong on failure.**
  This is a fundamental rule. Security systems should not tell an attacker which part of the offered identification data is incorrect. This rule should not be sacrificed for "ease of use."
- **Try to keep the same timing and operation for successful and failing authentications.**
  Where possible, an attacker should not be able to tell the difference between a successful authentication and a failing one based on the time it takes for a response to be produced. In some cases, this may mean that a

delay loop after detecting, for instance, a bad peer name is necessary. For EAP, this means that subsequent queries should still be made even if a prior query resulted in an erroneous response. When authentication fails, the peer should not be able to discern which of the responses was incorrect.

- **Do not use the same CHAP secret to validate both ends of a link.**
  Doing this enables a particularly simple break-in technique. The attacker simply echoes back the Challenge it receives from its peer. When the system issues its response, this is then played back as the attacker's response. If the CHAP secrets for each direction are the same, then these responses, given the same Challenges, will be the same. This implies, for the general case, that a system that has relationships with many peers must use separate lists of secrets for generating CHAP Response messages and validating received Response messages and that users must be carefully warned against having the same secret in both lists. Violating this rule effectively disables all CHAP security.

- **If you support both PAP and CHAP, do not use the same secret for both.**
  Sharing credentials between authentication protocols weakens both.

- **Limit the number of CHAP Challenges per second that are accepted.**
  Repeated Challenges have two possibly bad effects. First, they can constitute a denial-of-service attack, since the MD5 hash to generate the Response is computationally expensive. Second, they can theoretically be used to reveal the key using differential cryptanalysis.

- **Recognize Challenges that you would send, and send useless Responses.**
  Receiving Challenges that you would generate for a call in the same direction likely means that the peer is using your system as an *oracle*. This means that the peer is echoing back the Challenge that you sent on this or another port, and that it is expecting a Response calculated against the same secret. Of course, the same secret should not be used to validate both ends of the link, but this rule is sometimes broken by configuration errors. If you include a small amount of identifying information in your Challenges and generate random data in your Response messages when you see your own identification, you will prevent several types of simple attacks.

- **Do not respond correctly to a Challenge that has a peer name different from that of the first Challenge seen.**
  This tactic is used by peers that are fishing for valid responses or perhaps attempting to hide oracle-type attacks. Failing to respond will give useful clues to the attacker. Generating a meaningless random number or even a simple fixed string for the Response instead will frustrate the effort. In any event, such Challenges should be logged for review by an administrator.

- **Be very careful with pseudo-random-number generators.**
  Protocols, such as CHAP, that rely on the apparent unpredictability of these numbers as viewed from outside the system are compromised if these numbers are predictable, by either time of day (or time since boot) or the sequence of Challenge values. One good method of generating random numbers is to use a cryptographic hash of some secret along with the last number generated and the time of day. See RFC 1750, "Randomness Recommendations for Security."
- **Consider the system security and the PPP line security together.**
  If the system to which you are authenticating yourself is accessible to a large number of possibly untrustworthy people, consider using PAP instead of CHAP. With PAP, your password need not be stored in a reversible format on that possibly insecure system, while with either standard CHAP or MS-CHAP a copy of your password must be kept. For a system that only dials out, PAP is exactly equivalent to the traditional "username" and "password" prompts from a text-mode system. It is neither more nor less secure.
- **If using CHAP, invest as much effort as possible in making the inevitable list of secrets inaccessible in any form.**
  Reversible encryption helps only a little. Hiding the secrets on a dedicated Challenge/Response generating machine (perhaps running RADIUS) is much better. (Of course, this solution would require extensions to RADIUS, which does not support symmetric CHAP.)

Security References

Security is a broad and complex topic. Interested readers may wish to explore this topic through some of the many books written on the subject. The following is a list of suggested starting points.

- Schneier, Bruce, *Applied Cryptography*, 2nd ed. John Wiley & Sons, New York, 1996.
- Denning, D. E. *Cryptography and Data Security*. Addison-Wesley, Reading, MA, 1982.
- Garfinkel, Simson, and Gene Spafford. *Practical Unix and Internet Security*. O'Reilly & Associates, Sebastapol, CA, 1991.
- Hsiao, D. K., D. S. Kerr, and S. E. Madnick. *Computer Security*. Academic Press, New York, 1979.

- Rivest, R. L., A. Shamir, and L. Adleman. On Digital Signatures and Public Key Cryptosystems, *Communications of the ACM* 21, no. 2 (February 1978): 120–126.
- RFC 2408, *Internet Security Association and Key Management Protocol.*
- RFC 2574, *User-based Security Model for SNMPv3.*

Fast Reconnect

An example in Chapter 9 shows that PPP can fully negotiate even in complex cases within a few round-trip times and that this negotiation is easily faster than switched-circuit set-up times, even on ISDN.

Some people, however, view PPP negotiation as too slow for some applications, perhaps based on their experience with bad PPP implementations. Designers have often proposed complex mechanisms to maintain state across sessions in order to bypass normal PPP negotiation. These proposals are usually termed *fast reconnect* or *short hold*. These proposed protocols, such as expired `draft-ietf-pppext-scm-00.txt`, greatly weaken security by omitting the PPP authentication protocols during reconnection and are completely unnecessary since PPP, including normal authentication, can be made to run quite fast.

As the example in Chapter 9 (Multiple Protocols on page 269) shows, PPP is already faster than the inherent delays in switched-circuit set-up, but PPP can be made faster still, if necessary. A technique proposed by Vernon Schryver reduces this delay to a single round-trip time, at the expense of a minor but generally compatible violation of RFC 1661 and a possible time-out delay with some peers. It does not require any new PPP options or protocols.

The technique is simply to send without delay all of the Configure-Request and Configure-Ack messages that should bring up the link, rather than waiting after each message for the peer to respond. As long as both sides are in the right state (LCP transitioning to Req-Sent) at the start, this will cause the link to be up as soon as this burst is over. To the peer, it will seem as though the necessary negotiation message is always immediately available when it goes to read the next one. In the worst case, if the receiving peer requires a delay while switching state, this technique will cause LCP to reach Opened state, and the extra messages will be silently discarded. Negotiation will then proceed in the usual fashion after a time-out.

Implementing this technique requires prior knowledge of the messages that will be sent by the peer, including the ID numbers, and of the options it will attempt. This can be done by saving the negotiation options in stable storage during a "regular" call and using predictable ID numbers. For CHAP, it also requires prior knowledge of the CHAP Challenge value along with the ID. This can be achieved by prior agreement between the peers to use a secure pseudo-random-number generator for the Challenges and ID. A possible algorithm would be an MD5 hash of the last Challenge, the peer's secret, and the time of day to the nearest ten minutes. Another good algorithm would be to encrypt the last Challenge using DES and a key known only to the peers.

C H A P T E R   F I V E

The Network Layer Protocols

IN THIS CHAPTER

This chapter covers the network layer protocols, which form the links between PPP and the software outside PPP that handles the networking protocols, such as IP and AppleTalk. The network layers are where the real work of PPP is done. All common networking protocols, and many uncommon protocols, are represented, and new protocols are added as existing proprietary systems are converted over to standards-based protocols.

This chapter covers many of the more common network layer protocols for PPP, but some new protocols are still being introduced. Check with any of the standard document repositories listed in Chapter 11 for more information on particular protocols.

For each network protocol, there are usually two PPP protocol numbers. The first is the Network Control Protocol (NCP), which is distinguished by being chosen from the range 8000 through BFFF. The NCP is used by PPP to negotiate the use of the network protocol itself plus any parameters necessary for that network protocol. The second protocol number assigned is in the range 0000 through 3FFF, and is the same as the NCP number minus 8000. This is the network protocol and carries the user's data. For instance, the IP network protocol is assigned 8021 for IPCP, which negotiates IP addresses and other parameters, and is assigned network protocol 0021 for IP data.

Note that an implementation can use these defined protocol number ranges to direct intelligently the data through either a high-priority path for user data or a low-priority path for negotiation data. Such a split is common in embedded systems, such as routers, and most Unix systems. (Such an implementation would, of course, need to be extremely careful with the timing considerations between the data and the negotiation. In general, one must be ready to receive data when one sends the Configure-Ack message and must stop sending data when a Terminate-Request or Configure-Request is received.)

The negotiation process for each NCP uses the same message formats, code numbers, and state machine as LCP, which is described in Chapter 3. Code numbers 8 (Protocol-Reject) and above, however, are not used with the NCPs.

Of these protocols, IPCP is the most common and, for that reason, I give it more attention than the other protocols. IPV6CP has been proposed to supplant it but is rare as of this writing. IPXCP is the next most common. The others are less common, although not quite rare. The protocols are listed in order of their protocol numbers.

Internet Protocol (IP; IPCP)

The Internet Protocol Control Protocol (IPCP), described in RFC 1332, is protocol 8021, and the corresponding network protocol is 0021. This network layer transports IP Version 4 datagrams across a PPP link. See also RFC 791, which describes IPv4 itself, and the primary transport-level protocols ICMP (RFC 792), TCP (RFC 793), and UDP (RFC 768). Options 02 and 03 are common. Options 81, 82, 83, and 84 are specific to PCs. The others are rare. The negotiable IPCP options follow.

IPCP Option 01   IP-Addresses   Obsolete

This option is described in the obsolete RFC 1172. It contains eight octets of information: four for an IP source address (the local address of the Configure-Request sender) and four for an IP destination address (the address of the peer), as shown below. This option should not be implemented by any new PPP system. It has been deprecated due to convergence problems in some cases. The IP-Address option (described on page 131) should be negotiated instead.

01	0A	Source Address	Destination Address

IPCP Option 02   IP-Compression-Protocol   Common

This option is described in RFCs 1332 and 2509. The Data field of this option contains two octets for the compression protocol number, plus any additional octets defined by that protocol, as shown below.

02	Len	Protocol	Data . . .

The most common compression protocol number for this option is 002D, Van Jacobson (VJ) Compressed TCP/IP. The data for this protocol consist of two octets, as shown below.

02	06	00	2D	Max	Comp

Max is a single octet representing the maximum slot ID (number of slots minus 1), and Comp is a flag set to 00 if the slot identifier must not be compressed and to 01 if it may be. When this option is in use, three network protocols are used:

0021 Regular IP data (all non-TCP data)
002D Compressed TCP/IP
002F Uncompressed TCP/IP (IP protocol field has slot number)

(The obsolete RFC 1172 reserved 0037 for this protocol, but did not define the maximum slot ID or slot ID compression in the Data field, and this usage has been deprecated.)

VJ compression can reduce the standard TCP and IP headers from 40 octets to three octets under favorable conditions. It does not affect UDP or other IP protocols, and it does not compress the actual user data. The net effect is to improve latency greatly for interactive applications, such as TELNET, and to improve only slightly the throughput for bulk data applications, such as File Transfer Protocol (FTP) and large graphic images transferred by Hypertext Transfer Protocol (HTTP).

VJ compression assumes that a small number of long-lived TCP flows traverse the link, errors are rare and preferably detectable by the physical layer, and the link speed is relatively low compared with the CPU power available. Therefore, it should not be used on high-speed links or where large numbers of flows are expected, such as network-to-network links. Also, common HTTP usage generates large numbers of short-lived TCP flows, which are similarly ill-suited to VJ compression.

This compression technique is intricate, and a discussion of it is beyond the scope of this book. RFC 1144 contains both a detailed description of the algorithm and C language source code for a Berkeley kernel.

A new header compression technique, rare as of this writing, has been described in standards-track RFC 2508. This technique allows compression of both TCP and UDP over IP, and has a dedicated mode for compressing Real Time Protocol (RTP; RFC 1889) headers on point-to-point links. This compression algorithm is indicated, as described in the companion RFC 2509, with protocol 0061.

02	Len	0061
TCPSpace		NonTCP
MaxPeriod		MaxTime
MaxHeader	Suboptions . . .	

TCPSpace and NonTCP are similar to the maximum slot number in RFC 1144. Each represents the maximum context identification number that may be used, which is the same as the number of contexts minus 1. MaxPeriod is the maximum number of consecutively compressed non-TCP (UDP) headers that may be sent before one must be sent uncompressed to guarantee synchronization. Max-Time is the maximum time interval in seconds between transmission of uncompressed non-TCP headers. Both MaxPeriod and MaxTime may be set to zero to indicate that the given limit does not apply. Thus, if both are zero, uncompressed headers do not need to be sent. The MaxHeader value indicates the size in octets of the largest header that may be compressed.

The suboptions field is a bit unusual. This is a second level of type-length-value data structures, similar to regular PPP option encodings. The difference is that these suboptions are contained entirely within this single IPCP option. Currently, only a single suboption is defined. This is 01 02, which is a Boolean flag indicating that RTP data should also be compressed.

As with other options, this option is communicated from receiver to sender via Configure-Request. Thus, it is rarely necessary to send a Configure-Nak for this option. If the values sent by the receiver indicate that a smaller number of compression slots or header bytes may be used, the sender's compressor should limit itself to the receiver's values. If the receiver indicates that it can handle larger values than the compressor can send, no harm is done by acknowledging the larger value.

IPCP Option 03	IP-Address	Common

This configuration option is documented in RFC 1332. It contains a single four-octet IP address representing the address of the local system, as shown below.

03	06	Local Address

The address may be sent in Configure-Request as zero if the local address is not known, and Configure-Nak is then used by the peer to assign the local address. This option may, like any other option, be omitted, and the link run without any addresses at all, although doing so is often unwise.

Note that the IPCP Terminate-Request message will not terminate IPCP if it has not yet reached Opened state. If IPCP must be terminated due to addressing problems, then either use LCP Protocol-Reject or allow IPCP to reach Opened state with any options (send Configure-Ack for any received Configure-Request) and only then issue IPCP Terminate-Request.

See IP Addressing Issues on page 158 for a discussion of the issues involved in this option and IP addressing in general.

IPCP Option 04	Mobile-IPv4	Rare

This option is described in RFC 2290. The value contained in the option is a nonzero, four-octet home address for a mobile host, as shown below.

04	06	Home Address

This option is sent in a Configure-Request message only by a mobile node that is requesting a tunneled connection back to its home network. It should not be modified by Configure-Nak. If the peer is willing to establish the tunnel, a Configure-Ack should be sent. Otherwise, Configure-Reject is used to signal that tunneling is unavailable.

IPCP Option 81	Primary-DNS-Address	Microsoft
IPCP Option 82	Primary-NBNS-Address	Microsoft
IPCP Option 83	Secondary-DNS-Address	Microsoft
IPCP Option 84	Secondary-NBNS-Address	Microsoft

These four options are described in Informational (non-standards-track) RFC 1877. Each carries a single four-octet IP address for the indicated type of name server, where DNS is the standard Domain Name Service and NBNS is the NetBIOS Name Server. They are available in the pppd implementation through the ms-dns and ms-wins options.

These options work in an unexpectedly backward manner. An implementation sending Configure-Request containing any of these options is not specifying the addresses of its local name servers, as the implementor familiar with the IP-Address option would expect. Instead, it is specifying its current understanding of the addresses of the name servers that happen to be known to the peer.

In other words, a dial-up user is usually expected to send these options in an IPCP Configure-Request message but with invalid addresses, and the dial-in peer is expected to respond by sending the correct name server addresses that the dial-up user should use in an IPCP Configure-Nak message. Thus, use of these options usually involves multiple Configure-Requests. (This extra step can be avoided in some cases if the response from previous sessions is saved and used as the initial Configure-Request value.)

In addition to the odd semantics that were caused by a lack of peer review and the fact that these IPCP option numbers were taken without request from the Internet Assigned Numbers Authority (IANA), these options also have two rather severe design flaws. First, they are negotiated at the wrong level, since DNS and NBNS are application-layer services and IPCP is a network-layer negotiation. Second, they duplicate, at least for IP users, a service that already has a long history, which is Bootstrap Protocol (BOOTP, RFC 951) over PPP and is implemented in most major communications servers, such as those from Cisco Systems and Nortel Networks. Instead, the author of this RFC probably should have described options to transfer NBNS addresses via BOOTP in order to implement these new features.

To understand the importance of the layering flaw, consider a network in which a remote office has a small router attached to a wide-area link via PPP and a local network with a few devices attached via Ethernet. When IPCP is negotiated by the router, what name server address should be sent? If addresses are received, what should be done with them? In fact, this small router would probably neither know nor care about the location of any name servers, since this is, for many small routers, an irrelevant application-level detail. The local systems on the Ethernet will need to resort to using a BOOTP proxy across the PPP link to find this information, if necessary.

Consider also what happens when a PC implementing these options is disconnected from its PPP link and is plugged into an Ethernet or Token Ring network. If neither Token Ring nor Ethernet interfaces (which do not implement a similar negotiation) will be able to supply these addresses, where will the PC find them? It will then be necessary either to statically define the addresses through a user interface or to use a standard protocol such as BOOTP (or its cousin DHCP) to get them. But if BOOTP is available for the Ethernet connection, then why not also use it for the PPP configuration?

The advantage these options allow is a slight simplification of those few systems that have monolithic software architectures, where the applications and network layers are mixed together into a single program. This is often the case on PCs running some versions of Windows but is rarely true otherwise. The disadvantages, which generally include the lack of usefulness on many common architectures, argue that these options should not be implemented.

IPCP Option 89	Unused	Do not use

This option was described in `draft-ietf-pppext-ipcp-mip-01.txt`, the forerunner to RFC 2290 (Mobile-IPv4), using an option number unassigned by the IANA. No new implementation should use this option number.

IPCP Option 90	IP-Subnet-Mask	Do not use

This option was suggested on the IETF PPP mailing list, but was roundly rejected because the described feature was useful in only very narrow contexts and because the same problem can be solved using existing protocols, such as BOOTP and DHCP. (The option number is hex 90 or 144 decimal.) However, some ADSL vendors are reported to be implementing this option despite the advice of the working group. For that reason, I will give a brief description but caution that the option should not be implemented.

The option itself has a four-octet Data field containing the subnet mask, as shown below.

90	06	Subnet Mask

The implementation sending a Configure-Request with this option is requesting that it be granted a subnet of IP addresses for its use. If the receiver is in the business of allocating addresses through some type of security mechanism, rather than just using the addresses for routing purposes, this option allows it to allocate a block of addresses and grant these to the peer with Configure-Ack.

Open Systems Interconnection (OSI; OSINLCP)

The OSI Network Layer Control Protocol (OSINLCP) is described in RFC 1377. The control protocol is 8023, and the network protocol is 0023. The first octet of the network layer data is the Network Layer Protocol Identifier (NLPID), which indicates which OSI protocol is contained in the rest of the packet. Some example NLPID values follow (see ISO 9577 for a complete list of these protocol numbers).

```
00    null
01    pad
08    Q.933
80    SNAP
81    CLNP
82    ES-IS
83    IS-IS
8E    IPv6
C5    Blacker
CC    IPv4
CD    ISO IPv4
CF    PPP
DD    Netmon
```

OSINLCP is occasionally implemented in IP routers in order to use the Intermediate System to Intermediate System (IS-IS) routing protocol (see RFC 1195).

It also may be used in some SONET/SDH environments to provide support for Telecommunications Management Network (TMN) control (see ITU-T M.3100). There is only one option negotiated for OSINLCP.

OSINLCP Option 01   Align-NPDU   Common

This option requests alignment of Network Protocol Data Units (NPDUs) within the PPP information field by insertion of leading zero octets. The Data field of this option is a single octet whose value indicates the desired alignment. When this value is 01, 02, 03, or 04, that offset (modulo 4) from the beginning of the HDLC frame is requested. For instance, a value of 01 would result in the following alignment for the four ACFC and PFC combinations.

```
FF 03 00 23 00 <NPDU>      (neither ACFC nor PFC)
FF 03 23 00 00 <NPDU>      (PFC only)
00 23 00 00 00 <NPDU>      (ACFC only)
23 <NPDU>                  (both ACFC and PFC)
```

The 00 octets past the protocol number (23) are the added padding octets. Note that the example alignment of the NPDU is either 5 or 1 with a negotiated value of 01. The special value FF indicates that odd alignment (modulo 2) is necessary, and FE indicates even alignment.

If this option is negotiated, the sender must transmit data with the indicated alignment. However, all receivers must be able to receive packets with any alignment. If the Configure-Request option is rejected by the peer, data will be received without alignment changes, and the RFC requires that the link must operate in spite of the failure of this option.

Xerox Network Systems Internet Datagram Protocol (XNS IDP; XNSCP)

The XNS network protocol is 0025, and the control protocol is 8025 (XNSCP). The protocol is described in RFC 1764. XNS has no configuration options. To transport XNS data, each peer simply sends an empty Configure-Request and an empty Configure-Ack, like this:

```
A: FF 03 80 25 01 01 00 04 10 9A
B: FF 03 80 25 02 01 00 04 DD BF
B: FF 03 80 25 01 01 00 04 10 9A
A: FF 03 80 25 02 01 00 04 DD BF
```

Because this is always symmetric, I recommend implementing the LCP Magic Number option to prevent accidental loopbacks. XNS is extremely rare.

Xerox XNS and Novell IPX are essentially the same protocol. See also Internet Packet Exchange (IPX; IPXCP) on page 140.

There is no way to fragment XNS IDP datagrams, so all implementations must support a minimum MRU of 576.

Documentation on XNS IDP itself is available from Xerox as XNSS 029101, *Internet Transport Protocols.*

DECnet Phase IV Routing Protocol (DECnet; DNCP)

DECnet over PPP is described in RFC 1762. It is assigned network protocol number 0027 and network control protocol 8027. PPP supports only the routing messages, and not the other Phase IV messages, such as MOP, LAT, and the maintenance protocols. DNCP is very rare and is fading from use.

DECnet has no configuration options. Like XNS, negotiation of DECnet consists simply of an empty Configure-Request and Configure-Ack message. The network protocol messages consist of a two-octet Length field, which is in reverse byte order (LSB first), followed by the DECnet Data field.

Documentation on the DECnet protocol itself can be ordered from Compaq (formerly Digital Equipment Corporation) as AA-X436A-TK, *DNA Routing Layer Functional Specification.*

AppleTalk (AT; ATCP)

AppleTalk is the native protocol for Apple Macintosh computers. The AppleTalk Control Protocol for PPP is described in RFC 1378. The control protocol is 8029, and the network protocol is 0029. ATCP is not yet rare but is fading from use.

The data packets transferred via protocol 0029 begin with the extended Datagram Delivery Protocol (DDP) header. Fragmentation is not supported in AppleTalk, so implementations must support reception of AppleTalk frames with up to 599 octets in the PPP information field.

Implementors and testers of this protocol should refer to *Inside AppleTalk*, 2nd ed., by Gursharan S. Sidhu, R. Andrews, and Alan B. Oppenheimer (Addison-Wesley, May 1990) for information on AppleTalk protocols and routing.

Options 01, 06, 07, and 08 are common to ATCP implementations. Devices that implement ATCP often also implement the older proprietary ARAP protocol, which is not compatible with PPP.

ATCP Option 01	AppleTalk-Address	Common

This option indicates the AppleTalk network and local node number when sent as part of a Configure-Request message. The data in this option consist of an ignored octet, two octets for the network number, and one octet for the node number, as shown below. The network and node numbers must be in "non-extended" mode.

01	06	00	Network	Node

The network and local node numbers may be requested from the peer by sending a Configure-Request message with either network, node, or both set to zero. The peer should reply with a Configure-Nak message containing the correct network and node numbers, perhaps derived from a database look-up. A system that does not use AppleTalk addresses, such as a "half-router," will Configure-Reject this option. As with IP addresses, this option is useful for detecting configuration errors and should be implemented.

Note that only a single network number is negotiated for the link, but that a separate node number is negotiated for each end of the link. This means that the network number used in generating Configure-Requests should reflect the latest Configure-Nak or Configure-Request received from the peer. The node number, however, is symmetrically negotiated, so Configure-Requests must take only Configure-Nak values into consideration.

Unlike IPXCP, there is no higher-network-number rule for ATCP, so Configure-Nak is required if the peer suggests a different network number.

ATCP Option 02   Routing-Protocol   Uncommon

This option negotiates the routing protocol to be used on the link. By default, AppleTalk Routing Table Maintenance Protocol (RTMP) is expected. This option has a two-octet routing protocol number plus a variable-length Data field that depends on the particular routing protocol, as shown below.

02	Len	Protocol	Data . . .

The routing protocol numbers used here are not PPP Protocol numbers. The defined routing protocol numbers are 0000 for no routing information, 0001 for RTMP, 0002 for AURP, and 0003 for ABGP. None of these routing protocols uses the variable-length Data field.

ATCP Option 03   Suppress-Broadcast   Uncommon

This option specifies a variable-length list of octets, as shown below.

03	Len	DDP-Types . . .

Each octet is a DDP type code. The sender of Configure-Request for this option is requesting that the peer suppress forwarding of any DDP packet that was sent to the broadcast address on another link and has any of these type codes. This suppression may interfere with the selected routing protocol if it is not carefully chosen.

If the list is empty, then the peer is requesting that all DDP broadcasts be suppressed. An implementation that cannot filter based on DDP type code but can filter out all broadcasts might return an empty Configure-Nak in response to a Configure-Request list to indicate this.

Reasonable implementations should not implement this option at all, should implement it as a simple on/off flag to drop all broadcasts, or should permit an arbitrary list of protocol numbers to be specified. Otherwise, modifying the list and sending a Configure-Nak can lead to nonconvergence.

ATCP Option 04   AT-Compression-Protocol   Do not use

This option would negotiate the desired header compression protocol to be used, if any existed for AppleTalk. It defines a two-octet Protocol Number field followed by a variable-length Data field for the particular protocol chosen, as shown below.

04	Len	Protocol	Data . . .

No AppleTalk header compression algorithms are defined, and this option is not yet used.

ATCP Option 05   Reserved   Do not use

This option was originally derived from the old AppleTalk Remote Access Protocol (ARAP) connect-time feature. It was removed from ATCP by the IETF and placed into LCP as the Time-Remaining message, since it could be generally useful for many kinds of systems, not just ATCP-speakers.

ATCP Option 06   Server-Information   Common

This option provides information about the local implementation of AppleTalk to the peer. It should not be returned in a Configure-Nak. The data in this option include a two-octet "server class" number, a four-octet implementation ID, and a variable-length field for the name of the implementation in so-called AppleTalk ASCII, as shown below.

06	Len	Class	Implementation ID	Name . . .

All binary values, including 00, are legal in AppleTalk ASCII. For this reason, implementors must take care to use memcpy() and memcmp() rather than strcpy() and strcmp() when handling the ASCII data in any ATCP option.

The server class number can be 0001 for an AppleTalk PPP Dial-In Server, 0002 for a generic AppleTalk PPP, or 0003 for a Dial-In Server and Router. The implementation ID is a software version number and, if the server class is 0001, is specified as a single octet for the major version number, a single octet for the minor version number followed by two zero octets. The implementation ID is vendor specific for other server classes.

ATCP Option 07   Zone-Information   Common

This option provides the local AppleTalk zone name to the peer. It should not be returned in a Configure-Nak message unless its format is corrupt. The Data field of the option contains the name of the zone in AppleTalk ASCII, as shown below.

07	Len	Zone . . .

ATCP Option 08   Default-Router-Address   Common

This option is in the same format as the AppleTalk Address option. It specifies the network and node number of the local default router, as shown below.

08	06	00	Network	Node

Unlike the AppleTalk Address option, this option is advisory and not negotiated. It should not be included in a Configure-Nak.

Internet Packet Exchange (IPX; IPXCP)

Despite its name, IPX is generally not used on the global Internet. It is instead a protocol used chiefly by PCs running software from Novell on corporate networks (although there are at least partial implementations available for other types of computers). IPX is almost an exact subset of Xerox's original XNS protocol (see page 135), which has a separate PPP protocol number. IPXCP, described in RFC 1552, has been assigned PPP protocol number 802B, and the corresponding network layer for user data is 002B. IPXCP is fairly common but is gradually fading from use.

In addition to the following options, an implementation may also need to include Novell's IPX WAN protocol, which is documented in Informational RFC 1634. This RFC describes an application-level protocol used to maintain routing information on Novell wide-area links and restricts some of the information given in the following options. It is not possible to connect to a Novell MPR (Multi-Protocol Router) using IPXCP without IPXWAN support, although most other routers accept connections with or without IPXWAN. If your target market does not include direct connection to Novell dial-up routers over PPP links, the IPXWAN extension is not necessary for IPX support. All options except 04 are common to IPXCP implementations.

IPXCP Option 01   IPX-Network-Number   Common

This option negotiates a single four-octet unsigned integer representing the network number assigned to the link itself, as shown below. If both peers send Configure-Request messages for this parameter with nonzero values, the numerically larger network number is chosen. Both peers may send Configure-Ack in this case, even if the values are different, because the choose-larger rule is well known. Having the side that sent the larger network number also send a Configure-Nak is not necessary to correct the peer's lower number.

01	06	Network Number

The network number may also be configured as zero or omitted entirely, both of which mean that the link is not used for IPX LAN-to-LAN routing but is instead a link to a single node that is logically located on the peer's configured network in a manner analogous to proxy-ARP for IP. The receiver of a Configure-Request specifying zero may also reply with a Configure-Nak specifying a different number if LAN-to-LAN routing is desired by one peer.

This option is not symmetrically negotiated in each direction like other PPP options. Both sides must send either zero or nonzero for the network number. A link with the network number configured nonzero in one direction but zero or rejected in the other is illegal. There is only one network number for a given physical link, and the Configure-Request generating code in an implementation should take information from both Configure-Naks and Configure-Requests received from the peer.

IPXCP Option 02   IPX-Node-Number   Common

This option negotiates a unique six-octet number, which generally has a format similar to an Ethernet address, for the local system, as shown below. This number must be unique for the given network negotiated. Often a system that implements IPXCP will use an installed Ethernet adapter as the source for this number. Unlike the network number, this number is unique for each end of the link and is negotiated separately in each direction.

| 02 | 08 | | Node Number | | |

A system using no network number or number zero may send all zeros in its Configure-Request for this option. The peer should respond with a Configure-Nak specifying an available address. [Local use addresses, which start with bit 6 in the first octet set (hex 40), are useful in this case.] A system with a nonzero network number on the link should not send zero for this option.

IPXCP Option 03   IPX-Compression-Protocol   Common

This option negotiates a header compression algorithm. The negotiated value is a two-octet Protocol field specifying the compression algorithm, plus additional octets determined by the desired algorithm, as shown below.

| 03 | Len | Protocol | Data . . . |

The currently valid Protocol values are

0002   Telebit RFC 1553 compression. Two additional octets of information are given, one specifying the maximum slot ID number and the second specifying a number of Boolean option flags.

0235   Shiva Compressed NCP/IPX (Proprietary)

Unlike other negotiation options with a similar syntax, these values are not PPP Protocol numbers. They are merely identifiers for the particular compression algorithm in use.

Like IP compression, IPX compression compresses only header overhead and not the user data. Unlike IP compression, however, compressing IPX packets is mandatory once this option has been negotiated. The same protocol number (002B) is then used for the compressed data, and uncompressed data cannot be sent.

IPXCP Option 04   IPX-Routing-Protocol   Uncommon

This option negotiates the routing protocol to be used over the link. The value contained in this option is a two-octet integer representing a single routing protocol to be used, plus a variable-length Data field for information specific to that protocol, as shown below.

```
 04 | Len | Protocol | Data . . .
```

By default, a combination of Novell Routing Information Protocol (RIP) and Server Advertising Protocol (SAP) messages are expected. Unlike many options, this one may appear more than once in a Configure-Request message in order to request the use of multiple protocols on a link.

The routing protocol numbers are as follows.

0000	None.	RFC 1552
0002	Novell RIP/SAP.	RFC 1552
0004	Novell Netware Link State Protocol (NLSP).	RFC 1552
0005	Novell Demand RIP required.	RFC 1582
0006	Novell Demand SAP required.	RFC 1582
0007	Novell Triggered RIP required.	RFC 2091
0008	Novell Triggered SAP required.	RFC 2091

None of the current protocols requires any negotiated parameters in the Data field, and therefore each option has length 04. The sender of this option in a Configure-Request message is requesting the peer to send the indicated protocol to it (that is, the sender is indicating its willingness to receive the indicated protocol).

IPXCP Option 05   IPX-Router-Name   Common

This option provides a means for sending the name of the local IPX system (called the *file server name*) to the peer via Configure-Request. Since this option is simply advisory and is meant for logging functions, it is not actively negotiated. In particular, Configure-Nak must never be sent for this option.

The name should be 1 to 47 characters in length and should use ASCII A–Z, underscore (_), hyphen (-), and the commercial "at" sign (@).

IPXCP Option 06   IPX-Configuration-Complete   Common

This is a Boolean "option" meant to speed negotiations in the cases where convergence is not possible. If any option necessary for operation has been rejected by the peer or if the last message from the peer was a Configure-Nak that changed the value of an option to an unacceptable value, this option is not included. Otherwise, it is included with any Configure-Request message that could be acknowledged with Configure-Ack and that would result in a viable link.

Relying on this option is not recommended. A good implementation should offer this option in a Configure-Request sent, but should not expect the peer to include it in any Configure-Request received. Some implementations do not include it at all.

Bridging (BCP)

Bridging is a technique for forwarding messages from one physical network to another without reference to the network-layer information contained in the messages. In particular, bridging is useful in PPP for handling protocols that are otherwise unimplemented in a given router. BCP is uncommon.

The PPP bridging control protocol is described in RFC 1638 and is in the process of being updated by `draft-ietf-pppext-bcp-04.txt`. It is assigned "network" (data) PPP protocol number 0031 and control protocol number 8031. It also makes use of several special spanning tree protocol numbers, documented with that option below.

Two models of operation are supported by this protocol for Source Routed networks. One is the half-bridge model, where the two sides agree to behave as though they were a single larger bridge, and the PPP link is invisible for spanning tree calculations. The other model is the full, independent bridge, where the PPP link is visible as a separate segment in the spanning tree.

Usually, the default MRU of 1500 octets is not sufficient for BCP support. No standard exists for fragmentation at the MAC level, so the MRU must be large enough to handle a message forwarded from any interface that might be actively in use for bridging. For reference, a bridged Ethernet packet (including PPP bridging headers) is 1524 octets, and a bridged FDDI packet is 4377 octets with IP, or potentially as many as 4506 octets for arbitrary data (including 4500 octets of data plus PADS/MAC-type and LAN ID fields).

Alternatively, if the MRU cannot be negotiated large enough due to hardware or driver-imposed restrictions, MP with a large MRRU may be negotiated. MP can be used as a simple link-level fragmentation mechanism on a single link. See Chapter 7.

The data packet structure is complicated and contains a variety of optional fields. See the RFC for details.

The negotiable BCP options follow.

BCP Option 01   Bridge-Identification   Common

Negotiation of this option implies that the half-bridge model is in use for Source Routing. This option is mutually incompatible with the Line-Identification option. The data in this option consist of a two-octet field containing a 12-bit LAN segment number and a 4-bit bridge ID (both from IEEE 802.1D).

There is only one value for the bridge ID number for a given PPP link. This option is not negotiated symmetrically as are most PPP options. Instead, systems must either agree to disconnect if the configured number does not match or select the higher ID number of the two proposed in each Configure-Request.

BCP Option 02   Line-Identification   Common

Negotiation of this option implies that the full-bridge model is in use for Source Routing. This option is mutually incompatible with the Bridge-Identification option. The data in this option consist of a two-octet field containing a 12-bit LAN segment number and a 4-bit bridge ID (both from IEEE 802.1D).

There is only one value for the LAN segment number for a given PPP link. This option is not negotiated symmetrically as are most PPP options. Instead, systems must either agree to disconnect if the configured number does not match or select the higher segment number of the two proposed in each Configure-Request.

If neither this option nor the Bridge-Identification option is negotiated, the full-bridge model is assumed, and it is also assumed that the LAN segment number is correctly configured on both ends by an administrator. I do not recommend this mode of operation for Source Routing due to the likelihood of undetected misconfiguration. Misconfiguration may cause the creation of forwarding loops, which will make the attached networks unusable.

BCP Option 03	MAC-Support	Common

This option in a Configure-Request message announces support for a single MAC type to its peer. Since this is only an announcement, it must never be included in a Configure-Nak message. The Data field of the option is a single octet representing the MAC type, which is currently one of the following.

01 IEEE 802.3/Ethernet (with canonical addresses)
02 IEEE 802.4 (with canonical addresses)
03 IEEE 802.5 (with noncanonical addresses)
04 FDDI (with noncanonical addresses)
0B IEEE 802.5 (with canonical addresses)
0C FDDI (with canonical addresses)

Zero, 05-0A, and all numbers above 0C are reserved.

In general, the canonical forms of the addresses are used by most hardware. In canonical format, the Ethernet address 01:23:45:67:89:AB is sent in binary (LSB first) as 10000000 11000100 10100010 11100110 10010001 11010101. The noncanonical forms, sometimes known as "MSB" format, are usually found on older IBM Token Ring hardware, and have the bits in each byte reversed. The previous example would be rendered as 80:C4:A2:E6:91:D5 in noncanonical form. For a good description of the distinction between canonical and noncanonical address ordering, see RFC 2469.

An implementation that supports the canonical address form of 802.5 or FDDI must also support the noncanonical address form for backward compatibility.

Multiple copies of this option are sent in a Configure-Request message, with one for each supported MAC type.

BCP Option 04   Tinygram-Compression   Common

This option is a nonstandard Boolean flag. Unlike standard PPP Boolean flags, this option contains a single octet of data set to 01 to enable compression and 02 to disable it. Like a standard Boolean option, it is disabled with Configure-Reject, not Configure-Nak. The sender of Configure-Request for this option is declaring its support for decompression on receive.

Tinygrams are padded messages that appear on certain types of media, such as Ethernet. On Ethernet, the minimum PDU is 64 octets, but common frames in interactive applications are about two-thirds of that size, so many frames are padded out to meet the minimum PDU requirement. Compression of these frames means detecting and stripping out this padding and reconstructing it on the other side of the link.

This compression is done by removing octets equal to 00 from the end of the packet (or preceding the Ethernet CRC, if present) and setting the "Z" flag in the packet header. The receiver is expected to reconstruct the packet by padding out to 60 octets of data (not including the Ethernet CRC).

BCP Option 05   LAN-Identification   Uncommon

This option, which is deprecated in the new draft, is also a nonstandard Boolean flag. The Data field, as with the Tinygram-Compression option, is 01 to enable and 02 to disable. This option is an announcement only and must never be included in a Configure-Nak message.

When LAN identification is enabled, a four-octet integer, called the *LAN ID*, is added to each bridged PDU and a control flag is set to indicate that this value is present. The LAN ID field must be checked to separate traffic destined for separate interfaces. When identification is disabled (the default), any traffic carrying a LAN ID field must be dropped.

This option permits the implementation of multiple virtual LAN groups over a single bridging link, but does not support standard IEEE 802.1Q VLANs.

BCP Option 06   MAC-Address   Uncommon

This option announces the local Ethernet MAC address or is used to request that the peer assign the address. It is useful only with small bridges that have only a single Ethernet interface, and it is not defined for other media types. The data in the option consist of six octets, which are the Ethernet address in canonical format. If all six octets are zero, the sender of Configure-Request is asking the peer to send a Configure-Nak with the correct Ethernet address, perhaps derived from a look-up based on the system name provided during authentication. Otherwise, if it is nonzero, the peer should not send a Configure-Nak.

BCP Option 07	Spanning-Tree-Protocol	Common

This option, which is incompatible with the new Management-Inline option (described later), negotiates the spanning tree protocol in use. A spanning tree protocol detects and eliminates forwarding loops when multiple bridges are in use on a network.

There is at most one protocol negotiated for a given link, and in case of a conflict, the lower-numbered option of the two is chosen. This may result in no spanning tree protocol being selected. The RFC is somewhat unclear on the intention in this case, but a reasonable implementation should not bring up the link if it knows any spanning tree protocol at all. The link should be established with no spanning tree protocol only in the case where both peers have no protocol at all available.

A system may support no protocol at all. If it supports any protocol, however, it must support IEEE 802.1D (ID number 01).

The option data consist of a list of one or more protocol numbers represented as single octets chosen from the following list.

00   Null—no spanning tree protocol supported
01   IEEE 802.1D spanning tree protocol
02   IEEE 802.1G extended spanning tree protocol
03   IBM source route spanning tree protocol
04   DEC LANbridge 100 spanning tree protocol

The actual spanning tree protocol messages are sent using the following PPP protocol numbers.

0201   IEEE 802.1 (either 802.1D or 802.1G)
0203   IBM Source Route Bridge
0205   DEC LANbridge 100

Documentation for the IEEE protocols can be found in the following sources.

- *Media Access Control (MAC) Bridges,* ISO/IEC 15802-3:1998, ANSI/IEEE Std 802.1D.
- *Remote Media Access Control (MAC) Bridging,* ISO/IEC 15802-5:1998, ANSI/IEEE Std 802.1G.

Documentation for the IBM protocol can be found in

- *Token-Ring Network Architecture Reference,* 3rd ed., September 1989.

Documentation for the DEC LANbridge protocol is not available.

| BCP Option 08 | IEEE 802 Tagged Frame | Rare |

This new option, described in `draft-ietf-pppext-bcp-04.txt`, is a nonstandard Boolean option using the same format as the Tinygram-Compression option. When this option is enabled, the IEEE 802.1Q VLAN and Priority fields are present in the bridged datagrams.

| BCP Option 09 | Management-Inline | Rare |

This new option, also described in `draft-ietf-pppext-bcp-04.txt`, is a regular PPP Boolean option. When this option is enabled, the peers are expected to exchange standard IEEE interbridge protocols, such as Bridge Protocol Data Unit (BPDU) and Generic Attributes Registration Protocol (GARP) messages to implement Spanning Tree and exchange VLAN and multicast information.

Banyan Vines (VINES; BVCP)

RFC 1763 describes the standard method for carrying Banyan Vines data over a PPP link. The network protocol number is 0035 and the control protocol is 8035. Use of this protocol is quite rare.

Because of its history as a PC-based protocol, Vines is somewhat Ethernet-centric. Its MRU is fixed at 1500 octets, unless FRP is negotiated (see the options below). The negotiable BVCP options follow.

BVCP Option 01   NS-RTP-Link-Type

This Boolean option configures the behavior of the Nonsequenced Routing Update Protocol (NS-RTP). If it is present, then LAN-type updates are sent (a full table update every 90 seconds). If it is not present, then by default WAN-type updates are sent (a full table for the first three updates, then only changes for the next five updates, in a repeating pattern). This option has no effect if the newer (Version 5.5) Sequenced Routing Update Protocol (S-RTP) is used.

BVCP Option 02   FRP

This Boolean option configures the use of Vines Fragmentation Protocol (FRP). By default, no FRP header is sent with the Vines packets, and fragmentation is not possible.

The FRP header is a two-octet field prepended to the data packets and includes fragment begin and end flags and a sequence number, making it similar to standard PPP MP (RFC 1990; see Chapter 7). FRP is described in the Banyan documentation.

BVCP Option 03   RTP

This Boolean option suppresses the use of routing updates. By default, routing updates are sent on links. The sender of Configure-Request for this option is requesting that RTP messages not be sent to it. This is useful for dial-lines with static routes, where RTP would use up a significant portion of the bandwidth with no visible benefit.

BVCP Option 04   Suppress-Broadcast

This Boolean option suppresses Vines broadcast messages, except for ARP and RTP. Most such messages are not useful for simple dial-in systems, and suppression saves bandwidth. By default, all broadcasts are forwarded. The sender of Configure-Request for this option is requesting that broadcasts not be sent to it.

NetBIOS Frames Control Protocol (NetBIOS; NBFCP)

NetBIOS (formerly known as NetBEUI) is an older, nonroutable protocol used mostly with PCs. NBFCP is described in RFC 2097. The control protocol is 803F and the network protocol is 003F. NetBIOS itself is documented in IBM's *Local Area Network Technical Reference*, SC30-3383-2. NBFCP is rare.

Two special modifications to an otherwise straightforward PPP implementation are necessary to support NBFCP. First, instead of requiring an implementation to negotiate a large enough MRU before using this protocol, RFC 2097 requires that implementations disregard the negotiated MRU to send the large frames as needed. 1512 bytes of space for the PPP information field are required regardless of negotiation. Second, some of the actions required during negotiation can take a long time to complete. Implementations will need an adjustable Configure-Request time-out to support this. The negotiated options follow.

NBFCP Option 01   Name-Projection

This option is implemented strangely in that the value returned in the Configure-Ack message is not the same as the data in the corresponding Configure-Request due to the use of a result-code field. The negotiated value is a sequence of 17 octet blocks. The first 16 octets of each block constitute a network name string padded with null characters and not prepended with a Length field as are other PPP strings. The seventeenth octet is a field called "Added," which is 01 for *Unique Name* and 02 for *Group Name* in Configure-Request and Configure-Reject, but is changed to a result-code in Configure-Ack and Configure-Nak. Common result codes follow.

```
00    Name successfully added.
0D    Duplicate name in local name table.
0E    Name table full.
15    Name not found or cannot specify "*" or null.
16    Name in use on remote NetBIOS.
19    Name conflict detected.
```

```
30   Name defined by another environment.
35   Required system resources exhausted.
```

NBFCP Option 02   Peer-Information

This option is used as a means for one peer to inform the other of its software version and type numbers plus an identifying name. It should not be included
in Configure-Nak, since it is informational only and is not subject to negotiation.

NBFCP Option 03   Multicast-Filtering

This option allows the sender of Configure-Request to ask its peer to limit the
rate of NetBIOS multicasts forwarded over the link. To ask a peer to indicate
how often it wants to receive multicasts, an unsolicited Configure-Nak for this
option with the rate control set to the reserved value FFFF is used. By default, all
multicasts are forwarded.

NBFCP Option 04   IEEE-MAC-Address-Required

This Boolean option in a Configure-Request asks for the MAC addresses to be
added as the first 12 octets in each frame sent by the peer. If the source of the forwarded data is on Ethernet, this will expand the forwarded frame size to as large
as 1512 bytes, regardless of the negotiated MRU.

The addresses are sent in noncanonical (also known as "IBM") form. This
means that when standard Ethernet hardware is used, the bits within each byte
of the Ethernet destination and source address must be swapped. See RFC 2469
for more information.

Serial Data Transport Protocol (SDTP; SDCP)

This protocol, described in Informational RFC 1963, provides a method of transporting synchronous HDLC data or arbitrary asynchronous data using a protocol based on V.120 (see ITU-T V.120 on page 34). The transport uses protocol

0049 and the option negotiation is done using protocol 8049. The option negotiation protocol is called SDCP. SDTP is extremely rare.

The main differences between this protocol and standard V.120 are:

- The low-order 3 bits of the CS header are used to signal the actual length of non-octet-aligned synchronous data.
- One of the two reserved bits in the H header is used to signal end-to-end flow control.
- LAP-F is not used for error correction and flow control (but RFC 1663 numbered mode can be used for reliability).
- The CS and H bytes are (by default) placed at the end of the data frame.

The negotiated options follow. Since use of this protocol is rather rare, none of the options is particularly common.

SDCP Option 01   Packet-Format

This option negotiates a single octet with the value 00 (Header-Last) or 01 (Header-First). It is essentially a Boolean option but is not specified in the expected PPP manner.

Header-Last format is the default, but Header-First format is closer to the V.120 standard.

SDCP Option 02   Header-Type

This option negotiates a single octet with the value 00 (H-Only), 01 (H-and-CS), or 02 (H-and-CS-Always). This option controls the presence of the V.120 header bytes.

SDCP Option 03   Length-Field-Present

This option negotiates a single octet with the value 00 (no Length field), 01 (one octet), or 02 (two octets). This is intended for compatibility with the obsolete LCP Compound-Frames option.

SDCP Option 04   Multi-Port

>   This option negotiates a single octet representing the number of separate data
>   streams (called "ports" in the RFC) that the transport should support. Note that
>   this must be negotiated to be the same number in both directions. By default,
>   only one data stream is present.

SDCP Option 05   Transport-Mode

>   This option contains two octets of data. The first specifies the data stream and
>   the second is a flag set to 00 for synchronous HDLC (the default) or 01 for asyn-
>   chronous data.

SDCP Option 06   Maximum-Frame-Size

>   This option contains five octets of data. The first octet specifies the data stream.
>   The last four octets form a 32-bit unsigned integer representing the maximum
>   number of octets in a reassembled V.120 data frame. This option is meaningful
>   for synchronous HDLC streams only.

SDCP Option 07   Allow-Odd-Frames

>   This option has a single octet of data representing the data stream number. If this
>   option is requested, the sender should allow for odd bit alignments and preserve
>   non-octet-aligned data across the link. This option is meaningful for synchro-
>   nous HDLC streams only.

SDCP Option 08   FCS-Type

>   This option has two octets of data. The first selects the data stream. The second
>   is a flag value set to 00 to carry transparently the application's CRC across the

link (the default), 01 to strip and regenerate a CRC-16, or 02 to strip and regenerate a CRC-32. This option is meaningful for synchronous HDLC streams only.

SDCP Option 09   Flow-Expiration-Time

This option has two octets of data that specify a 16-bit number representing the minimum rate (in tenths of a second) at which the peer must send flow-off messages (FC bit in header H set to 1) in order to maintain the flow-control state. By default, this value is 100, so a flow-off message is cleared automatically after 10 seconds in case the flow-on message is lost.

Systems Network Architecture (SNA; SNACP)

SNA is a protocol primarily used by IBM mainframe computers. The SNA encapsulation for PPP is defined in RFC 2043. SNACP is rather rare and is found mostly on multiprotocol routers.

There are two protocols in use for SNA: raw SNA, used by IBM's Advanced Peer-to-Peer Networking High Performance Routing (APPN-HPR), and SNA over LLC 802.2. These protocols are assigned independent PPP protocol numbers 004D and 004B, respectively. Their control protocol numbers are 804D and 804B, although neither protocol has any negotiable parameters. Instead, only an empty SNACP Configure-Request is sent, and the reply is either an empty SNACP Configure-Ack or an LCP Protocol-Reject.

With protocol 004D, the HPR Network Layer Packet (NLP) is the only data in the PPP Information field. With protocol 004B, the PPP Information field contains the LLC (Lower-Level Compatibility) DSAP (Destination Service Access Point), SSAP (Source Service Access Point), and control fields before the SNA packet.

Internet Protocol Version 6 (IPv6; IPV6CP)

IPv6, also known as IPng, has gone by several names during its development as the next-generation replacement for IP. It provides significant enhancements over the venerable IPv4 protocol, including expanded addresses, automatic configuration, and better security. The network protocol is 0057, the control protocol is 8057, and the negotiation options are covered in RFC 2472. See also RFC 1883 for a description of IPv6 itself. IPv6 is not yet in common use.

The current IPV6CP options follow.

IPV6CP Option 01	Interface-Token	Common

This option negotiates a four-octet randomly chosen nonzero number at each end of the link. This number is then used to create the interface addresses by prepending FE000000000000000000000 to it, making it into an RFC 1884 "local use" address. (IPv6 addresses are 16 octets long, giving an address space that is more than 28 orders of magnitude larger than the IPv4 space.)

IPV6CP Option 02	IPv6-Compression-Protocol	Uncommon

The Data field of this option contains two octets for the compression protocol number, plus any additional octets defined by that protocol. The obsolete RFC 2023 allocated value 00 4F for this option. This protocol number is now historic.

RFC 2508 IP Header Compression should be used instead. The IPV6CP option is described in RFC 2509 and is identical to the new IPCP option described on page 130.

Simple Transportation Management Framework (STMF; STMFCP)

This protocol is being defined outside of the IETF for use in highway management and control. The network protocol number is 00C1 and the network control protocol is 80C1. No known STMFCP implementations exist.

The STMF protocol itself is, like ATM's Interim Local Management Interface (ILMI), a lightly modified version of SNMP. I believe that if the IETF PPP working group had been consulted in its development, the authors would likely have been told to use regular SNMP rather than inventing a new network layer.

Some, but not all, of the documentation is publicly available at the following Web site:

`http://www.ntcip.org/`

Multiprotocol Label Switching (MPLS; MPLSCP)

MPLS was originally specified as Cisco's proprietary Tag Switching protocol but is now a standards-track IETF protocol. It uses one control protocol—MPLSCP, which is 8281—and two data protocol numbers, 0281 for unicast and 0283 for multicast. These are described in `draft-ietf-mpls-label-encaps-07.txt`. MPLS is not yet in common use.

MPLS is a means of encapsulating arbitrary packet-oriented data for transport over a hop-by-hop explicitly routed network. In concept, it operates similar to Frame Relay except that the MPLS Label Switched Paths (LSPs), which are analogous to Frame Relay Virtual Circuits, are unidirectional.

MPLS can be used to connect routers together in an overlay network (for example, to connect together a VPN), to carry legacy proprietary data across a core network (Frame Relay or ATM replacement), or to implement traffic engineering. Traffic engineering is a way of calculating either additional explicit routes (for MPLS) or link weightings (for OSPF-OMP) such that links in a network are used in an optimal manner. Generally, this requires the insertion of routes that the routing protocols ordinarily would not have calculated—that is, paths that are not of optimal (shortest possible) length—in order to detour traffic around points of congestion.

There are no configuration options for MPLS over PPP. The negotiation of MPLSCP therefore consists of either the exchange of empty MPLSCP Configure-Request and MPLSCP Configure-Ack packets or MPLSCP Configure-Request followed by LCP Protocol-Reject for peers not supporting MPLS. Once MPLSCP goes to Opened state, either unicast or multicast packets may be sent.

The data packets have a stack of four-octet labels of the form

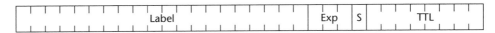

The Label value specifies a particular forwarding entry for this packet. The Experimental field, Exp, which was originally the Class of Service or CoS field, is reserved for future expansion, possibly to include explicit congestion notification, drop eligibility, or just additional label bits. The S bit is set to 1 for the last label before the encapsulated data (this label is known as the bottom of the stack). If S is 0, another MPLS label follows. If S is 1, the user datagram follows. The TTL is a hop-by-hop time-to-live counter, as with IPv4, and is used to prevent network damage due to temporary forwarding loops and to support traceroute-like applications in some cases. Depending on network configuration, the TTL is either copied from the encapsulated data or independent of it, and it is either decremented at each hop or predecremented for the LSP hop length at tunnel entry.

The Label values are assigned, generally using either CR-LDP or RSVP-TE, from egress to ingress of the LSP. In other words, the receiver tells the sender which Label value corresponds to the path being constructed, and the sender must then transmit data using the requested Label value.

Originally, this protocol was devised as a way to speed up relatively slow IP forwarding table look-ups. Now that hardware that forwards IP at line speed on fast interfaces is available, this is no longer a central focus of MPLS.

IP Addressing Issues

Dealing well with the IP-Address option can be difficult. This portion of an implementation has more interaction with the outside world—network stacks and address assignment mechanisms—and usually has many possible ways to be configured.

The primary purpose of the IPCP IP-Address option is to avoid the addressing problems that were inherent in SLIP. With SLIP, there is no negotiation of the addresses and it is very easy to misconfigure a SLIP link and cause a persistent routing loop or other failures. With this option, each peer can inform the other of its intended address, and misconfigurations can be detected before they cause trouble.

The address in a Configure-Request may be sent as 00000000 (also written as 0.0.0.0), in which case the peer is requested to send a Configure-Nak specifying the address of the local system, perhaps by looking up the authenticated peer name from PAP or CHAP in a database. This mechanism is usually used by a dial-up system (often a PC) to acquire an address from a dial-in "server." If the look-up fails, the IPCP protocol could be shut down either with a simple Protocol-Reject or by sending a Configure-Ack to go to Opened state and then sending a Terminate-Request message. Although more complex, many common implementations, including the freely available pppd (see Chapter 10), will do the latter because they detect the error while attempting to notify the IP layer that the interface is ready for use when IPCP goes to Opened state and because it allows IPCP to be reopened at a later time without restarting the link. Sending Protocol-Reject disables IPCP for the life of the link. Thus, one interpretation of IPCP going to Opened state and then immediately terminating is that the addresses negotiated were not acceptable.

This option may also be omitted from the Configure-Request and rejected with Configure-Reject if received. In this case, no IP addresses are negotiated on the link. If this is done, IP on PPP operates in a manner similar to SLIP, and any needed addresses must be configured into the network layer independently from PPP. The IP-Address option is occasionally rejected by half-bridge devices that do not have IP addresses assigned. However, I strongly recommend against this practice for three reasons. First, negotiation of addresses does not imply that the addresses are not in use for other purposes. In fact, it is quite reasonable to borrow the local IP address of another interface for IPCP negotiation purposes. The "ip unnumbered" configuration command on a Cisco router requires the user to specify another interface so that a source IP address is available for use in IP header generation. This same address is also used by a Cisco router for IPCP Configure-Request. It is explicitly not necessary to create a separate "subnet" for the link when negotiating addresses. Second, even if the addresses are not needed for any purpose, such as with half-bridges, it is still a good idea to negotiate for the addresses to avoid configuration and wiring errors. Finally, virtually all devices that speak IPCP have at least one IP address assigned that could be used for negotiation. For instance, any device that is manageable via SNMP must have a configured IP address. Sending this IP address to your peer via this option is a good practice.

An IP address of all zeros is often the source of trouble. Implementors should be aware that some systems will send an unsolicited Configure-Nak with the address set to 0 if the peer attempts to negotiate without revealing its address in a Configure-Request message. Such a Configure-Nak does not imply, as the normal convention specified in RFC 1661 would seem to indicate, that offering an IP address of all zeros to this peer is an acceptable response. Instead, a proper nonzero address should be sent in the next Configure-Request if possible. Also, some implementations (such as Windows 95 DUN) will erroneously send Configure-Ack with a zero IP address in response to a zero Configure-Request. If the peer of that system has no other local address to use, then IPCP should be shut down when this is detected, since it indicates a configuration error. Also, some ISPs give their own addresses as 0.0.0.0, since Windows 95 Dial-Up Networking (DUN) doesn't need a valid remote address. Other systems confronting this situation usually must Configure-Nak with an arbitrary address in order to make the link usable.

Good implementations allow both the local IP address (sent in Configure-Request) and the remote IP address (sent in Configure-Nak, if necessary) to be configured by an administrator. Depending on network topology and address assignment practices, it may be wise to allow a range or list of addresses to be specified in each case to allow for some latitude in the addresses requested by the peer.

Dial-in systems, in particular, need a variety of remote IP address assignment systems. The local address sent in Configure-Request is usually fixed to one convenient value for all callers. This address is often also the local address on a primary Ethernet interface. The remote IP address, however, can be assigned per port or channel, by a per-user security service, such as RADIUS (RFC 2138) or TACACS (RFC 1492), from a local address pool or from an external pool such as DHCP (RFC 2131). If any form of pooling is used, I suggest that a least recently used policy apply to new assignments and that the authenticated peer name be used to reclaim a previously held address if the address has not yet been reassigned.

Some Suggestions

Another issue that implementors face is dealing with the side effects of failing to negotiate optional items, such as the IP address. An implementation can be lenient in some cases because the negotiation of these options is not a security issue. (How the negotiated peer address is used may have security implications, because injecting bad data into routing protocols will disrupt network operation, but no implementation is compelled to use the data provided by the peer in that manner merely as a result of negotiation. Nor is it true that negotiating a particular local address obligates an implementation ever to send a packet using that address. There is no way to force a peer to use any particular address.)

The goal, then, is interoperability, not strictness of compliance. The following are some scenarios that can be dealt with.

- **Peer sends address as 0, but no local means of determining the peer's address is available.**
  On systems with only one interface, such as a typical dial-up PC, and a peer assumed to be providing access to the global Internet, this situation is easy to handle. Send a Configure-Nak for any RFC 1918 address, such as 192.168.1.1. This works around a misconfiguration that is now common in

many dial-in systems used by ISPs. Otherwise, for most other systems and situations, a Configure-Reject should be generated, which will lead to the peer omitting its address, a situation described below.

- **Peer sends a nonzero but unexpected or undesirable address.**

Send a Configure-Nak with the expected address as a hint. The peer may ignore this Configure-Nak. If it does, then IPCP should be shut down, since this situation indicates that the addresses have been incorrectly configured and an operator should intervene. Alternatively, Configure-Reject can be sent, leading to the same result as described below. This is effectively falling back to SLIP-like operation.

- **The peer refuses to provide its address.**

In most systems, a remote address is required on a point-to-point interface in order to establish the IP interface for the link in the network stack. One work-around is to allow IPCP to go to Opened state, but bring only the hardware `ifnet` (link layer) up, with IP forwarding disabled and without an IP routing table entry, and use implementation-dependent raw (non-IP) sockets to find the peer's identity by listening to the messages it sends.

If the link will eventually be used by Open Shortest Path First (OSPF, RFC 2328), then one particularly effective way to do this is to begin sending Hello packets. The local system sends OSPF Hello packets, setting the destination IP address to the assigned "AllSPFRouters" (224.0.0.5) multicast destination address. The peer will do the same, and its Hello packets will have its address as the IP source. With this configuration, OSPF will need to enforce any local rules concerning the peer's address that PPP would have used when OSPF decides to form an adjacency or to remain in state 2-Way.

Similarly, if the link will be used by Routing Information Protocol (RIP, RFC 2453), then RIP Request packets may be sent to the link-local broadcast address (255.255.255.255) with the source address set to the link's local address. The peer should respond with a RIP Response, and the source IP address will be the remote address on the link.

Finally, if no routing protocol is to be run on the link, then sending an ICMP (Internet Control Message Protocol) Echo to the link-local broadcast address may elicit an ICMP Echo-Reply from the peer.

- **Saved local address from previous session is available when peer is expected to assign local address.**

This is the mirror image of the last case above. It can occur with a dial-up system that usually gets an arbitrarily assigned address but would prefer to reacquire an address from a previous session, if possible. A Configure-Request with the saved local address is sent. If the peer sends Configure-Nak, then, for most dial-up systems, the peer's hint should be taken. If the peer's response is Configure-Reject, then I recommend saving a flag in stable storage to indicate that this peer cannot handle requested addresses and then sending Close and Open events into IPCP in order to restart with an address of 0. (Note that the stable storage must be present in order to implement the saved local address feature in the first place.)

- **Local address is unknown, and peer either sends Configure-Nak with address hint 0 or sends Configure-Reject.**

  The system can fall back in this case on BOOTP (RFC 951). A packet is formed as follows.

```
FF 03 - Standard Address and Control field
00 21 - PPP Protocol field for IP
45 00 - Version/IHL and TOS
01 48 - Total length (328 bytes)
00 00 - Identification
00 00 - Fragment flags and offset
02 11 - TTL 2, protocol 17 (UDP)
B7 A6 - IP header checksum
00 00 00 00
      - Source IP address (unknown)
FF FF FF FF
      - Destination IP address (broadcast)
00 44 - Source port (BOOTP client)
00 43 - Destination port (BOOTP server)
01 34 - UDP Length (308 bytes)
FB FD - UDP checksum
01    - op 1--BOOTREQUEST
00    - htype unknown
00    - hlen--no hardware address
00    - hops
00 00 00 01
      - xid
00 01 - seconds
00 00 - unused
00 00 00 00 00 00 00 00 00 00 00 00 00 00 00 00
```

```
             - ciaddr, yiaddr, siaddr, giaddr
   00 00 ... [272 bytes of zeroes]
             - chaddr, sname, file, vend
   C3 C1 - CRC
```

If the peer understands BOOTP over PPP, it will reply with a usable address. This request may need to be retried a few times using a timer. If the peer does not respond, the link must be dropped and failure reported to a user.

The Unnumbered Mode Controversy

Many implementations and implementors wrongly confuse the IP routing notions of "numbered" and "unnumbered" with the presence or absence of the IPCP IP-Address option. This issue probably causes more IPCP interoperability problems than any other.

To understand the confusion, it is necessary to understand some IP routing basics. There are two fundamental types of links,[1] called *broadcast* and *point-to-point*. On a broadcast interface, such as Ethernet, a given node will have at least one local address and a subnet mask. The local address on the interface must exist in order for the node to transmit on the link and receive data. The subnet mask segregates the world into those several nodes that are also on the same link and those many that must be on different links. When the node wants to send data to a particular IP address, it can use the subnet mask to determine if the message can be sent directly to the recipient on the same link or, if it is not on the subnet, if it must go through an intermediate router first. This test is done by comparing the destination address with the source address after logically AND-ing both with the subnet mask value.

An interesting corollary to the same link/other link distinction made by the subnet mask on broadcast interfaces is that no two links not connected by bridges may exist anywhere in the Internet that overlap in any portion of their given subnets.[2] In other words, on a broadcast interface, all IP addresses within

---

1. There are, of course, variants, such as the nonbroadcast LAN emulation used on ATM networks. These variants function in ways similar enough to the two fundamental types that they can be ignored for simplicity.
2. One exception to this general rule occurs with individual nodes on point-to-point links, where proxy-ARP for the remote node's IP address is reasonable because it represents just one ARP entry per link, rather than N entries for all hosts on the link. This is effectively bridging rather than routing.

the defined subnet must be reachable by a broadcast. If splitting of the subnet were permitted, then IP addresses would be ambiguous, at least for hosts not running a routing protocol. How would a router determine where to send a packet whose destination address lay in the overlapped region? It could not reasonably resolve the next hop, because the address would belong to two separate links (A and B in Figure 5.1) according to the subnet mask comparison. Worse still, consider what happens when a host unaware of this misconfiguration attempts to contact an address in the disputed region. It uses local address resolution (such as ARP) instead of forwarding to a router, as would be required.[3] Host 1 here will attempt to ARP for Host 2 rather than sending packets for Host 2 to the router. Host 2 will never see the ARP request and never be able to reply to it. Broadcasts and protocols that rely on them are even more adversely affected.

From this restriction, it follows that no broadcast interface can be configured whose local address lies within another interface's subnet, since this would clearly mean that any subnet mask given to the former would surely overlap some or all of the latter's subnet. Some IP implementations, however, have taken this idea to an extreme by prohibiting any interface—not just broadcast interfaces—from having a local address within another interface's subnet.

This extreme is clearly wrong for point-to-point links. Consider the configuration of routers connected only by point-to-point links in Figure 5.2. Node A could quite reasonably use the same local address for its links to both C and G, since that local address would define A's identity and would not be part of a subnet definition. Each node in this network may have a single unique and arbitrary IP address, and the entire configuration would still function as a part of an internet. The fact that node B has four links, each with the same local address, causes no harm. Even node E, which uses the same local address on a broadcast interface, is in no trouble, because the addresses are still distinct and the subnet does not overlap any address not physically connected to the broadcast link.

This configuration is known as "unnumbered mode" on a Cisco router. The point-to-point links on node E, for example, might be configured with

```
ip unnumbered ethernet0
```

3. For a few restricted cases, it is possible to do this by having the router respond to all ARP requests on the larger network on behalf of the smaller network. This solution, which amounts to a poor emulation of a bridge, does not scale as well as traditional routing and generally has little to recommend it.

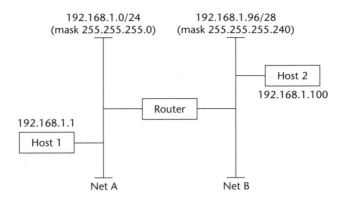

FIGURE 5.1 An undesirable configuration

This would configure the router to reuse the local IP address from the "ethernet0" interface (presumably 10.3.2.1 in this example) as the local IP address on the PPP links to B, D, and F. Note that the links still have IP addresses but the addresses are shared with other interfaces rather than being in distinct IP subnets.

IP implementations that require the local addresses to differ will obviously force the administrator to assign separate local addresses for each link. Node B in Figure 5.2 would consume at least four IP addresses. One reason for this software flaw is the result of the lack of a broadcast/point-to-point flag (known as IFF_POINTOPOINT on most Unix systems) in the link interface. Thus, since all links look like broadcast interfaces, a separate subnet must be created for each

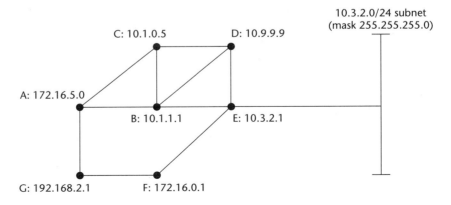

FIGURE 5.2 An internet

link even though there are only two peers, and the notion of "broadcasting" inherent in a subnet definition is irrelevant.

Note that for three links, as in Figure 5.3, a minimum of 12 IP addresses (four per link) are used if this problem exists. This is true because a subnet mask of 255.255.255.254 (also written "/31") generally cannot be used, and a 255.255.255.252 (/30) mask leaves 2 bits for host addresses, or four distinct IP addresses. Many WAN links running PPP are configured using /30 netmasks. This mode of operation is known as "numbered" mode to most router manufacturers, because each link is identified with a subnet number and a unique local address.

Clearly, for point-to-point links such as PPP, "numbered" mode need not exist. One reason numbered mode is popular with administrators is that a router generally allows the gross state of the interface (IPCP in Opened state) to determine whether it responds to a ping to the local IP address. By having separate local addresses for each link, a very primitive test of link status in a network can be made with just ping and traceroute. It is true, however, that a traceroute lacking a reply from one of these local addresses does not guarantee that the IPCP link is down, because corrupted (or locally inconsistent) routing data cause the same effect. Also, some systems cannot properly detect link failure and thus fail to remove the local IP address when the link has failed. I do not recommend the use of numbered mode links.

The confusion in IPCP is that some vendors have integrated the IP-Address option into this routing software problem. Normally, the IP-Address option serves only to detect configuration errors and to simplify administration. The IPCP option is not intended to affect routing issues, such as whether the link is marked as "unnumbered" for link-state protocols such as OSPF, which treats links to subnets and links to routers differently. However, on the implementations with this

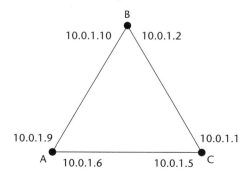

FIGURE 5.3 Numbered mode links. All subnet masks set to 255.255.255.252.

flaw, enabling IP-Address negotiation will also configure the unit for numbered mode, and disabling it reverts to unnumbered mode. Either way, the administrator must give up important functionality.

Good implementations of IPCP should separate these two options. If numbered mode is necessary, then the subnet definition should be configured separately from the option that controls whether or not IP-Address is included in the Configure-Request message. If the peer sends a Configure-Reject for IP-Address, then the obsolete IP-Addresses option may be tried. If both are Configure-Rejected, then, just like SLIP, any local address may be used without notifying the peer. If the peer refuses to send a Configure-Request with the IP-Address option, then after trying an unsolicited Configure-Nak, a guess at the peer's address may be taken (perhaps based on a database look-up of the authenticated peer name) or any reasonable address may be chosen to represent the peer.

I recommend going to great lengths to attempt to interoperate with peers that unwisely choose to reject the IP-Address option.

Proxy-ARP and Routing

Proxy-ARP is a simple way to make dial-in PPP clients appear on a local Ethernet or Token Ring network. It is simple because it generally doesn't require additional routing configuration. To use proxy-ARP, the remote client's address must be chosen such that it is in the same IP subnet as that assigned to one of the local broadcast interfaces. For example, if 172.16.0.0 with subnet mask 255.255.0.0 is used on an Ethernet interface, then a PPP link with remote address 172.16.0.100 is configured for proxy-ARP. The dial-in system then automatically answers ARP requests on that broadcast interface on behalf of the remote client.

The alternative to proxy-ARP is to use IP routing, by either distributing static routes among the systems on the network or running a standard routing protocol, such as RIPv2. This is more difficult to configure but is generally more flexible and reliable. Some of the proxy-ARP issues are as follows.

- **Trouble with Multiple Dial-in Servers and ARP Caches**
  If multiple dial-in servers are used, bad interactions with ARP caches on the local network are very likely. To avoid frequent broadcasting for IP address to MAC address translations (ARP requests), most systems cache the answers they get, sometimes for hours at a time. If a remote system disconnects and then reconnects to a different dial-in server, those local systems will be unable to communicate with the remote because their local cache

will still point to the previous dial-in server. One way to deal with this is to make ARP caches time out quickly and just accept the increased traffic. Another is to use RFC 1868 UNARP extensions, although many systems corrupt their caches when they receive UNARP.

- **Broadcasts and Multicasts**
  Since the remote host may think that it is attached to the LAN, it may try to rely on broadcasts and multicasts for various protocols. Most dial-in servers won't forward these messages between interfaces in order to avoid flooding the dial-up system with excessive traffic. This can lead to a variety of problems. The most common problem occurs with Windows systems, which make extensive use of chatty broadcast protocols to support the "Network Neighborhood" feature. One way to work around this problem is by configuring the dial-in server to forward broadcasts to specific numbered ports for particular dial-up users.

- **Multiple Addresses**
  If a remote site has multiple IP addresses, the dial-in server will need to be configured to proxy-ARP for each individual address. Most implementations do not have specific support for this case, and configuration can be cumbersome.

- **Routing Protocols**
  Many routing protocol implementations cannot deal well with proxy-ARP links. Proxy-ARP should be used for isolated dial-up nodes, such as common PCs, or for nodes using Network Address Translation (NAT).

In general, I recommend the use of proxy-ARP for very small installations (those with about 40 or fewer access lines). Larger sites should route.

The Transforming Layers

IN THIS CHAPTER

The two transforming layers defined in PPP are data compression (Compression Control Protocol, or CCP) and encryption (Encryption Control Protocol, or ECP). Technically, these layers are usually considered to be NCPs, but they are placed in this separate chapter because they share the following unusual properties.

- *Neither has an associated network interface.* These protocols, unlike the NCPs documented in the preceding chapter, such as IP and IPX, do not have an interface to a networking system outside of PPP.
- *Both reprocess data from other NCPs.* Data transmitted from other running NCPs are routed through these layers when they are active. The other NCPs process only user data.
- *Both have special definitions for use with Multilink PPP (MP).* These protocols define special protocol numbers to indicate their position in the flow of PPP data processing. They may be implemented logically above MP (at the aggregate link level) or below MP (in the multiple individual links).
- *Both can use patented error-recovery techniques (Reset-Request/Reset-Ack).* Both protocols can make use of techniques for which Motorola claims patent rights. However, many question the validity of these patents, unpatented work-arounds exist, and not all algorithms use this mechanism.
- *Both specify the use of encumbered algorithms.* Almost all compression algorithms are patented, and most encryption schemes are export controlled

by national governments. Normally, these kinds of restrictions are not permitted for IETF protocols (see RFC 1602), but a special variance for CCP and ECP was issued as RFC 1915. All of the patented algorithms are available for license, and the RFC for each algorithm provides licensing information. The existence of these problems means that implementors of these protocols may need to consult with patent and export lawyers before developing products including CCP and ECP. (See also the pointers to the LPF in Chapter 11.)

- *Both allow parallel negotiation of multiple algorithms.* This will be shown later.

The two relevant RFCs are 1962 for CCP and 1968 for ECP. I recommend reading both together, even if only one is to be used, since they are very similar, and since each can be used to clarify points made in the other.

Architecture

Architecturally, there is only one possible legal implementation when these protocols are not used with MP, according to RFC 1968. (See Chapter 7 for architectural details of CCP and ECP when used with MP.) The non-MP implementation corresponds to the diagram in Figure 6.1.

The encapsulation performed on transmit is shown in Figure 6.2. It is not necessary to use both CCP and ECP in all implementations. If both are used, however, data must first be compressed and then encrypted. This is required by RFC 1968 because compressed output is usually smaller, giving an eavesdropper less encrypted data to work with and thus providing greater security, and because encrypted data usually does not compress well. Note, however, that NCP negotiation traffic is not usually compressed but must be encrypted when both are employed.

Since these are PPP protocols, neither CCP nor ECP provides end-to-end service. Both IP payload compression and IPSec provide end-to-end service.

Negotiation Features

In both protocols, the goal of negotiation is to determine a preferred common algorithm for compressing or encrypting and to determine parameters for that

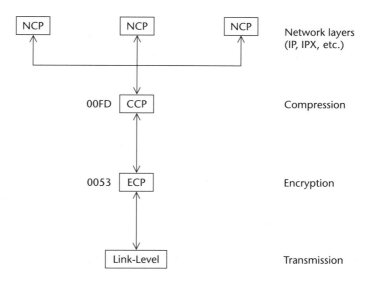

FIGURE 6.1 Non-MP compression and transmission

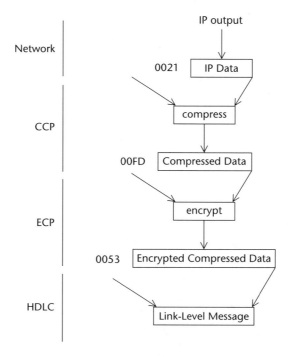

FIGURE 6.2 Encapsulation data flow

algorithm. In both CCP and ECP, the algorithms listed in the configuration messages take the familiar variable-length Type-Len-Data option format, with a single octet each for Type and Len and a variable number of octets for the Data field, depending on the parameters defined for the algorithm indicated by the Type field.

To negotiate the common algorithm, the decryptor or decompressor (let us call this peer the *decoder* for simplicity) sends a Configure-Request listing the algorithms it wishes to decode, in descending order of preference. The receiver replies with Configure-Reject if any of these algorithms are unknown. If all are known, but some are specified with unusable parameters, then Configure-Nak is sent. Finally, if all algorithms are known and have usable parameters the encryptor or compressor (the *encoder*) replies with Configure-Ack to agree to begin encoding.

These algorithms can be negotiated serially, with a separate Configure-Request sent for each single algorithm known by the decoder, or in parallel, with all algorithms listed at once. Although serial negotiation is simpler to implement, parallel negotiation usually converges faster, especially if a large number of algorithms are implemented.

An example negotiation for either CCP or ECP protocol might go as follows (watching only one side of the symmetric negotiation, with peer A as decoder and peer B as encoder and thus with encoded user data eventually flowing from B to A).

```
A: Configure-Request    ID:1 [ 1 2 15:0C 12:05 ]
B: Configure-Reject     ID:1 [ 1 2 12:05 ]
A: Configure-Request    ID:2 [ 15:0C ]
B: Configure-Nak        ID:2 [ 15:09 ]
A: Configure-Request    ID:3 [ 15:09 ]
B: Configure-Ack        ID:3 [ 15:09 ]
```

In this example, peer A offered to decode four algorithms, numbered 1, 2, 15, and 12. B does not implement 1, 2, or 12, so it Configure-Rejects these first. A offers the remaining algorithm 15 with parameter 0C. B implements this algorithm but does not agree to the parameter 0C, so it sends Configure-Nak with a hint of 09 instead. Finally, A offers algorithm 15 with parameter 09, and B accepts.

Note that it is also possible for peer A to offer several algorithms that are all known to B and that all have acceptable parameters. In this case, B has two choices: send Configure-Ack for all of the acceptable algorithms offered, in which case the actual algorithm used for decoding on A and encoding on B will be the first one in the list, or use Configure-Reject to disable the algorithms that are no longer wanted. B cannot send a Configure-Ack containing just the single desired algorithm from the list, because it is not legal to send a Configure-Ack with data that differ from the corresponding Configure-Request. The first possibility might appear as

```
A: Configure-Request    ID:1 [ 1 2 15:09 12:05 ]
B: Configure-Reject     ID:1 [ 2 12:05 ]
A: Configure-Request    ID:2 [ 1 15:09 ]
B: Configure-Ack        ID:2 [ 1 15:09 ]
```

and the second as

```
A: Configure-Request    ID:1 [ 1 2 15:09 12:05 ]
B: Configure-Reject     ID:1 [ 2 12:05 ]
A: Configure-Request    ID:2 [ 1 15:09 ]
B: Configure-Reject     ID:2 [ 15:09 ]
A: Configure-Request    ID:3 [ 1 ]
B: Configure-Ack        ID:3 [ 1 ]
```

The first option is fully supported by both of the RFCs, but the second is safer with peers that may not necessarily implement this feature correctly and also allows the encoder to choose a preferred algorithm that may not be the same as the decoder's preferred algorithm. In both cases, algorithm option 1 has been negotiated. (It is even possible to send a Configure-Ack if only the first option is acceptable even though the others are unknown or otherwise unacceptable. Doing so is faster but is risky and is not recommended.)

It is possible for there to be no common algorithm. For ECP, which is generally concerned with security, this means that the encryptor should tear down the link. For CCP, which generally has little security implication, either end may choose to terminate the CCP protocol using Protocol-Reject in response to Configure-Request, or simply to complete negotiation with no algorithms supplied in the Configure-Request and Configure-Ack messages. If the latter is done, CCP proceeds to Opened state but does not compress any data.

Although somewhat controversial, proceeding to Opened state in CCP with no chosen algorithm is often wise because the peer that is sending Configure-Request and finds no algorithms left to negotiate has no other option but to send an empty request. The implementor may want to send Protocol-Reject for the preceding Configure-Reject that caused the problem, but doing so will prohibit compression in the opposite direction as well, which may be an undesirable side effect.

Such an exchange appears as

```
A: Configure-Request    ID:1 [ 1 2 ]
B: Configure-Reject     ID:1 [ 1 2 ]
A: Configure-Request    ID:2
B: Configure-Ack        ID:2
```

One common implementation used by ISPs sends an empty Configure-Reject in response to an empty Configure-Request. This odd and rather poor behavior must be terminated by use of Protocol-Reject.

Once a single algorithm has been decided on, that algorithm is used to send data from the encoder (sender of Configure-Ack) to the decoder (sender of Configure-Request). Each direction must be separately negotiated and may well use different algorithms due to differences in configurations or system capacity. Encoding may even be run in only one direction if desired, leaving the opposite direction unencoded.

Error Recovery

Because these algorithms usually keep state between packets encoded, the encoder and decoder must be kept in synchronization. To do this, both protocols make use of a pair of special code numbers, called Reset-Request (code 0E) and Reset-Ack (code 0F), to recover from lost or corrupted messages. When the decoder detects a lost or corrupted packet, it sends a Reset-Request to the encoder and begins discarding all undecodable data received. When the encoder receives a Reset-Request, it clears any stored history, sends Reset-Ack to the receiver, and then resumes encoding. When the decoder receives a Reset-Ack, the next packet is known to be decodable from a predefined initial state, so discarding is disabled and normal operation is resumed.

Note that this mechanism implies that in a typical implementation, several resets will occur when there is an error, depending on the queuing and transmission delays in the system (see Figure 6.3). Note also that this system assumes that packets cannot be reordered on the wire; this fact is critical when running with MP or any of the tunneling techniques. See Chapters 7 and 8 for details on how each avoids reordering.

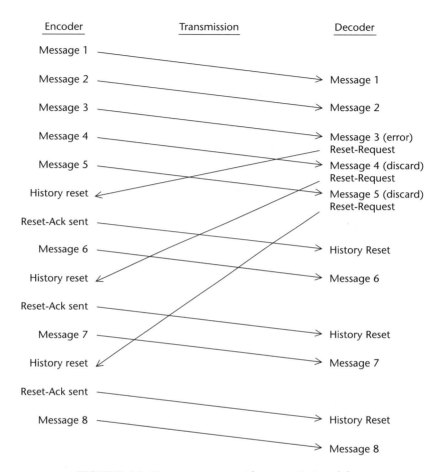

FIGURE 6.3 Error recovery with transmission delays

The decoder may elect not to send a Reset-Request for each failing message if it has an estimate of the round-trip time for the link. In this case, the decoder should simply silently discard the bad messages received until the round-trip time expires. If the Reset-Ack is not received within the estimated round-trip time, then another Reset-Request must be generated, since the prior request may have been lost.

U.S. Patent 5,130,993, assigned to Codex Corporation (a subsidiary of Motorola), entitled "Transmitting encoded data on unreliable networks," and expiring in 2009, claims to cover this Reset-Request/Reset-Ack technique of synchronization. I have reservations about this claim due to the apparent prior art available, such as the reset mechanisms available in well-designed TCP/IP VJ compression implementations and LAP-B. CCP implementors must take it on themselves to investigate this claim and to license or fight it as they deem reasonable. I can provide no guidance on this issue.

Other available techniques can be used as alternatives to the Reset-Request/Reset-Ack mechanism. For instance, the decoder can reset the encoder by sending a new Configure-Request message, which will take the encoder out of Opened state and cause encoding to be renegotiated. Several of the algorithms also define embedded flags for the request and ack states, which also make separate Reset-Request and Reset-Ack messages unnecessary.

Reportedly, Cisco IOS 10.3 returns CCP Code-Reject when Reset-Request is sent to it, and uses the CCP renegotiation technique to reset the peer if its decoder synchronization is lost. An implementation receiving CCP Code-Reject in response to Reset-Request must not use Reset-Request again and should drop back to using renegotiation of CCP to clear errors.

Interaction with Physical Layer

Modern modems normally implement MNP-5 or V.42bis data compression. Both of these algorithms automatically disable themselves when CCP is in use because the modem's compression ratio drops below a preset threshold. Despite the modem's ability to compress data, CCP is still somewhat useful since it reduces the number of characters that must be sent and received on the serial link to the modem.

Caution should be used when implementing CCP or ECP. If the physical layer is not highly reliable, as is the case when running PPP over L2TP, even very small losses are magnified by both of these protocols into unacceptable link performance. This performance loss occurs because packet loss and delay on the general Internet are far higher than on any single physical link. When a packet is lost, the compressor must be resynchronized, which requires a Reset-Request/Reset-Ack round trip and also causes all packets in flight to be discarded. Since the delay is longer, the number of these discarded packets is higher, and, coupled with the higher packet loss rate, this results in much higher overall data loss.

ECP's DES multiplies errors by a factor of 2, but errors with CCP can drop performance by an order of magnitude or more.

For compression protocols that support multiple histories, I recommend using zero histories (packet-by-packet compression mode) when tunneling over an unreliable physical layer. For those without multiple history support, I recommend simply disabling CCP. The features of ECP are probably more reasonably achieved in these cases by use of IPSec or application-layer security.

Compression Negotiation

CCP negotiation, described in RFC 1962, is done with protocol 80FD for non-MP implementations and MP implementations using compression above MP and with protocol 80FB for MP implementations that compress at the link level. The compressed data are passed with protocols 00FD and 00FB, respectively.

The RFC specifies that only 80FD be used if MP is not negotiated. However, CCP systems that do not implement MP and those that are not using MP on a given link should still support 80FB if requested by the peer or if 80FD is disabled by the peer using LCP Protocol-Reject. For individual PPP links, the two protocols are identical, and supporting both numbers allows better interoperability. Indeed, one major router vendor always uses 80FB instead of 80FD on non-MP synchronous links, presumably because its compression hardware works on individual links only.

The single-octet Type field indicates the algorithm, as selected from the following list.

```
00    Organization Unique Identifier (OUI)
01    Predictor type 1 (RFC 1978)
02    Predictor type 2 (RFC 1978)
03    Puddle Jumper
10    Hewlett-Packard PPC
      (draft-ietf-pppext-hpppc-00.txt)
11    STAC Electronics LZS (RFC 1974)
12    Microsoft PPC/PPE (RFC 2118 and drafts)
13    Gandalf FZA (RFC 1993)
14    V.42bis compression
15    BSD LZW Compress (RFC 1977)
17    LZS-DCP (RFC 1967)
18    Magnalink MVRCA (RFC 1975)
19    Not used (assigned as DCE for RFC 1976)
1A    Deflate (RFC 1979)
```

Codes 04–0F were originally reserved by RFC 1962 for freely available compression algorithms without license fees, although this scheme appears to have been abandoned. Codes 16 and 1B–FE are unassigned, and FF is reserved. Code 00 allows a vendor to use any proprietary algorithm desired without needing a number assigned by the IANA.

When a message is sent through CCP for transmission from an upper-level NCP, the protocol number is usually checked first. I recommend that if the protocol number is in the range 0001 through 3EFF, it should be compressed. Otherwise, it should be passed through to ECP or the link level without modification. I also suggest that NCPs be able to specify when network layer data should not be compressed; this is a design and administrator interface issue for implementors. Unfortunately, each compression algorithm defines a slightly different method for determining which data to compress. (Note that this problem does not occur with ECP; generally, all packets other than LCP are passed through the encryptor when ECP is in use.)

Generally, in order to compress the data, the original PPP protocol number used by the network layer, often referred to as the *inner protocol number,* is prepended to the user data, often using the Protocol Field Compression (PFC) technique even if PFC was not negotiated in LCP, and this entire message is then compressed using the chosen algorithm. The modified packet is then passed down to ECP or the link level for transmission with the CCP protocol number (00FD or 00FB), which is often referred to as the *outer protocol number* (see Figure 6.4). At the receiver's side, the packet is demultiplexed using the PPP protocol number, as usual. If that number is the CCP protocol number, the data are decompressed. The real NCP protocol number is then removed from the beginning of the resulting decompressed data, and the data are then passed back through the normal demultiplexing procedure. Note, however, that this is only a general outline. Each compression algorithm defines its own means of encapsulating the data for transmission.

Compression Algorithms

In general, choosing compression algorithms to implement and to use depends strongly on the expected environment. There is no one best algorithm, even for a specific purpose. The factors an implementor must weigh include availability and cost (since some algorithms are available only under license from the inventor and all are subject to patent concerns), memory consumption, CPU loading, compression ratios for various types of data, and asymmetry of compression and

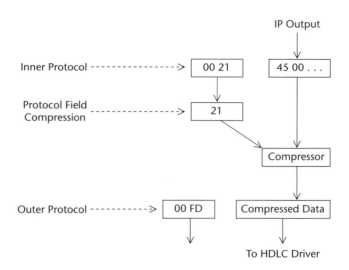

FIGURE 6.4 CCP data handling example

decompression. Table 6.1 lists results obtained with the Calgary Corpus with some of the CCP compression algorithms (higher numbers mean better compression; negative numbers indicate expansion). The last three files listed (img001) represent a large (683×1024) graphic image in three common file formats. Graphics represent the bulk of Internet traffic today.

For these tests, STAC was configured for performance mode 1, BSD Compress was set to 15 bits, and the Deflate window was set to 32KB. The CPU time in seconds, given for compression and decompression, was measured over all files on a 100MHz PowerPC running AIX, and is useful for comparing the algorithm performance. (All of the actual encapsulations have mechanisms for dealing with expansion, so the negative numbers in each case should be treated as zeros for comparison purposes.)

Perhaps the most important consideration, however, is the set of peers with which you plan to interoperate. This market decision causes most implementations to support STAC and MS-PPC first, probably followed by Predictor-1, BSD-Compress, and Deflate.

STAC compression is the most popular algorithm, in part because of its sparing memory requirements (one 20KB table for both transmit and receive) and because a C code implementation was once available from STAC for use in PPP without a license fee. Other algorithms also have strong adherents, and some additional market research may be required before choosing which algorithms

TABLE 6.1. Measured Compression Ratios

File Name	Predictor	STAC	BSD Compress	Deflate
bib	41%	43%	58%	69%
book1	28%	38%	56%	59%
book2	39%	46%	57%	66%
geo	19%	22%	25%	33%
news	34%	44%	49%	62%
obj1	34%	47%	35%	52%
obj2	43%	56%	45%	67%
paper1	34%	47%	53%	65%
paper2	33%	44%	56%	64%
paper3	28%	42%	52%	61%
paper4	24%	44%	48%	59%
paper5	24%	45%	45%	58%
paper6	35%	48%	51%	65%
pic	73%	84%	88%	89%
progc	37%	51%	52%	67%
progl	49%	63%	62%	77%
progp	50%	63%	61%	77%
trans	55%	56%	59%	80%
img001.jpg	−12%	−9%	−31%	0%
img001.gif	−12%	−10%	−35%	0%
img001.tif	−10%	0%	−2%	14%
CPU time (comp/decomp)	**3.64/3.13**	**4.67/1.42**	**9.53/3.64**	**22.69/1.59**

to support. In particular, it should be noted that Windows NT, unlike Windows 95 and 98, supports only MS-PPC and does not support STAC.

Many of the algorithms are mathematically similar and are based on original work by Lempel-Ziv (LZ) and later extensions by Welch (LZW). These techniques make use of dynamically constructed tables of substrings of the message and compress the message by producing pointers into these tables as output. In general, this class of algorithms uses more CPU time to compress than to decompress.

Most data compression algorithms operate a byte or two at a time and produce output that is a byte or two long. It is therefore useful to take advantage of the large data caches available in modern CPUs by doing the compression and decompression into regular data buffers, rather than into or out of the hardware-related uncached memory (mbufs). This means that a data copy is required after running the compressor or decompressor in order to get the data out of cached memory and into the buffers that DMA can use, but this is done with efficient word-at-a-time operations, and the overall effect is usually a performance gain.

Many of these algorithms also have available hardware implementations. These hardware devices, such as the Hi/fn 7811, can greatly increase the speed of a system using these compression algorithms, which are often highly computation intensive. Devices are also available that implement several algorithms simultaneously.

Motorola claims patent rights to much of the idea of compressing data and allocating memory for it through U.S. patent 5,245,614. Implementors of any data compression algorithms should investigate this claim first.

Implementors who need to support Windows machines should also note that Windows uses proprietary extensions to STAC and MPPC to support an encryption protocol called MPPE. These machines do not implement ECP. One of the side effects of this is that failure of CCP negotiation, which is normally harmless, can cause a link to a Microsoft system to fail, since encryption is normally considered a mandatory feature when enabled.

Many CCP implementations contain serious bugs. All implementations should therefore have a mechanism for allowing the user to disable CCP negotiation, and it is also worthwhile to implement an automatic means of shutting down a misbehaving CCP session, such as setting a maximum number of allowable Reset-Requests over a period of time.

| CCP Option 00 | Organization Unique Identifier (OUI) | Very rare |

The data for this option, shown in the diagram below, consist of three octets of identifier information, defined to be the first three octets of the manufacturer's assigned Ethernet physical address. (Despite the wording in the RFC, the Ethernet address is presented in normal canonical format. The first octet of an Ethernet address is the least significant byte of the address, not the most significant.) Presumably, a future draft of this RFC will permit the use of IANA-assigned identifiers as well. The next octet is a Subtype field for discriminating different algorithms supported by that manufacturer, and any additional octets are parameters for that algorithm.

| 00 | Len | OUI | Subtype | Data |

For example, this is OUI 00:80:2D (Xylogics), subtype 01, with additional data of 00 00 00 00:

```
00 0A 00 80 2D 01 00 00 00 00
```

(This example is fictitious. No known OUI implementations exist.)

| CCP Option 01 | Predictor Type 1 | Common |
| CCP Option 02 | Predictor Type 2 | Very rare |

These two algorithms are described in RFC 1978, which includes C source code. [Implementors should refer to the example source code distributed on SGI's ftp site (`ftp://ftp.sgi.com/other/ppp-comp/predictor1.c`) because it correctly implements the handling of incompressible data and is representative of a real implementation. The code in the RFC is based on a demonstration program that compresses and decompresses files, not packets.]

The Predictor algorithm requires no additional information to operate, so the options are Boolean types, as shown in the diagram below. CCP Configure-Nak should not be used with these options.

01	02
02	02

Predictor types 1 and 2 are basically the same, except that type 2 is a stream-oriented protocol that can pack multiple compressed frames into a single PPP frame, or segment a single compressed frame into many PPP frames. The RFC recommends the use of RFC 1663 Numbered Mode (LAP-B) operation if type 2 is used. For simplicity, most implementations use type 1 and, in fact, no known implementations of type 2 exist. The packet format is shown in the following diagram.

C	Uncompressed Length
Compressed Data . . .	
CRC–16 of Input	

The C bit is 1 if the data have been compressed, and it is 0 if they have not. The 15-bit Uncompressed Length field gives the original length of the packet before compression. An extra CRC-16 (in addition to the usual HDLC framing) is calculated with this algorithm to detect synchronization errors. This is done by first adding an optionally compressed (PFC) PPP protocol field to the input data, as described in the general CCP section. Then the length of this combined data is expressed as a two-octet integer in network byte order, and the CRC is calculated over these two octets followed by the combined protocol field and original data. Next, the data starting with the protocol field (not including the length field) are compressed using the Predictor algorithm. Finally, if the data did not expand in compression, the C bit is set to indicate that the data are compressed, and the CRC-16 calculated over the CCP input is appended to the end of the message. If the message is larger after compression, the original uncompressed data are sent with the C bit clear and with the same CRC.

Normally, of course, a Predictor implementation combines the CRC calculation with the compression encoding. The implementor must take care to start the CRC calculation with the original length information, then continue with both the CRC and the compression on the rest of the data, and finally append the resulting CRC to the end of the data.

If the data must be sent uncompressed and the addition of the Predictor length and protocol number header and CRC trailer would put the message over the peer's MRU, I recommend sending the data without CCP encapsulation, followed by a CCP Configure-Request to restart CCP and reset the peer. It is, of course, better to avoid this problem by negotiating an MRU of 1506 when Predictor is in use and setting an MTU of 1500 on the network interfaces (or, of course, negotiate 1500 and use 1494).

The algorithm itself is based on a hashing scheme that uses a value calculated from adjacent bytes in the message to predict the next byte. If the prediction is successful, a single bit is used to indicate the value. Otherwise, 9 bits are used. Thus, in the best case, this could compress a message by a factor of 8 to 1, or, in the worst case, expand it by 12.5 percent. Of course, if the data expand as a result of compression, the compressed flag should be cleared and the original uncompressed data sent.

The Predictor RFC does not recommend the use of Reset-Request or Reset-Ack messages. Instead, it uses the CCP Configure-Request technique to reset the compressor if a decoding error occurs.

The reader is cautioned that this algorithm may infringe on U.S. Patent number 5,229,768 assigned to Traveling Software. Novell, the author of the implementation in the RFC, has decided to allow copying of this source code without a license, but implementors wishing to use this algorithm may need to consult with a patent attorney because of this separate claim.

CCP Option 03	Puddle Jumper	Do not use

This algorithm was published in a now-obsolete Internet Draft. The algorithm was based on Huffman coding and allowed the table sizes to be negotiated. The author of the draft reports that it compressed about 10 to 15 percent better than Predictor 1. No known implementations exist, and the author has abandoned work on it.

CCP Option 10	Hewlett-Packard PPC	Do not use

This algorithm, which requires a license from Hewlett-Packard, was documented in `draft-ietf-pppext-hpppc-00.txt`, which has since expired. This document is no longer available from the official repositories, but it is available from the accompanying CD-ROM.

No parameters are negotiated, so the option appears in the list as just a type entry and a length entry, as shown below.

As with other compression methods, the optionally compressed (PFC) PPP Protocol field is prepended to the data and this entire message is compressed. Then a two-octet header similar to that used with Predictor is added, consisting of two octets of original length (including the PPP Protocol field), with the MSB set if the data are compressed. This packet format is shown below.

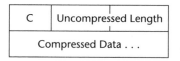

Unlike most other compression schemes, however, HPPC does not maintain state between packets and does not require sequencing or packet loss detection. Each packet is independently compressed. For this reason, no HPPC implementation should transmit a packet with the C bit set to 0. Incompressible data are instead sent without CCP encapsulation.

The draft does not describe the compression algorithm itself, although it does note that it is based on a variant of LZ, called LZ2. No known implementations exist.

CCP Option 11   STAC Electronics LZS   Common

STAC compression is documented in RFC 1974. As its name suggests, this is another variant of LZ compression.

Implementors of this algorithm must execute a license with Hi/fn, which bought the rights to the patents from STAC Electronics. Implementations of this compression algorithm are available from Hi/fn and several other vendors as hardware devices. See Chapter 11 for references. At one time, a license was available free of charge when the "low-performance" version of the STAC code was used as part of a PPP implementation, but it appears that this is no longer true. There are also free source-code implementations of STAC compression, but the patent encumbers these implementations as well.

The negotiation information consists of a two-octet History Count value followed by a single-octet Check Mode value, as shown below.

11	05	History Count	Check Mode

Some STAC implementations send one trailing pad byte in this option, probably because of the similarity to the MS-PPC option. A good implementation should be willing to accept and ignore any trailing pad octets in a STAC option with length greater than 5.

The History Count is used to allow multiple compression histories to be maintained by a compressor. This could be used, for instance, to separate data from certain network addresses or protocols to be compressed independently of other data on the link. Such use is up to the implementor to define. By default, and in most cases, the History Count is 1 to signify a single compression history. It can also be negotiated as 0 to compress each packet independently without maintaining a history. If this is done, then Reset-Request and Reset-Ack are not used.

The history-less form of STAC may also be used without CCP negotiation using PPP protocol 4021. If the peer replies with LCP Protocol-Reject, this mode must be disabled. The encapsulation for this mode is very simple. No header is used. The user data are prepended by the protocol number, STAC compressed, and sent. Use of this mode is rare.

The RFC erroneously describes the Check Mode octet as containing either left-aligned or right-aligned information (the text and diagram do not agree). The author of the RFC originally intended this to be a bit field. Instead, it is now by general agreement simply a single-octet enumerated value. The Check Mode value is one of the following.

```
00   No checking
01   Longitudinal Check Byte
02   Cyclic Redundancy Check
03   Sequence Number
04   Extended (Microsoft)
```

All implementations are required by the RFC to implement at least mode 3; however, several common implementations violate this requirement. In particular, Windows 95 implements only mode 4.

The Check Mode values are used to verify the integrity of the data so that a CCP Reset-Request can be generated when a packet is lost or damaged. The generated CCP Reset-Request and CCP Reset-Ack, despite the text of the RFC, must contain the affected History number, as shown below, even if only one history is used, since some existing implementations were based on one of the earlier drafts, which required this number. The receiver of these messages should, however, allow the two-octet History number to be omitted.

0E	ID	00 06	History

0F	ID	00 06	History

When in any mode except extended, the use of PFC on the inner protocol number is oddly conditional on the negotiation of PFC in LCP. If it is negotiated on, it may be used in CCP-STAC. If not, it must not be used.

The compressed packet format varies by the Check Mode and by the number of compression histories supported. The following table includes all legal formats.

```
Mode 0, 0 or 1 history:          (Compressed data)
Mode 0, 2 to 255 histories:      HH (Compressed data)
Mode 0, 256 or more histories:   HH HH (Compressed data)
Mode 1, 0 or 1 history:          LL (Compressed data)
Mode 1, 2 to 255 histories:      HH LL (Compressed data)
Mode 1, 256 or more histories:   HH HH LL (Compressed)
Mode 2, 0 or 1 history:          CC CC (Compressed data)
Mode 2, 2 to 255 histories:      HH CC CC (Compressed)
```

```
Mode 2, 256 or more histories:     HH HH CC CC (Compressed)
Mode 3, 0 or 1 history:            SS (Compressed data)
Mode 3, 2 to 255 histories:        HH SS (Compressed data)
Mode 3, 256 or more histories:     HH HH SS (Compressed)
Mode 4, 1 history:                 YY YY (Compressed data)
```

HH is the History number, in network byte order when expressed as more than one octet; LL is the XOR of hex FF and all of the uncompressed data (including the PPP protocol number); CC CC is the standard CRC-16 of the uncompressed data (the CRC is transmitted in LSB-first format, as with HDLC framing); SS is a sequence number (starting with 01 and wrapping from FF to 00); and YY YY is special 16-bit flag word for extended mode that is in this format (bitwise, MSB on left):

The A bit is set to 1 if the compressor was reset before compressing this packet. C is set to 1 if the packet is compressed. Both B and D are 0. The 12-bit Coherency Count is a sequence number starting at 0 for the first transmitted packet. For interoperability, packets that fail to compress are sent outside of compression through the normal data path. Thus, an observer will never see a packet with bit C set to 0 when this mode is used.

Extended mode is unlike most of the other compression techniques. The inner PPP protocol number prepended to the data before compression may not be compressed, regardless of the negotiation of Protocol Field Compression (PFC) in LCP. More strangely, the RFC requires that the outer 00 FD protocol number itself not be compressed using PFC, regardless of the state of PFC. This means that if STAC mode 4 is implemented, then ECP, MP, and the HDLC driver must all check for STAC mode 4 packets and temporarily disable PFC. Or, alternatively, an implementation may elect to disable all use of PFC if STAC mode 4 is negotiated. The original proponents of this algorithm state that their systems that support STAC mode 4 do not support PFC, so no conflict exists. However, compliance with the RFC poses implementation problems for others who have higher levels of functionality.

When in extended mode, CCP Reset-Request with the History number set to 1 is used to signal decompression failure or a missing sequence number, but CCP Reset-Ack is not issued by the compressor in response. Instead, the "A" bit is set on the next compressed packet to indicate that the compressor has been reset.

Cisco routers, on the other hand, have been noted to send CCP Configure-Request to reset the compressor. Either technique will work with a conforming and properly implemented peer.

No History number is included in the extended mode packet format, so only a single compression history is supported.

CCP Option 12   Microsoft PPC and PPE (MS-PPC/PPE; LZM/RC4)   Common

The compression part of this algorithm, which also requires a license from Hi/fn, is documented in RFC 2118. It is generally known as MPPC or MS-PPC, but within STAC and Microsoft it was known as LZM, since it is a variation on STAC's LZS technology.

Unlike all other vendors, who use ECP to negotiate encryption options and implement compression and encryption as separate protocols, Microsoft uses this CCP option to negotiate both compression and encryption. This implementation surprises many PPP users, since compression is never a requirement for proper operation of a link, but an NT system configured to "require encrypted connections" drops the link if CCP is rejected.

The encryption part of the negotiation was published in `draft-ietf-pppext-mppe-04.txt`. The encryption algorithm that is used with this option is RSA Data Security's RC4, which must be separately licensed from RSA. There are several available hardware devices that support both the compression and encryption algorithms for this option.

The negotiated value for this protocol consists of a single integer encoded as four octets in network byte order, as shown below. This integer is a bit-encoded mask of features supported.

12	06	Supported Bits

The legal Supported Bits values are

```
00 00 00 01     MPPC alone
00 00 00 10     MPPE with 40 bit key derived from LAN Manager
                form of user's password
00 00 00 20     MPPE with 40 bit key derived from NT version of
                user's password
```

```
00 00 00 40        MPPE with 128 bit key derived from NT version of
                   user's password
00 00 00 80        MPPE with 56 bit key derived from NT version of
                   user's password
01 00 00 00        Enable packet-by-packet encryption
```

These bits are logically ORed together to form the negotiated value. For instance, many NT servers send 00 00 00 71 to indicate that they support MPPE 128-bit and 40-bit encryption and keying from the LAN Manager password as well as MPPC compression. Some Microsoft technical documents describe another value, 00 00 02 00, for 40-bit keys derived from the NT version of the user's password, but this value has not been seen in the field. The key derivations, which are based on the MS-CHAP and SHA-1 functions, are too involved to describe here. See draft-ietf-pppext-mppe-keys-02.txt on the accompanying CD-ROM.

For compression, the data encapsulation is similar to STAC mode 4, except that the B bit is set if the packet was moved to the front of the history buffer, and the strange restriction prohibiting compression of 00FD down to FD at the link level has been removed. As with STAC mode 4, the inner prepended PPP Protocol field, which is passed through MS-PPC compression along with the user's data, may not be compressed.

If compression and encryption are both done, then the encapsulation is somewhat odd. The user's packet is prepended with the protocol number in the usual way, compressed, prepended with 00FD, encrypted, and finally prepended with 00FD again for transmission. This can only be described as a design flaw.

If both STAC and MS-PPC are implemented, be very careful with the ordering of options presented in the Configure-Request message. Windows 95 will terminate CCP if it sees STAC or other options first. Putting MS-PPC first seems to cure the problem. (This problem may be a side effect of the STAC option length bug.)

CCP Option 13   Gandalf FZA and FZA+   Rare

These algorithms, which must be licensed for a fee from Gandalf, are described in RFC 1993. These algorithms are also variants of LZ compression. Use of Gandalf FZA or FZA+ requires the use of RFC 1663 reliable transmission and RFC 1570 Self-Describing Padding.

The negotiated values, shown below, consist of a single octet representing the size of the history table as a power of 2 and an optional octet representing a version number, which is omitted for FZA and set to 01 for FZA+ (two variants of the algorithm).

13	03	History	

13	04	History	01

The History size value must be in the range 0C (4096 bytes) to 0F (32768 bytes). Because the compressor is not required to use the entire size indicated in the decompressor's Configure-Request, Configure-Nak should not be used to modify this value unless it is outside the range 0C to 0F. An FZA implementation should send Configure-Ack for any legal value requested by the peer, and should limit its compression to the lower of the peer's requested size or any internal resource limitation.

No header is used with the transmitted data. The output of the compressor is transmitted normally with PPP protocol number 00FD or 00FB, as negotiated.

Unlike most other compression algorithms, which either require or prohibit PFC-style compression of the PPP Protocol field prepended to the data before compressing, the RFC for FZA indicates that the Protocol field may be compressed using PFC only if PFC is negotiated by LCP. Also, data that expand beyond the peer's indicated MRU are sent in multiple consecutive frames. Since the algorithm may be run only on links with reliable transmission enabled, such frames can be unambiguously detected by the receiver during decompression based on features of the algorithm itself. Tracing and test equipment, however, generally cannot handle the data correctly.

CCP Option 14	V.42bis Compression	Do not use

This algorithm is available for licensing from several sources, including British Telecom. It is also a derivative of LZW. Unfortunately, no draft or RFC exists that describes the encapsulation or negotiation options. Since this compression algorithm is substantially similar to other algorithms already implemented, it has been abandoned.

CCP Option 15   BSD LZW Compress   Uncommon

This algorithm is described in RFC 1977, which includes C source code for a vaguely BSD-like Unix implementation with STREAMS buffers. It is available to anyone without a license. However, the basic LZW algorithm itself is subject to U.S. patent numbers 4,464,650 and 4,558,302 assigned to Unisys. Unisys has asserted its rights over other uses of LZW, such as the CompuServe GIF graphics file format.[1] Implementors should be aware of this restriction, which expires in 2003. IBM's U.S. patent 4,814,746 also covers the basic technology. (This list is incomplete. Designers must obtain competent legal counsel to avoid problems in this area.)

The negotiated value consists of a single octet, as shown below. The most significant 3 bits are a version number and must be set to binary 001. The least significant 5 bits, called Dict, represent the size of the compression dictionary as a power of 2. Valid values for this entire octet range from hex 29 (512-byte dictionary) to hex 30 (65,536 bytes).

The data packet format, shown below, is simply a two-octet Sequence number (initialized to zero) followed by the Compressed Data, which are formed from the original data prepended with a PFC-compressed PPP Protocol field. Unlike other compression schemes except Deflate, this one requires the use of PFC on the inner protocol number.

Sequence
Compressed Data . . .

Also unlike other compression formats, this one requires the decompressor to monitor the reception of uncompressed data as well as compressed data. When uncompressed data are received that would normally (based on the PPP protocol number) have been compressed by the peer, the decompressor's dictionary must be updated as though the compressed data have been received. This technique is used to guarantee that data are never expanded by this algorithm, since

---

1. Unisys has been rather insistent about its ownership of GIF, and for this reason there are no GIF images on my Web site. See `http://corp2.unisys.com/LeadStory/lzw-license.html`.

if expansion were to occur, the system would send the uncompressed data instead. Since the data will never expand on compression, BSD Compress does not suffer from the MRU-related problems that plague many of the other algorithms. (Alternatively, an implementation could simply renegotiate compression in these cases, although this would be likely to result in poor performance.)

Implementation of this algorithm requires a separate output buffer while compressing the data for transmission. If this output buffer is dynamically allocated (as with BSD mbufs) and compression fails due to a temporary lack of buffers, or if the resulting compressed data are larger than the original packet, then the original message is sent without compression. Note that Reset-Ack, which would normally reset the decompressor's dictionary, cannot be used to handle this case since it cannot be sent unsolicited—the ID number must be copied from the corresponding Reset-Request. Also, be aware that, to keep the dictionaries in synchronization, all data from the NCPs that are sent uncompressed due to failures must still pass through the compressor; the implementation must not abort the compression operation simply because of a lack of output buffer space. If this situation can occur, it is helpful to have a preallocated scratch buffer to receive the discarded output.

CCP Option 17   **LZS-DCP**   Very rare

This algorithm, described in RFC 1967, is just a variant packet format for the same STAC compression algorithm used in RFC 1974.

The negotiated values are, as shown below, a two-octet History number, a single-octet Check mode, and a single-octet Process mode. The History number is defined as in RFC 1974.

17	06	History	Check	Process

The Check mode is one of the following.

```
00    No checking
01    Longitudinal Check Byte
02    Sequence Number
03    Sequence Number and Longitudinal Check Byte
```

The default is 03. The Process mode is either 00 to indicate that uncompressed packets are not examined by the decompressor (the default) or 01 to indicate that the decompressor updates its state based on any uncompressed data received.

Transmitted packets are formed by prepending the PPP Protocol field, compressed with PFC if negotiated at LCP time, and compressing. If the Sequence Number option is negotiated, then a single octet is prepended to the resulting compressed data. Unlike the other compression schemes, the first transmitted packet will have sequence number 01. The sequence number is maintained separately for each history. If more than one history is in use, then a History number is prepended before the sequence number. This field is one octet if the number of histories is between 2 and 255, inclusive, and two octets if the total number of histories is 256 or greater. If the Longitudinal Check Byte option is negotiated, then a value is formed by exclusive-OR of all uncompressed data bytes and the value FF. This single octet is appended to the end of the compressed data.

Finally, the data are prepended with a single-octet header whose bits are defined as

E	C/U	R–A	R–R	0	0	0	C/D

The E (extension) bit is always set to 1. The header can be extended to multiple octets by setting this bit to 0 in the future. C/U indicates whether or not the enclosed data are compressed and is set to 1 for compressed data. R-A (Reset-Ack) is used to signal the decompressor that the compressor was reset before this packet was generated (as with RFC 1974 STAC mode 4 bit A). R-R (Reset-Request) is set to 1 in a message from the decompressor to the compressor to indicate that a reset is required. C/D is used for Frame Relay in other implementations, and must be set to 0.

Unlike other compression algorithms, this one requires a connection between the compressor and decompressor in a given implementation. The compressed messages are normally received by the decompressor, but the R-R bit received must be used to reset the compressor. This algorithm does not make use of the CCP Reset-Request and Reset-Ack messages.

CCP Option 18	Magnalink MVRCA	Very rare

This algorithm, which must be licensed from Telco Systems, is described in RFC 1975. The negotiated values are two octets, as shown below. The first octet contains 2 bits (FE) that are used for undocumented features, a single bit (P) to indicate if packet-by-packet compression is supported, and 5 bits (Hist) that specify the size of the history buffer in an undocumented manner. The second octet contains a value in the range 01 to 3F, and indicates the number of contexts for which history is maintained. If the P bit is set, then this number includes context zero, which by definition does not have a history and is used for packet-by-packet compression.

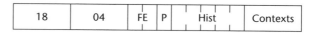

The inner protocol number is compressed only if the PFC option is negotiated at LCP time.

The packets transmitted are encapsulated with a two-octet header defined as:

C	E	Context	Integrity

The C bit is set to 1 if the data are compressed and to 0 if uncompressed. The Context number identifies one of 63 possible compression histories, or is 0 for packet-by-packet compression. The Integrity byte and the E bit are documented only in the Magnalink proprietary documentation and are not publicly described.

IBM and other vendors have compression devices that support this algorithm in hardware.

CCP Option 19   **DCE**   **Do not use**

This option number was apparently mistakenly allocated for RFC 1976, which defines an LCP (not CCP) option hex 19 (decimal 25). That RFC actually specifies several RFCs that should be supported by a class of equipment that includes CSU/DSUs.

CCP Option 1A   **Deflate**   **Uncommon**

This algorithm is documented in RFC 1979. It is available without licensing restrictions, although source-code distributions should include credit to the authors listed in the RFC. The algorithm is based on an LZ variant known as LZ77, which is used in GNU's "gzip" and PKWARE's PKZIP file compressors. The patent status of this algorithm is uncertain at this time, but the GNU Project and others have researched it extensively, and it is believed to be free of patent restrictions. Source code is copyrighted (not GNU "copyleft") and freely available over the Internet.

The negotiated values are contained in two octets, as shown below. The first octet contains two 4-bit integers. The upper half (Wind) is the window value, which is expressed as a power of 2, and ranges from binary 0000 for a 256-byte window to 1111 for an 8MB window.[1] The lower half is the method number, which must be 1000 for "zlib" compression. Zlib supports a maximum window size of 32KB, or a Wind value of 0111.

1A	04	Wind	8	00

The second octet contains 6 reserved bits. The least significant 2 bits are the Check mode, which must be 00 to specify the Sequence Number mode (no other Check modes are defined). The values negotiated thus range from 08 00 to 78 00 for a window size of 256 to 32KB.

The encapsulation format and general operation are identical to the procedure used by BSD LZW Compress in RFC 1977. The encapsulation consists of a two-octet Sequence Number field, which is initialized to zero for the first packet. The compressed data contain the inner PPP Protocol field that must be compressed with PFC and followed by the original data. An implementation must also process uncompressed packets that would normally have been compressed by updating its decompression dictionary. As with BSD Compress, this means that this algorithm never expands data and does not suffer from the MRU-related problems that the other algorithms exhibit.

Either of the CCP Reset-Request/Reset-Ack or CCP renegotiation mechanisms may be used to reset the compressor on error. Reset of the decompressor is unnecessary, so reception of CCP Reset-Ack is ignored.

A draft version of this algorithm incorrectly used option number 18 hex, now assigned to Magnalink. Since Magnalink is extremely rare, most implementations requesting algorithm 18 are actually asking for Deflate by its old number. (If necessary, the two cases can be distinguished by the final octet of the option data, which must be 00 for Deflate and nonzero for Magnalink.)

---

1. Do not use a window size of 256. The standard implementations will crash if this size is selected.

Encryption Negotiation

ECP negotiation, described in RFC 1968, is done with protocol 8053, for both non-MP implementations and MP implementations using encryption above MP, and with protocol 8055, for MP implementations that encrypt at the link level. The data are passed with protocols 0053 and 0055, respectively. Several interoperable implementations are now available. There are also many proprietary, non-ECP link-level encryption schemes in use by major vendors.

As with CCP, an ECP implementation should support 0055 if requested by the peer even if MP is not in use or even supported.

The single-octet Type field indicates the algorithm, as selected from the following list.

```
00    Organization Unique Identifier (OUI)
01    Data Encryption Standard Encryption (DESE)
02    Triple DES Encryption (3DESE)
03    DES Encryption version 2 (DESE-bis)
```

Codes 04 through FE are unassigned, and FF is reserved. Code 00 allows a vendor to use any proprietary algorithm desired without needing a new ECP option number assigned by the IANA.

As in CCP, the data received from upper layers are generally prepended with their protocol number and encrypted. The receiver employs the reverse process and sends the result back through the PPP protocol number demultiplexing procedure.

Unlike all current CCP algorithms, the encryption algorithms have special requirements for the input data. This is because DES requires that the data to be encrypted must be a multiple of eight octets in length. Also unlike CCP, negotiation of all other NCPs is held off until ECP negotiation is done for security reasons. Once the negotiation is done, all data except LCP and ECP itself are passed through the encryption procedure, including all NCP negotiation packets.

None of the current algorithms provides a keying mechanism. Keys may be retrieved from a database indexed on authenticated user name, statically configured per link, or by other means by prior arrangement with the peer. For instance, the peers could agree to use the first 56 bits of an MD5 hash of the last CHAP Challenge concatenated with a secondary, independent shared secret.

ECP fits in as one part of the security puzzle. Unlike authentication, it protects against a "man in the middle" attack and against most forms of wiretapping, but it does so only on the PPP link itself. Real security depends on encryption at higher layers, such as with IPSEC (IP Security), and within applications themselves, such as with PGP (Pretty Good Privacy).

There are other considerations for implementors. Quite unfortunately, many governments consider this type of technology to be of "national security" interest and classify systems containing encryption as "munitions" for export purposes. Consult a competent export lawyer before implementing any ECP algorithms. Protecting your customer's right to privacy may well cost you a stint in prison. I can recommend only caution. Don't dabble with this unless you are certain of what you are doing.

Note also that Windows negotiates encryption as a proprietary extension of CCP rather than implementing ECP.

The encryption algorithms follow.

| ECP Option 00 | Organization Unique Identifier (OUI) | Very rare |

This option is identical to the OUI option described for CCP.

| ECP Option 01 | Data Encryption Standard Encryption (DESE) | Uncommon |

This algorithm is described in RFC 1969. It is based on the U.S. National Bureau of Standards "DES" algorithm (FIPS PUB 46) in Cipher Block Chaining (CBC) mode. (This option code number is obsolete, although the general method is not; see the DESE-bis option below.)

The value given in Configure-Request, shown below, is an eight-octet initial Value (referred to by the RFC as a *nonce*, although it is not) provided by the decryptor to the encryptor that is used to seed the encryption algorithm in the same way that each packet seeds the encryption of following packets for CBC mode. This is used to prevent "replay" and chosen-plaintext attacks, among others.

| 01 | 0A | | | Initial Value | | | |

The Initial Value is data provided from decryptor to encryptor and is not negotiated using Configure-Nak.

Since each decryption depends on only one prior packet, losing a single packet means that two packets will be lost by the receiver, but that the receiver will recover without other intervention. For this reason, Reset-Request and Reset-Ack are not used.

The data packet format contains a simple sequence number, starting at zero, prepended as two octets to the ciphertext. The RFC complicates matters by attempting to document the standard RFC 1661 headers and both ACFC and PFC options as well.

The RFC generally recommends padding the input data from the NCPs with random data, where feasible, based on the upper-level protocol, such as with IP, and using Self-Describing-Padding (SDP) where this is not possible, such as with Bridging packets.

A shared secret (a key) must be held by both ends of the communication. Distribution and storage of this key are not covered by the RFC and are left to the implementor. Since the key itself must be configured into each peer that communicates using DESE, it is assumed that the method of key determination or exchange is also configured into the peers.

Distribution of keys is usually the most complex and vulnerable part of any encryption system. If it is not done often enough, key material that "leaks" into the data stream can allow an eavesdropper to decode the data. If it is done too often, the key distribution system itself can be more easily attacked.

ECP Option 02	Triple-DES (3DESE)	Rare

The Triple-DES algorithm is described in RFC 2420. The value given in the Configure-Request is an eight-octet initial value as with DESE, and the packet format is also the same. The padding requirements are identical to those of DESE-bis (see below).

This encryption is performed by running DES three times on each block of eight octets. In the first round, the data are encrypted with the first key. In the second round, they are decrypted using the second key. In the last round, they are encrypted again using the third key.

This operation increases the weak 56-bit DES key to a more robust, although not quite impenetrable, 168 bits.

ECP Option 03   DES Encryption Protocol, Version 2 (DESE-bis)   Very rare

The second version of DES encryption is described in RFC 2419. This is the replacement for RFC 1969. It is not intended to be compatible with the prior version and thus has been allocated a new option code number. In fact, an implementation supporting DESE-bis is required by the RFC to reject the older version if encountered.

The algorithm and packet format for DESE-bis is the same as for the original DESE option. The main difference between this RFC and RFC 1969 is that this version of the algorithm clearly describes how and when to pad the plaintext input using an SDP-like algorithm, but without specific negotiation of SDP at LCP time. The earlier mistake had caused some confusion among implementors.

The RFC describes the compression of the inner protocol number only in passing in Section 7. The inner protocol number compression is dependent on the LCP PFC negotiation. If PFC is negotiated at LCP time, the inner protocol number is compressed as well as the outer protocol number. If it is not, then neither is compressed.

Bandwidth Management and Call Control

IN THIS CHAPTER

Bandwidth management is an active area of both research and marketing. This situation is a result of pricing policies of telephone companies and governments, which generally mandate per-time-unit or per-information-unit charges rather than flat connectivity fees and place controls on technology and pricing. Variable charges drive users to search for means of limiting measured usage to the minimum amount necessary, and technological limits prompt work-arounds.

Bandwidth management techniques in PPP are fairly new and somewhat unsettled. This area is likely to change dramatically in the face of newer technologies such as wireless digital telephony and higher-speed dedicated lines to residences.

There are many bandwidth management techniques in use with PPP today. Examples follow.

- **Demand-Dialing.** Many PPP implementations can automatically establish a link when network traffic is present and tear it down when idle. This is known as *dial-on-demand* or *dynamic dialing*. These techniques often require sophisticated traffic filtering and protocol spoofing.
- **Aggregation of Multiple Links.** Frequently, acquiring several low-speed links, such as modems, costs less than the equivalent high-speed link, such as a dedicated line. Aggregation, which also goes by various other names (e.g., *multi-link, load balancing, bonding,* and *inverse multiplexing,* depending on

the underlying technology), allows an administrator to configure multiple low-speed links to behave as though they were a single higher-speed link. Aggregation is also used to combine channels on individual lines that inherently carry multiple independent data channels, such as Basic-Rate ISDN (BRI).

- **Active Bandwidth Management.** Several protocols have been invented to handle more gracefully the ebbs and flows of network traffic when used with dial-on-demand links. It is claimed that, by dropping individual links as soon as they become idle and avoiding dropping links that will soon be active, these techniques reduce expenses.
- **Cost Shifting.** In some economies, large companies have less expensive access to the public networks than do individuals. In others, reverse-toll lines (known in the United States as 800 numbers and in the United Kingdom as 0800 numbers) are more expensive than directly placed calls. In either case, it can be advantageous to have a designated party to the call pay for it, regardless of who initiates the contact.
- **Multiplexed Use of a Single Link.** Sometimes a higher-speed link, such as a Frame Relay connection, may be less expensive than a large number of individual slower links. Many variations of tunneling are used to support this technique, including ATM Virtual Circuits, MPLS, and L2TP.

These techniques are not mutually exclusive. In fact, each may complement the others in unexpected ways. For instance, MPLS LSPs may be used to carve out reserved bandwidth from an interface that is actually a load-balanced group of links.

Demand-Dialing

Demand-dialing is generally a proprietary technology, although the principle is simple. Filters that designate certain traffic as worthy of initiating a link and other traffic as important enough to keep the link up are normally required. For instance, with IP it is generally not desired that the link be brought up or kept up to send RIP updates. It may also be desired to keep the link up while SMTP (e-mail) is transferred but not to bring the link up if only SMTP traffic is detected. All other traffic, such as HTTP, will likely be configured to bring the link up and keep it up while present.

In some protocols, such as IPX and Windows Domain Browsing, extensive work is required to make demand-dialing function properly, because both of these systems are designed for LAN use and send frequent messages (called *keepalive* or *hello* messages) to detect what is available on the network and to detect failed connections. These messages must be spoofed and filtered from the demand-dialing system or the link will never go idle.

Even on TCP/IP networks, spoofing or other changes are likely to be required. For instance, RIP sends broadcasts on every link at characteristic 30-second intervals and OSPF sends multicasts at 10- to 30-second intervals. TCP connections may send keepalive messages at 2-hour intervals. Good demand-dialing implementations include mechanisms for handling these cases plus extensive troubleshooting support for installation-specific problems.

Spoofing

Spoofing is the deliberate falsifying of responses to protocol and application time-outs. It is done when these time-outs, which often are not under the user's control and are done even though no data need to be transferred, would cause either an unconnected dial-on-demand link to initiate dialing or, if the link were not to be reestablished, the application to fail.

As of this writing, only a single proposal has been made to negotiate use of spoofing with PPP links. This proposal, called the PPP Protocol Spoofing Control Protocol (PSCP), was presented as an Internet Draft (`draft-ietf-pppext-spoof-00.txt`) in February 1996.

This proposal, which has since expired and has not been advanced, provided a means of negotiating which protocols should be spoofed when the link was down, a means of identifying the "same" link being brought back up, and a means of setting various timers. Unfortunately, the proposal contained extraneous matter, such as callback numbers, and was fairly ISDN specific.

Spoofing and filtering for demand-dialed links are generally handled using proprietary configuration parameters rather than any standard protocol. The main reason for this is that any spoofing must function properly when there is no connection between the peers.

Aggregation of Multiple Links

This particular wheel has been invented many times, with varying results. Some of these inventions are as follows.

- **Inverse Multiplexing.** Multiplexing allows multiple streams to flow over a single link. Inverse multiplexing, therefore, is any technique for spreading a single stream of data over multiple links, as shown in Figure 7.1. This is a rather generic term that is often applied to physical layer solutions. These solutions generally consist of some component, external to PPP, that uses proprietary means to spread traffic across multiple links. An example of this would be a short haul modem that is able to use multiple channels or frequencies to transmit but has a single serial port and uses ISO LAP-B Multi-link to make those channels appear as one link to the user. Inverse multiplexing is also the term used for multilink ATM. Since these techniques are invisible to PPP, except perhaps for the latency variances that occur when an individual link is added or dropped, they will not be discussed further here.

- **BONDING.** This is a particular hardware-based inverse-multiplexing scheme invented, in general terms, for use with consumer-grade ISDN lines, as shown in Figure 7.2, and is actually an acronym for "Bandwidth On Demand." BONDING is done at the bit level and requires tightly controlled timing relationships between the two B channels being bonded. These restrictions, which must also be supported by each of the telephone company switches in the path between caller and callee using special call set-up commands (encoded in the ISDN Bearer Capability), make this a niche solution. In general, BONDING is far more expensive, less often available, and less capable than the other PPP-based solutions. It has, however, the marginal benefit of the lowest possible latency, although the latencies of the other techniques can be within 16 bit-times of BONDING. It has the drawback of being unable to change bandwidth on the fly; it requires the connection to be torn down for any change.

- **Load Balancing.** This technique is not specific to PPP and can be used by any point-to-point technology, such as SLIP or ATM VCs. The general

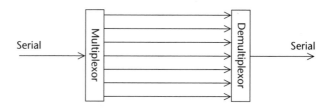

FIGURE 7.1 Inverse multiplexing

FIGURE 7.2 BONDING

technique, as it concerns PPP, is to run separate copies of PPP on each of the individual links but to insert a layer between these PPP implementations and the network layers, as shown in Figure 7.3. This inserted layer then parcels out outgoing packets bound for a single "virtual" network link (which represents the load-balancing group) among the individual links.

- **Multilink.** This is the name given to the RFC 1990 protocol used in PPP to spread traffic over multiple links by sending part of each packet over each link, as shown in Figure 7.4. It does not suffer from packet reordering, as can load balancing, nor does it require special telephone company or ISDN support, as does BONDING, and it runs over existing equipment, unlike inverse multiplexing. It can also change bandwidth by adding or dropping links dynamically without interrupting the connection. It has drawbacks, such as multiplying the error rates for those interfaces that drop packets with a given probability rather than corrupt individual octets, and having indeterminate latency on some types of media, but these drawbacks are usually outweighed by the benefits. It requires specific support in both peers' implementations of PPP. It is not possible to run MP if one of the two peers does not support the protocol.

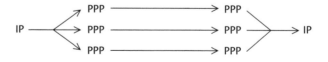

FIGURE 7.3 Load balancing

FIGURE 7.4 Multilink PPP

Load Balancing

Load balancing is usually most appropriate with very-high-speed links and with large numbers of independent flows. In order to make effective use of the available links, the traffic should be distributed among the links as evenly as possible. Because prediction or control of packet order between the links is rarely possible, packets should not be assigned to links using a simple algorithm such as round-robin or random selection. The resulting reordering of packets within an individual stream is undesirable because it will break some network layer assumptions and, with IP in particular, lower performance by triggering TCP fast retransmit. To prevent reordering within streams, identifying marks for the streams should be used to select the outbound link for each packet. Balancing the links thus relies on statistics; large numbers of flows are needed, and link selection must be as uniform as possible.

One effective technique for IP is to calculate a CRC over the IP source and destination addresses and, at lower data rates, the TCP or UDP port numbers as well. A few bits selected from the CRC are then used to select the output link. Because this technique places all of the packets for a particular TCP stream on a single link, connections that have small numbers of TCP flows, such as single-user PCs or even small corporations, will not necessarily see the expected benefit. Any of the other techniques described here—inverse multiplexing, BONDING, or MP—would be a better choice in these cases.

The CRC hashing technique can be used with encapsulated flows as well by looking past one or more levels of encapsulation and extracting flow-identifying information there. This technique is useful with IP over MPLS and IP-IP tunneling.

One benefit of load balancing is simplified fail-over. If a link fails, the system need only redirect the affected traffic over any remaining link. Only a small amount of traffic is affected—ideally just the packets in flight at the time of failure but actually 1/N (N is the number of links) of all packets from the moment of failure to the eventual redirection of traffic among the remaining links. All of the other techniques described in this chapter affect a greater proportion of the traffic during failure recovery.

Some routing protocols, such as OSPF and IS-IS, can determine equal-cost paths to network destinations. Use of these paths generally requires an implementation of a type of load balancing, at least for the network-layer-forwarding path, although there are subtle differences of interest to routing protocol engineers. These routing-protocol-determined paths can work in place of or in addition to link-level load balancing.

Multilink PPP (MP)

This protocol is described in RFC 1990. MP, sometimes incorrectly called "MLP," "MPPP," or "MLPPP," specifies a way to break each packet into multiple fragments, transmit each fragment on a different link, and then reassemble the fragments into whole packets at the receiving end. This makes a group of links appear as though it were a single, higher-speed link.

If the links are given the same constraints as necessary for BONDING, MP's header adds as little as two octets to the data to be transferred. Latency over MP can thus be nearly equivalent to the best achievable.

The RFC specifies a means of negotiating MP mode, detecting the establishment of new links (termed *bundling*), detecting fragment loss, and fragmenting and reassembling messages. It does not specify when (or even if) additional links should be established, when to drop links, or how to acquire necessary telephone numbers or other access information. These other tasks can be handled by configuration parameters, rules of thumb, or special protocols, as described later. The MP system architecture is shown in Figure 7.5.

When MP is used with CCP or ECP, there are three possible configurations. The most common is with both CCP and ECP at the bundle level (Figure 7.6). The data flow for transmission in this case is shown in Figure 7.7.

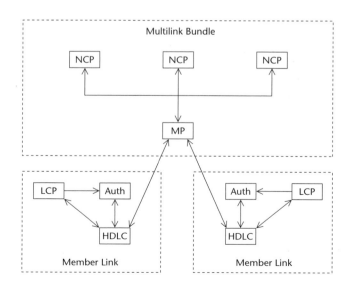

FIGURE 7.5 MP system architecture

Less commonly, ECP is moved to the member links, as shown in Figure 7.8. This is usually done because of the use of a dedicated link-level hardware encryption device, since encrypting at the bundle level would require that the hardware be separate from the link-level drivers. The corresponding data flow is shown in Figure 7.9.

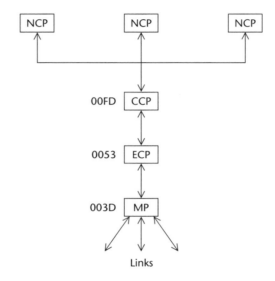

FIGURE 7.6 MP with CCP and ECP

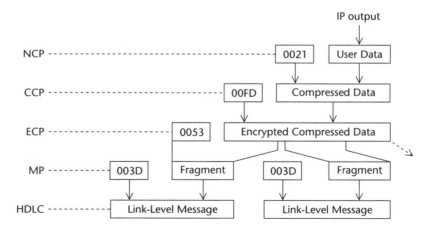

FIGURE 7.7 MP with CCP and ECP data flow

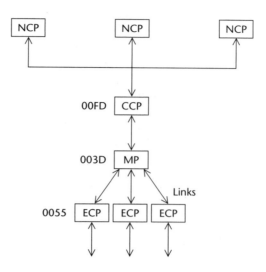

FIGURE 7.8 ECP in member links architecture

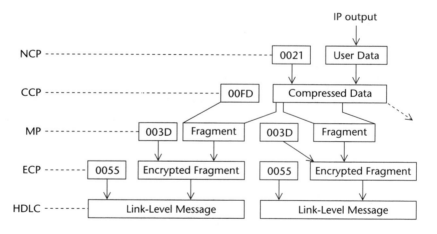

FIGURE 7.9 Data flow with ECP in member links

Least commonly, both CCP and ECP are done in the member links as in Figure 7.10. The corresponding data flow is shown in Figure 7.11.

When CCP and ECP are used with MP, the compress-then-encrypt semantics must be retained, but it is possible to negotiate separate compression and encryption at the bundle level and at each link level. This can lead to an explicitly illegal

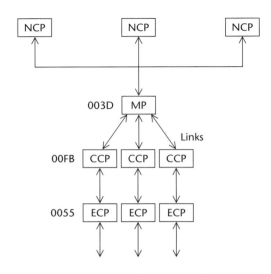

FIGURE 7.10 Link-level CCP and ECP architecture

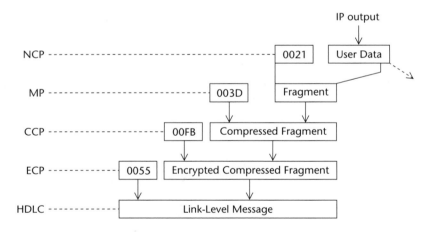

FIGURE 7.11 Link-level CCP and ECP data flow

(by RFC 1968) state in which encryption is negotiated at the bundle level and compression at the link level. This must be avoided. For security reasons, ECP is generally negotiated before any other NCP, including CCP. An implementation using both protocols that allows link-level compression must disable subsequent negotiation of per-link CCP if bundle-level ECP is negotiated. A good implementation should also disable the link-level alternatives of both of these protocols if the corresponding bundle-level protocol is accepted by the peer.

To minimize memory usage and the number of security relationships, preserve security in distributed MP systems, and maximize the compression ratio, I recommend implementing both CCP and ECP at the bundle level with MP. Implementations at the individual link level might be desirable in systems with special link-level compression or encryption hardware, but this is the exception rather than the rule and often is not as widely interoperable.

As a PPP protocol, MP is an oddball. The parameters for it are negotiated using LCP options, not NCP options, and the data are passed using a network-layer protocol (003D) without a corresponding NCP negotiation after authentication is complete. The reason is that when MP is negotiated, the link becomes part of the bundle where there is only one set of NCPs. If MP were an NCP by itself, it would be negotiated alongside the other NCPs, and joining an existing bundle would be much more difficult since it would involve merging or terminating duplicate NCPs.

Normally, all data received by the member links except authentication (such as CHAP Challenges), LQM, and LCP negotiation messages are forwarded to the bundle level. The messages not forwarded to the bundle must be processed at the member-link level. Special code is required to segregate the LCP messages that a member link handles—usually codes 01–07 and 09–0B—and those that are forwarded to the bundle for processing. In particular, Protocol-Reject (LCP code 08) must be forwarded to the bundle. If CCP or ECP is done at the member-link level, protocol numbers 0055, 00FB, 8055, and 80FB must be handled at the member-link level, while others are forwarded to the bundle level.

MP may also be used on a single link to increase the effective MRU for the network-layer protocols when the LCP MRU is too small for the intended application and when the LCP MRU cannot be changed due to hardware or serial driver restrictions. Usually the MRRU, a software construct, has no such restrictions and can be made as large as desired. In this case, MP functions as a link-layer fragmentation mechanism.

The parameters negotiated with LCP for MP are as follows.

LCP Option 11	Maximum Receive Reconstructed Unit (MRRU)	Common

The MRRU sent in an LCP Configure-Request, shown below, is the number of octets an implementation can concatenate together for a given reconstructed frame. It is analogous to the MRU at the link level.

In a non-MP system, the MRU is the maximum PPP Information field size at the link level and is used as the MTU advertised to network-layer interfaces, such as IP, on the peer's side. In an MP system, the MRRU sent by the peer's Configure-Request is used as the MTU for the network-level interfaces, and the peer's MRU is used as the maximum message size within MP fragmentation. If the MRRU given by the peer is less than or equal to its MRU+6, it is not necessary to support fragmentation (although reassembly will still be required).

Unlike MRU, this parameter must be actively negotiated in order to enable MP, even if the desired value is the default (1500 octets). The presence of this option in a Configure-Request signals the desire of that peer to initiate MP mode. If the link is joining an existing bundle, the MRRU offered must be same as the MRRU initially negotiated for the bundle. It must also be either negotiated in both directions or not at all, since MP cannot be run unidirectionally on a link.

The developer implementing MP should also refer to the obsolete RFC 1717 for MP, since this RFC recommended slightly different rules for initiating MP. (In particular, it specified that the presence of the following Short Sequence Number option was enough to enable MP.) These differences may affect compatibility in some cases.

LCP Option 12   Short Sequence Number Header Format   Common

This Boolean option, shown below, allows a 12-bit sequence number instead of the default 24-bit sequence number to be used for efficiency on low-speed links. If this option is used on any link in a bundle, it must be used on all links.

The default long-sequence-number MP header is four octets long. The first octet contains just two single-bit flags defined as follows:

    40   End-of-fragment (E bit)
    80   Beginning-of-fragment (B bit)

The remaining three octets are the sequence number of the fragment in network byte order. The MP header with Short Sequence Number mode enabled is two

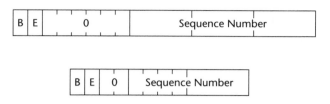

FIGURE 7.12 MP sequence number headers

octets long. The first octet reserves the most significant 4 bits for flags, of which two are defined as above. The remaining 4 bits plus the second octet form the sequence number in network byte order. These two formats are shown in Figure 7.12.

As long as the peak rate of transmitting fragments (in fragments per second) is less than 4096 divided by the maximum time delay skew between the links, short sequence numbers are viable. If the skew becomes too large for the transmit rate, the sequence numbers become ambiguous and reassembly fails.

LCP Option 13   Endpoint-Discriminator (ED)   Common

This option acts as a unique system identifier to disambiguate links from two separate peers with the same authenticated name. The negotiated value is intended to be simply accepted by the peer and is not intended to be included in a Configure-Nak. This value consists of a single octet encoding the discriminator class followed by a variable-length Address field, as shown below.

| 13 | Len | Class | Address |

The Class options are

```
00 Null class (equivalent to not specifying ED)
01 Locally assigned address (any value up to 20 octets)
02 IP address (four octets of address)
03 Ethernet MAC address (six octets of address)
04 Magic number block (four to 20 octets)
05 Public switched network directory number (up to 15
   octets; E.164 address)
```

I recommend using these values only as suggested methods of displaying the negotiated parameters for diagnostic purposes. The Class and Address values have no defined usage in the protocol other than as a "magic cookie" used to identify links that should be bundled together. A reasonable implementation may, therefore, treat the value (both the Class and the Address) it receives from its peer for this option as an opaque object that is simply compared for strict byte-for-byte equality with other ED objects. Good implementations should not attempt to validate or restrict the peer's choice of Class or Address values.

Some implementations, however, use the enclosed values for special purposes. For instance, the directory number (telephone number) class can be useful for supplying a new telephone number for the peer to use for subsequent links. This is done when a main access telephone number is configured on one side and this number maps into a telephone-company-controlled rotary spanning many separate units on the other side. Since the links normally cannot terminate on separate units, a direct telephone number that bypasses the rotary for the unit reached on the first call is supplied through the ED, and then subsequent calls are placed through this number. Such usage, though, is generally obsolescent given the release of multichassis MP by many manufacturers (see Layer-Two Tunneling and MP on page 222 and L2TP in Chapter 8).

Another view of this option is that it forms an unauthenticated extension of the peer name, which is normally established during authentication. In fact, a reasonable implementation could concatenate the ED and the peer name together in some form when forwarding the data to an authentication server, and base its authentication decisions on the complete value.

Detecting New Links in a Bundle

Detecting that a newly negotiated link is actually a new link in an existing bundle is accomplished by scanning an internal list of established bundles. This scan terminates when the same combination of peer name and peer-supplied Endpoint Discriminator is found, or when no matching bundle can be found. When comparing peer name and discriminator, it is possible for some bundles to have either no peer name (security was not enabled), no discriminator (none was supplied by the peer during LCP negotiation), or neither of these. These cases will still match an identical link being established if it lacks the same information. Thus, if neither a peer name nor an Endpoint Discriminator is supplied by the peer, all such links are simply bundled together. In this way, the peer name and

Endpoint Discriminator can be thought of as being logically concatenated for purposes of comparison. Note, however, that if the special Null Class (00) discriminator is seen, it must be treated as though the discriminator were omitted from the LCP options.

The default bundling algorithm described above uses the authenticated peer name only. The Name field included in the CHAP Challenge message must not be used in the bundling decision. If the only peer name known is from CHAP Challenge, this should be treated as if no name at all were known.

Once the bundle has been identified, the MRRUs, MRUs, and Short Sequence Number options must be checked. These must be identical to the other links already in the bundle. If they are not, LCP should be renegotiated with the newly discovered correct values for these options.

Many implementations have timing problems with the bundle identification algorithm. Note that it is necessary to do the scan and either to establish a new bundle (if none matches) or to join an existing bundle (if a match is found), all without permitting other processes to do the same scan concurrently. Otherwise, it is possible for two links from the same peer brought up at the same time to establish separate bundles mistakenly. This timing situation is very common with ISDN, since many TAs immediately dial both B channels when a link is requested. Also, it is highly desirable to be prepared to handle MP encapsulated data as soon as security is complete, whether or not the link is joining an existing bundle, since NCP negotiation is done over the bundle.

It is possible to defer the encapsulation of data transmitted in MP headers until more than one link is in use. If this is desired, MP headers must be enabled as soon as the second link is detected and joins the bundle. The first MP packet sent should also be sent over the previously existing link rather than the newly established link in order to avoid out-of-order packet delivery.

The Default Bundle

If neither an authenticated peer name nor an Endpoint Discriminator is received from the peer but MRRU is negotiated, then RFC 1990 indicates that all such links should be joined together into a default bundle.

This operation makes some implementors nervous. On some systems, such as a small router with an Ethernet port and two PPP links over ISDN dialing into an access server that does not identify itself, it may be quite reasonable, whereas on others, such as the access server itself, it may not be useful. There are several legal ways out of this problem, as follows.

- Refuse connections from unauthenticated peers. Since many of the concerns about the default bundle are related to security, this solution solves both problems at once. Authenticated peer name alone is almost always enough to distinguish MP bundles correctly.
- Send LCP Configure-Reject for the MRRU option if the peer doesn't include an Endpoint-Discriminator option or if it sends LCP Configure-Reject for the Authentication-Protocol option. (Note that you may need to formulate a new LCP Configure-Request if the peer Configure-Rejects the Authentication-Protocol option after it Configure-Acks your request.)
- Use prior configuration to select any useful external source of information, such as ANI, to distinguish the bundles.

By prior arrangement, any method at all may be used to identify new links for a bundle. For instance, a configured list of physical port numbers could be used. Any such usage is legal but outside the scope of RFC 1990.

Another Way to Handle New Links

This method, posted to the pppext mailing list in January 1998 by Vernon Schryver, is compatible with most RFC 1990 implementations but is much more elegant than the standard search-after-authentication algorithm. It rests on the recognition that for MP-speaking devices, there typically is at most one bundle connected to any single peer device. This means that the Endpoint-Discriminator received in an LCP Configure-Request can be used without authentication to perform the bundle look-up operation during LCP negotiation. With the proper bundle in hand, it is always possible to identify the correct MRRU, MRU, and Short-Sequence-Number values to use and the correct settings for the other MP options, and with the preliminary identification, other options (such as PFC) can be preset to expected values, shortening negotiation time.

After this preliminary assignment of the link to the bundle with NCP packet reception disabled, the Authenticate phase is entered for the link. At this point, the possibilities are more restricted than for RFC 1990 MP. The peer must identify itself as the same peer as it did for the other links, or the link should be terminated.

This method precludes having multiple simultaneous bundles that have the same peer Endpoint-Discriminator but different authentication data, which is an unusual case supported by RFC 1990. In practice, this is not an important distinction, since functioning MP implementations must offer different ED values when executed on different nodes anyway (unless layer-two techniques are used to make multiple nodes appear to be a single unit for MP purposes).

Fragmentation and Reassembly

The RFC does not specify an exact method for fragmenting the message for transmission. It specifies the header formats and the correct way to handle these headers, but it does not specify exactly how large to make each message or how to distribute the message among the member links, although it does include some suggestions. This imprecision is intentional. The authors wish to allow implementors to decide what fragmentation policies are acceptable to them and to allow for future innovation.

As fragments are received over the member links, they are placed in a reassembly queue, sorted by sequence number. As the messages are reconstructed, they are removed from this queue in sequence number order. Thus, as long as the fragments are numbered correctly by the sender, the messages will be delivered in the same order as they were sent, even if some links experience delays. This property is very important, since out-of-order delivery will break CCP and ECP at the bundle level, as well as many network protocols.

For readers interested in IP, the description of MP above should sound familiar. IP fragmentation performs a similar function in a similar manner: both adapt a large MTU to a smaller MTU, and neither relies on retransmission or acknowledgment. They are different in the following ways.

- Nonfinal IP fragments must be multiples of eight octets, but MP fragments packets on any octet boundary.
- Each IP fragment carries an offset that gives its position in the reassembled datagram and implies the size of the missing portion. MP has only a serial number that gives the order of reassembly; it says nothing about the size of the missing portion.
- IP fragmentation and reassembly use only an arbitrary ID number to identify portions of an IP packet, and thus usually cause fragmented packets to be delivered out of order; MP does not reorder packets.
- IP fragmentation uses timers to discard stale fragments in place of MP's increasing-sequence-number rule. (An MP implementation may use timers for robustness if desired, but this is not required.)

- IP fragments may be reordered during transit by an intermediate router, or even refragmented. MP fragments are not routed and may not be reordered on any link.
- Depending on network conditions, received IP fragments may have overlapping data portions, and the receiver must remove the duplicate segments. Since no complex network exists between the MP peers, this problem cannot happen with MP.
- IP fragmentation is end-to-end, so a lost or delayed fragment does not affect delivery of other packets in the intermediate routers or in other applications on the same host. MP fragmentation is on a single virtual link only and can cause delays for all traffic over that link when a single fragment is lost or delayed.

Implementation Issues

A large number of issues must be addressed during implementation of MP. Examples are as follows.

- **The First Link.** There is nothing special about the first link in a bundle. Some MP implementations erroneously terminate operation of the bundle if the first link is shut down. The bundle should exist as long as there is at least one link in it, and in a good implementation it should be possible for any of the links to come and go at any time.
- **Idle Links.** Idle links hamper the effectiveness of the fragment loss detection logic and increase the buffer space required by the peer, because the algorithm specifies that sequence numbers newer than the oldest sequence number last seen on all links must be kept. If one link is not receiving new fragments, its last sequence number will not change, and no more lost fragments will be detected and dropped. Any lost fragments at that point will cause all subsequent fragments to be buffered indefinitely and cause in-order reassembly to stop. Thus, a good implementation should attempt to avoid ever allowing a member link to go idle for an extended period. Fragments should be fairly distributed among the member links, and occasional null fragments, which have both the B and E bits set but contain no data bytes, should be sent when no new data packets are available in order to update the peer's minimum sequence number for the link. If a link from a peer is idle for a long (configurable) period of time and is causing reassembly difficulty, that link should be terminated.

- **Arbitrary Discard.** It is possible for a misbehaving peer to send large amounts of data that cannot be reassembled and simply consume ever larger amounts of storage in the reassembly queue. To avoid this situation, an implementation can employ several mechanisms that discard fragments. One method is to place a limit on the amount of storage used, based on either an estimate of the round-trip time or the bundle's fair share of available memory. Another method is to use timers to discard fragments that remain unassembled for a long period.

- **Link Loss.** In the event of catastrophic loss of a link, there still may be fragments enqueued for transmission on that link. These fragments cannot in general be requeued on another link because of the increasing-sequence-number rule. Thus, it is important to make use of the LCP Terminate-Request and Terminate-Ack messages to remove a link from a bundle gracefully. In this case, LCP Terminate-Request is sent on a link that is no longer needed. Received data from that link are still processed, but no new fragments are sent over it. When LCP Terminate-Ack is received, the link is finally dropped from the bundle. This procedure violates RFC 1661's rules on the use of LCP Terminate-Request, because this message is to be sent only when leaving Opened state and packet reception must then be disabled, but this modification is quite common to MP implementations, eliminates unnecessary data loss, and is generally regarded as safe by most members of the IETF PPP working group. If the link loss leaves just one link in the bundle, it is safe to turn off MP encapsulation (if desired for efficiency reasons) when the LCP Terminate-Ack is received or when one-half of the current round-trip time has elapsed.

- **Out-of-Order Delivery.** MP is permitted to deliver some network-layer data out of normal order, either by removing it from the reassembly queue early or by transmitting it without the normal MP header. Implementors who do this for some defined purpose, such as meeting performance constraints, must also consider the effects on layers above MP. In particular, out-of-order delivery breaks most CCP and ECP implementations, breaks Van Jacobson compression in TCP/IP (although IP by itself tolerates reordering), and breaks several entire network protocols, such as SNA. The example MP code given on the accompanying CD-ROM avoids out-of-order delivery by doing fragment enqueuing, reassembly, and frame loss detection in a single pass.

    Although reordering plain TCP itself is generally permissible, reordering can cause very poor performance by disabling common header-prediction-based optimizations and by triggering TCP's fast-retransmit mechanism.

- **Synchronization.** Many systems support multiple concurrent tasks, and some support multiple processors. These systems pose special problems for MP implementations. For instance, when a message is being fragmented for transmission, it is necessary to assign sequence numbers to the fragments and transmit these fragments on the links without violating the increasing-sequence-number rule on any link. Since the process of enqueuing a message for transmission on a link may involve a task switch, it is possible for another network-layer entity to attempt to transmit while the first sender is in a suspended state and has not completed fragment queuing. If this happens, it results in misordered fragments and the loss of both messages. The implementor either must guarantee that no task switch occurs from the time the sequence numbers are assigned to the fragments until they are safely enqueued on each link or must provide a means of detecting this occurrence when the second entity attempts to transmit and must place the second entity's data on a queue for later MP transmission rather than transmitting it immediately.

- **Native Encapsulation.** Some messages, such as LCP Protocol-Reject, are often sent using native encapsulation (with no MP header) on the link. Others, such as the NCPs, may optionally be sent this way, although they usually are not. Since the NCPs are generally constructed logically "above" the MP layer, except for the per-link ECP and CCP options, this means that the implementation must have a means of forwarding these non-MP messages (such as LCP Protocol-Reject) from any link layer to the bundle and acting on them without the normal MP headers as though they were received as normal MP-encapsulated messages. This generally implies that a flag or switch accompanies the message that was passed up to indicate whether or not the source PPP protocol number was MP, so that the headers may be stripped when necessary.

- **Mismatched MRRU.** The RFC states that a system that is joining a link to an existing bundle must use the same MRRU used for the initial link. Since this negotiation is done at LCP time, before the peer is properly identified, this can pose a problem. What is to be done when a link is identified as part of a bundle after going through authentication but either this system or the peer has offered an MRRU different from that of the previous links to that bundle? This can occur if different MRRUs are accidentally configured or if the layer-two techniques of Chapter 8 are used with multiple systems having different configurations. One possibility is to renegotiate LCP but use the newly discovered "correct" MRRU values as the defaults. When the peer supplies an ED value, this problem can be avoided entirely; see Another Way to Handle New Links on page 216.

- **Rules of Thumb.** Establishing and tearing down calls can be done on demand in a reliable manner without resort to additional protocols. There are three common rules of thumb for doing this. First, either peer may establish a call, but only the peer that established a call may tear it down. This prevents thrashing, since the system that determines that a need for a new link exists also determines when that need has passed. This rule is modified slightly when MP is used with callback; the initiator of the callback request, not the party doing the callback, is the one that controls teardown for the subsequent call. Whenever possible, the party ultimately responsible for paying for the call should be the initiator. Second, if a link is torn down by the peer that was not the initiator of the call, this is an error condition, and another link should not be established until a "damping" time-out occurs. If possible, an operator should also be notified, since this may represent some kind of system failure. Third, a new link should be established when traffic is heavy in either direction (transmit or receive) for a given period of time.

  It may come as a surprise, but it is true that both peers have precisely the same information on the traffic intensity available for this calculation. Measuring transmit traffic is rather easy, since examining queue depths on the member links gives this information readily. Measuring receive traffic turns out to be also rather easy. To do this, the utilization of the link must be tracked by the receiver. Since, by traditional queuing theory, a utilization that approaches the known bandwidth of the link indicates that the peer's transmit queues are growing without bound, this provides a gauge for establishing a new link.

Establishing a new link for a bundle is very much like establishing the first link. In both cases, if the low-level link fails to establish for any reason, then it is necessary to back off and retry at some later point. It is also necessary to limit the number of consecutive failed attempts, since a configuration error, such as a miskeyed telephone number, could cause pathological behavior.

The rules of thumb serve well in the vast majority of cases. One possible problem with them is that, depending on the usage of reverse-toll lines or callback, it is possible that the initiator of a call could be the peer that is not paying for it. If this peer is malicious, or simply unintelligent, it could cause the payer to pay for unnecessary links. Since the payer did not establish the call, he or she cannot terminate it without risking thrashing and is on the hook for charges he or she cannot control.

Another problem is that if MP is used with callback, each new link should be established by the peer that called back. These links sometimes cannot be established automatically, since even when callback is used, the system doing the callback usually does not ultimately pay for the call, since the charges are simply tallied and billed to the original caller. This means that establishing additional links requires a separate call and callback pair and, probably, additional charges.

The problem of the malicious or stupid peer can be solved administratively: if your ISP forces you to pay too much for connectivity, then find another one. Using a bandwidth management protocol could possibly solve the problem, but it is often better simply not to do business with such an outfit. Good implementations measure link utilization and report abnormal conditions, such as continued high usage with no new links and low usage with too many links. If, on the other hand, you own both ends of the link, it is up to you to find implementations that dial only when necessary and to configure them properly.

The second problem involving callback is not very common but is a good candidate for a simple separate protocol that allows the original initiator of a callback to request an additional link. (Since this side is also the initiator for link termination purposes, it is not necessary to have a special protocol to determine when to tear down the link; the rules of thumb work correctly.) Unfortunately, the proposed bandwidth management protocols are far, far more complex than this trivial problem and attempt to solve problems that do not exist here, as we will see in the Active Bandwidth Management section starting on page 226.

Layer-Two Tunneling and MP

Early in the development of MP, a fundamental problem was discovered with MP implementation. For reliability and scalability, large installations need to have many physically separate systems to handle PPP calls and need to use services that automatically distribute incoming calls among those systems. However, standard MP will not work in this environment, since each individual link must terminate on the same system in order for fragment reassembly to function.

To fix this problem, developers have taken two routes. One group has proposed mechanisms for steering the additional links to the right individual system. This is the idea behind BACP. The other group has proposed means of discovering that a new link has landed on the wrong system and of forwarding the data over local high-speed networks to the right system using layer-two tunneling.

There are several advantages of layer-two techniques. First, the dial-in users do not need to implement any new protocols other than MP, so it is compatible with existing equipment. Second, complete utilization of equipment without arbitrary denial of service is possible. If you use BACP and your first link unfortunately lands on a system that is already busy, you might not be able to start a second link, even though all the other systems may be idle. With layer-two tunneling, your second connection can land on any system, and the data will be forwarded to the right place.

The next chapter deals with tunneling PPP in more detail. The next three subsections describe three MP-specific mechanisms that are in common use with these tunneling protocols.

Nortel's Multi-link Multi-node Bundle Discovery

This protocol, documented in Informational RFC 2701, provides a simple mechanism for a PPP system to discover another system on a local network that has an existing MP bundle with the same authentication and endpoint identifier as a newly negotiated link. If an existing MP bundle is located, the new link is tunneled to that bundle using RFC 2661 L2TP. Otherwise, a new bundle is established.

This protocol uses IP multicast to an IANA-allocated address (224.0.1.69) and with an allocated well-known port (581).

I recommend the use of this protocol for large, multichassis dial-up systems.

Ascend's Multi Chassis MP

Ascend's solution, also called "Stacks," is based on a simple protocol that performs both discovery and tunneling. To find a possible bundle head when a new link comes up, the Ascend MAX sends out seven request messages within 1 second. If no response is seen, then this link must represent a new bundle. Otherwise, it is joined to the existing bundle indicated in the response.

The messages are sent, by default, to UDP port 5151 with UDP checksumming disabled. The Query messages are sent as Ethernet multicast messages to 01:C0:7B:00:00:01. The first three octets of that Ethernet address are assigned to Ascend. At the IP level, the messages are sent to the local broadcast address (255.255.255.255), perhaps because Ascend has not registered an IP multicast address with the IANA.

The data inside the UDP message have the formats shown in Figure 7.13. In this diagram, the initial 01 octet appears to be a revision number. The other fields are described below.

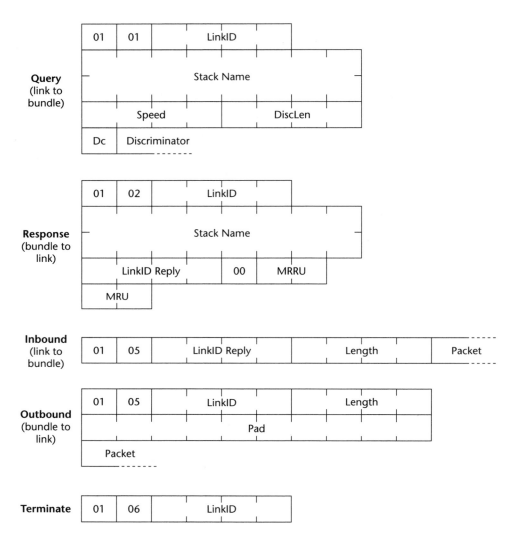

FIGURE 7.13 Ascend Stacks messages

LinkID is a four-octet integer assigned sequentially by the system that received the new link. (Messages from the bundle head will use this number to contact the link with outbound data.)

Stack is a 16-octet ASCII string that names the group of boxes that will be exchanging links. This allows many boxes within a multicast domain to be partitioned into logical groups for administrative reasons.

Speed is a four-octet integer representing the link speed in bits per second.

DiscLen is a four-octet integer representing the length of the peer's Endpoint Discriminator, including the class identifier.

Dc is the Endpoint Discriminator class.

Discriminator is the variable-length Endpoint Discriminator received from the peer.

LinkIDReply is a four-octet integer that is assigned by the bundle head to identify the new link. (Messages from the link will use this number to contact the bundle head with inbound data.)

MRRU is a two-octet integer representing the negotiated peer's MRRU.

MRU is a two-octet integer representing the negotiated peer's MRU.

Length is a four-octet integer representing the data length. It does not include the Pad, if any.

Pad is a ten-octet fill of apparently random data that appears only in outbound messages from the bundle head to the link. Its function is unknown but may serve to avoid situations where one link ends up joining to another link or a bundle head joins to another head due to errors.

Packet is the PPP message itself, including Address and Control fields but not including FCS.

Only the initial Query message is sent as a multicast. All other messages are sent as unicast messages directly to the peer.

A start-up and shut-down exchange might look like this:

```
Query:
    01 01 00 00 00 04 48 69 00 00 00 00 00 00 00 00 00
    00 00 00 00 00 00 00 FA 00 00 00 00 04 01 14 7E 5B
```

The LinkID is 00000004, the stack name is "Hi," the link speed is 0000FA00 (64Kbps), and the discriminator is locally assigned (type 01) as 147E5B.

```
Response:
    01 02 00 00 00 04 48 69 00 00 00 00 00 00 00 00
    00 00 00 00 00 00 00 00 00 19 00 05 DC 05 F4
```

This is a reply to LinkID 00000004 in stack "Hi." The LinkIDReply value to get back to the bundle is 00000019, the MRRU is 05DC (1500), and the MRU is 05F4 (1524).

```
Data:
    01 05 00 00 00 19 00 00 00 08 FF 03 C0 21 05 06 00 04
```

This is a message from link to bundle, eight octets long (LCP Termination-Request.)

```
Data:
    01 05 00 00 00 04 00 00 00 08 00 00 00 00 00 00 00
    00 00 00 FF 03 C0 21 06 06 00 04
```

This is a message from bundle to link, eight octets long (LCP Termination-Ack.) Note the padding before the Address and Control fields.

```
Tear-down:
    01 06 00 00 00 04
```

This is the final tear-down request from bundle to link, sent four times. This simple protocol allows a group of Ascend servers to appear to be one large server to dial-up users. It is not yet publicly documented, so compatible implementations are unlikely.

Cisco's Stack Group Bidding Protocol (SGBP)

Cisco's SGBP is roughly equivalent to the other protocols described above, except that it makes provisions for distribution based on CPU load and is usually used with Cisco's L2F. It is not publicly documented and is rumored to be the subject of a patent application.

Active Bandwidth Management

Several protocols have been proposed to control establishment and tear-down of MP links. The rules of thumb discussed in the preceding section make these protocols unnecessary for proper and efficient operation of a demand-dialed system, but the proponents of these protocols have been able to garner significant market support, and the protocols are advancing in the standards process. Due in part to competition in the marketing rather than the technical arena, this area is extremely contentious.

MP+

Ascend Communications (now Lucent) has been one of the proponents of active bandwidth management. Its proprietary protocol for bandwidth control, MP+, is described in Informational RFC 1934. This protocol is quite complex (47 pages) and includes its own reliable delivery layer plus extensive remote control and remote management functions (which are otherwise often done with SNMP).

I do not recommend implementing this protocol. The RFC contains significant errors, it does not provide sufficient information to make interoperable implementations, and the functions the protocol provides are better implemented in other ways. For instance, most parameters that might be transferred via the REMOTE_MGMT_RX_REQ command can be negotiated through normal PPP options or by use of standard protocols, such as BOOTP, TFTP, SNMP, and even TELNET. If necessary, the bandwidth management portions of this protocol can be implemented using BACP.

Most of the errors in the RFC are in the description of the state machine, which has erroneous states and events. Marco S. Hyman sent me the corrected state machine, which is summarized in Table 7.1.

The state machine has three states and is initialized in Stopped state. For each event, the table entries give the numbered action to perform and the next state. The actions are substantially similar to the RFC description and are not further described here. The events are as follows.

TABLE 7.1.   Corrected State Machine

Event	Current State		
	Stopped	Idle	Pending
Start	1,Idle	**	**
Stop	9,Stopped	9,Stopped	9,Stopped
Send	**	3,Pending	8,Pending
RxAckEqual	**	2,Stopped	5,Idle/Pending
RxDataEqual	**	6,Idle	6,Pending
RxDataMinus1	**	7,Idle	7,Pending
RxBadSeq	**	**	**
RxInvalid	**	2,Stopped	2,Stopped
Timeout	**	**	4,Stopped/ Pending

Start	Request to start state machine; normally invoked automatically when state machine is instantiated.
Stop	Request to shut down state machine.
Send	Request to transmit an MP+ message.
RxAckEqual	Receive Ack message with same sequence as last transmitted message.
RxDataEqual	Receive Data message with expected sequence number.
RxDataMinus1	Receive Data message with last (duplicate) sequence.
RxBadSeq	Receive any message with any other sequence number.
RxInvalid	Receive any invalid (not Data or Ack) message.
Timeout	Retransmission timer expiry.

Bandwidth Allocation Control Protocol (BACP)

The Bandwidth Allocation Control Protocol is described in RFC 2125. This protocol defines an additional LCP option (hex 17) called a *Link Discriminator,* plus two PPP control protocols, C02B (BACP) and C02D (BAP).

The LCP option, described on page 90, negotiates a two-octet integer that is intended to be a unique identifier for a link within a multilink bundle and is used as a reference for the *Link-Drop-Query-Request* BAP message. If either end of the connection is using one of the layer-two-forwarding techniques described below, then assigning this number is slightly more difficult at LCP time. One option is to use some of the upper bits of the Link Discriminator to identify the system negotiating LCP among a group of dial-in systems, so that assigned Link Discriminators are always known to be unique within a bundle. Any such scheme would be proprietary and may not work reliably in a heterogeneous environment. Another option is to renegotiate LCP from the device with the bundle head after finding that the link is part of an existing bundle.

BACP provides a means of requesting permission to add a link, requesting the addition of a dial-back link, and requesting that a link be dropped. It also provides a way of passing information, such as telephone numbers and link characteristics, between the peers. BACP has a single configuration option that must be negotiated before BAP can be used to send these requests.

BACP Option 01   Favored-Peer   Uncommon

This option negotiates a four-octet integer that determines the peer that "wins" in the case of a tie, where both peers request the same action. This is not an option; it must be implemented in all BACP implementations. The RFC says that this tie-breaker is to be used when the actions are requested at the same time, which should be interpreted to mean that if after the request is sent and before a reply is received an identical request is received, the favored peer (with the higher value) should send Nak and the unfavored peer (with the lower value) should send Ack.

Once BACP has reached Opened state, BAP packets are permitted. These messages take the familiar Code-ID-Length format. Responses to BAP messages have an additional single octet after the Length that specifies the status of the message, using 00 for *Ack*, 01 for *Nak* ("maybe later"), 02 for *Reject*, and 03 for *Full-Nak* ("at my limit"). The defined Code values are

    01   Call-Request
    02   Call-Response
    03   Callback-Request
    04   Callback-Response
    05   Link-Drop-Query-Request
    06   Link-Drop-Query-Response
    07   Call-Status-Indication
    08   Call-Status-Response

Following this is a variable-length Data field that contains Type-Len-Data fields encoding parameters for the operation. These option types are

    01   Link-Type
    02   Phone-Delta
    03   No-Phone-Number-Needed (Boolean)
    04   Reason (string)
    05   Link-Discriminator
    06   Call-Status

Should BACP Be Used?

Often, the main reason BACP is implemented is to fulfill a marketing rather than a technical requirement. For instance, ISPs usually have customers using Ascend

Pipeline routers, and they are therefore likely to ask for this protocol whether or not the actual configuration requires it.

Of the BACP protocol features, the "request to add" (Call-Request) is not useful in most situations, since the rules of thumb generally suffice to handle any call rejection. In fact, it is necessary for all systems, with or without BACP, to be able to handle call rejection gracefully and handle misdirection, as detected by failed authentication or an unexpected Endpoint Discriminator, either on the first link or on subsequent links. On systems with BACP, the successful Call-Request negotiation provides only the indication that the peer believes that the call might succeed. It may still fail for any number of reasons—for example, switch congestion or low-level negotiation failure (modem training or V.120 SABME exchange). Since such handling is already required and since, at least for commercial services, full servers mean lost customers and servers will thus rarely reject the request, this feature adds little benefit.

A secondary reason offered for use of Call-Request is to receive the phone number of a line that is more likely to land on a particular system in a multi-system implementation. This reason is less than compelling, because (1) the first call in a bundle may land on a busy system, and additional links will then need to be handed out to other systems with the use of layer-two forwarding or tunneling; (2) any system that implements layer-two forwarding does not need to use this option at all; and (3) management of the telephone number deltas themselves is likely to be difficult or impossible in nontrivial configurations, which may involve nonlocal call routing during peak periods—precisely the situation in which the Call-Request feature is needed.

The Callback-Request feature is useful in those situations where the initial link was created via callback and the initiator of that callback wishes to establish additional links without additional calls. Implementation of this option in other circumstances is discouraged, since it permits the nonpaying peer to demand additional links.

The Link-Drop-Query-Request may seem odd at first glance, but it does have a narrow purpose. If both sides of the conversation are actively establishing links, then some links will be under the control of one peer and others under the control of the other peer. This means that when traffic is light, both peers are configured with the same link-drop thresholds, and a link should be dropped, it is possible that both peers may accidentally elect to drop a link, resulting in too little bandwidth, at least until a new link is established. In extreme cases, this could cause oscillation as both sides establish, then tear down, a single link in each direction. Fortunately, it is very rarely the case that both sides actively establish links, and in these cases it is usually quite satisfactory simply to set the link-drop thresholds differently for the two peers. Thus, this option is generally not necessary.

The Link-Drop-Query-Request is also suggested for use when one side of the link is not sufficiently sophisticated to monitor usage. It seems rather unlikely that an implementation would include a complex protocol such as BACP but would not include simple link utilization monitoring.

Another suggested use of BACP is with metered leased lines. With this type of line, the user pays only when data are sent, but the link is not dialed, so there is no identifiable "caller" or "called" party. However, again, it is true that only one party is ultimately paying for the additional links, and that party must be the one that establishes and tears down links as necessary. If the other party is bringing up links, it is simply guilty of fraud and should be disabled or replaced.

Still another possible use for BACP is to communicate MP usage policy decisions from a central site to dial-up clients. Of course, a central site that wishes to disallow use of MP need only renegotiate LCP and Configure-Reject the MRRU option and also not offer the MRRU option to new sessions that start during the disabled period. Since most current dial-up MP implementations use only one or two links, turning MP on or off, rather than attempting to regulate the number of allowable links, provides exactly as much control as necessary. Again, good implementations can behave gracefully with arbitrary restrictions without using BACP.

Always On Dynamic ISDN (AO/DI)

"Always On Dynamic ISDN" is described in `draft-ietf-pppext-aodi-01.txt`. It is not a separate protocol for use with PPP, but rather a summary of one manufacturer's modifications to several standard protocols.

This draft has several serious problems. First, it requires the use of BACP, although BACP is logically independent of the goals of the draft—either one or both could be successfully implemented. Second, it attempts to modify in incompatible ways every protocol it comes in contact with, including RFC 1990 MP, RFC 1598 PPP in X.25, and RFC 2125 BACP. Finally, the wording of the draft is such that interoperable implementations are unlikely.

I recommend against implementing the feature as specified in this draft.

Cost Shifting

Callback

Callback is generally used as a form of cost shifting and is occasionally used for security. It allows a dial-in system to disconnect a caller and immediately call back to establish the PPP session. There are two current means for requesting this behavior. The first is documented in RFC 1570 and is a Proposed Standard. The second is a Microsoft proposal that is used in Windows Dial-Up Networking and described in documents available on their FTP site and the accompanying CD-ROM.

The RFC 1570 callback mechanism uses a single LCP option to request the callback. The negotiated value consists of a single-octet operation code and an optional variable-length Message field. The operation code is one of the following.

00   Call back to predetermined location based on authenticated peer name. The Message field is omitted.

01   Message field contains a dialing string. An implementation sending this code must have prior knowledge of a valid format for the receiver's dialing device in order for this to work.

02   Message field contains a location identifier that should be looked up by the receiver in a database to find the dialing string. This identifier is arbitrary, but could be a text string such as "home."

03   Message contains an E.164 address (similar to a telephone number).

04   Message field contains an X.500 distinguished name.

06   Use Microsoft CBCP (not described in RFC 1570).

When the specified operation code is one of the RFC 1570 values (00 through 04), the initial call proceeds through authentication and then is terminated. The callback then occurs, and the callback option is not negotiated on the called-back link.

The RFC 1570 form of callback leaves a problem besides the need for the first call to request the callback. The problem is that acceptance of the callback option is done at LCP time when the peer's identity is still unknown. What should be done if callback is not acceptable once the peer has been identified? Authentication should not be allowed to complete, since the peer will then expect a callback that is not going to occur.

Instead, two possibilities exist. First, the system detecting this condition can send LCP Configure-Request again and restart LCP without replying to the PAP

Authentication-Request or CHAP Response. This should restart the peer, and then, during this second time through LCP, callback can be disabled with Configure-Reject. This will allow the call to continue to an established state without the expected dial-back. (Of course, an error should also be logged so that an operator can correct this misconfiguration.) Note that the call must not be terminated in anticipation of a callback until the authentication is complete.

The second alternative is to send an Authenticate-Nak even though the peer is correctly identified and to include a message saying, "your log-in was valid, but you're not authorized to use callback." This has the advantage of alerting an operator to the condition that should be corrected.

One of these two options should be implemented, although which is implemented depends on whether it is more desirable to allow misconfigured links to operate or to prevent the wrong party from paying for the call.

Microsoft Callback Control Protocol

The Microsoft Callback Control Protocol (CBCP), described in the now-expired `draft-ietf-pppext-callback-cp-02.txt`, is an extension to RFC 1570. It claims that the RFC 1570 callback is not interoperable and presents a security hole, despite the fact that multiple interoperable RFC 1570 implementations exist, that initially agreeing to callback during LCP does not require the callback to occur, and that authentication is used on both the initial and callback calls.

CBCP defines a new operation value 06 in addition to the values 00 through 04 described by RFC 1570. Negotiation of this new value indicates that CBCP should be negotiated after authentication is complete. CBCP, PPP protocol number C029, negotiates a callback instead of running other NCPs by using three messages. This effectively introduces a new PPP phase (Callback) between Authenticate and Network, where any received NCP messages should be silently dropped. This phase is similar in concept to ECP negotiation (see Chapter 6).

Like the authentication protocols, CBCP does not use the familiar NCP negotiation message code numbers or packet formats. The CBCP message types are described below.

CBCP Code 01   Callback-Request   Uncommon

This is the first CBCP message sent on a link, and it is sent by the system that will be calling back—the system that had sent LCP Configure-Ack for the callback option above—called the "answerer" in the CBCP draft.

01	ID	Length	Callback Option List

The message format is shown above. The option list consists of one or more options from which the caller will choose a preferred callback address and type. Each option has the format shown below.

Type	Len	Dly	Addresses

The single-octet Type field may be 01 (*No Callback*), 02 (*User Specified Number*), 03 (*Pre-Specified Number*), or 04 (*Number List*). The Dly field is a single octet indicating the number of seconds that the answerer must wait before initiating the callback. The answerer normally sets this to zero, and the caller modifies it as needed to account for modem reset time in the Callback-Reply message. (But see More About CBCP below.)

Within each of these options are zero and more addresses (telephone numbers). These are formatted as shown below.

AType	Address

The AType octet is 01 to indicate that the address is a dialing string composed of ASCII digits "0" through "9," plus the special characters "*," "#," "T," "P," "W," "@," "-," comma, space, and parenthesis. The string, unlike other PPP strings, is not prefixed with a count, but is rather terminated with an octet set to 00. A complete Callback-Request is shown below

```
FF 03 C0 29 01 01 00 11 04 0D 00 01 35 35 35 2D 31 32
31 32 00 02 54
```

which decodes as

```
FF 03      - Address/Control
C0 29      - CBCP Protocol
01         - Callback-Request
01         - ID 1
00 11      - Length (17 octets)
04         - Number List
0D         - Length (13 octets)
00         - Delay
```

```
01              - Telephone number
35 35 35 2D 31 32 31 32 00
                - "555-1212"
02 54           - CRC-16
```

CBCP Code 02   Callback-Response   Uncommon

This is the second message, and is a reply to Callback-Request. This message, shown below, allows the caller to choose one of the callback options provided by the answerer. The Data field consists of exactly one of the options selected from the corresponding Callback-Request.

02	ID	Length	One Option from Callback-Request

CBCP Code 03   Callback-Ack   Uncommon

This is the reply from the answerer to the Callback-Response message and indicates whether the callback will be performed as requested. The contents of this message, shown below, are simply copied from the Callback-Response.

03	ID	Length	Data Field from Callback-Response

Once the caller receives the Callback-Ack, he or she should disconnect and wait for the callback to occur.

At least one dial-in server (the Ascend MAX) is known to send code 05 to request termination of CBCP on an idle link. This is not documented, but appears to be an attempted reuse of the LCP Terminate-Request code.

More About CBCP

Unfortunately, the data types used in the CBCP negotiation messages are not at all compatible with standard telenetworking equipment or even standard PPP itself. For example, the telephone numbers are specified as ASCIIZ strings (a nonportable MS-DOS concept) when, in contrast, PPP strings are always defined to be counted strings, not null terminated. The phone numbers also are defined to contain optionally the strange characters *, #, T, P, W, @, etc., which are all defined in the command sets of certain common consumer-grade modems but which are not at all applicable to standard equipment used at carrier-class installations, and are therefore useless to most service providers.

Due to the lack of interoperability and standardization, I do not recommend implementation of this protocol. However, given the Windows hegemony, some servers may need to support it. Here are a few hints on the implementation and use of CBCP provided to me by Gary Greenberg, who implemented CBCP on a remote access server.

- Windows 95 does not allow the user to enable or disable CBCP. It is enabled at all times and must be disabled by the peer if callback is not desired. (Windows NT, however, allows the user to control CBCP.)
- Since the Windows 95 client will always ask for callback, dial-up server devices supporting CBCP generally must have a per-user list to keep track of which users do and do not actually want callback. Since CBCP is agreed to at LCP time, however, it is usually not possible to disable callback until after Authentication has been run. Instead, when CBCP itself is negotiated during Network phase, the answerer must send a Callback-Response packet with Callback-Type set to *No-Callback* (value 01) in response to the dial-up user's initiating Callback-Request packet. The Windows 95 caller will respond with a Callback-Response packet with the Callback-Type also set to No-Callback.
- Windows 95 does not examine the contents of the Callback-Ack message, but Windows NT does. When supporting NT users, a dial-up server must send Callback-Ack with both Callback-Type and Callback-Delay options copied from the received Callback-Response. If this is not done, the NT client will resend its Callback-Response, leading to a looping condition until the link is dropped.
- The answerer sets the Callback-Delay parameter. The client has no control over this. NT has a registry setting for this value, but it affects the RAS (server) and not the DUN (client). This means that the server must somehow guess what an appropriate reset delay time for the user's modem might be or allow per-user configuration of this time.
- When an NT server calls back, the ACCM option is not set to the RFC 1662 default. Instead, it retains the value negotiated in the previous call. This often leads to callback failures when NT is used with standards-compliant implementations (pppd's "receive-all" option is a work-around; many other implementations cannot be configured to deal with this flaw).

- CBCP is not interoperable with RFC 1570 mechanisms. Devices that support only RFC 1570 callback, unfortunately, must send LCP Configure-Reject if the callback operation field is set to 6, indicating that the peer uses CBCP. This problem occurs because NT clients will not properly handle LCP Configure-Nak for callback and will instead loop on LCP Configure-Request for CBCP until the connection drops. Devices that do not support callback at all, of course, should always send an LCP Configure-Reject to disable callback.
- The modem properties on Windows 95 sometimes disable the auto-answer capability by default. This capability is necessary to use any form of callback. In order to reenable it, select Control Panel -> Modems -> your modem -> Properties -> Connection -> Advanced and insert "S0=1" into the Extra Settings box.

Tunneling PPP

IN THIS CHAPTER

Tunneling is a term for the process of running one network protocol on top of another, especially when the upper protocol is generally considered to represent a lower or equal layer in the OSI protocol stack in comparison with the protocol over which it is run.

PPP may be tunneled over several other protocols, including L2TP, L2F, PPTP, and Ethernet. This section deals with the issues involved in tunneling PPP and the implementation of these specific protocols.

Why Tunnel PPP?

Tunneling may be used for a variety of purposes. One common reason is to provide "virtual private network" (VPN) services, as shown in Figure 8.1. A VPN allows a service provider or customer to construct an isolated network on top of an existing network, such as the Internet. Such services are not common as of the writing of this book, but telephone companies and some large Internet service providers believe that corporations with commuting employees will use these services to link them to corporate systems over inexpensive public networks.

One way to create a VPN is to tunnel PPP over another network. In the case shown in Figure 8.1, the Access device encapsulates the PPP packets in another IP packet and addresses them to the Gateway. The Gateway then decapsulates

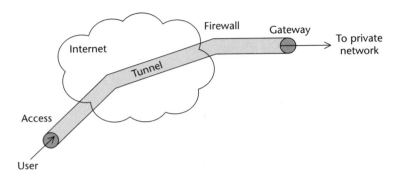

FIGURE 8.1 General VPN model

the PPP frame, runs the PPP state machines, and delivers the user's data to the private network.

There are other ways to construct VPNs, rather than using tunneled PPP. Among these are protocols such as MPLS, IP-IP, IP-GRE, IPSec, and ssh. These alternatives are more generally applicable and will likely work at higher speeds than devices employing any of the PPP tunneling protocols. Worse yet for the service providers planning to charge extra for VPN service, all but MPLS can be employed today by Internet users without having to pay extra for the feature.

Since VPNs generally require creation of small holes in existing firewalls, security is extremely important in any VPN design and is another reason for users to be very cautious when choosing a technology. This issue is beyond the scope of this book.

Another reason to tunnel PPP, described in Chapter 7, is to link together multiple PPP-speaking systems so that they behave as though they were one large system for Multilink PPP operation. This allows better scaling of dial-up sites. This solution, shown in Figure 8.2, is in common use at large dial-in access sites run by ISPs.

Yet another reason to tunnel PPP is to multiplex multiple PPP sessions over a common link. Although tunneling is used for this purpose, a better mechanism for multiplexing is Frame Relay. The HDLC Address field in the PPP frame can be used to multiplex sessions using PPP in Frame Relay (RFC 1973) encapsulation.

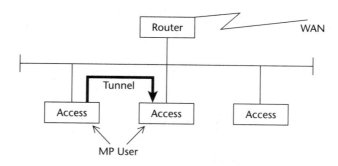

FIGURE 8.2 Tunneling for distributed MP

PPP Tunneling Protocols

These services work by extending the link between the HDLC driver and the rest of PPP over a separate network. Since PPP is at layer two (data-link) in the OSI protocol stack, the underlying technology is sometimes called *layer-two forwarding*.

The first proposal for a layer-two technique was Cisco's Layer Two Forwarding Protocol (L2F). The main features of this proposal are that it can carry both SLIP and PPP, it runs over any connectionless network service (the RFC mentions use over UDP/IP, but any datagram service would work), it contains an optional message sequencing mechanism without flow control, and it uses a small management protocol to establish and tear down tunnels.

The second proposal to appear was Microsoft's Point-to-Point Tunneling Protocol (PPTP). This is a PPP-specific protocol that was designed to run over a combination of TCP and raw IP. At 57 pages, it is far more complex than L2F, but it also includes important call-setup information, such as link speed and calling number, and support for dial-out, none of which were included in L2F. It does not, however, include any form of security other than that provided by PPP itself, which means that its dial-out mechanism is free for use by unauthorized parties. (Most implementations include a fairly weak protection based on an unauthenticated "host name" string.)

At the Montreal IETF meeting in June 1996, these two proposals were merged into a single working proposal called Layer Two Tunneling Protocol (L2TP). The result of this merger has been published as RFC 2661 and is now a separate IETF working group. At 80 pages, L2TP is extremely complex, and includes

PPTP's reinvention of the TCP round-trip-time estimation and flow control mechanisms for the control portion of the tunnel.

An alternative tunneling mechanism called "PPP over Ethernet" was published as Informational RFC 2516. This protocol, which was not designed within the IETF, is peculiar to ADSL devices.

PPP may also be tunneled using a variety of ad hoc mechanisms, such as running AHDLC over TELNET or raw PPP frames over UDP. The former is usually done to bypass firewalls, create inexpensive VPNs, and test new implementations. The latter is used within some proprietary systems.

Layer Two Forwarding—L2F

This protocol is described in RFC 2341, which has Historic status, indicating that it has been superseded by L2TP and that L2F does not define a standard.

L2F is a Cisco-developed protocol for tunneling PPP, SLIP, and potentially other link-layer protocols over arbitrary packet-based networks. For PPP, this connection is described as being between a NAS ("Network Access Server," a dial-in access point) and a Home Gateway (which runs the PPP state machines). It is a simple and flexible forerunner to the standards-track L2TP protocol.

L2F uses an encapsulation derived from GRE (Generic Routing Encapsulation) for the PPP or SLIP frames and does not provide flow control, error control, or message ordering by default. Data may be optionally protected against reordering. L2F has a tunnel control protocol that uses a simple lock-step message exchange. It also has a simple keyed security mechanism to prevent unauthorized use. Typically, L2F is run over UDP, but it may be run over any datagram layer.

It does not directly describe how LCP parameters that affect the HDLC operation, such as ACCM and FCS Alternatives, are to be handled. A reasonable implementation would likely allow the NAS to inspect and modify on the fly any LCP negotiation messages between the Home Gateway and the dial-up user.

The RFC describes only the so-called "mandatory tunneling" mode of operation, where the HG is identified by the NAS using PPP authentication information. "Voluntary tunneling" with L2F is still possible but is not likely to be interoperable.

U.S. Patent 5,918,019 (issued to Andrew Valencia of Cisco) covers both L2F and L2TP. Anyone planning to implement either of these protocols should investigate this patent first.

Point-to-Point Tunneling Protocol—PPTP

PPTP, described in Informational RFC 2637, is a Microsoft-developed protocol for tunneling only PPP between a PAC ("PPTP Access Concentrator," a dial-in access point) and a PNS ("PPTP Network Server," equivalent to the L2F Home Gateway).

Like L2F, PPTP uses a GRE variant to carry the PPP frames between the PAC and the PNS. Unlike L2F, it uses GRE over raw IP rather than UDP and uses a TCP control connection to signal the use of the tunnels. This means that PPTP is tied specifically to IP networks and, unlike L2F, cannot be run by itself over other networks, such as Frame Relay.

PPTP is significantly more complex than L2F. Most significantly, it uses an ill-advised mechanism to make the tunneled PPP data connection between the PAC and the PNS more reliable by asserting end-to-end flow control. This mechanism uses sequencing and windowing without retransmission but does not have TCP's more sophisticated congestion control. This may lower performance by presenting TCP with highly variable delays if acknowledgments are lost, triggering needless retransmit within TCP itself.

The control messages between the PAC and the PNS are extensive. They include ISDN call parameters, hardware error counter statuses, and other information not present in L2F control messages.

The control messages in PPTP also include a Set Link Info (SLI) message to carry ACCM information, but not FCS Alternatives, between the PAC and the PNS. Using this message is likely to be more error prone and complex than snooping the LCP messages on the fly.

No security at all is present in PPTP. If a PAC supports dial-out, PPTP allows arbitrary Internet users to make free PPP telephone calls. If a PNS is used, the network behind it is vulnerable to several types of attacks.

I do not recommend the use of this protocol. If you do plan to implement or use PPTP, you should consult `http://www.counterpane.com/pptp.html` first.

Layer Two Tunneling Protocol—L2TP

L2TP, described in RFC 2661, is the IETF standards-track mechanism for tunneling PPP between an LAC ("L2TP Access Concentrator," a dial-in access point) and an LNS ("L2TP Network Server," the same as the PPTP PNS and L2F

Home Gateway) over other protocols. As a combination of L2F and PPTP, it contains features and failings of both and is more complex than either.

L2TP repairs many mistakes in PPTP. First, it does away with PPTP's flow controlled data channel. The PPP messages tunneled over L2TP may be sequenced to prevent reordering if desired, but are never delayed for flow control.[1] Second, L2TP does not require the use of TCP for the control connection. Third, L2TP has integral security mechanisms, including control connection authentication and simple encryption of some control data. Fourth, L2TP uses an Attribute-Value-Pair (AVP) mechanism that is easier to extend than PPTP's fixed control message formats. Finally, L2TP may run over non-IP networks.

L2TP also covers some omissions in L2F. It allows the control protocol to be windowed for practical use on networks with long latencies, although at a great expense of complexity (the suggested algorithms in the specification are essentially a reinvention of TCP and are rarely implemented). L2TP includes mechanisms for supporting ISDN and other dial-up connection types and carrying external information back to the LNS.

Unfortunately, it also includes the SLI mechanism from PPTP, which is unnecessary because the needed information is easily extracted from the data stream and architecturally unsound because it requires the LNS to understand the configuration and limitations of the serial connection attached to the LAC.

It also has at least one largely undocumented design flaw: implementations must tunnel HDLC headers (the Address and Control fields) in addition to the actual PPP frame. For dial-up systems, this is not generally a problem. However, for all other systems (such as PPP over ATM or Frame Relay), this means that the HDLC header must be synthesized when entering the L2TP tunnel and removed in the opposite direction.

Richard Shea's *L2TP Implementation and Operation,* published by Addison-Wesley, contains a far more detailed explanation of the operation of L2TP and the ways in which it interacts with PPP. If you implement or use L2TP, I recommend this book.

U.S. Patent 5,918,019 on L2F makes claims that also cover L2TP operation.

---

1. An old draft of L2TP included flow control on the tunneled data. This was moved into a separate draft and briefly kept alive at Microsoft's request, but has since fallen from favor.

PPP over Ethernet (PPPoE)

This protocol, described in Informational RFC 2516, is not the result of any IETF work. Instead, it is a protocol designed within the ADSL Forum.

RFC 2516 is very simple. It begins with a four-way DHCP-like handshake where a PPP user finds other PPPoE systems on the local Ethernet by broadcasting a PPPoE Active Discovery Initiation (PADI) packet with Ethertype 8863. The systems that allow access reply with PPPoE Active Discovery Offer (PADO) messages. The user then picks one of the offers and replies to this server with a PPPoE Active Discovery Request (PADR) message. The selected server returns a PPPoE Active Discovery Session-confirmation (PADS) message that gives a unique session ID number for the new PPP user. PPP can then be tunneled using a distinguished Ethertype (8864) and the specified session ID.

In the usual ADSL configuration, the PPPoE server system is an access concentrator reachable through an ADSL modem that acts as an Ethernet bridge. The access concentrator, which may reside at the telephone company central office or at a remote location over ATM links, communicates with the user's PPP system and establishes the PPPoE tunnel.

Unfortunately, since PPPoE runs directly over Ethernet with no fragmentation facilities and adds additional headers, RFC 2516 fixes the MRU to a maximum of 1492, in violation of RFC 1661. This problem can be corrected by use of MP within a single session, although no known implementation does this. The LCP MRU must be no greater than 1492, but the MRRU may be any convenient larger value.

Worse still, PPPoE essentially has no security at all. The PPPoE Active Discovery Terminate (PADT) message is unauthenticated. Any user on the local link can terminate or disrupt another user's PPP session by sending forged PADT messages and by sending false PADO messages. Since, unlike L2TP, PPPoE cannot be run over a secure facility such as IPSec, users may also inject arbitrary packets into existing PPP sessions.

It would be hard to justify the use of this protocol. The ADSL devices that use this protocol could just as easily use a combination of L2TP and DHCP or implement PPP and traditional routing or bridging themselves. Several easily implemented combinations of existing standards would solve the same problems as PPPoE without requiring the invention of a new protocol.

Ad Hoc Tunneling

Many nonstandard tunneling mechanisms are also used to tunnel PPP. Generally, these mechanisms are used to create secure remote access, link separate networks, bypass firewalls, and test new PPP implementations.

One such mechanism is running PPP over a remote login protocol, such as Telnet, rlogin, or ssh, the last of which provides data compression and encryption as well. The *pty* option in the new versions of pppd allows this to be configured quite easily. The user must be careful to use the appropriate "binary" options on the remote login command (usually a "-8" command line flag) when doing this and to use chat appropriately. This mechanism works reasonably well on highly reliable local networks but tends to perform quite badly when run over the general Internet. All of these remote login protocols themselves run over TCP, and the combination of TCP over IP over PPP over TCP again is often unstable in the face of congestion and packet loss.

The pty option is also very useful for testing new PPP implementations. To do this, the implementation under test is linked to pppd using the pty option to invoke the new program. This avoids many unnecessary complexities dealing with serial ports and associated hardware. It can also be used to link together two physically separate implementations for compatibility testing over the Internet. Using a local high-speed network, such as Ethernet, this feature can be used to stress-test an implementation with higher-speed data than are possible over standard serial ports.

Another tunneling mechanism is called "httptunnel." This is free software (released under GNU's GPL) that establishes port forwarding between a tiny client and server application that look to a Web proxy as though they were a Web browser and server. Using this, you can set up a bidirectional connection through most traditional firewalls and then run telnet over that connection. Using the technique above, PPP can then be run over this telnet session.

Here is an example of the use of PPP over telnet using pppd version 2.3.9 on a Linux system:

```
pppd debug noauth 10.0.0.1:10.0.0.2 user carlson pty
"telnet -8E 127.1" connect "chat -v ogin: carlson
word: mypass % 'pppd debug user carlson'"
```

There are two instances of PPP being run here. The first runs the "telnet" remote login program and then uses "chat" to start the second copy of PPP. The two instances of PPP then negotiate with each other and begin passing packets. The resulting configuration appears in Figure 8.3.

To link two machines over telnet using PPP, the "127.1" IP address in the example above would be changed to the address of the remote machine. The options being used are as follows.

debug Debug mode is enabled on both sides.

noauth The local system is not authenticating the peer.

10.0.0.1:10.0.0.2 The local system specifies its address and provides one to its peer.

user carlson This specifies the user name used to authenticate to the peer.

pty "telnet -8E 127.1" This creates the connection between the two copies of pppd. It invokes the standard telnet utility with two flags: -8 to enable 8-bit data (also called "binary mode") and -E to disable the escape character (usually Control-]). The address given here is the standard IP loopback address (127.1), so both copies of pppd will run on the local machine in this example.

connect "chat -v ogin: carlson word: mypass %" . . . This logs into the remote system, waits for the usual Unix "%" command-line prompt, and then invokes pppd on that system. Note the separate set of single quotes (') necessary to deliver the pppd invocation as a single line to the remote system.

If rlogin were used instead of telnet, an additional "escape 0xff" option would need to be added to avoid problems with the rlogin window-size-change message. In the resulting debug logs, first the initial copy of pppd runs, sets up the telnet connection, and then runs chat to invoke pppd on the peer.

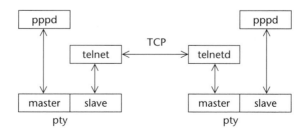

FIGURE 8.3 PPP over telnet

```
Nov 12 22:48:06 linux pppd[1327]: pppd 2.3.9 started
by root, uid 0
Nov 12 22:48:06 linux chat[1329]: expect (ogin:)
Nov 12 22:48:06 linux chat[1329]: Trying 127.0.0.1...
Nov 12 22:48:06 linux chat[1329]: Connected to 127.1.
Nov 12 22:48:06 linux chat[1329]: Escape character is
'off'.
Nov 12 22:48:06 linux chat[1329]: ^M
Nov 12 22:48:06 linux chat[1329]: Red Hat Linux
release 5.0 (Hurricane)^M
Nov 12 22:48:06 linux chat[1329]: Kernel 2.0.32 on an
i586^M
Nov 12 22:48:06 linux chat[1329]: login:
Nov 12 22:48:06 linux chat[1329]: -- got it
Nov 12 22:48:06 linux chat[1329]: send (carlson^M)
Nov 12 22:48:06 linux chat[1329]: expect (word:)
Nov 12 22:48:06 linux chat[1329]:  carlson
Nov 12 22:48:06 linux chat[1329]: Password:
Nov 12 22:48:06 linux chat[1329]: --got it
Nov 12 22:48:06 linux chat[1329]: send (mypass^M)
Nov 12 22:48:06 linux chat[1329]: expect (%)
Nov 12 22:48:06 linux chat[1329]:
Nov 12 22:48:07 linux PAM_pwdb[1331]: (login) session
opened for user carlson by (uid=0)
Nov 12 22:48:07 linux chat[1329]: Last login: Fri Nov
12 22:41:46 from localhost
Nov 12 22:48:07 linux PAM_pwdb[1331]: LOGIN ON ttyp3
BY carlson FROM localhost
Nov 12 22:48:07 linux chat[1329]: %
Nov 12 22:48:07 linux chat[1329]: --got it
Nov 12 22:48:07 linux chat[1329]: send (pppd debug
user carlson^M)
Nov 12 22:48:08 linux pppd[1327]: Serial connection
established.
Nov 12 22:48:08 linux pppd[1327]: Using interface
ppp1
Nov 12 22:48:08 linux pppd[1327]: Connect: ppp1 <-->
/dev/ttyp2
```

Now that chat is complete, the two copies of pppd are now communicating
with each other using AHDLC over the telnet connection. LCP begins to negotiate. Pay attention to the process ID (PID) numbers in brackets. The first invocation is [1327] and the second is [1350].

```
Nov 12 22:48:08 linux pppd[1350]: pppd 2.3.9 started
by carlson, uid 1001
Nov 12 22:48:08 linux pppd[1350]: Using interface
ppp0
Nov 12 22:48:08 linux pppd[1350]: Connect: ppp0 <-->
/dev/ttyp3
Nov 12 22:48:08 linux pppd[1350]: sent [LCP ConfReq
id=0x1 <asyncmap 0x0> <auth pap> <magic 0xffff8001>
<pcomp> <accomp>]
Nov 12 22:48:09 linux pppd[1327]: sent [LCP ConfReq
id=0x1 <asyncmap 0x0> <magic 0xffff0001> <pcomp>
<accomp>]
Nov 12 22:48:09 linux pppd[1327]: rcvd [LCP ConfReq
id=0x1 <asyncmap 0x0> <auth pap> <magic 0xffff8001>
<pcomp> <accomp>]
Nov 12 22:48:09 linux pppd[1327]: sent [LCP ConfAck
id=0x1 <asyncmap 0x0> <auth pap> <magic 0xffff8001>
<pcomp> <accomp>]
Nov 12 22:48:09 linux pppd[1350]: rcvd [LCP ConfReq
id=0x1 <asyncmap 0x0> <magic 0xffff0001> <pcomp>
<accomp>]
Nov 12 22:48:09 linux pppd[1350]: sent [LCP ConfAck
id=0x1 <asyncmap 0x0> <magic 0xffff0001> <pcomp>
<accomp>]
Nov 12 22:48:09 linux pppd[1350]: rcvd [LCP ConfAck
id=0x1 <asyncmap 0x0> <auth pap> <magic 0xffff8001>
<pcomp> <accomp>]
Nov 12 22:48:09 linux pppd[1327]: rcvd [LCP ConfAck
id=0x1 <asyncmap 0x0> <magic 0xffff0001> <pcomp>
<accomp>]
```

After LCP, authentication is done. In this case, the peer is configured to request
authentication. The system is configured with user "carlson" and password "baz"

in the pap-secrets file. Note that one packet was lost here on the transition from
LCP to authentication.

```
Nov 12 22:48:09 linux pppd[1327]: sent [PAP AuthReq
id=0x1 user="carlson" password="baz"]
Nov 12 22:48:12 linux pppd[1327]: sent [PAP AuthReq
id=0x2 user="carlson" password="baz"]
Nov 12 22:48:12 linux pppd[1350]: rcvd [PAP AuthReq
id=0x2 user="carlson" password="baz"]
Nov 12 22:48:12 linux pppd[1350]: sent [PAP AuthAck
id=0x2 "Login ok"]
Nov 12 22:48:12 linux pppd[1327]: rcvd [PAP AuthAck
id=0x2 "Login ok"]
Nov 12 22:48:12 linux pppd[1327]: Remote message:
Login ok
```

Now IPCP comes up. The peer gives its address as one of its defaults. Since we
have a configured address for the peer, we suggest that address with Configure-
Nak, and the peer accepts it.

```
Nov 12 22:48:12 linux pppd[1327]: sent [IPCP ConfReq
id=0x1 <addr 10.0.0.1> <compress VJ 0f 01>]
Nov 12 22:48:12 linux pppd[1327]: rcvd [IPCP ConfReq
<addr 192.168.5.121> <compress VJ 0f 01>]
Nov 12 22:48:12 linux pppd[1327]: sent [IPCP ConfNak
id=0x1 <addr 10.0.0.2>]
Nov 12 22:48:12 linux pppd[1350]: sent [IPCP ConfReq
id=0x1 <addr 192.168.5.121> <compress VJ 0f 01>]
Nov 12 22:48:12 linux pppd[1350]: rcvd [IPCP ConfReq
id=0x1 <addr 10.0.0.1> <compress VJ 0f 01>]
Nov 12 22:48:12 linux pppd[1350]: sent [IPCP ConfAck
id=0x1 <addr 10.0.0.1> <compress VJ 0f 01>]
Nov 12 22:48:12 linux pppd[1350]: rcvd [IPCP ConfNak
id=0x1 <addr 10.0.0.2>]
Nov 12 22:48:12 linux pppd[1350]: sent [IPCP ConfReq
id=0x2 <addr 10.0.0.2> <compress VJ 0f 01>]
Nov 12 22:48:12 linux pppd[1327]: rcvd [IPCP ConfAck
id=0x1 <addr 10.0.0.1> <compress VJ 0f 01>]
```

```
Nov 12 22:48:12 linux pppd[1327]: rcvd [IPCP ConfReq
id=0x2 <addr 10.0.0.2> <compress VJ 0f 01>]
Nov 12 22:48:12 linux pppd[1327]: sent [IPCP ConfAck
id=0x2 <addr 10.0.0.2> <compress VJ 0f 01>]
Nov 12 22:48:12 linux pppd[1327]: local  IP address
10.0.0.1
Nov 12 22:48:12 linux pppd[1327]: remote IP address
10.0.0.2
Nov 12 22:48:12 linux pppd[1327]: Script /etc/ppp/ip-
up started (pid 1352)
Nov 12 22:48:12 linux pppd[1350]: rcvd [IPCP ConfAck
id=0x2 <addr 10.0.0.2> <compress VJ 0f 01>]
Nov 12 22:48:12 linux pppd[1350]: local  IP address
10.0.0.2
Nov 12 22:48:12 linux pppd[1350]: remote IP address
10.0.0.1
Nov 12 22:48:12 linux pppd[1350]: Script /etc/ppp/ip-
up started (pid 1354)
Nov 12 22:48:12 linux pppd[1327]: Script /etc/ppp/ip-
up finished (pid 1352), status = 0x0
Nov 12 22:48:12 linux pppd[1350]: Script /etc/ppp/ip-
up finished (pid 1354), status = 0x0
```

Debugging Links

Approach

When PPP fails to function properly, a fair bit of detective work is sometimes required to find the source of the problem. In general, the problems users see fall into three categories: communications, negotiation, and networking. Of course, only the negotiation is actually part of PPP, but it is necessary to isolate the problem to one part of the system in order to repair it.

Network-Layer Problems

Networking problems are usually the easiest to isolate. If the link comes up, but no data pass, or only a few hosts are reachable, it is likely to be a networking problem. A general rule of thumb for establishing that the problem is indeed related to networking is to disable all optional protocols, such as compression, and establish the link. If the problem still appears, networking is suspect.

Debugging of networking problems usually requires an intimate knowledge of the routing and forwarding techniques used. Some general hints are as follows.

- *Check the addresses used.* The network-layer addresses used must be properly assigned in order to communicate with other systems on the network. They usually cannot be picked arbitrarily. For IP, 10.0.0.0/8, 172.16.0.0/12, and 192.168.0.0/16 are reserved addresses. They can be routed within an organization, but they cannot be routed on the general Internet. If these addresses are in use, a NAT or proxy server must be installed to reach the Internet.

- *Check the routing tables.* Examine the network-layer routing tables not only on the machine exhibiting the problem but on the peer's side as well, and on any other routers on either side of the link that are in the path to the destination system. It is very common for networking problems, especially those that result in only some hosts being reachable, to be due to misconfiguration of those intermediate routers. Don't forget to check both the path to the destination and the path back; more often than not, the problem is in the return path.

- *Check the optional features.* Most systems do not forward network packets by default, so this must be explicitly enabled if the system is used as a router. This is done with different commands on different systems:

```
ndd -set /dev/ip ip_forwarding 1                    Solaris
echo 1 > /proc/sys/net/ipv4/ip_forward              Linux 2.0
echo 1 > /proc/sys/net/ipv4/conf/all/forward        Linux 2.2+
sysctl -w net.inet.ip.forwarding=1                  FreeBSD
no -o ipforwarding=1                                AIX
nettune -s ip_forwarding 1                          HP/UX
```

Some systems, such as recent versions of Linux (kernel Version 2.2 and above), do not proxy ARP by default, even if pppd is configured with the "proxyarp" option. If proxy ARP is to be used, it must also be enabled with this command:

```
echo 1 > /proc/sys/net/ipv4/conf/all/proxy_arp
```

- *Check the available statistics.* Most network-layer implementations provide several counts, such as packets received and packets forwarded. If the peer system is not too busy, it is often possible to check the statistics, attempt to contact a host, then reexamine the statistics and find which ones changed. If this does not reveal a problem, check the same statistics on the next router or the destination host itself.

For instance, if "netstat -s" shows an increasing number of "IP packets not forwardable" or "ICMP input destination unreachable," it is likely that this system is missing a needed route. If it shows an increasing number of "ICMP time exceeded" errors (and the "traceroute" utility is not in use at the time), the problem is likely to be a forwarding loop—two routers are set to forward the same destination address to each other, and the packets bounce back and forth until the TTL (time-to-live) expires. Finally, if it shows an increasing number of "redirects sent" or "redirects received," the problem may be a misconfigured network mask on a broadcast interface. (The names of these counters will vary depending on the system used. For instance, the Solaris names that correspond to the five counters discussed above are "ipOutNoRoutes," "icmpInDestUnreachs," "icmpInTimeExcds," "icmpOutRedirects," and "icmpInRedirects," respectively.)

- *Check the name service configuration.* If the name service is misconfigured, you may find that numeric network addresses work but symbolic names do not, or that commands such as "netstat," "ping," "route," "tcpdump," and "traceroute" hang unless the "-n" flag is given. On Unix-like systems, name service is configured through /etc/resolv.conf. This file usually looks like this:

```
domain myisp.com
nameserver 192.168.1.1
```

On Windows machines, this will appear in the Control Panel -> Network menu. The actual domain name and address will be different in your configuration. Contact your ISP to obtain the correct address.

Negotiation and Communications

The distinction between negotiation problems and communications problems can be difficult to discern sometimes. Some are obvious, such as chat script failures. Some types of communications problems, however, such as bad ACCM settings, can look like negotiation problems. Listed below are some of the symptoms of communications errors.

- **Very long delays between received messages.**
  On a PC Linux system, this is usually caused by the wrong IRQ level configured for the serial port with the setserial utility. The debug messages have a characteristic 19- or 20-second interval when this failure occurs.

- **Link terminates with "too many Configure-Requests" message.**
  This usually means that one system cannot hear the other. Possible causes include bad cabling, incorrect bit-rate settings, broken flow control, and chat script failure.

  On a PC Linux system, this can also be caused by improper `setserial` configuration in `/etc/rc.d/rc.serial`, including setting "uart 16450" when "uart 16550A" should be set. Improper configuration of the serial driver causes the hardware receive FIFO to be disabled, which often leads to overruns and corrupted serial data.
- **Link terminates with "possibly looped-back" message.**
  This is most often caused when the peer is not actually running PPP, but is rather left sitting at some kind of command-line prompt due to a chat script error. This is not a PPP failure.

  When dialing into ISPs, the chat script failure is usually due to the use of user name and password scripting when this is either not required or not allowed by the ISP. Some ISPs will say that you should "use PAP" instead—this means that no scripting is required. The last line of the chat script for these ISPs should be:

  ```
  CONNECT      '\d\c'
  ```

  Another possible cause of this problem, although much rarer, is that PPP authentication data are incorrectly configured and the peer has silently stopped running PPP due to the misconfiguration.
- **LCP comes up, but all protocols above that fail or exhibit unexpected CRC errors.**
  This is usually caused by an incorrectly set ACCM. Try setting the ACCM back to the standard default of FFFFFFFF, or to the Windows default of 000A0000.
- **LCP comes up, but link terminates shortly afterward.**
  This can be caused by an incorrect password, depending on how the peer implements the security protocols. In MP systems, this can be caused by a failure to match the expected Endpoint-Discriminator, MRRU, MRU, or Short Sequence Number options.
- **IPCP comes up and terminates immediately.**
  This is usually the result of IP address configuration errors, such as missing or duplicate addresses. If no local errors are evident, check the debug logs for the peer.

- **Very low performance.**
  This can be due to flow control configuration errors, modem set-up errors, and DTE rates configured either too low or above what the system is able to handle. On Linux, this is sometimes cured with the "spd_vhi" option to `setserial`, which sets the data rate to the maximum of 115.2Kbps when pppd requests 38.4Kbps.

The PPP debugging Web pages referenced in Chapter 11 can be a big help in isolating these problems for particular implementations.

Configuration Problems

Listed below are some common problems in PPP configuration.

- **IP-Address option is Configure-Rejected or fails.**
  This often occurs when no remote IP address is configured and the peer refuses to provide one. For PPP links pointing to the Internet as a default route (the usual case for a link to an ISP), the remote address is irrelevant and can be supplied on the pppd command line like this:

  ```
  0:192.168.1.1
  ```

- **"Peer is not authorized to use remote address 1.2.3.4" log message.**
  This occurs when pppd is used as a server because the remote address for the dial-up user is not listed in the pap-secrets file. Adding an extra "*" at the end of the associated entry will cure the problem.
- **LCP "No network protocols running" right after IPCP Configure-Ack.**
  This occurs on Linux systems running a version of pppd that is incompatible with the kernel. PPP should be updated in this case.
- **Can communicate with everything except one network.**
  On Windows machines, this is caused by having the Ethernet interface configured with a static IP address but not connected. This problem occurs most often with laptop machines that are plugged into an Ethernet at work and used for dial-up on the road. The solution is either to disable the Ethernet interface manually through the Control Panel when using PPP or to switch to DHCP for address assignment on the Ethernet.

- **Cannot negotiate CCP and connection is dropped.**
  Normally, the failure of CCP (data compression) does not cause the link to fail. However, if the peer is an NT server and the "Require Microsoft Encryption" option has been selected in RAS, then failure of CCP will cause the link to terminate. NT does not implement ECP but rather attempts to negotiate Microsoft-proprietary RC4 encryption as part of CCP. If this fails, the link is terminated.

Link Failure

Low-Level Communications Hardware

The normal result of a failure in communications hardware when a link is started is LCP remaining in Req-Sent state until it fails due to too many Configure-Requests having been sent. This can mean that the peer is not actually running the PPP protocol or that data loss is so high that nothing gets through. On asynchronous lines, a well-implemented PPP system will notice if the data received always contain the same LCP Magic Number. This condition indicates what is termed a *loop-back*. Generally, this means that the peer is sitting at some kind of text-mode prompt, probably because of a failure of the start-up script.

LCP failure while in Ack-Sent state due to too many Configure-Request messages usually points to a unidirectional link. The system that fails in this way is able to receive data from the other system, but nothing transmitted is getting through. This can be due to flow control or to character transmission problems, such as parity errors.

Authentication or NCP failure in an Ack-Sent state often points to a problem with link transparency. In debugging this kind of problem, a good first start is to set the ACCM back to the default of FFFFFFFF. Some broken implementations assume the value 000A0000 at all times, so this should also be tried. If either of these solutions fixes the problem, then at least one of the control characters is interfering in data transmission. (On SLIP links, an analogous problem sometimes occurs. If software XON/XOFF flow control is accidentally enabled, TCP will get through somewhat but may behave poorly, and sessions will lock up occasionally. Ping, which is based on ICMP, may work for "small" packets but not for large ones. UDP services, like DNS, will fail completely, because UDP's protocol number is 11 hex, which is the same as the XON control character.)

Authentication

Although all PPP authentication protocols include a means of gracefully notifying the peer that the identification has not been accepted, it is still necessary to interpret either a hardware-level hang-up (such as loss of DCD on a modem) or an LCP Terminate-Request as the failure of authentication if a PAP Authenticate-Request or CHAP Response has been sent.

NCP Convergence

NCPs normally fail to converge when one side or the other is not configured properly. For instance, IPCP will fail while sending Configure-Requests if the peer believes that the address being sent is incorrect, perhaps due to some kind of peer-name-to-address translation table being used on its end or to an address reuse policy set by an external system such as DHCP. In these cases, both peers become intransigent; one sends Configure-Request repeatedly, and the other sends Configure-Nak. Each side should maintain counters for the numbers of Configure-Requests, Configure-Rejects, and Configure-Naks sent and should terminate the NCP if the counter passes some configurable threshold (with a suggested default of 10). When done properly, this protects an implementation from lock-up when presented with a misbehaving peer that may not have implemented these counters.

Another possible anomalous behavior is looping. This can occur even with well-implemented PPP systems that obey the above-mentioned rules. The usual reason for this failure is that the peer detects something in an NCP negotiation that forces it to drop back to an earlier stage to renegotiate a parameter. For instance, attempted negotiation of BCP (bridging) may cause an implementation to return to LCP in order to request a larger MRU. Since RFC 1661 doesn't specify any maximum number of times that this pattern may repeat, it is possible that it repeats indefinitely due to bugs on either side. To fix this, I suggest implementing a counter that is incremented each time a lower layer reopens and that is reset to zero when all layers are open. If this counter passes some preset threshold, PPP should be terminated.

Common Implementation Errors and Effects

Bad State Machine Transitions

The most common state-machine-related problem in implementations observed in the field is a failure to handle Configure-Request messages correctly. This manifests itself as the link cycling LCP up and down several times and then terminating. The problem is that the failing implementation gets its state machine out of synchronization if it is the recipient rather than the sender of the first Configure-Request message.

A good implementation should have a configuration option to delay the initial transmission of an LCP Configure-Request message for a single time-out period in order to communicate with the many peers that have this bug. This allows the peer to issue its Configure-Request first and receive a Configure-Ack before your implementation does the same. On properly implemented peers, the order does not matter, but on those with this bug, the order matters greatly.

One of the many systems with this problem is an embedded system intended as an appliance for the general public. Since this problem is incorporated into widely distributed firmware, it is likely that it will persist in the field for quite some time. This problem is often related to the general race condition problem described below.

LCP-to-NCP-Transition Race Conditions

In order to make the software easier to understand, designers often implement each layer as a separate module and pass messages between them. But in order to satisfy performance constraints, they usually need to handle input data immediately, usually with an asynchronous interrupt mechanism. A common side effect of these two choices is that the first Configure-Request message for the next layer brought up (Authentication after LCP, or NCP after Authentication) is lost because the lower layer has just sent the Up message to the next layer but the system has not yet scheduled the task for that layer to run by the time the message arrives. Since the next higher layer is not yet at least in Req-Sent state, the state machine must ignore the message.

This problem also occasionally occurs between the PPP implementation itself and the external network-layer entities or between routing or naming dæmons. The result is that the NCP goes to Opened state, but the external interfaces, routing tables, or name databases have not yet become operational. This causes the first few user data packets to be lost.

There are three possible solutions to this problem in PPP.

1. Fix the broken implementation so that it puts negotiation messages at the end of the same queue that is used for the messages between the software layers, and make sure that the software messages are always placed at the front of the queue.
2. Fix the broken implementation so that it disables reception of interrupts for received data when a layer goes to Opened state, and reenable when the next layer changes state.
3. If the broken implementation is unfixable, as is often the case with systems that are shipped without source code, the correctly functioning implementation may need to have a short delay added after sending Configure-Ack in each layer. In the broken implementations I have seen, 300 milliseconds appears to be adequate. This delay, of course, should be configurable, but may be enabled automatically if a known broken peer is detected. The LCP Identification message can be useful for this purpose.

For the networking and naming problems, the fixes depend strongly on the network protocol being used, but some suggestions are as follows.

- Use routing protocols and binding services that can quickly and reliably synchronize with the establishment of the PPP NCP, and delay sending the NCP Configure-Ack until the changes have been propagated on other links. Note that these protocols may have to propagate the changes to many other systems before synchronization is achieved.
- Use static routing and static name binding instead of or in addition to dynamic routing protocols and name binding services.
- Implement a delay of a few seconds after the NCPs go up before data are forwarded to other interfaces. During the delay period, network packets should be queued.

Parameter Change Race Conditions

This failure mode is more subtle than LCP-to-NCP-transition race conditions, but the effects are similar. A well-designed implementation of LCP, in order to be as liberal as possible, should set its receive ACCM when the Configure-Request message from the peer is seen and should set its transmit ACCM only after waiting for all output to drain after transitioning LCP to Opened state. (Renegotiation is a special case, and the receive ACCM should be left unchanged until Configure-Request is seen, but the transmit ACCM should be immediately set back to the default of FFFFFFFF.)

However, since AHDLC encoding and decoding are byte-intensive operations, and most routers are optimized to operate better on a packet-by-packet basis, AHDLC handling is often delegated to separate dedicated processors. This means that setting ACCM masks requires a communication between the two CPUs, and this synchronization is an occasional source of failure. The most common failure occurs when the transmit ACCM is set to the final value either before or even during the transmission of the LCP Configure-Ack message. This causes at least some unescaped characters to be sent, and, if the peer is strict in setting its receive ACCM, the packet will be dropped with a corrupt FCS.

Following the rules above in order to make an implementation as liberal as possible in receiving data and as strict as possible in sending it will avoid this problem in most cases.

Renegotiation Failure

Many implementations have trouble with renegotiation of one or more layers. If you want to renegotiate LCP, you must be prepared for the peer to fall apart completely. Common responses range from immediate termination to negotiation loops (LCP negotiates up, then authentication starts, and LCP restarts). In particular, Shiva engineers have noted that both the ShivaRemote and Windows 95, which uses code developed at Shiva, will immediately terminate the telephone connection if LCP renegotiation is attempted.

Compression Failure

When compression fails due to a corrupted dictionary or to implementation errors, the most obvious result is strange-looking LCP Protocol-Reject messages from the peer. Some of the compression techniques do not detect data corruption well, and the result is a decompressed packet with an illegal protocol number prepended. This causes the receiver to issue the LCP Protocol-Reject for this illegal number and to forward the rest of the bad data. This can be confusing because the compressor never appeared to send data that contained this bad protocol number.

Message Field Validation

Not all implementations validate the various fields of the messages they receive. Some common commercial implementations do not bother to check that the ID field in the Configure-Ack, -Nak, or -Reject matches the last Configure-Request sent. Some do not bother to check the various Length fields, and a few will even crash if presented with bad lengths.

The lack of ID field checking can be a nuisance during lengthy authentication requests, since a straightforward implementation will start the authentication with the first message and will queue subsequent messages. If the peer sending the authentication information times out and resends the message, the first peer will enqueue this new one. When the authentication is complete, it will reply to ID 1, then read the second request from the queue and immediately return a reply for this second message (which may be ID 1 or 2). The broken peer will read and accept the first reply, since it is not looking at the ID number, and may become confused on seeing the second reply. A work-around for this problem is to read in the messages from the queue after completing authentication but before sending the response, then to send the response using the latest ID number seen.

Strings

Some implementors seem to think that strings should be terminated by an ASCII NUL (00) byte. Of course, with PPP, all strings are bounded by a separate length, so there is no need for explicit termination of the string with NUL. In order to interoperate with these peers, it is sometimes necessary to discard extra NULs at the ends of some messages.

When implementing with languages or libraries that are designed around NUL-terminated strings, such as C, be careful in handling PPP strings. It is perfectly legal for strings to contain embedded NUL bytes, so the usual `strncpy()` and `strncmp()` functions will not work as expected. Instead, use `memcpy()` and `memcmp()`, especially with the AppleTalk zone name.

Missing Reject Messages and Handling

I have seen at least one implementation that fails to send LCP Protocol-Reject if it recognizes the protocol sent by the peer but does not want to use the protocol (for example, a system that has CCP implemented but has a configuration option to disable it). This results in the NCP sending Configure-Request messages until reaching a limit and disabling the NCP. In this case, because other NCPs establish themselves properly, it can be useful to detect this error and issue an appropriate diagnostic message, since the user may mistakenly believe that the properly functioning implementation is broken because it will log an error indicating that it "failed" as a result of having sent too many Configure-Requests.

Incorrect Use of Terminate-Request

The Terminate-Request message will shut down a protocol that is in Opened state. However, it will not shut down a protocol that is still negotiating but rather will push it back to the start of negotiation. For this reason, Terminate-Request (triggered by a Close event) should not be sent to terminate a misbehaving protocol. Some implementations erroneously attempt to use Terminate-Request instead of Protocol-Reject to shut down a protocol that is failing to negotiate. This behavior appears in the log file as a Configure-Request/Terminate-Request/Terminate-Ack loop. The only available fix is to disable the affected protocol administratively. (Since this is most often seen only with CCP, and since the Configure-Request counter should eventually terminate the failing protocol, it should not affect normal PPP operation.)

Example Traces

The following examples show the raw hexadecimal frames sent by each peer, followed by the decoded interpretation of each message. On a particular medium, the actual data captured will differ due to HDLC or AHDLC encapsulation. If you are working with the low-level data, you may want to convert it to raw hexadecimal form first by decoding the HDLC format. For instance, on an asynchronous line, every 7D XX sequence should be replaced with (XX XOR 20) and every 7E marks the end of a frame.

Later, in Getting Traces from Common PPP Software (page 277), I will cover the logging and debugging mechanisms used by common PPP implementations.

Simple IP Example

This simple but complete example shows LCP, PAP authentication, and IPCP negotiation. The options negotiated include Address and Control field compression and

Protocol field compression in LCP. Peer A is configured to be IP address 10.1.0.1 and peer B is 10.2.0.5.

```
1A:    FF 03 C0 21 01 01 00 0C 03 04 C0 23 07 02 08 02 5A B8
2B:    FF 03 C0 21 01 01 00 0C 03 04 C0 23 07 02 08 02 5A B8
3B:    FF 03 C0 21 02 01 00 0C 03 04 C0 23 07 02 08 02 B4 3F
4A:    FF 03 C0 21 02 01 00 0C 03 04 C0 23 07 02 08 02 B4 3F
5A:    C0 23 01 01 00 12 05 50 65 65 72 41 07 41 53 65 63 72 65
       74 6D CE
6B:    C0 23 01 01 00 12 05 50 65 65 72 42 07 42 53 65 63 72 65
       74 04 B0
7B:    C0 23 02 01 00 17 12 50 65 72 6D 69 73 73 69 6F 6E 20 67
       72 61 6E 74 65 64 EB 2D
8A:    C0 23 02 01 00 05 00 FD 30
9A:    80 21 01 01 00 0A 03 06 0A 01 00 01 96 51
10B:   80 21 01 01 00 0A 03 06 0A 02 00 05 D6 F8
11B:   80 21 02 01 00 0A 03 06 0A 01 00 01 FF 25
12A:   80 21 02 01 00 0A 03 06 0A 02 00 05 BF 8C
```

The notations "1A," "2B," and so on indicate the relative sequence of the message, and the identity of the sending peer (A or B). These references are used in the detailed decodings below.

The trace above assumes that both peers have reached Req-Sent state at the same time. If one peer reaches Req-Sent state before the other, its Configure-Request message is usually lost, and the exchange is somewhat easier to read than this example since each side will end up negotiating separately.

The first two messages (1A and 2B) are byte-for-byte identical. Decoded in detail, one of these messages is as follows.

```
1A:    LCP Configure-Request 1 [PAP PFC ACFC]
       FF 03 - HDLC Address and Control Field
       C0 21 - PPP Protocol field (LCP)
       01    - Configure Request
       01    - ID 1
       00 0C - Length 12 octets
       03    - Option 3 (Authentication Protocol)
       04    - Length 4 octets
       C0 23 - PAP
```

```
07     - Option 7 (Protocol Field Compression)
02     - Length 2 octets
08     - Option 8 (Address and Control Field Compression)
02     - Length 2 octets
5A B8  - CRC
```

The Configure-Request messages above are sent at nearly the same time in opposite directions on the link, one by peer A and one by peer B. At this point, LCP
on both peers is in Req-Sent state. When these messages arrive at the other end
of the link, both peers issue identical Configure-Ack messages, numbered 3B and
4A and shown below, and transition to Ack-Sent state.

```
3B:    LCP Configure-Ack 1 [PAP PFC ACFC]
       FF 03 - HDLC Address and Control Field
       C0 21 - PPP Protocol field (LCP)
       02    - Configure-Ack
       01    - ID 1
       00 0C - Length 12 octets
       03    - Option 3 (Authentication Protocol)
       04    - Length 4 octets
       C0 23 - PAP
       07    - Option 7 (Protocol Field Compression)
       02    - Length 2 octets
       08    - Option 8 (Address and Control Field Compression)
       02    - Length 2 octets
       B4 3F - CRC
```

These two messages pass each other in flight. On reception, both peers transition
LCP from Ack-Sent to Opened state, and send an "Up" event to security. The
security layer (PAP in this example) on both peers then sends an Authenticate-
Request and proceeds to Req-Sent state. Note that because the Address and
Control Field (ACFC) option was negotiated, these fields (normally FF 03) are
no longer present.

```
5A:    PAP Authenticate-Request 1 ["PeerA" "ASecret"]
       C0 23 - PPP Protocol field (PAP)
       01    - Authenticate-Request
       01    - ID 1
```

```
            00 12 - Length 18 octets
            05    - Name length is 5 octets
            50 65 65 72 41 - Peer name is "PeerA"
            07    - Password length is 7 octets
            41 53 65 63 72 65 74 - Password is "ASecret"
            6D CE - CRC

  6B:       PAP Authenticate-Request 1 ["PeerB" "BSecret"]
            C0 23 - PPP Protocol field (PAP)
            01    - Authenticate-Request
            01    - ID 1
            00 12 - Length 18 octets
            05    - Name length is 5 octets
            50 65 65 72 42 - Peer name is "PeerB"
            07    - Password length is 7 octets
            42 53 65 63 72 65 74 - Password is "BSecret"
            04 B0 - CRC
```

On reception of these messages, each peer verifies the identity of the peer, sends an Authenticate-Ack message, and proceeds to Ack-Sent state. Note that peer B chooses to send a friendly "Permission Granted" string, while peer A chooses simply to acknowledge the identity of the peer. These are, of course, equivalent from the point of view of the protocol.

```
  7B:       PAP Authenticate-Ack 1 ["Permission Granted"]
            C0 23 - PPP Protocol field (PAP)
            02    - Authenticate-Ack
            01    - ID 1
            00 17 - Length 23 octets
            12    - Message Length is 18 octets
            50 65 72 6d 69 73 73 69 6F 6E 20 67 72 61 6E 74 65 64
                  - Message "Permission Granted"
            EB 2D - CRC

  8A:       PAP Authenticate-Ack 1
            C0 23 - PPP Protocol field (PAP)
            02    - Authenticate-Ack
            01    - ID 1
```

```
00 05 - Length 5 octets
00    - Message Length is 0 octets (no message)
FD 30 - CRC
```

On reception of the two messages above, both peers change PAP to the Opened state. Note that if only one side is authenticating the other (this is not a recommended configuration, although it is quite common in commercial dial-up systems), the side that is demanding authentication starts off in Ack-Rcvd state and the side that is providing its identity (peer name and password) starts off in Ack-Sent state.

Both peers now send Up events to all of the NCP state machines. In this example, only IPCP is being used, so each side transitions IPCP to Req-Sent state and sends an IPCP Configure-Request message.

```
9A:    IPCP Configure-Request 1 [10.1.0.1]
       80 21 - PPP Protocol field (IPCP)
       01    - Configure-Request
       01    - ID 1
       00 0A - Length 10 octets
       03    - Option 3 (IP Address)
       06    - Length 6 octets
       0A 01 00 01 - Address 10.1.0.1
       96 51 - CRC

10B:   IPCP Configure-Request 1 [10.2.0.5]
       80 21 - PPP Protocol field (IPCP)
       01    - Configure-Request
       01    - ID 1
       00 0A - Length 10 octets
       03    - Option 3 (IP-Address)
       06    - Length 6 octets
       0A 02 00 05 - Address 10.2.0.5
       D6 F8 - CRC
```

On reception of these messages, both peers transition IPCP to Ack-Sent state, and send the following messages.

```
11B:   IPCP Configure-Ack 1 [10.1.0.1]
       80 21 - PPP Protocol field (IPCP)
```

```
                02    - Configure-Ack
                01    - ID 1
                00 0A - Length 10 octets
                03    - Option 3 (IP-Address)
                06    - Length 6 octets
                0A 01 00 01 - Address 10.1.0.1
                FF 25 - CRC

      12A:      IPCP Configure-Ack 1 [10.2.0.5]
                80 21 - PPP Protocol field (IPCP)
                02    - Configure-Ack
                01    - ID 1
                00 0A - Length 10 octets
                03    - Option 3 (IP-Address)
                06    - Length 6 octets
                0A 02 00 05 - Address 10.2.0.5
                BF 8C - CRC
```

On reception of these two messages, IPCP is transitioned to Opened state by both peers, and the IP network layer is notified that it can now begin sending data.

Multiple Protocols

With multiple protocols in use, the interleaving of the messages becomes more complex. In this example, peer A supports IP, IPX, and CCP, while peer B supports IP, IPX, AppleTalk, and MP. The authentication is bidirectional using standard CHAP, and parameter negotiation is required due to the configuration.

```
      1A:    FF 03 C0 21 01 01 00 13 02 06 00 0A 00 00 03 05 C2 23 05
             07 02 08 02 00 18
      2B:    FF 03 C0 21 01 01 00 1B 01 04 05 F4 03 05 C2 23 05 05 06
             11 26 55 10 07 02 08 02 11 04 05 DC EB AE
      3B:    FF 03 C0 21 03 01 00 0A 02 06 10 0A 00 00 CD 93
      4A:    FF 03 C0 21 04 01 00 0E 05 06 11 26 55 10 11 04 05 DC 90
             AD
      5A:    FF 03 C0 21 01 02 00 13 02 06 10 0A 00 00 03 05 C2 23 05
             07 02 08 02 E8 43
```

```
 6B:    FF 03 C0 21 01 02 00 11 01 04 05 F4 03 05 C2 23 05 07 02
        08 02 66 45
 7B:    FF 03 C0 21 02 02 00 13 02 06 10 0A 00 00 03 05 C2 23 05
        07 02 08 02 22 FE
 8A:    FF 03 C0 21 02 02 00 11 01 04 05 F4 03 05 C2 23 05 07 02
        08 02 77 75
 9A:    C2 23 01 01 00 1A 10 C7 C8 3D BE 83 5F 84 D9 DA 55 29 61
        87 E6 90 1C 50 65 65 72 41 19 FE
10B:    C2 23 01 01 00 1A 10 FC 93 B0 B3 81 AD B3 41 63 22 A2 71
        41 F7 8A D3 50 65 65 72 42 C5 A3
11B:    C2 23 02 01 00 1A 10 6B ED CC 2D 05 7A DF 6D BC C5 03 F6
        3C 5B 75 DD 50 65 65 72 42 26 CF
12A:    C2 23 02 01 00 1A 10 80 3E 61 29 D1 33 F2 CA F3 B0 9A 63
        BA 2E 0C F3 50 65 65 72 41 54 47
13A:    C2 23 03 01 00 0B 57 65 6C 63 6F 6D 65 A3 5A
14B:    C2 23 03 01 00 09 48 65 6C 6C 6F A4 CA
15B:    80 21 01 01 00 10 02 06 00 2D 0F 01 03 06 84 F5 0B 0A 29
        8E
16B:    80 2B 01 01 00 1A 01 06 00 00 00 33 03 06 00 02 0F 00 05
        08 53 45 52 56 45 52 06 02 9E EF
17B:    80 29 01 01 00 15 01 06 00 17 E8 9B 07 05 6D 61 63 08 06
        00 17 D4 16 D3 B0
18A:    80 21 01 01 00 0A 03 06 00 00 00 00 6D C6
19A:    80 2B 01 01 00 0A 01 06 00 00 00 00 B3 D9
20A:    80 FD 01 01 00 0F 11 05 00 01 04 12 06 00 00 00 01 D9 A9
21A:    80 21 04 01 00 0A 02 06 00 2D 0F 01 F8 30
22A:    80 2B 02 01 00 1A 01 06 00 00 00 33 03 06 00 02 0F 00 05
        08 53 45 52 56 45 52 06 02 7F B0
23A:    FF 03 C0 21 08 03 00 1B 80 29 01 01 00 15 01 06 00 17 E8
        9B 07 05 6D 61 63 08 06 00 17 D4 16 94 81
24B:    80 21 03 01 00 0A 03 06 84 F5 0B D1 84 57
25B:    80 2B 03 01 00 0A 01 06 00 00 00 33 E5 82
26B:    FF 03 C0 21 08 03 00 15 80 FD 01 01 00 0F 11 05 00 01 04
        12 06 00 00 00 01 9D 81
27B:    80 21 01 02 00 0A 03 06 84 F5 0B 0A 93 B1
28A:    80 21 01 02 00 0A 03 06 84 F5 0B D1 CD D9
29A:    80 2B 01 02 00 0C 01 06 00 00 00 33 06 02 A9 10
30A:    80 21 02 02 00 0A 03 06 84 F5 0B 0A FA C5
```

```
31B:    80 21 02 02 00 0A 03 06 84 F5 0B D1 A4 AD
32B:    80 2B 02 02 00 0C 01 06 00 00 00 33 06 02 47 97
```

Unlike the simple IP exchange above, a terser decoding is provided for this example.

```
 1A:    LCP Configure-Request ID 1 [ACCM 000A0000 CHAP PFC ACFC]
 2B:    LCP Configure-Request ID 1 [MRU 1524 CHAP Magic 11265510
                                    PFC ACFC MP-MRRU 1500]
 3B:    LCP Configure-Nak ID 1 [ACCM 100A0000]
 4A:    LCP Configure-Reject ID 1 [Magic 11265510 MP-MRRU 1500]
 5A:    LCP Configure-Request ID 2 [ACCM 100A0000 CHAP PFC ACFC]
 6B:    LCP Configure-Request ID 2 [MRU 1524 CHAP PFC ACFC]
 7B:    LCP Configure-Ack ID 2 [ACCM 100A0000 CHAP PFC ACFC]
 8A:    LCP Configure-Ack ID 2 [MRU 1524 CHAP PFC ACFC]
 9A:    CHAP Challenge 1 [rand1 "PeerA"]
10B:    CHAP Challenge 1 [rand2 "PeerBv"]
11B:    CHAP Response 1 [MD5(1,secret-ab2,rand1) "PeerBv"]
12A:    CHAP Response 1 [MD5(1,secret-ba1,rand2) "PeerA"]
13A:    CHAP Success 1 ["Welcome"]
14B:    CHAP Success 1 ["Hello"]
```

Note that any well-configured PPP system using CHAP will have at least two secrets if calls can be made in only one direction, and will have four secrets if either peer may call the other. In this case, "secret-ab2" is peer B's secret used to authenticate itself to peer A when peer A has initiated the call, and "secret-ba1" is peer A's secret used to authenticate itself to peer B when peer A has initiated the call. The other two secrets for this link, secret-ab1 and secret-ba2, are not used in this example, but would be used if peer B had called peer A.

The function "MD5" above is the MD5 hash of the ID field (the byte 01 in the example above), the secret, and the challenge value (the random number supplied by the peer). This is the standard CHAP response value calculation specified in RFC 1994. Of course, rand1 and rand2 are random challenge values.

Now that security is complete, both sides send an "Up" message from the authentication layer to the NCPs chosen for the link. These NCPs then send Configure-Request messages. The following six messages, three from B and three from A, are likely to be sent nearly simultaneously by both sides. Peer B is requesting use of IP, IPX, and AppleTalk, while peer A is requesting IP, IPX, and

CCP. Peer A does not have its network-layer addresses configured, so it specifies these as zero to request that peer B supply them, and, for IPXCP, it leaves off the option 6 flag, since it does not want the peer to bring up the link if it would agree to this number. (Note that if peer A could "hear" the Configure-Request from peer B for IPXCP before sending its own Configure-Request, it should pick up the network number specified in that message rather than sending zero. Since these messages are sent out nearly simultaneously, that does not happen in this case.)

```
15B:    IPCP Configure-Request 1 [VJComp 15/1 132.245.11.10]
16B:    IPXCP Configure-Request 1 [Net 33 Telebit 15/0 "SERVER"
                                     complete]
17B:    ATCP Configure-Request 1 [6120.155 "mac" rtr 6100.22]
18A:    IPCP Configure-Request 1 [0.0.0.0]
19A:    IPXCP Configure-Request 1 [Net 0]
20A:    CCP Configure-Request 1 [STAC mode 4, MPPC]
```

On reception of the messages above, both sides must decide on appropriate replies. In this case, peer A does not want to do VJ header compression (21A) or AppleTalk (23A). It also completely agrees with the parameters sent for IPXCP by peer B. It thus transitions IPXCP to Ack-Sent state and sends a Configure-Ack message, and leaves both IPCP and CCP in Req-Sent state.

Peer B detects the zero addresses in the IPCP and IPXCP messages, so it sends Configure-Nak for each with the appropriate addresses. It does not recognize CCP, so it sends a Protocol-Reject for this. All three NCPs (IPCP, IPXCP, and ATCP) are left in Req-Sent state. (The Protocol-Reject ID numbers are 3, since the last LCP message sent by each—the Configure-Ack—had ID 2.)

```
21A:    IPCP Configure-Reject 1 [VJ Comp 15/1]
22A:    IPXCP Configure-Ack 1 [Net 33 Telebit 15/0 "SERVER"
                                 complete]
23A:    LCP Protocol-Reject 3 [8029; ATCP]
24B:    IPCP Configure-Nak 1 [132.245.11.209]
25B:    IPXCP Configure-Nak 1 [Net 33]
26B:    LCP Protocol-Reject 3 [80FD; CCP]
```

When these messages are received, peer B turns off VJ header compression in IPCP and generates a new Configure-Request. IPXCP is transitioned to Ack-Rcvd state, ATCP is transitioned to Closed state, and IPCP is still in Req-Sent state.

Peer A updates its IP address based on the Configure-Nak message from peer B and resends Configure-Request. IPCP stays in Req-Sent state. IPXCP resends its Configure-Request message based on the network number learned from peer B's Configure-Request (remember: there is only one IPX network number for a given link) and the match received in the Configure-Nak message. IPXCP stays in Ack-Sent state. CCP is transitioned to Closed state.

```
27B:     IPCP Configure-Request 2 [132.245.11.10]
28A:     IPCP Configure-Request 2 [132.245.11.209]
29A:     IPXCP Configure-Request 2 [Net 33 complete]
```

Peer A agrees to the IP address sent by peer B, so it transitions IPCP to Ack-Sent state and sends Configure-Ack. IPXCP is left in Ack-Sent state. Peer B agrees to the IP address and the IPXCP network number sent by peer A, so it transitions IPCP to Ack-Sent state and IPXCP to Opened state and sends Configure-Ack messages.

```
30A:     IPCP Configure-Ack 2 [132.245.11.10]
31B:     IPCP Configure-Ack 2 [132.245.11.209]
32B:     IPXCP Configure-Ack 2 [Net 33 complete]
```

Finally, peer B receives the IPCP Configure-Ack message from peer A and transitions IPCP to Opened state. Peer A receives the Configure-Ack messages for IPCP and IPXCP and transitions each to Opened state.

Negotiation is now complete, with IPCP and IPXCP open and ATCP and CCP closed. The reader should note here that, although a total of 32 messages have been sent, the negotiation above should happen rapidly on well-designed PPP implementations. In each round, the messages sent are triggered by reception of the peer's message, and not by a time-out, and there are only 11 exchanges of messages. Since the messages are short, the time of transmission is likely for most media to be dominated by the delay across the link for each burst of messages instead of the message size divided by the actual bit rate. Thus, the total negotiation time in this rather complex case is just 11 times the link delay.[1] On a V.34

---

1. Link delay, also called latency, is not the same as throughput. The two are completely unrelated. Latency measures the time required for a given bit to traverse the system between two known points. Throughput measures the number of bits per second that can be sent across the link per unit of time. The product of these two is the number of bits in flight at one time.

modem, for instance, the total time is well under 1 second, which is dwarfed by the typical 2-to-3-second call set-up time through the telephone switches and the 15-to-20-second modem negotiation time.

A technically illegal, although very interesting, optimization is possible here that will reduce this time still further. To do this, it is necessary for each peer to know in advance what the other will send, which is practical for some installations. Each peer precalculates its side of the entire exchange and sends it all as one burst, resulting in only a single link delay for the entire negotiation. The "technically illegal" part of this trick is that a PPP implementation that follows RFC 1661 closely should not be sending Configure-Request for the next layer before the current layer is up. In the best case, this will very quickly establish the link. In the worst case, even if the predicted value of the CHAP Challenge is wrong or if the peer will not cooperate with this trick, the extra messages will be silently dropped, and both peers can fall back to an LCP or Authentication layer time-out to continue standard negotiation. See Fast Reconnect on page 125 for a more complete description of this technique.

Network Data

Once the link is up, network-layer data will be sent over it. In general, the encapsulation is just 1 or 2 bytes of PPP protocol number followed by the raw network-layer information. For example, a complete IP packet from an Ethernet network is shown in Figure 9.1. That same packet, as sent over a PPP link with both Address and Control Field and Protocol Field compression enabled is shown in Figure 9.2.

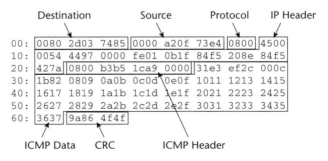

FIGURE 9.1 IP packet from Ethernet

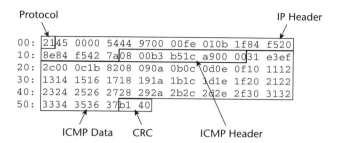

FIGURE 9.2 IP packet sent over PPP

Chapters 5 and 11 contain references to other books that cover these upper-level protocols, such as IP and ICMP, in detail. In particular, I recommend W. Richard Stevens' *TCP/IP Illustrated*.

For reference, IP, TCP, and UDP headers are shown (without explanation) in Figure 9.3. Each line represents 32 bits (four octets).

Ver	IHL	DSCP	CU	Total Length		
Identification			0 D M	Fragment Offset		
Time to Live		Protocol		Header Checksum		
Source Address						
Destination Address						

IPv4 Header (RFCs 791 and 2474)

Source Port						Destination Port
Sequence Number						
Acknowledgment Number						
Offset	Reserved	U	A	P	R	S	F	Window
Checksum						Urgent Pointer

TCP Header (RFC 793)

Source Port	Destination Port
Length	Checksum

UDP Header (RFC 768)

FIGURE 9.3 Standard TCP/IP headers

MP, CCP, and ECP

These protocols do not change the basic nature of negotiation as shown in the examples above, but they do make it more difficult to follow. In particular, after MP is negotiated by sending MRRU at LCP time and then going through authentication, most implementations send all messages with MP headers over all of the links. Thus, in order to debug an MP link using external monitors, it is necessary to watch all of the data on all of the member links, even during NCP negotiation. Another oddity is that each link has its own LCP and Authentication layers, but the bundle has only one set of common NCPs. Thus, a lost CHAP Success message, for instance, may cause the loss of any MP fragments on that link and can cause the CHAP Response to be resent after a time-out. This CHAP Response is generated by a CHAP state machine that is local to the link, but the MP fragments seen on the link (and dropped) may contain NCP negotiations, which are global to the MP bundle. And, of course, if LCP renegotiates, the link leaves the bundle and the LCP negotiation is done with the link's individual copy of LCP.

With CCP and ECP, the decoding of each packet depends on the successful decoding of prior packets and, to a small degree, on knowing which packets may have been lost by the peer. This makes the job of tracing a link using these protocols very difficult. In general, if the trace is taken at an arbitrary point during the life of the link (say, perhaps, at the start of some detected failure condition), instead of at the start of the link, it usually cannot be decoded. This means that tracing an intermittent failure with these protocols requires either storage of the entire history of the link or a method of storing only the data since the last Reset-Ack message.

Here is how the packet from Figures 9.1 and 9.2 might be fragmented for transmission over two links using MP with the Short-Sequence-Number option enabled. The first fragment has the "B" (begin) bit set, sequence number 0, the first 43 octets of the original packet, and its own CRC.

```
3d 80 00 21 45 00 00 54 44 97 00 00 fe 01 0b 1f 84 f5
20 8e 84 f5 42 7a 08 00 b3 b5 1c a9 00 00 31 e3 ef 2c
00 0c 1b 82 08 09 0a 0b 0c 0d 79 6d
```

The second fragment has the "E" (end) bit set, sequence number 1, the last 42 octets, and another CRC.

```
3d 40 01 0e 0f 10 11 12 13 14 15 16 17 18 19 1a 1b 1c
1d 1e 1f 20 21 22 23 24 25 26 27 28 29 2a 2b 2c 2d 2e
2f 30 31 32 33 34 35 36 37 3e 4c
```

Decoding this is as simple as pasting together all of the sequentially numbered fragments between the one with the B bit set and the one with the E bit set. Note that this presents problems for some real-time analyzers that decode each packet individually, since fragments other than the first one do not have any indication of the next layer protocol in use.

Appearance of Packets on Various Media

If you are examining PPP data at the lowest level, perhaps using an oscilloscope, you should know that most communications hardware, such as standard synchronous interfaces and asynchronous RS-232, present the data bits in backward order, with the LSB first. So, to read these data from the screen, you need to read the bits from right to left and the octets from left to right. Also remember that, on asynchronous links, LCP negotiation of the ACCM parameter alters the escaping of transmitted data when LCP reaches Opened state. This issue does not exist on synchronous lines.

If you are examining data from a synchronous hardware interface, it is commonly the case, although not always, that the hardware will verify and remove the CRC automatically and that the CRC will not appear in the data received. This is usually true on PC-based synchronous cards. On most synchronous hardware, this is a selectable feature that can be controlled through configuration registers.

Getting Traces from Common PPP Software

Usually, debugging is done by reading logs provided by the PPP software packages or by use of specialized hardware. This section presents a few of the more common PPP implementations and the logging information they provide. This is not intended to be a comprehensive list of available PPP implementations, nor does it show everything that can be done with each implementation. Readers may want to view these logs, however, to get a feel for what to expect when debugging, and implementors in particular may wish to see various techniques for logging in order to choose their favorites.

Some of the examples below are long and difficult to read. In the longer traces, the important pieces to examine are given in **boldface** type. See also Chapter 11, which has pointers to sites carrying this software and various on-line help texts, and the accompanying CD-ROM.

Unix Systems

ppp-2.3

Also known as pppd, ppp-2.3 is a very high quality, freely available implementation of PPP that runs on most standard Unix systems. It is the result of the efforts of many people, but has been released and maintained by Paul Mackerras at the Australian National University Department of Computer Science. For more information about ppp-2.3, see Chapter 10.

There are two pieces that users must deal with. First, the chat mechanism dials the telephone through the modem, and then PPP negotiates. Both of these steps can cause trouble. To debug either of them, you must first properly configure syslogd on your system to log debug-level messages to a file. This is highly system specific but often consists of placing lines such as those below in /etc/syslog.conf.

```
daemon.debug        /var/log/debug
local2.debug        /var/log/debug
```

After setting this up, the named log file must exist (use touch if it doesn't) and syslogd must be sent a SIGHUP to reread its configuration.

The chat utility has a "-v" switch on it to enable verbose logging via syslog facility local2, while the pppd daemon has a "debug" option to enable its logging. Usually, it is wise to enable both, as with

```
pppd debug connect 'chat -vf /users/carlson/.chatrc'
```

The chat logs look like this:

```
Aug 11 19:21:52 madison chat[16014]: send (^M)
Aug 11 19:21:52 madison chat[16014]: send (atdt1-508-555-1212^M)
```

```
Aug 11 19:21:53 madison chat[16014]: expect (CONNECT)
Aug 11 19:22:19 madison chat[16014]: ^Matdt1-508-555-1212^M^M
Aug 11 19:22:19 madison chat[16014]: CONNECT -- got it
Aug 11 19:22:19 madison chat[16014]: expect (sername:)
Aug 11 19:22:19 madison chat[16014]:  38400/V32b 14400/V42b^M
```

By examining both the messages presented and the timing, it is usually possible to determine any kind of chatting failure. Typically, when chat fails, it is the result of having not received the expected response string from the peer. It will hang for an extended period, then time out at 45 seconds by default. This appears in the logs as follows.

```
Apr 26 11:53:00 madison chat[13702]: expect (sername:)
Apr 26 11:53:45 madison chat[13702]: alarm
Apr 26 11:53:45 madison chat[13702]: Failed
Apr 26 11:53:45 madison pppd[17540]: Connect script failed
Apr 26 11:53:45 madison pppd[17540]: Exit.
```

In many cases, you may need to use a terminal-mode dial-in program, such as kermit, miniterm, or cu, to verify that login on the target system is possible and that PPP will run on that system.

The chat script is sometimes a difficult-to-write piece of the system. I have used the following example to dial into an ISP's Annex terminal server.

```
ABORT BUSY
ABORT 'NO CARRIER'
REPORT CONNECT
"" ""
"" "atdt1-508-555-1212"
CONNECT \c
TIMEOUT 3 sername:--sername: carlson
ssword: \qbigsecret
nnex: ppp
```

This somewhat odd style ("ssword:" instead of the expected "Password:") is common in chat scripts. Omitting one or two of the initial characters makes the script more reliable in case of communications errors. The \q code in front of the password means that it should not be logged via syslog when debugging is enabled.

This script is almost certainly wrong for your application. Most ISPs require the script to end with the CONNECT string, as follows.

```
ABORT BUSY
ABORT 'NO CARRIER'
REPORT CONNECT
"" ""
"" "atdt1-508-555-1212"
CONNECT \d\c
```

If you see something like the following in your log, the peer is already in PPP mode but the chat script has not terminated correctly. It is likely that the chat script is waiting for some string for which it should not be waiting.

```
Apr 20 16:36:04 madison chat[15420]: ~^?}#@!}!}!} }4}"}&} } } }
```

Once chat has run successfully, pppd begins negotiating with the peer. An annotated log of a pppd session can be found at the end of Chapter 8. Once the link is up, the pppstats utility can be used to display link statistics.

```
% pppstats
    in   pack  comp uncomp   err |   out  pack  comp uncomp    ip
   330    17      0      0     0 |     0    15     0      0    15
     0     0      0      0     0 |     0     0     0      0     0
```

An extension to pppd is available that supports MS-CHAP. See the README.MSCHAP80 file in the pppd-2.3 distribution or the resources in Chapter 11. If you use this extension to connect to an NT system, remember that your local name entered in the chap-secrets file will actually be the combined NT domain and user name (which must also be specified with the "name" option) and the remote peer name entered will be the name you assign for that system using the "remotename" option (this name is arbitrary, but must be present, since NT does not identify itself). If you are being called by an NT or 95 system, the reverse is true. For example, put the following in chap-secrets to call an NT system that demands MS-CHAP from you.

```
ntdomain\\username remotenamehere userpassword
```

dp

dp is a variant of pppd that supports dial-on-demand links on Solaris and SunOS systems. The extensions that permit dial-on-demand operation have not been ported to other Unix systems as of this writing.

xisp

xisp is a graphical interface for configuring pppd.

Unix Vendor PPP Implementations

AIX

This PPP system does not support much in the way of debugging syslog messages. The few messages that are given are fairly rudimentary. Here is an example from AIX 4.1.3.

```
Apr 20 17:33:39 madison pppattachd[18958]: starting attachment
    daemon
Apr 20 17:33:39 madison pppattachd[15376]: open /dev/tty0
Apr 20 17:34:36 madison pppattachd[15376]: attachd name
Apr 20 17:34:36 madison pppattachd[15376]: ctl msg badebe08
Apr 20 17:34:36 madison pppattachd[15376]:  attachment
    connection established
Apr 20 17:34:36 madison pppattachd[15376]: ctl msg badebe07
Apr 20 17:34:38 madison last message repeated 9 times
Apr 20 17:34:39 madison pppattachd[15376]: ctl msg badebe07
Apr 20 17:34:39 madison pppattachd[15376]: ctl msg badebe08
Apr 20 17:34:39 madison /usr/sbin/pppcontrold[19458]: msgid
    badebe01
Apr 20 17:34:39 madison /usr/sbin/pppcontrold[19458]: LOWERUP
    5dc
Apr 20 17:34:39 madison /usr/sbin/pppcontrold[19458]: msgid
    badebe03
```

```
Apr 20 17:34:39 madison /usr/sbin/pppcontrold[19458]: msgid
        badebe03
Apr 20 17:34:39 madison pppattachd[15376]: ctl msg badebe07
Apr 20 17:34:42 madison last message repeated 5 times
Apr 20 17:34:42 madison /usr/sbin/pppcontrold[19458]: msgid
        badebc03
Apr 20 17:34:42 madison /usr/sbin/pppcontrold[19458]:
        /etc/ifconfig pp0 132.245.11.229 132.245.11.106 netmask
        255.255.255.0 >/dev/null 2>&1
Apr 20 17:34:45 madison pppattachd[15376]: ctl msg badebe07
```

Here are a few syslog messages excerpted from AIX 4.2. These syslog messages have been improved here, but they are still insufficient to debug PPP itself.

```
Jul  1 16:36:49 lacroix /usr/sbin/pppcontrold[11720]: msgid
        badeb101
Jul  1 16:36:49 lacroix /usr/sbin/pppcontrold[11720]: DEMAND
        REQUEST  0 / etc/ppp/dial_out.rhesus
Jul  1 16:36:49 lacroix pppattachd[14690]: Str 0 converted 0
Jul  1 16:36:49 lacroix pppattachd[14690]: starting attachment
        daemon
Jul  1 16:36:49 lacroix pppattachd[14690]: open /dev/tty0
Jul  1 16:36:49 lacroix pppdial[12134]: send (at^M)
Jul  1 16:36:49 lacroix pppdial[12134]: expect (OK)
Jul  1 16:36:49 lacroix pppdial[12134]: O CARRIER^M
Jul  1 16:36:50 lacroix pppdial[12134]: at^M^M
Jul  1 16:36:50 lacroix pppdial[12134]: OK -- got it
Jul  1 16:36:50 lacroix pppdial[12134]: send (atdt9,2364104^M)
Jul  1 16:36:50 lacroix pppdial[12134]: expect (CONNECT)
Jul  1 16:36:50 lacroix pppdial[12134]: ^M
Jul  1 16:36:50 lacroix /usr/sbin/pppcontrold[11720]: msgid
        badeb101
```

AIX does, however, have a sophisticated kernel debugging mechanism that can be used to debug PPP connections once the chat file has been modified to establish a link correctly (this script is usually /etc/ppp/dial_out.system, which is entered in the "Demand Command" section of the PPP demand interface configuration menu in smit).

To invoke kernel tracing, run "smit trace" and enable hooks 2AB, 2AC, 2AD, and 2AE (leave the "EVENT GROUPS" blank and enter these as "ADDITIONAL EVENTS"). Stop tracing once the interface has run and failed. Then start with "trcrpt -Oids=off -d2AE" to produce the following.

```
ELAPSED_SEC    DELTA_MSEC    APPL    SYSCALL KERNEL   INTERRUPT


25.044231168*                               PPP DATA lcp_send data
                                            protocol=C021 Conf-req id=0001
                                            01 04 05 DC 02 06 00 00 00 00 0
25.332675712*                               PPP DATA lcp_input data
                                            protocol=C021 Conf-req id=0001
                                            02 06 00 00 00 00 03 04 C0 23 0
25.332828160*                               PPP DATA lcp_send data
                                            protocol=C021 Conf-Rej id=0001
                                            13 0B 05 33 31 33 32 33 33 33 3
25.621775744*                               PPP DATA lcp_input data
                                            protocol=C021 Conf-req id=0002
                                            02 06 00 00 00 00 03 04 C0 23 0
25.621921408*                               PPP DATA lcp_send data
                                            protocol=C021 Conf-ACK id=0002
                                            02 06 00 00 00 00 03 04 C0 23 0
28.044558976*                               PPP DATA lcp_send data
                                            protocol=C021 Conf-req id=0001
                                            01 04 05 DC 02 06 00 00 00 00 0
28.358268672*                               PPP DATA lcp_input data
                                            protocol=C021 Conf-ACK id=0001
                                            01 04 05 DC 02 06 00 00 00 00 0
29.341080448*                               PPP DATA ipcp_send data
                                            protocol=8021 Conf-req id=0001
                                            03 06 84 F5 42 79 02 06 00 2D 0
29.436894208*                               PPP DATA lcp_send data
                                            protocol=C021 Protocol-Rej id=02
                                            80 FD 01 03 00 07 15 03 29
29.771947520*                               PPP DATA ipcp_input data
                                            protocol=8021 Conf-req id=0004
                                            03 06 84 F5 42 7C
```

The other trace IDs besides 2AE allow you to capture other events inside the system, such as HDLC errors (2AC), TCP/IP interface events (2AB), and the protocol multiplexing information (2AD).

Solaris

The SunSoft Solaris PPP daemon, called aspppd, writes a log file called /etc/asppp.log. This file contains information about the demand-dialing interface and the PPP negotiation.

Before it is configured, you are likely to see logs such as:

```
09:48:09 Link manager (99) started 03/03/97
09:48:09 parse_config_file: no paths defined in /etc/asppp.cf
09:48:09 parse_config_file: Errors in configuration file
         /etc/asppp.cf
09:48:09 Link manager (99) exited 03/03/97
```

The PPP parameter configuration is done in a file called /etc/asppp.cf. This file has entries that look like the example below, which is set up to dial into a system named "rhesus" with a local user name of "carlson" and password "notmine."

```
ifconfig ipdptp0 plumb carlson rhesus up
path
        interface ipdptp0
        peer_system_name rhesus
        will_do_authentication pap
        pap_id carlson
        pap_password notmine
        negotiate_address on
        debug_level 9
```

Notice that "will_do_authentication" is necessary even with the PAP credentials included in the entry. Without this configuration option, aspppd will reject PAP.

If you are dialing into an NT server, you will need to use PAP, but set the local user name to "NTDomain\\NTAccount" in the ifconfig line and the pap_id.

After inserting a path in the /etc/asppp.cf file, you may see the following. This indicates that you need to run the ifconfig utility manually to install the ipdptp0 interface. (The ifconfig command in the configuration file is run only at system start-up.)

```
14:09:13 Link manager (1605) started 04/29/97
14:09:13 parse_config_file: Successful configuration
14:09:13 register_interfaces: IPD_REGISTER failed
```

You will also need to set up at least /etc/uucp/Systems in order to get the dialer to make an outgoing call.

```
rhesus Any ACU 38400 19785551212
```

You can test the dialer itself by using the cu utility.

```
cu -dL rhesus
```

The following is an example of a fairly common connection failure. In this case, the dialing process is successful, but the remote end is not yet in PPP mode, so aspppd sends LCP Configure-Request, times out, sends it again, and repeats until a counter reaches its maximum value.

```
14:10:43 process_ipd_msg: ipdptp0 needs connection
conn(rhesus)
Trying entry from '/etc/uucp/Systems' - device type ACU.
Device Type ACU wanted
Trying device entry 'cua/b' from '/etc/uucp/Devices'.
processdev: calling setdevcfg(ppp, ACU)
fd_mklock: ok
fixline(8, 38400)
gdial(hayes) called
Trying caller script 'hayes' from '/etc/uucp/Dialers'.
expect: ("")
got it
sendthem (DELAY
APAUSE
TE1V1X1Q0S2=255S12=255^M<NO CR>)
```

```
expect: (OK^M)
ATE1V1X1Q0S2=255S12=255^M^M^JOK^Mgot it
sendthem (ECHO CHECK ON
A^JATTDDTT99,,22336644110044^M^M<NO CR>)
expect: (CONNECT)
^M^JCONNECTgot it
getto ret 8
call cleanup(0)


14:11:12 000001 ipdptp0 SEND PPP ASYNC 23 Octets LCP Config-Req
    ID=00 LEN=18 MRU=1500 MAG#=117a0953 ProtFCOMP AddrCCOMP
14:11:15 000002 ipdptp0 SEND PPP ASYNC 23 Octets LCP Config-Req
    ID=01 LEN=18 MRU=1500 MAG#=117a0953 ProtFCOMP AddrCCOMP
14:11:18 000003 ipdptp0 SEND PPP ASYNC 23 Octets LCP Config-Req
    ID=02 LEN=18 MRU=1500 MAG#=117a0953 ProtFCOMP AddrCCOMP
...
14:11:42 process_ppp_msg: PPP_ERROR_IND Maximum number of
    configure requests exceeded
14:11:43 000011 ipdptp0 PPP DIAG CLOSE
```

After correct configuration of the remote end to answer the call in PPP mode,
the log of a successful connection is as shown below. Note that although both
CCP and IPX are being rejected here, the trace is somewhat hard to follow
because the information in the protocol rejects does not include the actual PPP
protocol number being rejected.

```
14:12:46 process_ipd_msg: ipdptp0 needs connection
conn(rhesus)
Trying entry from '/etc/uucp/Systems' - device type ACU.
Device Type ACU wanted
Trying device entry 'cua/b' from '/etc/uucp/Devices'.
processdev: calling setdevcfg(ppp, ACU)
fd_mklock: ok
fixline(10, 38400)
gdial(hayes) called
Trying caller script 'hayes' from '/etc/uucp/Dialers'.
expect: ("")
got it
```

```
sendthem (DELAY
APAUSE
TE1V1X1Q0S2=255S12=255^M<NO CR>)
expect: (OK^M)
ATE1V1X1Q0S2=255S12=255^M^M^JOK^Mgot it
sendthem (ECHO CHECK ON
A^JATTDDTT99,,22336644110044^M^M<NO CR>)
expect: (CONNECT)
^M^JCONNECTgot it
getto ret 10
call cleanup(0)
```

```
14:13:14 000012 ipdptp0 PPP DIAG OPEN
14:13:14 000013 ipdptp0 SEND PPP ASYNC 23 Octets LCP Config-Req
     ID=0a LEN=18 MRU=1500 MAG#=aeacb38e ProtFCOMP AddrCCOMP
14:13:14 000014 ipdptp0 RECEIVE PPP ASYNC 23 Octets LCP
     Config-ACK  ID=0a LEN=18 MRU=1500 MAG#=aeacb38e ProtFCOMP
     AddrCCOMP
14:13:16 000015 ipdptp0 RECEIVE PPP ASYNC 38 Octets LCP
     Config-Req  ID=01 LEN=33 ACCM=00000000 Auth=PAP
     MAG#=a8a89d4f ProtFCOMP AddrCCOMP {Unknown OPTION=13 l=9}
14:13:16 000016 ipdptp0 SEND PPP ASYNC 18 Octets LCP Config-REJ
     ID=01 LEN=13 {Unknown OPTION=13 l=9}
14:13:16 000017 ipdptp0 RECEIVE PPP ASYNC 29 Octets LCP
     Config-Req  ID=02 LEN=24 ACCM=00000000 Auth=PAP
     MAG#=a8a89d4f ProtFCOMP AddrCCOMP
14:13:16 000018 ipdptp0 SEND PPP ASYNC 29 Octets LCP
     Config-ACK ID=02 LEN=24 ACCM=00000000 Auth=PAP
     MAG#=a8a89d4f ProtFCOMP AddrCCOMP
14:13:16 000019 ipdptp0 SEND PPP ASYNC 25 Octets AuthPAP
     Authenticate  ID=01 LEN=20 Peer-ID-Length= 7 Peer-ID:
     63 61 72 6c 73 6f 6e Passwd-Length= 7 Passwd: 6e 6f
     74 6d 69 6e 65
14:13:19 000020 ipdptp0 SEND PPP ASYNC 25 Octets AuthPAP
     Authenticate  ID=02 LEN=20 Peer-ID-Length= 7 Peer-ID:
     63 61 72 6c 73 6f 6e Passwd-Length= 7 Passwd: 6e 6f
     74 6d 69 6e 65
```

```
14:13:20 000021 ipdptp0 RECEIVE PPP ASYNC 10 Octets AuthPAP
     Auth ACK  ID=02 LEN=5 Msg-Length= 0
14:13:20 000022 ipdptp0 SEND PPP ASYNC 21 Octets IP_NCP
     Config-Req  ID=0b LEN=16 VJCOMP MAXSID=15 Sid-comp-OK
     IPADDR=132.245.66.121
14:13:20 000023 ipdptp0 RECEIVE PPP ASYNC 19 Octets
     {Unrecognized protocol: 80fd }
14:13:20 000024 ipdptp0 SEND PPP ASYNC 25 Octets LCP Proto-REJ
     ID=0c LEN=20 Rej_proto=103 Rej_info: 01 03 00 0e 01 02 11
     05 00 01 03 15 03 2c
```

The two logs above show that the peer attempted to negotiate CCP (protocol 80fd). This Solaris system doesn't support CCP, so it sends an LCP Protocol Reject to shut it down.

```
14:13:20 000025 ipdptp0 RECEIVE PPP ASYNC 15 Octets IP_NCP
     Config-Req  ID=04 LEN=10 IPADDR=132.245.66.124
14:13:20 000026 ipdptp0 SEND PPP ASYNC 15 Octets IP_NCP
     Config-ACK  ID=04 LEN=10 IPADDR=132.245.66.124
14:13:21 000027 ipdptp0 RECEIVE PPP ASYNC 37 Octets IPX_NCP
14:13:21 000028 ipdptp0 RECEIVE PPP ASYNC 15 Octets IP_NCP
     Config-REJ  ID=0b LEN=10 VJCOMP MAXSID=15 Sid-comp-OK
14:13:21 000029 ipdptp0 SEND PPP ASYNC 43 Octets LCP Proto-REJ
     ID=0d LEN=38 Rej_proto=105 Rej_info: 01 05 00 20 01 06
     00 00 00 00 02 08 00 80 2d 05 4a bb 04 04 00 02 05 0a
     4c 4d 30 35 34 41 42 42
```

In this case, the two boldface log messages show the arrival of an IPXCP negotiation message and the reply with LCP Protocol-Reject. Unlike the CCP case, the Solaris system recognizes IPXCP (and may even support it), but it has been administratively disabled for this user and thus must be disabled.

```
14:13:21 000030 ipdptp0 SEND PPP ASYNC 19 Octets IP_NCP
     Config-Req  ID=0e LEN=14 OLD_VJCOMP IPADDR=132.245.66.121
14:13:21 000031 ipdptp0 RECEIVE PPP ASYNC 13 Octets IP_NCP
     Config-REJ  ID=0e LEN=8 OLD_VJCOMP
14:13:21 000032 ipdptp0 SEND PPP ASYNC 15 Octets IP_NCP
     Config-Req  ID=0f LEN=10 IPADDR=132.245.66.121
```

```
14:13:21 000033 ipdptp0 RECEIVE PPP ASYNC 15 Octets IP_NCP
    Config-ACK  ID=0f LEN=10 IPADDR=132.245.66.121
14:13:21 start_ip: IP up on interface ipdptp0, timeout set
    for 120 seconds
14:13:39 000034 ipdptp0 SEND PPP ASYNC 89 Octets IP_PROTO
14:13:39 000035 ipdptp0 RECEIVE PPP ASYNC 89 Octets IP_PROTO
14:13:56 000036 ipdptp0 SEND PPP ASYNC 89 Octets IP_PROTO
14:13:56 000037 ipdptp0 RECEIVE PPP ASYNC 89 Octets IP_PROTO
```

The last four logs above show ICMP Echo and ICMP Echo-Reply messages (from "ping").

IRIX

Because the ppp program on IRIX can use the UUCP control files, the best way to install a PPP connection is first to install a simple UUCP connection. So, one first creates appropriate entries in the /etc/uucp/Dialers, the /etc/uucp/Devices, and the /etc/uucp/Systems files and then "debugs" the connection with "cu -d remotesystem." (*Note:* Do not attempt to debug an ISDN connection with cu; cu is not supported with internal ISDN adapters.) For example, you might have the following.

```
/etc/uucp/Systems
    rhesus Any ACU 38400 9,2364104
/etc/uucp/Devices
    ACU ttyf2 null 38400 212 x hayes24
/etc/ppp.conf
    rhesus      remotehost=rhesus
                uucp_name=rhesus
                send_username=irix
                send_passwd=irix-test
                debug=4
                -del_route
```

To debug the PPP connection itself, start with -dddd on the command line or with debug=4 in the /etc/ppp.conf file. Start with a configuration such as the one shown above. If dial-on-demand is desired, add the keyword quiet to the ppp.conf file once a nailed-up connection has been debugged.

The configuration above was run with ppp -r rhesus. Shown below is an excerpt from the syslogs generated when the IP address is configured incorrectly.

```
Jul  2 16:11:43 3D:itra-irix6 ppp[13583]: rhesus AUTH1:
     receive PAP Ack ID=0x7d containing ""
Jul  2 16:11:43 3D:itra-irix6 ppp[13583]: rhesus 1:
     entering Network Phase
Jul  2 16:11:43 3D:itra-irix6 ppp[13583]: rhesus  LCP1:
     set async,acomp=1,pcomp=1,rx_ACCM=0,tx=0,pad=0
Jul  2 16:11:43 3D:itra-irix6 ppp[13583]: rhesus IPCP1:
     event Open
Jul  2 16:11:43 3D:itra-irix6 ppp[13583]: rhesus IPCP1:
     action TLS
Jul  2 16:11:43 3D:itra-irix6 ppp[13583]: rhesus IPCP1:
     Initial(0)->Starting(1)
Jul  2 16:11:43 3D:itra-irix6 ppp[13583]: rhesus IPCP1: event Up
Jul  2 16:11:43 3D:itra-irix6 ppp[13583]: rhesus IPCP1:
     send Configure-Request ID=0x28
Jul  2 16:11:43 3D:itra-irix6 ppp[13583]: rhesus IPCP1:
     16 slot VJ compression without compressed slot IDs
Jul  2 16:11:43 3D:itra-irix6 ppp[13583]: rhesus IPCP1:
     ADDR our address 132.245.33.131
Jul  2 16:11:43 3D:itra-irix6 ppp[13583]: rhesus 1: send
     0x10 bytes: index=25 proto=0x8021 01 28 00 10 02 06
     00 2d 0f 00 03 06 84 f5 21 83
Jul  2 16:11:43 3D:itra-irix6 ppp[13583]: rhesus IPCP1:
     Starting(1)->Req-Sent(6)
Jul  2 16:11:43 3D:itra-irix6 ppp[13583]: rhesus 1: read
     0x7 bytes: proto=0x80fd 01 02 00 07 15 03 29
Jul  2 16:11:43 3D:itra-irix6 ppp[13583]: rhesus  CCP1:
     dropping Configure-Request packet because in Initial(0)
Jul  2 16:11:43 3D:itra-irix6 ppp[13583]: rhesus 1: read 0xa
     bytes: proto=0x8021 01 03 00 0a 03 06 84 f5 42 7c
Jul  2 16:11:43 3D:itra-irix6 ppp[13583]: rhesus IPCP1:
     receive Configure-Request ID=0x3
Jul  2 16:11:43 3D:itra-irix6 ppp[13583]: rhesus IPCP1:
     accept its address 132.245.66.124 from ADDR Request
```

```
Jul  2 16:11:43 3D:itra-irix6 ppp[13583]: rhesus IPCP1:
     event RCR+
Jul  2 16:11:43 3D:itra-irix6 ppp[13583]: rhesus IPCP1:
     send Configure-ACK ID=0x3
Jul  2 16:11:43 3D:itra-irix6 ppp[13583]: rhesus 1: send 0xa
     bytes: index=25 proto=0x8021 02 03 00 0a 03 06 84 f5 42 7c
Jul  2 16:11:43 3D:itra-irix6 ppp[13583]: rhesus IPCP1:
     Req-Sent(6)->Ack-Sent(8)
Jul  2 16:11:44 3D:itra-irix6 ppp[13583]: rhesus 1: read
     0x20 bytes: proto=0x802b 01 04 00 20 01 06 00 00 00
     00 02 08 00 80 2d 05 4a bb 04 04 00 02 05 0a "LM054ABB"
Jul  2 16:11:44 3D:itra-irix6 ppp[13583]: rhesus 1:
     Protocol-Rejecting IPX Protocol
Jul  2 16:11:44 3D:itra-irix6 ppp[13583]: rhesus  LCP1:
     send Protocol-Reject ID=0x9d
Jul  2 16:11:44 3D:itra-irix6 ppp[13583]: rhesus 1: send 0x26
     bytes: index=25 proto=0xc021 08 9d 00 26 80 2b 01 04 00
     20 01 06 00 00 00 00 02 08 00 80 2d 05 4a bb 04 04 00 02
     05 0a "LM054ABB"
Jul  2 16:11:44 3D:itra-irix6 ppp[13583]: rhesus 1: read 0xa
     bytes: proto=0x8021 04 28 00 0a 02 06 00 2d 0f 00
Jul  2 16:11:44 3D:itra-irix6 ppp[13583]: rhesus IPCP1:
     receive Configure-Reject ID=0x28
Jul  2 16:11:44 3D:itra-irix6 ppp[13583]: rhesus IPCP1:
     peer is rejecting header compression
Jul  2 16:11:44 3D:itra-irix6 ppp[13583]: rhesus IPCP1:
     event RCN
Jul  2 16:11:44 3D:itra-irix6 ppp[13583]: rhesus IPCP1:
     send Configure-Request ID=0x29
Jul  2 16:11:44 3D:itra-irix6 ppp[13583]: rhesus IPCP1:
     ADDR our address 132.245.33.131
Jul  2 16:11:44 3D:itra-irix6 ppp[13583]: rhesus 1: send 0xa
     bytes: index=25 proto=0x8021 01 29 00 0a 03 06 84 f5 21 83
Jul  2 16:11:44 3D:itra-irix6 ppp[13583]: rhesus IPCP1:
     Ack-Sent(8)->Ack-Sent(8)
Jul  2 16:11:44 3D:itra-irix6 ppp[13583]: rhesus 1: read 0xa
     bytes: proto=0x8021 03 29 00 0a 03 06 84 f5 42 79
```

```
Jul  2 16:11:44 3D:itra-irix6 ppp[13583]: rhesus IPCP1:
     receive Configure-NAK ID=0x29
Jul  2 16:11:44 3D:itra-irix6 ppp[13583]: rhesus IPCP1:
     peer says 132.245.66.121 instead of 132.245.33.131
     for our address
```

This log shows an exceptional condition that eventually leads to negotiation failure. The peer stubbornly refuses to accept our locally configured IP address.

```
Jul  2 16:11:44 3D:itra-irix6 ppp[13583]: rhesus IPCP1:
     event RCN
Jul  2 16:11:44 3D:itra-irix6 ppp[13583]: rhesus IPCP1:
     send Configure-Request ID=0x2a
Jul  2 16:11:44 3D:itra-irix6 ppp[13583]: rhesus IPCP1:
     ADDR our address 132.245.33.131
Jul  2 16:11:44 3D:itra-irix6 ppp[13583]: rhesus 1: send 0xa
     bytes: index=25 proto=0x8021 01 2a 00 0a 03 06 84 f5 21 83
Jul  2 16:11:44 3D:itra-irix6 ppp[13583]: rhesus IPCP1:
     Ack-Sent(8)->Ack-Sent(8)
Jul  2 16:11:44 3D:itra-irix6 ppp[13583]: rhesus 1: read
     0xa bytes: proto=0x8021 03 2a 00 0a 03 06 84 f5 42 79
Jul  2 16:11:44 3D:itra-irix6 ppp[13583]: rhesus IPCP1:
     receive Configure-NAK ID=0x2a
Jul  2 16:11:44 3D:itra-irix6 ppp[13583]: rhesus IPCP1:
     peer says 132.245.66.121 instead of 132.245.33.131
     for our address
[...]
Jul  2 16:11:45 3D:itra-irix6 ppp[13583]: rhesus IPCP1:
     event RCN
Jul  2 16:11:45 3D:itra-irix6 ppp[13583]: rhesus IPCP1:
     send Configure-Request ID=0x32
Jul  2 16:11:45 3D:itra-irix6 ppp[13583]: rhesus IPCP1:
     ADDR our address 132.245.33.131
Jul  2 16:11:45 3D:itra-irix6 ppp[13583]: rhesus 1:
     send 0xa bytes: index=25 proto=0x8021 01 32 00 0a
     03 06 84 f5 21 83
Jul  2 16:11:45 3D:itra-irix6 ppp[13583]: rhesus IPCP1:
     Ack-Sent(8)->Ack-Sent(8)
```

```
Jul   2 16:11:45 3D:itra-irix6 ppp[13583]: rhesus 1: read 0xa
      bytes: proto=0x8021 03 32 00 0a 03 06 84 f5 42 79
Jul   2 16:11:45 3D:itra-irix6 ppp[13583]: rhesus IPCP1:
      receive Configure-NAK ID=0x32
Jul   2 16:11:45 3D:itra-irix6 ppp[13583]: rhesus IPCP1:
      peer says 132.245.66.121 instead of 132.245.33.131
      for our address
Jul   2 16:11:45 3D:itra-irix6 ppp[13583]: rhesus IPCP1:
      giving after 11 Configure-NAKs
```

This means that the IRIX system tried to report its IP address to the peer using IPCP Configure-Request, but the peer insisted on sending Configure-Nak every time. The IRIX system eventually gave up and shut down IPCP.

```
Jul   2 16:11:45 3D:itra-irix6 ppp[13583]: rhesus IPCP1:
      event RXJ-
Jul   2 16:11:45 3D:itra-irix6 ppp[13583]: rhesus IPCP1:
      action TLF
Jul   2 16:11:45 3D:itra-irix6 ppp[13583]: rhesus IPCP1:
      event Close
Jul   2 16:11:45 3D:itra-irix6 ppp[13583]: rhesus IPCP1:
      Stopped(3)->Closed(2)
Jul   2 16:11:45 3D:itra-irix6 ppp[13583]: rhesus  LCP1:
      event Close
Jul   2 16:11:45 3D:itra-irix6 ppp[13583]: rhesus  LCP1:
      send Terminate-Request ID=0x9e
```

The last two logs above show that when the last NCP (IPCP in this case) is closed, a Close event is sent into LCP. This causes the failing link to be torn down. This is normal error handling for most implementations.

```
Jul   2 16:11:45 3D:itra-irix6 ppp[13583]: rhesus 1: send 0x4
      bytes: index=25 proto=0xc021 05 9e 00 04
Jul   2 16:11:45 3D:itra-irix6 ppp[13583]: rhesus  LCP1:
      action TLD
Jul   2 16:11:45 3D:itra-irix6 ppp[13583]: rhesus  LCP1:
      set async,acomp=0,pcomp=0,rx_ACCM=0,tx=0xffffffff,
      pad=0
```

```
Jul  2 16:11:45 3D:itra-irix6 ppp[13583]: rhesus IPCP1:
     event Down
Jul  2 16:11:45 3D:itra-irix6 ppp[13583]: rhesus IPCP1:
     Closed(2)->Initial(0)
Jul  2 16:11:45 3D:itra-irix6 ppp[13583]: rhesus  LCP1:
     Opened(9)->Closing(4)
Jul  2 16:11:45 3D:itra-irix6 ppp[13583]: rhesus 1:
     entering Terminate Phase
Jul  2 16:11:45 3D:itra-irix6 ppp[13583]: rhesus IPCP1:
     Ack-Sent(8)->Initial(0)
Jul  2 16:11:45 3D:itra-irix6 ppp[13583]: rhesus 1:
     read 0x4 bytes: proto=0xc021 06 9e 00 04
Jul  2 16:11:45 3D:itra-irix6 ppp[13583]: rhesus  LCP1:
     receive Terminate-Ack: 06 9e 00 04
Jul  2 16:11:45 3D:itra-irix6 ppp[13583]: rhesus  LCP1:
     event RTA
Jul  2 16:11:45 3D:itra-irix6 ppp[13583]: rhesus  LCP1:
     action TLF
Jul  2 16:11:45 3D:itra-irix6 ppp[13583]: rhesus 1:
     entering Dead Phase
Jul  2 16:11:45 3D:itra-irix6 ppp[13583]: rhesus  LCP1:
     Closing(4)->Closed(2)
Jul  2 16:12:46 3D:itra-irix6 ppp[13583]: rhesus:
     received signal 2
```

Notice that, although these logs are quite large, they are also quite friendly and easy to read. In particular, the messages for the IPCP Configure-Nak failure give a very clear picture of the problem. This makes the PPP implementation in IRIX quite easy to configure.

The implementation also supports running of IP effectively unnumbered—it does not exhibit the point-to-point addressing problems mentioned in Chapter 5. Any available addresses may be negotiated as desired.

Here is an excerpt from a connection that succeeds:

```
Jul  2 16:23:31 3D:itra-irix6 ppp[13689]: rhesus IPCP1:
     event Open
Jul  2 16:23:31 3D:itra-irix6 ppp[13689]: rhesus IPCP1:
     action TLS
```

```
Jul  2 16:23:31 3D:itra-irix6 ppp[13689]: rhesus IPCP1:
     Initial(0)->Starting(1)
Jul  2 16:23:31 3D:itra-irix6 ppp[13689]: rhesus IPCP1: event Up
Jul  2 16:23:31 3D:itra-irix6 ppp[13689]: rhesus IPCP1: send
     Configure-Request ID=0x6b
Jul  2 16:23:31 3D:itra-irix6 ppp[13689]: rhesus IPCP1:
     16 slot VJ compression without compressed slot IDs
Jul  2 16:23:31 3D:itra-irix6 ppp[13689]: rhesus IPCP1:
     ADDR our address 132.245.33.131
Jul  2 16:23:31 3D:itra-irix6 ppp[13689]: rhesus 1: send
     0x10 bytes: index=26 proto=0x8021 01 6b 00 10 02 06
     00 2d 0f 00 03 06 84 f5 21 83
Jul  2 16:23:31 3D:itra-irix6 ppp[13689]: rhesus IPCP1:
     Starting(1)->Req-Sent(6)
Jul  2 16:23:31 3D:itra-irix6 ppp[13689]: rhesus 1: read
     0x7 bytes: proto=0x80fd 01 02 00 07 15 03 29
Jul  2 16:23:31 3D:itra-irix6 ppp[13689]: rhesus  CCP1:
     dropping Configure-Request packet because in Initial(0)
Jul  2 16:23:32 3D:itra-irix6 ppp[13689]: rhesus 1: read
     0xa bytes: proto=0x8021 01 03 00 0a 03 06 84 f5 42 7c
Jul  2 16:23:32 3D:itra-irix6 ppp[13689]: rhesus IPCP1:
     receive Configure-Request ID=0x3
Jul  2 16:23:32 3D:itra-irix6 ppp[13689]: rhesus IPCP1:
     accept its address 132.245.66.124 from ADDR Request
Jul  2 16:23:32 3D:itra-irix6 ppp[13689]: rhesus IPCP1:
     event RCR+
Jul  2 16:23:32 3D:itra-irix6 ppp[13689]: rhesus IPCP1:
     send Configure-ACK ID=0x3
Jul  2 16:23:32 3D:itra-irix6 ppp[13689]: rhesus 1: send
     0xa bytes: index=26 proto=0x8021 02 03 00 0a 03 06
     84 f5 42 7c
Jul  2 16:23:32 3D:itra-irix6 ppp[13689]: rhesus IPCP1:
     Req-Sent(6)->Ack-Sent(8)
Jul  2 16:23:32 3D:itra-irix6 ppp[13689]: rhesus 1: read
     0x20 bytes: proto=0x802b 01 04 00 20 01 06 00 00 00
     00 02 08 00 80 2d 05 4a bb 04 04 00 02 05 0a "LM054ABB"
Jul  2 16:23:32 3D:itra-irix6 ppp[13689]: rhesus 1:
     Protocol-Rejecting IPX Protocol
```

```
Jul  2 16:23:32 3D:itra-irix6 ppp[13689]: rhesus  LCP1:
     send Protocol-Reject ID=0x8a
Jul  2 16:23:32 3D:itra-irix6 ppp[13689]: rhesus 1: send
     0x26 bytes: index=26 proto=0xc021 08 8a 00 26 80 2b
     01 04 00 20 01 06 00 00 00 00 02 08 00 80 2d 05 4a
     bb 04 04 00 02 05 0a "LM054ABB"
Jul  2 16:23:32 3D:itra-irix6 ppp[13689]: rhesus 1:
     read 0xa bytes: proto=0x8021 04 6b 00 0a 02 06 00
     2d 0f 00
Jul  2 16:23:32 3D:itra-irix6 ppp[13689]: rhesus IPCP1:
     receive Configure-Reject ID=0x6b
Jul  2 16:23:32 3D:itra-irix6 ppp[13689]: rhesus IPCP1:
     peer is rejecting header compression
Jul  2 16:23:32 3D:itra-irix6 ppp[13689]: rhesus IPCP1:
     event RCN
Jul  2 16:23:32 3D:itra-irix6 ppp[13689]: rhesus IPCP1:
     send Configure-Request ID=0x6c
Jul  2 16:23:32 3D:itra-irix6 ppp[13689]: rhesus IPCP1:
     ADDR our address 132.245.33.131
Jul  2 16:23:32 3D:itra-irix6 ppp[13689]: rhesus 1: send 0xa
     bytes: index=26 proto=0x8021 01 6c 00 0a 03 06 84 f5 21 83
Jul  2 16:23:32 3D:itra-irix6 ppp[13689]: rhesus IPCP1:
     Ack-Sent(8)->Ack-Sent(8)
Jul  2 16:23:32 3D:itra-irix6 ppp[13689]: rhesus 1: read
     0xa bytes: proto=0x8021 02 6c 00 0a 03 06 84 f5 21 83
Jul  2 16:23:32 3D:itra-irix6 ppp[13689]: rhesus IPCP1:
     receive Configure-Ack ID=0x6c
Jul  2 16:23:32 3D:itra-irix6 ppp[13689]: rhesus IPCP1:
     event RCA
Jul  2 16:23:32 3D:itra-irix6 ppp[13689]: rhesus IPCP1:
     action TLU
Jul  2 16:23:32 3D:itra-irix6 ppp[13689]: rhesus IPCP1:
     Ack-Sent(8)->Opened(9)
```

The message above means that IPCP has successfully negotiated on this link, and IP traffic can now flow. The next message gives details on the negotiated endpoint addresses and VJ compression parameters.

```
Jul  2 16:23:32 3D:itra-irix6 ppp[13689]: rhesus IPCP1: ready
     132.245.33.131 to 132.245.66.124, rx_vj_comp=n,tx=n
     rx_compslot=n,tx=n rx_slots=16,tx=16
```

The IRIX implementation can also be configured to run RFC 1990 Multilink with the following options.

```
maxdevs=2          # use at most two links
mindevs=2          # always start up two links
mp_headers         # enable MP
mp_send_ssn        # request short sequence numbers
mp_recv_ssn        # allow short sequence numbers
```

Personal Computer Software

Windows 95 and 98 Dial-Up Networking (DUN)

To enable PPP tracing on Windows 95 or 98, select the Control Panel from the "My Computer" icon. Select (double-click) "Network" in the Control Panel, then click once on the "Dial-Up Adapter." Press the "Properties" button and select the "Advanced" tab. Finally, change the "Record a log file" property from "No" to "Yes." Now click on "OK" to exit the "Adapter Properties" and "Network" menus. This places a text file called "ppplog.txt" in the \WINDOWS directory. This file contains output similar to the following.

```
06-13-1997 10:24:01.01 - Remote access driver log opened.
06-13-1997 10:24:01.01 - Installable CP VxD SPAP     is loaded
06-13-1997 10:24:01.01 - Server type is  PPP (Point to Point
      Protocol).
06-13-1997 10:24:01.01 - FSA : Software compression disabled.
06-13-1997 10:24:01.01 - FSA : Adding Control Protocol 803f
      (NBFCP) to control protocol chain.
06-13-1997 10:24:01.01 - FSA : Adding Control Protocol 8021
      (IPCP) to control protocol chain.
06-13-1997 10:24:01.01 - FSA : Adding Control Protocol 802b
      (IPXCP) to control protocol chain.
```

```
06-13-1997 10:24:01.01 - FSA : Adding Control Protocol c029
    (CallbackCP) to control protocol chain.
06-13-1997 10:24:01.01 - FSA : Adding Control Protocol c027
    (no description) to control protocol chain.
06-13-1997 10:24:01.01 - FSA : Encrypted Password required.
06-13-1997 10:24:01.01 - FSA : Adding Control Protocol c223
    (CHAP) to control protocol chain.
06-13-1997 10:24:01.01 - FSA : Adding Control Protocol c021
    (LCP) to control protocol chain.
06-13-1997 10:24:01.01 - LCP : Callback negotiation enabled.
06-13-1997 10:24:01.01 - LCP : Layer started.
06-13-1997 10:24:04.16 - LCP : Received and accepted ACCM of 0.
06-13-1997 10:24:04.17 - LCP : NAK authentication protocol 23c0
    with protocol c223 (CHAP).
06-13-1997 10:24:04.17 - LCP : Naking possibly loopback magic
    number.
06-13-1997 10:24:04.17 - LCP : Rejecting unknown option 19.
06-13-1997 10:24:04.30 - LCP : Received and accepted ACCM of 0.
06-13-1997 10:24:04.30 - LCP : NAK authentication protocol 23c0
    with protocol c223 (CHAP).
06-13-1997 10:24:04.30 - LCP : Naking possibly loopback magic
    number.
06-13-1997 10:24:04.43 - LCP : Received and accepted ACCM of 0.
06-13-1997 10:24:04.43 - LCP : Received and accepted
    authentication protocol c223 (CHAP).
06-13-1997 10:24:04.43 - LCP : Received and accepted magic
    number cc9ea55d.
06-13-1997 10:24:04.43 - LCP : Received and accepted protocol
    field compression option.
06-13-1997 10:24:04.43 - LCP : Received and accepted
    address+control field compression option.
06-13-1997 10:24:07.14 - LCP : Received configure reject for
    callback control protocol option.
06-13-1997 10:24:07.29 - LCP : Layer up.
06-13-1997 10:24:07.29 - CHAP : Layer started.
06-13-1997 10:24:08.03 - CHAP : Login failed: username,
    password, or domain was incorrect.
06-13-1997 10:24:08.03 - LCP : Received terminate request.
```

```
06-13-1997 10:24:08.03 - LCP : Layer down.
06-13-1997 10:24:11.04 - LCP : Layer finished.
06-13-1997 10:32:37.92 - Remote access driver is shutting down.
06-13-1997 10:32:37.92 - CRC Errors              0
06-13-1997 10:32:37.92 - Timeout Errors          0
06-13-1997 10:32:37.92 - Alignment Errors        0
06-13-1997 10:32:37.92 - Overrun Errors          0
06-13-1997 10:32:37.92 - Framing Errors          0
06-13-1997 10:32:37.92 - Buffer Overrun Errors   0
06-13-1997 10:32:37.92 - Incomplete Packets      0
06-13-1997 10:32:37.92 - Bytes Received          310
06-13-1997 10:32:37.92 - Bytes Transmittted      380
06-13-1997 10:32:37.92 - Frames Received         8
06-13-1997 10:32:37.92 - Frames Transmitted      9
06-13-1997 10:32:37.92 - LCP : Layer started.
06-13-1997 10:32:37.92 - Remote access driver log closed.
06-13-1997 10:32:57.65 - Remote access driver log opened.
```

Of course, in this example, the user's password is incorrect, as noted by the message shown in boldface. Note that "CHAP" in these logs is actually MS-CHAP. Older Windows 95 systems support standard MD5 CHAP only with a patch available from Microsoft, while Windows 98 and 2000 both support standard CHAP.

The next example shows an interface establishing itself normally. This system does not have "ISDN Accelerator Pack" installed, which implements RFC 1990 standard MP (over modems as well as over ISDN, despite the moniker), so option decimal 19 (hex 13), the Multilink Endpoint-Discriminator, is rejected. Also note that the IP addresses are displayed as 32-bit hexadecimal numbers rather than as the more familiar decimal dotted quads.

```
06-13-1997 10:34:46.07 - Installable CP VxD SPAP    is loaded
06-13-1997 10:34:46.07 - Server type is  PPP (Point to Point
    Protocol).
06-13-1997 10:34:46.07 - FSA : Software compression disabled.
06-13-1997 10:34:46.07 - FSA : Adding Control Protocol 803f
    (NBFCP) to control protocol chain.
06-13-1997 10:34:46.07 - FSA : Adding Control Protocol 8021
    (IPCP) to control protocol chain.
```

```
06-13-1997 10:34:46.07 - FSA : Adding Control Protocol 802b
    (IPXCP) to control protocol chain.
06-13-1997 10:34:46.07 - FSA : Adding Control Protocol c029
    (CallbackCP) to control protocol chain.
06-13-1997 10:34:46.07 - FSA : Adding Control Protocol c027 (no
    description) to control protocol chain.
06-13-1997 10:34:46.07 - FSA : Adding Control Protocol c023
    (PAP) to control protocol chain.
06-13-1997 10:34:46.07 - FSA : Adding Control Protocol c223
    (CHAP) to control protocol chain.
06-13-1997 10:34:46.07 - FSA : Adding Control Protocol c021
    (LCP) to control protocol chain.
06-13-1997 10:34:46.07 - LCP : Callback negotiation enabled.
06-13-1997 10:34:46.07 - LCP : Layer started.
06-13-1997 10:34:49.22 - LCP : Received and accepted ACCM of 0.
06-13-1997 10:34:49.22 - LCP : Received and accepted
    authentication protocol c023 (PAP).
06-13-1997 10:34:49.22 - LCP : Received and accepted magic
    number 4849ece6.
06-13-1997 10:34:49.22 - LCP : Received and accepted protocol
    field compression option.
06-13-1997 10:34:49.22 - LCP : Received and accepted
    address+control field compression option.
06-13-1997 10:34:49.22 - LCP : Rejecting unknown option 19.
```

Note the rejection of the RFC 1990 Multilink Endpoint-Discriminator option. This version of Windows does not support MP.

```
06-13-1997 10:34:49.34 - LCP : Received and accepted ACCM of 0.
06-13-1997 10:34:49.34 - LCP : Received and accepted
    authentication protocol c023 (PAP).
06-13-1997 10:34:49.34 - LCP : Received and accepted magic
    number 4849ece6.
06-13-1997 10:34:49.34 - LCP : Received and accepted protocol
    field compression option.
06-13-1997 10:34:49.34 - LCP : Received and accepted
    address+control field compression option.
```

```
06-13-1997 10:34:52.20 - LCP : Received configure reject for
    callback control protocol option.
06-13-1997 10:34:52.33 - LCP : Layer up.
06-13-1997 10:34:52.33 - PAP : Layer started.
06-13-1997 10:34:53.72 - PAP : Login was successful.
06-13-1997 10:34:53.72 - PAP : Layer up.
06-13-1997 10:34:53.72 - IPXCP : Layer started.
06-13-1997 10:34:53.72 - IPCP : Layer started.
06-13-1997 10:34:53.72 - IPCP : IP address is 0.
06-13-1997 10:34:53.72 - NBFCP : Layer started.
06-13-1997 10:34:53.83 - FSA : Sending protocol reject for
    control protocol 80fd.
```
**06-13-1997 10:34:54.38 - IPCP : Received and accepted IP address
    of 84f5427c.**

The hex number in the message above is commonly written as 132.245.66.124. To convert, take pairs of hex digits starting from the rightmost and convert them to produce the decimal numbers printed from the right. In this case, 0x7c is 124, 0x42 is 66, 0xf5 is 245, and 0x84 is 132.

```
06-13-1997 10:34:54.38 - IPCP : Turning off IP header
    compression.
06-13-1997 10:34:54.94 - IPXCP : Accepted matching net
    number 0.
06-13-1997 10:34:54.94 - IPXCP : Received and accepted peer
    node number 0 80 2d 5 4a bb.
06-13-1997 10:34:54.99 - FSA : Received protocol reject for
    control protocol 803f.
06-13-1997 10:34:54.99 - NBFCP : Layer finished.
06-13-1997 10:34:55.07 - IPXCP : Accepted matching net
    number 0.
06-13-1997 10:34:55.07 - IPXCP : Received and accepted peer
    node number 0 80 2d 5 4a bb.
06-13-1997 10:34:55.07 - IPXCP : Received and accepted routing
    protocol 0.
06-13-1997 10:34:55.07 - IPXCP : Received and accepted router
    name LM054ABB.
```

```
06-13-1997 10:34:55.07 - IPXCP : Layer up.
06-13-1997 10:34:56.95 - IPCP : Changing IP address from 0 to
    84f54279.
06-13-1997 10:34:57.06 - IPCP : Layer up.
06-13-1997 10:34:57.07 - FSA : Last control protocol is up.
```

Windows NT

On these machines, debug logging is enabled by a registry setting. Run "REGEDT32.EXE." Then, from the HKEY_LOCAL_MACHINE subtree, go to the following key.

```
System\CurrentControlSet\Services\RasMan\PPP
```

Select the "Logging" value, then select "DWORD" in the Edit menu. Enter 1 and click on OK. Then reboot the computer to have the setting take effect. The resulting log file is found in

```
C:\winnt\system32\ras\ppp.log
```

MacPPP

This free software package for the Apple Macintosh from Merit Network is sometimes also referred to as ConfigPPP, since this is the utility that the user sees when configuring this package. Its log files look like the following.

```
LCP: Sending Configuration Request.
LCP: >> Async Map = 0x00000000.
LCP: >> Magic Number = 0xDAC00914.
LCP: >> Protocol Compression On
LCP: >> Address/Control Compression On
LCP: Received Configuration Request.
LCP: >> Async Map = 0x00000000.
LCP: >> Auth Protocol = 0x0000C027.
LCP: >> Magic Number = 0x33F221A0.
LCP: >> Protocol Compression On
LCP: >> Address/Control Compression On
```

Communications Servers and Routers

Cisco IOS

From an "enabled" terminal session, the interactive user can use the "debug ppp negotiation" and "debug ppp packet" commands to enable a fairly verbose debug display. The log below contains excerpts from the start-up of an IP unnumbered V.35 synchronous interface using RFC 1663 Numbered Mode between two Cisco 7200 routers.

```
Se2/0 PPP: Phase is ESTABLISHING, Active Open
Se2/0 LCP: O CONFREQ [Closed] id 65 len 14
Se2/0 LCP:    MagicNumber 0x67643E1B (0x050667643E1B)
Se2/0 LCP:    ReliableLink window 7 addr 05 (0x0B040700)
Se2/0 PPP: I pkt type 0xC021, datagramsize 18
```

The boldface line above is from the "debug ppp packet" portion of the requested output. It shows a received packet with PPP protocol C021 (LCP) and total length 18 octets.

```
Se2/0 LCP: I CONFREQ [REQsent] id 15 len 14
Se2/0 LCP:    MagicNumber 0x67643E20 (0x050667643E20)
Se2/0 LCP:    ReliableLink window 7 addr 05 (0x0B040700)
```

This is the continuation of the decode from "debug ppp negotiation." It shows the details of the options set, both as plain text and as a hex string.

```
Se2/0 LCP: O CONFNAK [REQsent] id 15 len 8
Se2/0 LCP:    ReliableLink window 7 addr 362 (0x0B040703)
Se2/0 PPP: I pkt type 0xC021, datagramsize 18
Se2/0 LCP: I CONFREQ [REQsent] id 16 len 14
Se2/0 LCP:    MagicNumber 0x67643E20 (0x050667643E20)
Se2/0 LCP:    ReliableLink window 7 addr 3119 (0x0B040703)
[...]
Se2/0 UNKNOWN(0x0001): I UNKNOWN(63) [Not negotiated] id 235 len
      57102
Se2/0 LCP: O PROTREJ [Open] id 68 len 7 protocol UNKNOWN(0x0001)
      (0x00013F)
```

The two logs above represent a harmless race condition in Cisco's implementation of RFC 1663. The peer has begun sending LAP-B SABM messages, but this system has not yet started its LAP-B protocol. The messages are misinterpreted as corrupted PPP frames and are rejected.

```
[...]
Se2/0 PPP: I pkt type 0x8021, datagramsize 14
Se2/0 IPCP: I CONFREQ [REQsent] id 9 len 10
Se2/0 IPCP:    Address 10.1.2.1 (0x03060A010201)
ip_get_pool: Se2/0: validate address = 10.1.2.1
set_ip_peer_addr: Se2/0: address = 10.1.2.1 (3)
Se2/0 IPCP: O CONFACK [REQsent] id 9 len 10
Se2/0 IPCP:    Address 10.1.2.1 (0x03060A010201)
```

These lines show the handling of the peer's IP address in some detail. Note that the Cisco system goes through several validation steps before returning the IPCP Configure-Ack message.

```
Se2/0 IPCP: I CONFACK [ACKsent] id 11 len 10
Se2/0 IPCP:    Address 172.20.0.147 (0x0306AC140093)
Se2/0 IPCP: State is Open
Se2/0 IPCP: Install route to 10.1.2.1
```

This is the end of the normal IP start-up. The peer's IP is entered into the routing system as a reachable address.

```
Se2/0 PPP: O pkt type 0x0021, datagramsize 66
```

The log above is from IP traffic on the link.

```
Se2/0 LCP: O ECHOREQ [Open] id 1 len 12 magic 0x67643E1B
Se2/0 LCP: echo_cnt 1, sent id 1, line up
Se2/0 PPP: I pkt type 0xC021, datagramsize 16
Se2/0 PPP: I pkt type 0xC021, datagramsize 16
Se2/0 LCP: I ECHOREQ [Open] id 1 len 12 magic 0x67643E20
Se2/0 LCP: O ECHOREP [Open] id 1 len 12 magic 0x67643E1B
Se2/0 LCP: I ECHOREP [Open] id 1 len 12 magic 0x67643E20
Se2/0 LCP: Received id 1, sent id 1, line up
```

The idle link sends periodic LCP Echo-Request messages as keepalive messages.

```
Se2/0 PPP: O pkt type 0x0207, datagramsize 309
Se2/0 PPP: I pkt type 0x0207, datagramsize 320
```

The messages above are caused by Cisco's proprietary CDP (Cisco Discovery Protocol). They are generally seen only on links to other Cisco routers.

Xyplex

Xyplex servers log PPP state transitions in syslog:

```
IPCP  Event: DOWN State: OPEN    => STARTING
IPXCP Event: DOWN State: INITIAL => INITIAL
LCP   Event: DOWN State: OPEN    => STARTING
IPCP  Event: DOWN State: STARTING => STARTING
IPXCP Event: DOWN State: INITIAL => INITIAL
```

Nortel Annex

Annex terminal and communications servers were originally designed by Encore Computer, then sold to Xylogics, which was bought by Bay Networks, which in turn was bought by Nortel Networks.

Annex servers log state transitions, significant events, and a summary of the state in case of failure to syslog. The event logs look like this:

```
May  8 17:42:48 guenevere ppp[2559]: Port-
     Begin:asy42:PPP::::[local]
May  8 17:42:48 guenevere ppp[2559]: ppp:asy42:ADM Start LCP
May  8 17:42:48 guenevere line_adm[1298]: started mp on mp126 as
     PID 2573
May  8 17:42:48 guenevere system[0]: ppp:asy42:detach link from
     bundle mp126
May  8 17:42:48 guenevere mp[2573]: ppp:mp126:terminating:
     errno: Success
May  8 17:42:51 guenevere ppp[2559]: ppp:asy42:LCP Started LCP
```

```
May  8 17:42:52 guenevere ppp[2559]: ppp:asy42:Security Started
     PAP
May  8 17:42:55 guenevere ppp[2559]: ppp:asy42:ipxcp started
May  8 17:42:55 guenevere ppp[2559]: ppp:asy42:rejecting unknown
     protocol 803F
May  8 17:42:55 guenevere ppp[2559]: ppp:asy42:send protocol
     reject for 803F
May  8 17:42:55 guenevere ppp[2559]: ppp:asy42:LCP:received
     protocol reject for 8029 (ATCP)
May  8 17:42:55 guenevere ppp[2559]: ppp:asy42:NCP Closed ATCP
May  8 17:42:55 guenevere ppp[2559]: ppp:asy42:NCP Started IPCP
May  8 17:42:55 guenevere ppp[2559]: ifconfig asy42 local
     132.245.11.10 remote 132.245.11.92 mask 255.255.255.255
     metric 1
```

The summary is printed if no NCPs go to Opened state. It appears like this:

```
Apr 18 08:09:55 annex ppp[20817]: ppp:asy2: *** LCP SYSLOG
     HISTORY ***
Apr 18 08:09:55 annex ppp[20817]: ppp:asy2:Rcv cfg req: Send cfg
     req with MRU: 1500
Apr 18 08:09:55 annex ppp[20817]: ppp:asy2:Rcv cfg req: Sending
     ACCM of: a0000
Apr 18 08:09:55 annex ppp[20817]: ppp:asy2:Rcv cfg req:
     Requesting CHAP security
Apr 18 08:09:55 annex ppp[20817]: ppp:asy2:Rcv cfg req: Request
     for ACFC
Apr 18 08:09:55 annex ppp[20817]: ppp:asy2:Rcv cfg req: Sending
     random magic number
Apr 18 08:09:55 annex ppp[20817]: ppp:asy2:Rcv cfg req: Request
     PFC
Apr 18 08:09:55 annex ppp[20817]: ppp:asy2: *** END LCP HISTORY
     ***
```

Lucent PortMaster

The PortMaster was originally designed by Livingston, which has been bought
by Lucent.

From a command prompt, the administrator can enable debug mode 0x51, which displays the raw PPP data (minus the AHDLC Address and Control fields, and the PPP Protocol field) as well as notes on the state transitions (such as the "LCP Open" message below).

```
> set console
> set debug 0x51
Setting debug value to 0x51
Sending LCP_CONFIGURE_REQUEST to port S2 of 24 bytes containing:
01 02 00 18 01 04 03 ee 02 06 00 00 00 00 05 06
83 59 4b 5e 07 02 08 02
Received LCP_CONFIGURE_ACK on port S2 of 20 bytes
      containing:
02 02 00 18 01 04 03 ee 02 06 00 00 00 00 05 06
83 59 4b 5e 07 02 08 02
S2: LCP Open
```

These logs can be decoded into more readable text by copying them into a "decoder ring" Web page set up by Livingston technical support at

```
http://www.livingston.com/Tech/Support/dring.shtml
```

This Perl script will decode each option as a separate line of text with a verbose expansion of the option values.

The PortMaster also logs PPP conditions to any syslog host.

```
Mar 1 18:01:23 pma dialnet: port S2 ppp_sync failed dest
      1.2.3.4
```

Lucent MAX

The MAX communications server was originally designed by Ascend, which has been bought by Lucent.

From a terminal-mode command line, the Ascend devices allow the administrator to enable various levels of PPP debug messages. Shown below are the "pppfsm" (finite state machine) and "pppif" (interface) levels of debug. Note that the actual data are not shown and that the messages include internal software implementation notes.

```
> pppfsm
PPPFSM state display is ON
> pppif
PPPIF debug is ON
> PPPIF: open: routeid 372, incoming YES
PPPIF-105: vj comp on
PPPIF-105: _initAuthentication, mpID=0
PPPIF-105: auth mode 3
PPPIF-105: PAP/CHAP/MS-CHAP auth, incoming
PPPFSM-105: Layer 0   State INITIAL      Event OPEN...
PPPFSM-105: ...New State STARTING
PPPFSM-105: Layer 0   State STARTING     Event UP...
PPPFSM-105: ...New State REQSENT
PPPIF-105: Link Is up.
PPPFSM-105: Layer 1   State INITIAL      Event UP...
PPPFSM-105: ...New State CLOSED
PPPFSM-105: Layer 2   State INITIAL      Event UP...
PPPFSM-105: ...New State CLOSED
```

3COM Netserver Plus

The syslog messages produced by the Netserver/HiperArc are not as friendly as
those sent from some of the other servers cited above.

```
Dec 12 17:12:39 nsp ModemFSM: state = InCall   , event =
    CallEstabRspPlus, mod:1
Dec 12 17:12:49 nsp At 17:12:47, Facility "Call Initiation
    Process", Level "VERBOSE":: CIP: Login succeeded on
    interface mod:1 for joe
Dec 12 17:12:52 nsp At 17:12:50, Facility "IP", Level
    "CRITICAL":: User joe is configured for an existing IP
    network address (01000000).
Dec 12 17:12:52 nsp At 17:12:50, Facility "PPP", Level
    "UNUSUAL":: ../../ src/ppp_main.c: PPP Get Option Rejected,
    (bad status).
Dec 12 17:12:52 nsp ModemFSM: state = InCall   , event =
    DropCallReq, mod:1
```

These products have an interactive command—"monitor ppp"—that displays traces in a more usable format. This is shown below.

```
Select a letter for one of the following options:
        C) Monitor PPP Call Events.
        I) Monitor a specific interface.
        N) Monitor the next session that starts up.
        U) Monitor a specific user.
        X) Exit the monitor.
     Please Enter Your Choice :
   Monitoring the next session to start up.
Decode tracing started, press ESCAPE to stop; press X for hex
     tracing.


Outgoing PPP Data on interface: slot:2/mod:7 Time: 24-FEB-2000
     14:19:50
     LCP         CFG_REQ             MRU             05 ea
                                     ASYNC_MAP       00 00 00 00
                                     AUTH_TYPE       c2 23 05
                                     MAGIC_NUM       4d 83 90 32
                                     PROTO_COMP
                                     AC_COMP
                                     MPP_MRRU        05 ea
                                     MPP_ENDPTID     00


Incoming PPP Data on interface: slot:2/mod:7 Time: 24-FEB-2000
     14:19:50
     LCP         CFG_REQ             ASYNC_MAP       ff ff 00 00
                                     MAGIC_NUM       ff ff 82 89
                                     PROTO_COMP
                                     AC_COMP


Outgoing PPP Data on interface: slot:2/mod:7 Time: 24-FEB-2000
     14:19:50
     LCP         CFG_ACK             ASYNC_MAP       ff ff 00 00
                                     MAGIC_NUM       ff ff 82 89
                                     PROTO_COMP
```

```
                                    AC_COMP
[...]
Outgoing PPP Data on interface: slot:2/mod:7 Time: 24-FEB-2000
        14:19:54
        CHAP         CHALLENGE        10 5f 43 d8 03 33 3d 1d
                                      86 12 62 d7 2d 90 94 ce
                                      a8 48 69 50 65 72


Incoming PPP Data on interface: slot:2/mod:7 Time: 24-FEB-2000
        14:19:54
        CHAP         RESPONSE         10 06 bc cd d7 79 03 ce
                                      7d 75 d3 b0 8c c6 42 e7
                                      48 61 62 63


Outgoing PPP Data on interface: slot:2/mod:7 Time: 24-FEB-2000
        14:19:54
        CHAP         SUCCESS          00


Outgoing PPP Data on interface: slot:2/mod:7 Time: 24-FEB-2000
        14:19:54
        IPCP         CFG_REQ          COMPR_TYPE    00 2d 0f 00
                                      NEW_ADDRS     95 70 d6 b2


Incoming PPP Data on interface: slot:2/mod:7 Time: 24-FEB-2000
        14:19:55
        IPCP         CFG_REQ          NEW_ADDRS     01 01 01 01
```

Test Tools

Two main types of specialized test tools are available for networking protocols, including PPP. These tools are conformance or stress testers and analyzers.

Many developers are able to get by with ad hoc tools for both functions, usually using ppp-2.3's "pty" option and Perl scripts to test conformance plus modified versions of tcpdump for analysis. Dedicated tools are also available and, for some developers, can help speed implementation and testing.

Conformance Testing

One very well-known tool for conformance testing of many network protocols, including PPP, is ANVL from Midnight Networks (now known as Hammer Technologies). This tool consists of an automated test harness along with hundreds of functional, boundary, and error test cases written in C.

ANVL is useful for "smoke testing" (automated testing of regular builds before hand-off from engineering to a test organization) and finding bad error handling (such as buffer overruns). In my experience, it is not as useful in stress or compatibility testing, both of which require test time against fully functioning peers.

Analyzers

Dedicated analyzers provide a good bit more detail than the debug logs from most implementations, are usually easier to use, and are very useful when the implementation under test may be failing in a way that is not recorded in the standard logs. They range in price from free to a few hundred dollars for software-only implementations to $75,000 or more for dedicated hardware that runs at SONET data rates. For the extra money, dedicated systems are usually more reliable, decode more protocols, offer specialized test modes, and can run at much higher speeds than the software-only systems. If you are working with asynchronous PPP on RS-232 lines, the software versions are quite capable. If you are working with high-speed telecommunications lines, the dedicated systems are worth investigation.

A very important feature of analyzers is that they are much more objective than the log file from a PPP implementation. They show what is on the wire, and only what is on the wire. Occasionally, when the bug being investigated is inside the HDLC driver, the PPP log files may show things that simply did not take place. An analyzer is then the best way to settle the matter.

Using analyzers sometimes requires a bit more practice than reading the debug logs. Since most parts of PPP have shared state between the peers (such as the negotiation state machines, the negotiated parameters themselves, and the CCP compression history), it is sometimes difficult for a third party observing the communication to determine correctly the meaning of the data. This results in occasional misleading data in the verbosely decoded sections of the output, so the user often must read the hexadecimal data to interpret the frame.

WinPharaoh

This PC-based analyzer from GN Nettest can monitor data on BRI (Basic Rate ISDN) links using an external module that attaches to the S/T interface between the NT1 and the unit under test.

The logs produced by this system are representative of the type of output available from most stand-alone analyzers. (Note that this is CCP over MP and is misinterpreted as sequence 253 because the analyzer never saw the Short Sequence Number option in LCP.)

```
Seconds  Bytes Ad Ctl PID      PPP Protocol           Type
      Description
18:07:53    19  ff  03 003d      Multilink (Seq=253)    PPP
      Multilink PPP


                            Point-to-Point Protocol Layer
      Time Stamp: 18:07:53.294109    Inter-frame Gap(uSecs):
       >65535
      Frame Source:  DTE              PPP Header: x'FF03'
      Protocol Identifier: x'003D' (PPP Multilink)
                                 Multilink PPP
      Fragment indicator: x'C0'
          1... ....  Beginning of fragment
          .1.. ....  End of fragment
          ..00 0000  Reserved
      Sequence number: 253
                                 Hexadecimal Frame
      0000    ff 03 00 3d c0 5c 00 fd 04 d5 7f f9 80 70 00
      ...=@\.}.U.y.p.
      -------------------------------------------------------------
```

SerialView and ISDNView

SerialView and ISDNView are PC-based analyzers produced by Klos Technologies, Inc. The asynchronous version uses two standard serial ports on an IBM PC-compatible system to monitor data passing in each direction. It can correctly handle in-band flow control (XON/XOFF) and standard AHDLC escaping, which makes reading the PPP frames much less tedious.

The following example shows a portion of an LCP exchange.

```
=================================================================
PPP:
     From Port B to Port A      Size: 0035  Number:       8
                                             Time:   31.025

MAC DATA:
0000  FF 7D 23 C0 21 7D 21 7D-20 7D 20 7D 39 7D 22 7D   .}#@!}!}
      } }9}"}
0010  26 7D 20 7D 20 7D 20 7D-20 7D 23 7D 25 C2 23 80   &} } } }
      }#}%B#.
0020  7D 25 7D 26 7D 20 7D 20-62 3C 7D 27 7D 22 7D 28   }%}&} }
      b<}'}"}(
0030  7D 22 7D 33 BB                                    }"}3;

+++++++++++++++++++++++++++++++++++++++++++++++++++++++++++++++++

PPP:
     From Port B to Port A      Size: 0019  Number:       8
                                Type: C021  Time:   31.025

LCP:
     Code: Configure-Request (1)
     Identifier:   0  Length: 0019

Option 2 - Async-Control-Character-Map
     Length = 6
     ACCM = 00000000
Option 3 - Authentication-Protocol
     Length = 5
     Protocol = C223 (CHAP)
     Data = 80 (Microsoft)
Option 5 - Magic-Number
     Length = 6
     Magic Number = 0000623C
Option 7 - Protocol-Field-Compression
     Length = 2
```

```
Option 8 - Address-and-Control-Field-Compression
    Length = 2


====================================================================

PPP:
    From Port A to Port B      Size: 0034   Number:      9
                                            Time:   31.035

MAC DATA:
0000  FF 7D 23 C0 21 7D 22 7D-20 7D 20 7D 39 7D 22 7D    .}#@!}"}
      } }9}"}
0010  26 7D 20 7D 20 7D 20 7D-20 7D 23 7D 25 C2 23 80    &} } } }
      }#}%B#.
0020  7D 25 7D 26 7D 20 7D 20-62 3C 7D 27 7D 22 7D 28    }%}&} }
      b<}'}"}(
0030  7D 22 9E B7                                        }".7


++++++++++++++++++++++++++++++++++++++++++++++++++++++++++++++++++++

PPP:
    From Port A to Port B      Size: 0019   Number:      9
                                            Type: C021   Time:   31.035

LCP:
    Code: Configure-Ack (2)
    Identifier:   0   Length: 0019

Option 2 - Async-Control-Character-Map
    Length = 6
    ACCM = 00000000
Option 3 - Authentication-Protocol
    Length = 5
    Protocol = C223 (CHAP)
    Data = 80 (Microsoft)
Option 5 - Magic-Number
    Length = 6
    Magic Number = 0000623C
```

```
Option 7 - Protocol-Field-Compression
    Length = 2
Option 8 - Address-and-Control-Field-Compression
    Length = 2


===================================================================
```

Summary

Most PPP packages can be coaxed into providing debugging information that can help isolate and identify the commonly encountered problems, although the information provided is often incomplete. If you support a large number of PPP users or if you are developing a PPP implementation, I highly recommend the use of stand-alone analyzers.

One PPP Implementation

IN THIS CHAPTER

This chapter describes the internal operation of one available implementation in detail. This implementation, Paul Mackerras' ppp-2.3, often called pppd, runs on a variety of machines, is freely available as C source code, and serves as a good example of a complete, well-written PPP implementation.

Overview

The pppd package has several components. These components are

kernel	Kernel portions for different operating systems.
pppd	Daemon that implements the PPP state machines.
chat	Utility program to dial modems and initiate PPP on the peer system.
pppdump	Utility program to display captured binary data in a readable format.
pppstats	Utility program to display internal PPP statistics.

The kernel portion is very system specific. Its role is to handle the serial data I/O, process AHDLC (for asynchronous interfaces), and demultiplex incoming data among network stacks. For performance reasons, all of the user data are transferred to and from the network stacks by direct function calls within the kernel. Only "unrecognized" protocols (LCP and the other negotiation protocols) are passed along to the daemon, which treats the kernel portion as a packet-oriented serial port.

On some systems, such as those using microkernel operating systems, the kernel portion of pppd is nonexistent; its functionality is merged into either the system interface portion of pppd or a separate user-space task. Unfortunately, although such adaptations do exist, the pppd distribution includes none of them, apparently because all of these versions are proprietary.

The pppd daemon is a user-level process, shown in Figure 10.1, that opens the kernel portion as a serial device and runs the PPP state machines. Through a system interface module it uses ioctl() calls to control the escape characters, assigned addresses, and other attributes within the kernel.

The chat utility is typically invoked by the "connect" option in pppd. Chat is a separate program that communicates via standard I/O and runs a fixed script composed of expect and send pairs. If it reaches the end of the script, it exits successfully. Otherwise, it reports an error. This utility is used to send "AT" commands to the modem to set it up and dial the telephone, and to communicate with the peer if necessary to start the PPP process on that system.

The other two utilities, pppdump and pppstats, are useful for debug and testing of the pppd daemon. They are, however, not normally used during the operation of a typical link.

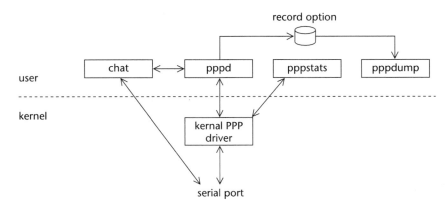

FIGURE 10.1 Components of pppd

Kernel Details

There are two basic styles of kernel drivers supported by pppd, depending on the operating system in use. One is the "line discipline" style, used mostly on BSD-like systems, and the other is the "STREAMS driver," used mostly on System V–like systems.

The Linux Kernel Driver

The Linux driver distributed with ppp-2.3 is an example of the line discipline style of implementation. There are four source files involved in the kernel driver, all in the linux subdirectory: the main driver ppp.c., the CCP Deflate implementation zlib.c and ppp_deflate.c, and the CCP BSD Compress implementation bsd_comp.c. The ppp.c. module has four major sections: line discipline (tty emulation) support, network interface support, CCP support, and frame-level handling.

The internal architecture is shown in Figures 10.2 and 10.3. In these diagrams, I show the names of the major functions involved in input and output processing. These functions include interfaces to the kernel for network input (netif_rx), network output (ppp_dev_xmit() called through the hard_start_xmit function pointer), serial input (ppp_tty_receive() called through the receive_buf function pointer), and serial output (direct calls to the driver.write function pointer). The connection to the pppd process takes place through queues, since the driver runs inside the kernel and the pppd process is in user space.

As of Linux kernel Version 2.3, this driver is being replaced with a rewritten driver. The new driver is under GNU Public License, unlike most of the rest of the ppp-2.3 code, and has been divided into a ppp_generic module, which implements the various compression interfaces (PPP header compression, VJ compression, and CCP data compression), and the ppp_async module, which implements the AHDLC framing and the tty interface. This split simplifies the implementation of synchronous and ISDN PPP drivers. Otherwise, the code is similar to the ppp-2.3 supplied module.

The line discipline driver is attached to the serial I/O subsystem by the pppd daemon when it calls ioctl(tty_fd,TIOCSETD,&ppp_disc) to set the tty line discipline to N_PPP (value 3). This causes the kernel to call through the ppp_tty_open() routine, which allocates and attaches the PPP state structure to the tty. Input on the tty then causes the kernel to call the ppp_tty_receive()

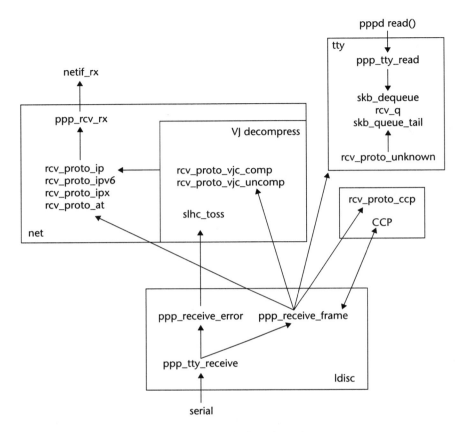

FIGURE 10.2 Linux PPP line discipline—input

routine, which decodes the AHDLC data into packets and calls `ppp_receive_`
`frame()` for each decoded packet.

No flow control is ever asserted on the received serial data stream. In all cases,
the data received are either discarded due to errors or put on a queue, either as
network-layer input or as "unknown" negotiation packets to be sent to the pppd
daemon. If any of these input queues reaches a preconfigured maximum, the oldest packet on the queue is discarded.

Output from the daemon enters the driver as a call to `ppp_tty_write()`. This
function prepares the packet for transmission and calls through to `ppp_send_`
`frames()`. If the output portion isn't already busy with prior output, the driver
selects the oldest packet on the output queue and the call eventually goes down
to `ppp_tty_push()`, which loops and calls the underlying serial tty driver to start

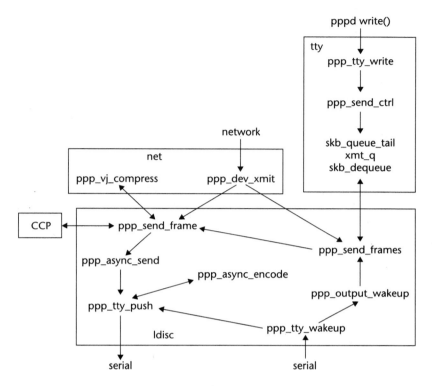

FIGURE 10.3 Linux PPP line discipline—output

the output operation. This loop terminates either when the tty driver output buffer is full or when all data have been enqueued in the tty driver. If the tty driver output buffer becomes full, the PPP state structure is marked as busy and subsequent callbacks from the tty driver to the `ppp_tty_wakeup()` function, which occur when room becomes available in the output buffer, fetch the next batch of data and repeat the cycle.

Thus, the output path operates in two modes: an idle mode, where output calls go straight to the tty driver, and a busy mode, where output calls merely enqueue the data and later upcalls from the tty driver cause these queues to be drained. When all queued data have been sent, the PPP driver clears the busy flag and returns to idle mode.

Network output calls through the `hard_start_xmit` function pointer, which points to `ppp_dev_xmit()`. The rest of the Linux kernel operates with Ethernet type codes to identify network-layer protocols, so these protocols must be translated into PPP protocol numbers in this routine. On input, the PPP protocol number is translated back to an Ethernet type code by each network-layer protocol stub before calling the `ppp_rcv_rx()` function. Since this translation is not one-to-one, it is impossible to transmit arbitrary PPP packets using raw sockets. Since the negotiation packet input is delivered directly to the pppd tty interface, it is also impossible to monitor all of the link traffic using raw sockets.

Unlike the output handler for the daemon, network output is not queued. This is done so that priority-based queuing at the network layer will function properly. If the PPP output driver is not ready for a new packet—because it is currently transmitting another network packet or because the daemon is transmitting data—the `mark_bh(NET_BH)` function is called and an error is returned to the caller. This caller is `do_dev_queue_xmit()` in `net/core/dev.c`, which is part of the general Linux networking stack. This routine puts the packet back on a priority-based queue in the `device` structure.

The call to `mark_bh(NET_BH)` causes an idle polling loop in `kernel/sched.c` to call `do_bottom_half()` in `kernel/soft-irq.c`, and then to `net_bh()` and `dev_transmit()` in `net/core/dev.c`. This routine calls through to the `ppp_dev_xmit()` routine to try again. This process is repeated as long as the system is idle.

The Solaris Kernel Driver

The Solaris kernel driver uses a System V STREAMS module. The bulk of this code is in the modules subdirectory in files called ppp_ahdlc.c and ppp.c. The basic flow of control is shown in Figure 10.4.

The big difference between the STREAMS modules and the line discipline driver is in the flow of control. In the line discipline case, control is transferred by calling through function pointers. In the STREAMS modules, control is transferred either by a call to `putnext()`, which calls through to the "put" routine in the next module, or by an external scheduler that calls into the "srv" routines for each module in turn when `putq()` has been called to defer execution.

The STREAMS module implementation supports priority queuing and multiple kernel threads.

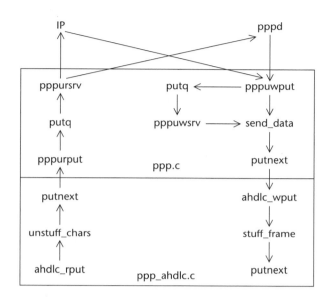

FIGURE 10.4 Solaris PPP STREAMS modules

The pppd Daemon

The daemon itself is relatively straightforward in comparison with the tricks necessary inside the Unix kernel. The daemon consists of the files in the pppd subdirectory. These files are as follows.

main.c	The main loop; this routine initializes the PPP link phases (as shown in Figure 3.1 on page 48) and dispatches timer events and packets received.
options.c	This module parses the options files and command line and sets the internal data structures based on user configuration.
fsm.c	This module implements the XCP (LCP and NCP) finite state machines (as shown in Figure 3.6 on page 53). This is the main part of PPP negotiation.
*xxx*cp.c	These are the control protocols, including lcp, ipcp, ipv6cp, ipxcp, cbcp, and ccp.
chap.c	RFC 1994 CHAP authentication.
md5.c	Implementation of the Message Digest 5 algorithm used in CHAP.

chap_ms.c	MS-CHAPv1 algorithm 80 glue code (requires an external DES library not distributed with pppd).
md4.c	MD4 algorithm used in MS-CHAPv1.
upap.c	RFC 1334 PAP authentication.
auth.c	Authentication support functions to read password files and implement linkage among authentication protocols, LCP, and the NCPs through the PPP link phases.
magic.c	A wrapper around calls to the standard mrand48() library function plus a few compatibility definitions for systems lacking this function; this is used to generate data for the LCP Magic Number option and the Challenge values for CHAP.
eui64.c	Implements eui64_ntoa() for IPv6 (prints IPv6 addresses).
demand.c	Support functions for demand-dialing interfaces; includes packet queuing and playback.
utils.c	String manipulation, logging functions, and portable file locking.
sys-*name*.c	This contains the small amount of system-dependent glue to make pppd operate, including routines for detecting the presence of the necessary kernel modules, and system-dependent usage of routines such as select() and poll(). Porting to a new system generally requires modification of only the routines found here.

The main control protocols (LCP, authentication, and the NCPs) work through a set of function pointers declared in a data structure called the protent. These functions are invoked by fsm.c. This structure is declared in pppd.h and has functions for all of the events that can occur, except time-outs, plus linkage from LCP to the NCPs for handling received Protocol-Reject messages (the protrej function) and a generic packet print function pointer to allow each implemented protocol to log packets in a human-readable format. Time-outs are handled separately through a callout mechanism similar to the BSD timeout interface.

After setting up logging and reading the options files, the main() routine calls get_input() to service the received packets. For each received packet, this routine searches the list of known protocols and delivers the packets through the input function pointer in the appropriate protent structure, or sends LCP Protocol-Reject if the protocol received is unknown.

When LCP goes to Opened state, it calls link_established() in auth.c. This routine determines if any authentication is to be run. If any is to be run, it calls directly into the authentication protocol code to start the authentication process. The authentication protocols are then responsible for calling network_phase()

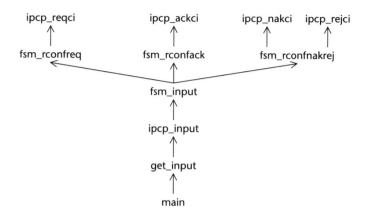

FIGURE 10.5 Call path on IPCP reception

to kick off the NCPs. Otherwise, if no authentication is in use, link_authentication() calls network_phase() itself to start the NCPs immediately.

This main packet-handling loop continues until the link_terminated() function is invoked to transition to "dead" phase. This is done if the modem hangs up (detected as an end-of-file condition on the connection to the kernel driver) or if LCP triggers the "this layer finished" action in the finite state machine. The latter case usually results from the shut-down of all of the NCPs.

Figure 10.5 shows the function call path from the main loop to the IPCP option processing functions on IPCP packet reception. The call from get_input() to ipcp_input() is made through the ipcp_protoent.input function pointer. The call from fsm_rconfreq() to ipcp_reqci() is made through the ipcp_callbacks.reqci function pointer. In each case, the IPCP option processing function returns a code to the FSM to indicate whether or not the options were accepted so that the FSM can take the appropriate state transition.

The Utility Programs

chat

This utility is normally invoked by pppd using the "connect" option. It is, however, a free-standing program and is not specific to PPP. Chat reads a script on the command line, reads and writes to standard I/O, and terminates with return code 0 if all parts of the script have run without error, or with nonzero if any errors have occurred.

pppdump

This utility is intended for testing CCP data compression, MTU handling, AHDLC framing, and other implementation problems. It produces a raw hex dump of all data sent and received on a PPP link from the binary file produced by the pppd "record" option. Unlike the usual pppd debug trace facility, it can decode compressed data. However, it does not decode PPP negotiation and is therefore not suitable for general use in link debugging.

pppstats

This utility calls into the kernel driver using ioctl code SIOCGPPPSTATS. This retrieves the `ppp_stats` structure, which contains various implementation-specific counters, such as input and output byte and packet counts. These counters are then printed on standard output in a human-readable form.

Modifying pppd

Adding a New Protocol

Adding a new network-layer protocol to pppd generally involves four main code changes. First, the NCP for the new protocol is created. The easy way to do this is to copy an existing NCP implementation (ipcp.c and ipcp.h serve as a good template) and edit the names as needed. Second, edit main.c and add the header file for the new protocol and a new entry to the `protocols[]` array. Third, the appropriate sys-*name*.c file must be edited to add any necessary network interface support functions, such as `sifaddr()`. Finally, the kernel portion for the appropriate system must be updated to connect into the new network layer and to support the `ioctl()` functions added to sys-*name*.c.

The appropriate Makefile for the added modules in pppd will need to be updated as well as documentation, such as README files and man pages.

You might also want to add debug wrapper macros to pppd.h if your code is instrumented with unit-test debug messages. Most new protocols do not do this but probably should. When adding debug messages of this type, do not omit detailed error messages for the user. It should not be necessary to recompile pppd with debug enabled in order to troubleshoot configuration or common compatibility errors.

Porting to a New Platform

This task can be much more difficult than adding a new protocol. First, you must be intimately familiar with the low-level serial I/O mechanisms and with the network-layer implementation. On Unix systems, these generally have either a STREAMS-like or a BSD-like implementation, and one of the existing ports can be used as a starting point. On other systems, the distinction between kernel and user may not exist, or portions of serial I/O or networking may exist outside of the kernel. These differences are hidden from pppd in the sys-*name*.c module.

The general tasks to be accomplished on a new system are to implement AHDLC for asynchronous ports, attach to network layer processing, and, if necessary, create control mechanisms similar to Unix ioctl() to link together the kernel and sys-*name*.c portions, allowing pppd to set serial and network parameters. The time-critical portions of PPP—the AHDLC processing and network packet handling—are usually optimized and integrated into a single module for the kernel. Any other tasks are deferred to the pppd daemon and are implemented in sys-*name*.c.

Differences from RFC 1661

There are several differences between pppd and the protocol described in RFC 1661. These differences are described below.

- The RFC has just five link phases. Pppd adds five more to handle serial ports better (PHASE_INITIALIZE, PHASE_SERIALCONN, and PHASE_HOLDOFF), add demand-dialing (PHASE_DORMANT), and support callback (PHASE_CALLBACK). See Figure 10.6. Not shown in this diagram are transitions from any phase to PHASE_DEAD; this phase can be entered at any time by a modem hang-up signal.
- Unlike the RFC, pppd does not invoke the "this layer finished" action when going from Starting state to Initial state due to a Close event. This appears to be a bug.

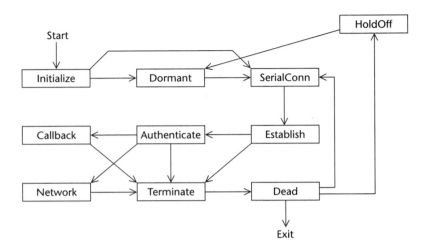

FIGURE 10.6 PPPD link phases

- The Up event in pppd when in Starting state does not necessarily go to Req-Sent state. Pppd has an option (called *silent* mode) in which it transitions instead to Stopped state and awaits negotiation messages from the peer. Similarly, in Closed state an Open event will send it into Stopped state when this option is enabled. (The RFC has a similar mode called *passive,* but it does not alter the operation of the Starting or Closed state.)
- The "this layer finished" action is not invoked by pppd if silent mode is enabled and a TO– event occurs in Req-Sent, Ack-Rcvd, or Ack-Sent state.
- The RFC makes a distinction between fatal and nonfatal Code-Reject and Protocol-Reject messages. Pppd simplifies this and calls any Code-Reject nonfatal (RXJ+) and any Protocol-Reject fatal (RXJ–). This means that, contrary to the RFC, pppd ignores errant Code-Rejects of standard messages, such as Configure-Request. Fortunately, peer systems rarely have bugs that would generate such messages, and ignoring them is arguably safer than the handling suggested in the RFC. Unfortunately, this does mean that pppd does not implement the Code-Reject handling according to the RFC if the peer rejects an extended code number. It is required to cease transmission of the affected code number, but it has no mechanism to handle this. If the peer Code-Rejects CCP Reset-Request or LCP Echo-Request, pppd ignores this and continues to send the offending code number.

- Pppd can transition to Stopped state from Req-Sent or Ack-Sent states on event RCN based on flags from CCP (a negative return value from the rejci function). This is a special feature intended to allow CCP to cease negotiation when no more algorithms remain to be negotiated. The RFC always remains in the same state on this event.

Listed below are the mappings between the events in RFC 1661 and the functions that handle these events in pppd.

```
Up         fsm_lowerup()
Down       fsm_lowerdown()
Open       fsm_open()
Close      fsm_close()
TO+        fsm_timeout() (f->retransmits>0)
TO-        fsm_timeout() (f->retransmits<=0)
RCR+       fsm_rconfreq() (reqci gives CONFACK)
RCR-       fsm_rconfreq() (reqci() != CONFACK)
RCA        fsm_rconfack()
RCN        fsm_rconfnakrej()
RTR        fsm_rtermreq()
RTA        fsm_rtermack()
RXJ+       fsm_rcoderej()
RXJ-       fsm_protorej()
```

The RUC (receive unknown code) event is handled directly inside `fsm_input()`, which is responsible for dispatching messages with known codes to the functions listed above.

Log Messages

Below is a summary of some of the more common error and status messages that pppd can place in the system log during operation. Not all possible messages or corrective actions are listed here.

protocol: timeout sending Config-Requests

The negotiation is not converging or the peer is not responding at all to Configure-Request messages. When this occurs to LCP, it generally indicates that a low-level communications problem, such as a chat script failure, exists. For CCP, this is usually not an error at all. It means that the peers have no algorithms in common and cannot compress data. The link is still operational. You may want to specify "noccp" in this case in order to speed convergence.

```
Received bad configure-ack: packet
Received bad configure-nak/rej: packet
```

These messages are triggered by bugs in the peer implementation. They mean that the Configure-Ack, -Nak, or -Reject sent by the peer was unacceptably formed. One possible problem, for instance, is that the peer's Configure-Ack does not match the last Configure-Request sent. It is not legal to modify any part of a message returned in Configure-Ack. (The one exception to this rule is the NBFCP Name-Projection option described on page 151.)

When this error occurs, it is often quite troublesome. When a peer malforms one of these packets, it usually does so quite repeatably. This means that either the peer must be repaired or pppd must be patched to accept or work around the malformed data.

```
protocol terminated by peer (string)
protocol terminated by peer
```

These messages are emitted for the Terminate-Request message. They mean that the peer has shut down the indicated protocol. If the peer included an optional text message, it is included in this message as well. Some implementations, such as Windows NT, send baroque binary error codes instead of plain text strings when errors occur. Some of the more common codes for that system are listed in Section 8 of RFC 2433 and on page 112 of this book.

These messages do not always signify an error condition. For instance, CCP rarely works between pppd and any commercial PPP implementation, since pppd implements only freely available algorithms, and most commercial implementations have only proprietary algorithms. In these cases, CCP is often shut down, and this is the expected result. To speed negotiation, the "noccp" option should be specified in these cases.

```
protocol: Rcvd Code-Reject for code number, id number
```

This message indicates only that a Code-Reject message was received; it does not indicate that any specific failure has occurred. This can be caused by CCP Reset-Request messages or by Identification messages, where implemented.

Pppd does not properly implement Code-Reject handling, and will continue to send the offending code number, so if this message occurs in the debug log, it is likely to occur many times.

```
Protocol-Reject for unsupported protocol 0xXXXX
```

This message means that pppd has received an LCP Protocol-Reject message indicating that pppd itself has somehow sent a protocol that it doesn't implement to the peer.

There are two common causes of this message. The first is that Version 2.3.7 of pppd is in use and the "debug" option was specified. This version of pppd has a bug that causes pppd to send text debug messages over the link rather than to the system log file, and the peer will reject these messages as unknown PPP protocols. The fix is to upgrade to 2.3.8 or later. The other common cause is CCP compressor corruption. If these messages occur frequently, the "noccp" option should be used.

```
Unsupported protocol "name" (0xXXXX) received
Unsupported protocol (0xXXXX) received
```

This is usually not an error. It usually indicates that the peer is offering to run a network protocol not implemented in pppd. The unsupported protocol will be rejected, and the link will continue to operate normally. The messages are errors when the peer is offering to run ECP, protocol 8053, where refusal to negotiate will cause the link to be terminated, and when the errors are due to CCP decompressor corruption, or peers that have the 2.3.7 bug. The current pppd does not implement ECP and cannot be used with peers that require it. If CCP runs into trouble, it should be disabled with "noccp." If the peer is using pppd-2.3.7, it should be upgraded.

```
Hangup (SIGHUP)
```

The modem has hung up the telephone connection. This can be caused by modem problems, chat script errors, authentication problems, and idle timers on the remote system. A more extensive debugging effort is often necessary to discern the cause of an unexpected hang-up.

```
Terminating on signal number.
```

Pppd has received an unexpected signal. This includes Control-C or "kill" (SIGTERM) by the user. This error also occurs on Linux systems when the serial port is misconfigured with setserial. On other systems, it can represent initd problems or failing cron jobs. In general, completely unexpected signals are very difficult to debug since Unix offers no tracing facilities for interprocess signals.

```
Receive serial link is not 8-bit clean:
Problem: all had bit 7 set to 1
Problem: all had bit 7 set to 0
Problem: all had odd parity
Problem: all had even parity
```

These errors occur in two cases. The most common case is that the peer is not running PPP at all but rather is running a text-mode command line and is simply echoing the received data back to pppd. Some command-line implementations will strip the upper bit of the bytes received, leading to the messages above. The less common case is that the link is configured for 7-bit operation. PPP cannot be run over 7-bit links.

```
Serial line is looped back.
```

This error is given when pppd receives too many (ten or more) LCP Configure-Naks. This usually indicates that the peer is not running PPP, and pppd is receiving its own output echoed back. This usually is not a problem in pppd configuration, but rather is a chat script error.

```
No response to count echo-requests
Serial link appears to be disconnected.
```

These two messages are always logged together. They indicate that the "lcp-echo-failure" option was specified and that the peer has failed to respond to the specified number of consecutive LCP Echo-Request messages. This usually indicates that the peer is no longer running PPP or that the physical link itself has failed.

```
Connection terminated.
```

This means that LCP has terminated operation, either due to a hang-up signal from the modem (if any) or due to the state machine invoking the "this layer finished" action in LCP.

```
peer refused to authenticate: terminating link
```

The "auth" option was specified, meaning that the peer was required to authenticate itself, but the peer either sent Configure-Reject for the LCP Authentication option or sent Configure-Nak for all known protocols. Note that the current pppd implementation assumes that authentication is required if the host system has a default route. Many small stand-alone systems using pppd to connect to the general Internet are misconfigured with an errant default route on some other interface, and the usual fix for this problem is to remove the mistakenly configured route. The privileged "noauth" option must be used if the default route must be retained and this behavior is not desired.

```
No secret found for PAP login
No CHAP secret found for authenticating us to name
```

The peer has requested a PAP peer name and password or CHAP authentication from pppd, but neither the "password" option nor any matching entries in the pap-secrets or chap-secrets file were found. This means that we cannot log into our peer.

```
Terminating connection due to lack of activity.
```

The "idle" option was specified with a time limit, and no network activity has been detected recently.

```
Connect time expired
```

The "maxconnect" option was specified with a time limit, and that absolute limit has been reached, regardless of network activity.

```
The remote system (name) is required to authenticate itself but
    I couldn't find any suitable secret (password) for it to
    use to do so.
```

This error often occurs because pppd is being used on a system that has a default route and the peer is a regular ISP, which usually does not offer to authenticate itself to dial-up users. If this is the case, the right fix is to remove the default route before starting pppd. This route is usually erroneous.

Another possible cause of this problem is that the pap-secrets or chap-secrets file is misconfigured.

```
By default the remote system is required to authenticate itself
    (because this system has a default route to the internet)
    but I couldn't find any suitable secret (password) for it
    to use to do so.
```

This error message is new as of Version 2.3.11. It better explains the problem described above.

```
The remote system is required to authenticate itself but I
    couldn't find any secret (password) which would let it use
    an IP address.
```

This error usually occurs after upgrading of a pppd dial-in system from an older pppd version. The pap-secrets and chap-secrets files now have a required fourth field for dial-in users. This field must list any valid IP address for the dial-in user or specify "*" to allow any address.

```
The remote system is required to authenticate itself but I
    couldn't find any suitable secret (password) for it to use
    to do so. (None of the available passwords would let it use
    an IP address.)
```

This error message is also new as of Version 2.3.11. It better explains the problem described above.

```
no PAP secret found for name
No CHAP secret found for authenticating name
```

The peer is attempting to identify itself using PAP or CHAP, but no local pap-secrets or chap-secrets entry for the remote system exists.

```
PAP authentication failed
CHAP peer authentication failed for remote host name
```

The peer has rejected our credentials and returned either PAP Authenticate-Nak or CHAP Failure. This means that the locally configured user name or password is incorrect for the remote system. This can be caused by an incorrect or missing name in the "user" option or a lack of correct quoting of any special characters in the pap-secrets or chap-secrets file or command-line options.

```
No response to PAP authenticate-requests
Peer failed to respond to CHAP challenge
```

This means that pppd attempted to identify itself to its peer using PAP or to identify the peer using CHAP, but the peer never responded. One common cause of this problem is a bad value in the "asyncmap" option, which sets the ACCM. If this value is bad for the current link (that is, if it permits raw transmission of control characters that are not handled by the link itself) or if the peer has ACCM-related bugs (unfortunately, many do), then LCP negotiates properly and goes to Opened state. Once LCP is up, the ACCM is set to the negotiated value and the next protocol to run fails.

One way to fix this problem is to use the "debug" option, note the "asyncmap" value in the peer's LCP Configure-Request messages, and then specify this in the pppd options.

For PAP, another possible cause of this problem is that the peer is sending malformed PAP Authenticate-Ack messages and the pppd version is prior to 2.3.11. Some Windows NT systems omit the required message-length octet from this packet, and the older pppd versions have a bug that causes pppd to ignore these packets entirely. Upgrading to 2.3.11 or later fixes this problem.

```
PAP authentication failure for name
CHAP authentication failed
```

The peer's password is invalid. This can be caused by a misconfigured peer or by errors in the pap-secrets or chap-secrets file.

```
PAP login failure for name
```

The pap-secrets file has a blank password for the indicated peer and the "login" option was set, but the peer's password does not validate against the system password file.

```
Can't open PAP password file name: error
Can't open chap secret file name: error
cannot stat secret file name: error
can't open indirect secret file name
```

These are access errors on the pap-secrets and chap-secrets files. The nonprivileged "user" and "password" options can usually be used to work around this problem. (Since pppd can invoke external scripts and will not give up privileges when it does so, it is not a good idea to run pppd while logged in as root as a possible work-around.)

```
Warning - secret file name has world and/or group access
```

This message warns that the system is possibly insecure because the pap-secrets or chap-secrets file, which may contain actual user passwords, is readable by someone other than the privileged root user. You can fix this with the Unix "chmod go-rwx name" command.

```
Could not determine remote IP address
Could not determine local IP address
```

These errors occur when IP attempts to go to Opened state and either the remote or local IP address on the link is still 0.0.0.0. Some ISPs fail to supply their own IP addresses, and simply adding an arbitrary remote address to the link (using an option such as ":192.168.1.1") is sufficient to make the link operational. See IP Addressing Issues, on page 158, for more details.

```
Peer is not authorized to use remote address IP
```

The peer has negotiated an IP address that is not listed in the corresponding pap-secrets or chap-secrets entry.

```
not replacing existing default route to interface [gateway]
```

This message occurs when pppd is run with the "defaultroute" option on a system that already has a configured default route. Usually, this is a mistake and leads to trouble. The most frequent cause of this is that a mistaken default route as been installed on an available Ethernet interface. If the dial-up PPP session is connecting to the global Internet, this session should get the default route rather than the Ethernet. Otherwise, if the PPP session is actually a dial-in user, the "defaultroute" option should usually be omitted.

```
Cannot determine ethernet address for proxy ARP
```

Proxy ARP is generally used for dial-in clients and works by having one of the local Ethernet interfaces generate ARP replies on behalf of the peer's IP address. Therefore, in order to use proxy ARP, the remote IP address on the PPP link must be within a subnet defined by one of the configured Ethernet interfaces. This error message indicates that the remote IP address is not in any of those subnets and, therefore, that no proxy ARP entry can be determined. If the peer's address is not in the same subnet as one of the Ethernet interfaces, then packets must be routed to it and proxy ARP cannot be used.

```
Compression disabled by peer.
```

This is not necessarily an error. CCP has been shut down because the peer sent CCP Terminate-Request while CCP was in Opened state. This usually happens because the peers have no algorithms in common. The "noccp" option can be used to disable CCP.

```
modprobe: can't locate module char-major-108
modprobe: can't locate module ppp-compress-26
modprobe: can't locate module ppp-compress-24
```

These are common and harmless messages issued when pppd is run on pre-2.3 Linux kernels. On 2.2 and earlier kernels, you can add this line to /etc/conf.modules to quiet down the first error:

```
alias char-major-108 off
```

On 2.3 and above, this should be changed to load the new PPP driver:

```
alias tty-ldisc-3 ppp_async
alias char-major-108 ppp_generic
```

On all kernels, these lines should be used to load compression modules:

```
alias ppp-compress-21 bsd_comp
alias ppp-compress-24 ppp_deflate
alias ppp-compress-26 ppp_deflate
```

These modules may also be specified as "off" to disable the corresponding error message without loading the module. For example, you may use this link to disable the obsolete Deflate option number:

```
alias ppp-compress-24 off
```

Other Notes

The "connect" option can specify a script that uses the stty utility to change the line to 7 bits, even parity, runs chat, and then changes back to 8 bits, no parity to run PPP. This can be used to support old or nonstandard systems that require parity during the login process.

The current pppd implementation assumes that authentication is required if the host system has a default route. Since this feature is rather unobvious, I recommend using an explicit "auth" or "noauth" as needed. Note, however, that "noauth" is a privileged option. This means that by default ordinary (nonroot) users invoking pppd on a system with a default route will always be required to authenticate the remote peer.

If you use the "login" option for PAP peers, you must still list each user permitted to use PPP in the pap-secrets file and specify the password as blank (""). Don't specify a real password, or the user's password will always need to match both this password and the system password. Be careful with this option, since the peers listed this way in the pap-secrets file will be allowed access with no password at all if pppd is accidentally invoked without the "login" option. Use of this option is demonstrated in the example configuration in the next section.

One useful but not well-documented feature of pppd is that some options can be specified in the pap-secrets and chap-secrets files. To do this, place two dashes (--) between the authorized IP addresses and the additional options. This is useful if one user has trouble with VJ compression or some users would like to run optional network protocols.

Pppd directly supports BSD Compress (because it is distributed from Australia, where the Unisys patent does not hold) and Deflate and has hooks to support Predictor-1, although the latter is not shipped with the code due to other patent problems.

Pppd has supported CBCP as a dial-up client since Version 2.3.5. There is a CBCP server-side implementation available on the Internet, but it is rough and unsupported.

The pppd Configuration Options

Pppd options can be hard to understand. In addition to having 170 options, pppd also reads options from several sources: three main configuration files, the command line, the secrets files, and other optional files. Also the order of evaluation is significant, and the privilege rules are different for some files.

On start-up, pppd always reads these sources of options in the following order:

1. /etc/ppp/options   System-wide options, such as "lock" or "auth"
2. ~/.ppprc   User-specific options, such as "user"
3. /etc/ppp/options.*ttyname*   Per-tty options, such as dynamic IP addresses
4. command line   Invocation options, such as "call" and "debug"

The first file, /etc/ppp/options, is special in two ways. First, if it does not exist, regular users are not permitted to run pppd; only the root user may run it. Second, all options read from this file are treated as though the user were privileged. This allows special system-wide defaults to be set for all users.

The second file, ~/.ppprc, is processed if it exists. It is not an error for this file to be missing, and most configurations do not make use of this file. Any options read from this file are treated as unprivileged for ordinary users and as privileged for root users.

The third file, /etc/ppp/options.*ttyname,* is also processed if it exists. As with the first file, all options read from this file are treated as privileged. This file is most often used with dial-in servers to set a single IP address per serial port. (Most ISPs supporting dial-up users do not have enough IP addresses for all customers. Instead, they assign users IP addresses dynamically on connection, and assigning one IP address to each port is the easiest way to configure this operation.)

The command line is processed last. Like the second file, it is read with the user's privilege level.

Two special options, *file* and *call*, can be used to read options from another file. The first option works as an "include" statement—the options read from that file are read with the same privilege level as that in effect at the location at which the option was read. The second option is special. This causes pppd to read options from a named file in the directory /etc/ppp/peers/. All options in that file are treated as privileged. The purpose of this option is to allow the administrator to set up specific peers that ordinary (nonroot) users may call when necessary.

Finally, an undocumented feature allows options to be read from /etc/ppp/pap-secrets and /etc/ppp/chap-secrets. These options, which are placed at the end of a matching entry after a double-dash (--) separator, are treated as privileged and are interpreted and set at the point where pppd transitions from Authenticate to Network phase. Since these options are interpreted after LCP and authentication have both passed, they are limited in use. They are usually used to enable or disable network protocols for special users or to configure options (such as VJ compression) on a per-user basis.

Option Privilege

There are three basic types of options. Most options may be invoked by either privileged or unprivileged users. The following options may be invoked by privileged users only.

```
allow-ip        name        plugin
linkname        noauth      privgroup
```

The options listed below, all of which specify external scripts to run when particular events occur, are usually available to both privileged and unprivileged users. However, if a privileged source (one of the special files specified above) specifies the option, the value specified cannot be overridden by an unprivileged user.

```
connect         init        welcome
disconnect      pty
```

This special override feature protects the scripts by root and is used to support the "call" option. These options—especially "connect"—are usually used in the /etc/ppp/peers/*name* file, and this restriction prevents ordinary users from redirecting the call to another site.

Deprecated Options

All of the options with a leading "+" or "−" character have been deprecated. The following list gives equivalents from old to new option names, where direct equivalents exist.

Old	New	Old	New
+chap	require-chap	-detach	nodetach
+ipx	ipx	-ip	noip
+pap	require-pap	-ipv6	noipv6
-ac	noaccomp	-ipx	noipx
-am	default-asyncmap	-mn	nomagic
-as	asyncmap	-mru	default-mru
-bsdcomp	nobsdcomp	-p	passive
-ccp	noccp	-pap	refuse-pap
-chap	refuse-chap	-pc	nopcomp
-crtscts	nocrtscts	-predictor1	nopredictor1
-d	debug	-proxyarp	noproxyarp
-defaultroute	nodefaultroute	-vj	novj
-deflate	nodeflate	-vjccomp	novjccomp

In a few cases, however, direct equivalents do not exist. These options are summarized below.

−all   Disables all LCP and IPCP options. This might be helpful on the pppd command line to return the options to a known state if multiple option files are in use during debugging.

−h   Prints a very short help string and exits.

+ipv6   Enables IPV6CP negotiation. Unlike the "ipv6" option, this option is a Boolean option and thus takes no additional arguments.

+ua   Undocumented option that takes a single argument, which is the name of a file from which pppd will read a user name and password (each on a separate line) for use in authenticating to the peer with PAP. The file must be readable by the user invoking pppd and should not be readable by others.

Other Undocumented Options

Listed below are several options that were accidentally left undocumented in Version 2.3.11 but should appear in future versions of the documentation. (I have included updated "man" pages on the accompanying CD-ROM for these options.)

callback	This option takes a single text-string argument representing the callback telephone number for use with Microsoft CBCP.
ipv6cp-accept-local	Allows IPV6CP to accept the peer's suggestion of a local interface identifier.
ipv6cp-use-ipaddr	Use the local IPv4 address as the local interface identifier by default.
ipv6cp-use-persistent	Uses a special persistent value for the local interface identifier. (Available only on Solaris.)
ipxcp-restart	Takes a single numeric argument and sets the IPXCP restart interval (retransmission timer) in seconds. The default is 3 seconds.
ms-lanman	If using MS-CHAPv1 authentication, use LAN Manager style authentication, rather than Windows NT.
nocdtrcts	This was mistakenly documented as "nodtrcts."
nodeflatedraft	Disables use of the improperly assigned algorithm number (hex 18) for Deflate in CCP. This was once used in an Internet Draft.
nologfd	An alias for "nolog."
password	Sets the PAP password for authenticating oneself to the peer.

The following options are undocumented and probably will remain so.

-- help	Same as –h.
-- version	Prints the version of pppd and exits.
pdebug	This option is intended to set the debug level in libpcap on systems supporting packet filtering, but is not currently implemented. This option takes a single-integer argument.

Example Configuration

In this example, a machine running pppd is to be used to provide Internet access to typical Windows 98 dial-up clients. This machine, named "fred," is connected to a local Ethernet, configured with local address 172.16.1.1 and subnet mask 255.255.255.0. Since the remote machines are just dial-up systems, proxy-ARP will be used to give them access to the local network.

First, we configure mgetty for two ports. Alternatively, users could dial in and invoke "pppd" themselves using a terminal window or a script, but mgetty makes things much easier.

```
/etc/inittab
    S0:345:respawn:/usr/local/sbin/mgetty ttyS0
    S1:345:respawn:/usr/local/sbin/mgetty ttyS1


/usr/local/etc/mgetty+sendfax/login.config
    /AutoPPP/ - ppp /usr/sbin/pppd
```

Next, we set up the default pppd options. None of our PPP links should be used as a routing interface, so we disable those options. For convenience of the Windows users, we also set up DNS server addresses.

```
/etc/ppp/options
    lock                  # ensure exclusive access
    auth                  # must authenticate peers
    nodefaultroute        # peers never route for us
    hide-password         # caution on logging
    idle 3600             # disconnect if idle for an hour
    172.16.1.1:           # specify our address
    ms-dns 172.16.1.1     # specify a name server
    ms-dns 172.16.1.2     # specify a secondary
    noccp                 # don't bother with compression
    noipx                 # don't use IPX
    nolog                 # don't log messages
    proxyarp              # remote peers are on local net
    nodetach              # don't detach from tty
    name fred             # our official name
```

Now we set up the per-port configuration. By putting a remote address here, we are allowing per-port (often called "dynamic") addressing. This is very useful when the population of potential users is greater than the number of available addresses.

```
/etc/ppp/options.ttyS0
   :172.16.1.240        # dynamic IP address for peer
/etc/ppp/options.ttyS1
   :172.16.1.241        # dynamic IP address for peer
```

Finally, we set up the secrets file. This one is more complicated than most, and illustrates some of what can be done with pppd. Sue is a regular dial-up user. Bob is a dial-up user with an assigned static IP address—every time he dials in, he gets the same address, and no other user will be assigned his address. Sam has an encrypted password (the plaintext is "dog") and uses dynamic addresses, but he cannot use VJ compression because of bugs in his system. Finally, Sally keeps her password in a local file (readable only by her) rather than in the system pap-secrets file.

```
/etc/ppp/pap-secrets
   sue fred "suzie" 172.16.1.240/28
   bob fred "i123" 172.16.1.100 # static IP for Bob
   sam fred "gAYqX/XYXtB8E" 172.16.1.240/28 -- novj
   sally fred @/usr/sally/.secret 172.16.1.240/28
```

Here is a simple program that generates valid encrypted passwords for use in the pap-secrets file. It is included on the accompanying CD-ROM as "crypt.c."

```
#include <stdio.h>

int main(argc,argv)
int argc;
char **argv;
{
    char salt[2];
    int i;
    static char saltchrs[] =
"ABCDEFGHIJKLMNOPQRSTUVWXYZabcdefghijklmnopqrstuvwxy"
    "z0123456789./";
```

```
        if (argc < 2 || argc > 3) {
           fprintf(stderr,
               "Usage:\n\t%s passwd [salt]\n",*argv);
           return 1;
        }
        if (argc > 2) {
           if (!strchr(saltchrs,salt[0] = argv[2][0]) ||
               !strchr(saltchrs,salt[1] = argv[2][1])) {
               fprintf(stderr,
                   "Illegal salt characters; must be in the"
           "range [A-Za-z0-9\\./]\n");
               return 1;
            }
        } else {
           srand(time(NULL));
           i = rand();
           salt[0] = saltchrs[i % 64];
           salt[1] = saltchrs[(i / 64) % 64];
        }
        puts(crypt(argv[1],salt));
        return 0;
    }
```

Resources

Any list of resources for an actively evolving technology such as PPP will almost immediately be outdated. In addition to the various sources listed below, I encourage you to seek out the latest information from your local library, Internet search services, and bookstores that specialize in technical publications.

The CD-ROM accompanying this book contains all of the RFCs and many other public documents, references, and links that are current as of publication. Unfortunately, because most of the PPP-related protocols are covered by patents, I have been forced to omit all of the publicly available source code.

I also maintain an up-to-date reference list at `http://people.ne.mediaone.net/carlson/ppp/` and at `http://www.workingcode.com/ppp/`. These sites have links to the available source code.

Other PPP-Related Books

Richard Shea, *L2TP: Implementation and Operation*, Addison-Wesley, ISBN 0-201-60448-5.

This book covers the Layer Two Tunneling Protocol (L2TP) and PPP's operation over this protocol in great detail. If you need to implement or use L2TP, this is the book to get.

Andrew Sun, *Using and Managing PPP*, O'Reilly & Associates,
ISBN 1-56592-321-9.

This is the other PPP book. It focuses on PPP usage rather than on implementation or debugging, and it covers other matters such as DNS and server
configuration.

Related Books and Other Publications

W. Richard Stevens, *TCP/IP Illustrated*, vol. 1, Addison-Wesley,
ISBN 0-201-63346-9.

This book, part of a series on networking, does a superb job of describing the
IP network layer and the transport and application layers above it. If you implement or use IPCP over PPP, this book will help you design and debug your system once PPP is running.

Douglas E. Comer, *Internetworking with TCP/IP: Principles, Protocols
and Architecture*, vols. 1 and 2, Prentice-Hall, ISBN 0-13-216987-8 and
0-13-125527-4.

This is another good series of books on the TCP/IP suite of protocols. It is
referred to often enough in the Internet world that most people simply call it
"Comer."

Marshall Kirk McKusick et al., *The Design and Implementation of the 4.4 BSD
Operating System*, Addison-Wesley, ISBN 0-201-54979-4.

4.4 BSD is a reference version of Unix produced by the University of California at Berkeley. It contains several networking-related mechanisms that are
typical of high-performance implementations of TCP/IP and PPP. If you need
more information about how to design a networking system from scratch, this is
a good place to start.

Ian Wade, *NOSintro: TCP/IP Over Packet Radio: An Introduction to the
KA9Q Network Operating System*, Dowermain, ISBN 1-897649-00-2.

This is a book specifically about the MS-DOS-based KA9Q networking system, which includes PPP drivers and many common TCP/IP applications.

G. Sidhu, R. Andrews, A. Oppenheimer, *Inside AppleTalk*, 2d ed., Addison-Wesley, ISBN 0201550210.

This is the standard reference for the AppleTalk networking protocols.

Local Area Network Technical Reference, IBM, SC30-3383-2.

This is the standard reference for NetBEUI/NetBIOS.

Internet Transport Protocols, Xerox, XNSS 029101.

This is the standard reference for XNS.

DNA Routing Layer Functional Specification, Digital Equipment Corporation, AA-X436A-TK.

This is the standard reference for DECNet.

Media Access Control (MAC) Bridges, ISO/IEC 15802-3:1998, ANSI/IEEE Std 802.1D; *Remote Media Access Control (MAC) Bridging*, ISO/IEC 15802-5:1998, ANSI/IEEE Std 802.1G.

These two documents describe the IEEE bridging (spanning tree) protocols.

Token-Ring Network Architecture Reference, 3rd ed., September 1989.

This is the standard reference for Token Ring bridging and other MAC details.

Bob Quinn and Dave Shute, *Windows Sockets Network Programming*, Addison-Wesley, ISBN 0-201-63372-8; Karen Hazzah, *Writing Windows VxDs and Device Drivers: Programming Secrets for Virtual Device Drivers*, 2nd ed., R&D Books, ISBN 0-87930-438-3; Tom Shanley and Don Anderson, *Plug and Play System Architecture*, Addison-Wesley, ISBN 0-201-41013-3.

These are three reference books that PC programmers might find useful. There are a very large number of similar books on the market today.

Bruce Schneier, *Applied Cryptography*, 2nd ed., John Wiley & Sons, ISBN 0-471-11709-9; Dorothy Elizabeth Denning, *Cryptography and Data Security*, Addison-Wesley, ISBN 0-201-10150-5; Simson Garfinkel and Gene

Spafford, *Practical Unix and Internet Security,* O'Reilly & Associates, ISBN 1-56592-148-8; David K. Hsiao, D. S. Kerr, S. E. Madnick, *Computer Security,* Academic Press, ISBN 0-12357-650-4; R. L. Rivest, A. Shamir, L. Adleman, On Digital Signatures and Public Key Cryptosystems, *Communications of the ACM,* vol. 21 no. 2 (February 1978): pp. 120–126.

These are a few of the standard references on computer security. Bruce Schneier's Web site, `http://www.counterpane.com/`, has more information about his books and several useful documents on security.

Getting RFCs, Internet Drafts, and Other Documents

There are a large number of repositories of the IETF standards-related documents. Visit the RFC editor's Web page at `http://www.rfc-editor.org/` and the IETF home page at `http://www.ietf.org/` for up-to-date lists of repositories. The current primary RFC repositories are as follows.

`nis.nsf.net`	`ftp.rfc-editor.org`
`ftp.isi.edu`	`wuarchive.wustl.edu`
`src.doc.ic.ac.uk`	`ftp.ncren.net`
`ftp.sesqui.net`	`ftp.nic.it`
`ftp.imag.fr`	`ftp.ietf.rnp.br`
`www.normos.org`	

These documents are also retrievable via e-mail to `rfc-info@isi.edu`. Simply put the words "help: help" in the body of your message to retrieve full instructions for both e-mail and ftp access.

To start, the reader should use anonymous FTP to connect to `ftp.isi.edu`, then retrieve the following files from the "`in-notes`" directory.

`rfc1661.txt`	`rfc1662.txt`	
`rfc1332.txt`	`rfc1334.txt`	`rfc-index.txt`

See Appendix A for a list of other RFCs you may want to read. Current protocol numbers are available from `http://www.iana.org/`. (Ignore the "Assigned

Numbers" RFC 1700; this is out of date.) All current RFCs are also on the accompanying CD-ROM.

UUNET maintains a secondary archive with an extensive collection of documents. The archive list is `ftp://ftp.uu.net/archive/inet/ls-lR.Z`.

Current Internet Draft documents are available from `ftp://ftp.ietf.org/internet-drafts/`. The Microsoft proprietary extensions are available from `ftp://ftp.microsoft.com/developr/rfc/`.

InfoMagic (11950 N. Highway 89, Flagstaff, AZ 86004, USA) publishes CD-ROMs containing source code as well as RFCs and other documents. Call +1-520-526-9565. The Web site is at `http://www.infomagic.com`.

Official Standards Organizations

A variety of governmental and professional organizations set standards for telecommunications equipment, including devices running PPP. Unlike the IETF, most of these organizations charge for membership and for document access.

- The International Telecommunications Union (ITU), a UN organization.

  `http://www.itu.int/`

- The International Organization for Standardization (ISO).

  `http://www.iso.ch/`

- European Telecommunications Standards Institute (ETSI).

  `http://www.etsi.org/`

- The American National Standards Institute (ANSI).

  `http://www.ansi.org/`

- The Electronic Industries Association (EIA).

  `http://www.eia.org/`

- Institute of Electrical and Electronics Engineers (IEEE).

  `http://www.ieee.org/`

All of the official documents can be conveniently ordered from Global Engineering Documents, 15 Iverness Way, Englewood, CO 80112-5704. Call +1-303-397-7956 or, in the United States or Canada, 800-854-7179. The Web site is at `http://www.ihsengineering.com/`.

A handy searchable index of U.S. Federal Communications Commission (FCC) rules and regulations is at `http://www.hallikainen.com/FccRules/`. The official FCC Web site is at `http://www.fcc.gov/`, and most official U.S. documents (including FCC rules) can be found at `http://www.gpo.gov/`.

Other Standards Organizations

These other groups focus on ITU-related protocols. Some allow easier access to relevant documentation than do the official groups.

- The Frame Relay Forum (FRF).

  `http://www.frforum.com/`

- The Asynchronous Transfer Mode Forum (ATMF).

  `http://www.atmforum.com/`

- The Optical Internetworking Forum (OIF).

  `http://www.oiforum.com/`

- Access Technologies Forum (ACTEF; previously known as VIA).

  `http://www.actef.org/`

Help Sites

- Livingston/Lucent PortMaster "PPP Decoder Ring."

  `http://www.livingston.com/Tech/Support/dring.html`

- Livingston/Lucent Java-based PPP decoder.

  `http://www.livingston.com/tech/docs/release/pppdecoder.html`

- PPP tips for SGI from an SGI employee.

  `http://reality.sgi.com/scotth/dialup-support.html`

- PPP tips for SGI from a user.

  `http://www.mindspring.com/~sholben/`

- Linux PPP FAQs from RedHat.

  `http://www.redhat.com/support/docs/tips/Dialup-Tips/`
  `    Dialup-Tips.html`
  `http://www.redhat.com/support/docs/tips/PPP-Client-Tips/`
  `    PPP-Client-Tips.html`

- The Linux PPP how-to document.

  `http://metalab.unc.edu/mdw/HOWTO/PPP-HOWTO.html`

- Jonathan Marsden's Linux PPP troubleshooting checklist.

  `http://www.xc.org/jonathan/linux/linux-ppp-setup.txt`

- Bill Unruh's "How to Hook up PPP in Linux" FAQ.

  `http://axion.physics.ubc.ca/ppp-linux.html`

- Setting up callback on Linux.

  `http://www.icce.rug.nl/docs/programs/callback/callback.html`

- "Pedantic PPP Primer" for FreeBSD.

  `http://www.freebsd.org/tutorials/ppp/ppp.html`

- Solaris PPP "how-to."

  `http://photon.nepean.uws.edu.au/ppp/ppp.html`

- Solaris 2.X FAQ.

  `http://www.wins.uva.nl/pub/solaris/solaris2.html`

- Sun's Solaris AnswerBook documentation.

  `http://docs.sun.com/`

- Solaris to Demon (UK) connection instructions.

  `http://www.firstalt.co.uk/drive/_suntodemon.html`

- Khalid Aziz' Solaris dial-up instructions.

  `http://www.info2000.net/~aziz/solaris/ppp.html`

- IBM's AIX Hints and Tips.

  `http://service.software.ibm.com/rs6k/techdocs`

- Cisco's IOS configuration manual.

  `http://www.cisco.com/univercd/cc/td/doc/`

- Bay/Nortel server documentation.

  `http://support.baynetworks.com/library/tpubs`

- Bay/Nortel ISP help page, mail archive; includes 5399 modem settings.

  `http://bay-isp.bit.net.au/rindex.php3`

- MacOS Networking.

  ```
  http://developer.apple.com/macos/opentransport/
  ```

- Coping with MS Windows Dial-Up Networking (DUN).

  ```
  http://www.annoyances.org/win95/dun.html
  ```

- Pages of pointers to TCP/IP information.

  ```
  http://www.private.org.il/tcpip_rl.html
  http://www.faqs.org/faqs/internet/tcp-ip/resource-list/
  ftp://rtfm.mit.edu/pub/usenet-by-group/news.answers/
      internet/tcp-ip/resource-list
  ftp://rtfm.mit.edu/pub/usenet-by-hierarchy/comp/protocols/
      tcp-ip/TCP_IP_Resources_List
  ```

- A comprehensive guide to CRCs by Ross Williams.

  ```
  http://www.geocities.com/SiliconValley/Pines/8659/crc.htm
  ```

- A guide to HDLC framing by Markus Kuhn.

  ```
  ftp://ftp.informatik.uni-erlangen.de/pub/doc/ISO/async-HDLC
  ```

USENET News Groups

Before posting or e-mailing a question anywhere, please read the list of Frequently Asked Questions (FAQ) for PPP and for the group. Many of the folks on the Internet can be quite abrupt if the question you are asking has already been answered many times. The FAQ lists for most USENET groups are archived at MIT. The FTP server is `ftp://rtfm.mit.edu/pub/usenet-by-group/`. In this directory you will find a single subdirectory for each USENET group; a copy of the FAQ list for each group is kept in those subdirectories.

To access newsgroups, you should use the news server provided by your ISP. This is usually an NNTP server located at address news.yourisp.com. If your ISP does not provide a news server, you might use one of the public news sites, such as `http://www.deja.com/`.

comp.protocols.ppp

This is the main PPP news group. If you have questions about PPP in general, this is the place to turn. This is not the right place to ask questions about networking problems or about application programs, so if your e-mail program or browser is not working right over PPP, look for a different group. A Web version of the FAQ for this group is kept at `http://www.faqs.org/faqs/ppp-faq/part1/index.html`, and a slightly more readable version is kept at `http://cs.uni-bonn.de/ppp/faq.html`.

comp.protocols.tcp-ip

This is the main TCP/IP discussion group. Of course, PPP supports many more protocols than just TCP/IP, but this is an important enough use that many folks debugging PPP problems end up here.

comp.dcom.servers

This is the group for discussing data communications servers. If you have a problem with your IPX file server or Microsoft DCOM system, you need to post your question elsewhere, but if you are using terminal servers or communications servers, this is the right place.

comp.dcom.frame-relay

comp.dcom.cell-relay

comp.dcom.isdn

comp.dcom.modems

comp.dcom.xdsl

These groups are all related to link-layer technologies that can use PPP.

comp.os.linux.networking

This group is dedicated to the Linux operating system networking features. Linux is a free Unix-like implementation available at many FTP sites and runs on several platforms, including IBM PC compatibles, DEC ALPHA RISC, and Apple PowerPC systems.

comp.os.ms-windows.networking.ras

This group discusses the Remote Access Services for Microsoft Windows. This should be the first place to turn if you have problems with the PPP implementation that comes with Windows.

comp.os.ms-windows.nt.admin.networking

This is for administrators of Windows-NT networks. Administrators of sites using the NT PPP implementation should follow this group.

comp.os.os2.networking.misc

This is the IBM OS/2 networking group.

comp.unix.*

For most Unix systems, the vendor's newsgroup is the right place to ask questions about the vendor's implementation of PPP. For instance, IBM's AIX is covered by `comp.unix.aix`.

Meetings and Mailing Lists

Internet Engineering Task Force

The IETF holds a week-long meeting approximately once every four months. The meetings are open to anyone interested in the standards process, although a registration fee is required. To be notified of upcoming IETF events, send a subscription request to `ietf-announce-request@ietf.org`.

No fee is charged for participating in the group itself through the various e-mail lists. The work of the IETF is conducted on the mailing lists, not at the IETF meetings, so it is not necessary to attend these meetings to be a part of the standards-setting process. Many people who are very active in the standards process by way of the mailing lists have never been to an IETF meeting.

pppext

This is the IETF's PPP extensions working group. The working group charter is available at `http://www.ietf.org/html.charters/pppext-charter.html`.

The official working group mailing list, ietf-ppp, discusses issues related to the PPP protocol for developers. If you are developing a PPP implementation or want to listen in on the discussions that go on during development of new protocols, send your subscription request to `ietf-ppp-request@merit.edu`. The mailing list archives are located at `ftp://ftp.merit.edu/mail.archives/ietf-ppp-archive/`.

Do not post inappropriate questions to this list, such as those that relate to specific implementations, user-level interfaces, or troubleshooting. This is not the purpose of this mailing list, and the responses you get will probably be much less helpful than you would imagine.

l2tpext

This is the IETF's L2TP extensions working group. The charter is at `http://www.ietf.org/html.charters/l2tpext-charter.html`, the mailing list is at lt2p-request@ipsec.org, and the mailing list archive is at `http://www.zendo.com/vandys/l2tp-mail` (up to February 1, 1999) and `http://www.ipsec.org/email/l2tp/` (from February 1 through November 11, 1999). Unfortunately, no known archives exist beyond this point.

Bake-offs

Bake-offs are informal get-togethers of the implementors of the IETF protocols. They are organized and announced on the mailing lists for the various working groups. In a bake-off, preproduction code for new protocols is tested between the participating implementors in order to shake out compatibility problems and specification errors. These meetings are generally not as open as the IETF meetings and are intended for active developers only.

One frequently organized bake-off is primarily for ISDN-based implementations of PPP that include MP and BACP. This is sponsored by PacBell in California.

NetWorld/Interop

NetWorld/Interop is a major networking trade show that is run about twice a year. This is a marketing and sales show; most of the attendees are the people who will buy the products. Demonstrations of new products are done at Interop, but these are not testing events for developers. The Web site is `http://www.interop.com/`.

Publicly Available Source Code

PPP Implementations

The best-known implementation of PPP for Unix systems is ppp-2.3. It runs on a wide variety of systems and is available from `ftp://cs.anu.edu.au/pub/software/ppp/` and newer versions from `ftp://linuxcare.com.au/pub/ppp`. A modified version for NeXTSTEP machines is at `http://www.peak.org/next/ppp/`.

Dp, which runs on only SunOS and Solaris systems, is a demand-dialing version of pppd. It is available from `http://www.ces.purdue.edu/dp/`.

Another freely available implementation is "iij-ppp," which runs only on older HP-UX systems. More information is available from `http://www.interex.org/~borg/ppp.html`.

Phil Karn wrote an IBM PC-based PPP implementation called "ka9q" (named after his ham radio call sign). It has been ported to other small computers, such as the Atari, by many volunteers. One copy of this implementation is at `ftp://ftp.fu-berlin.de/pc/msdos/network/ka9q/`. You can fetch the original from `http://people.qualcomm.com/karn/code/ka9qnos/`.

Related Sources

Several MP implementations exist, including mpd on FreeBSD at `ftp://ftp.whistle.com/pub/archie/mpd` and patches for pppd on Linux at `http://linux-mp.terz.de/` and `ftp://ftp.east.telecom.kz/pub/src/networking/ppp/multilink/`.

SGI has made working Predictor-1 source code available on their ftp site at `ftp://ftp.sgi.com/other/ppp-comp/predictor1.c`.

A DES library (called "libdes-3.06") for implementing MS-CHAP is available from `ftp://ftp.psy.uq.oz.au/pub/Crypto/DES/`.

Patches to pppd's authentication mechanisms to support TACACS+ are available from `http://ceti.com.pl/~kravietz/progs/tacacs.html`.

Support for Microsoft's proprietary PPTP on Linux in client mode is available at `http://www.pdos.lcs.mit.edu/~cananian/Projects/PPTP/`. Server mode is `http://www.moretonbay.com/vpn/pptp.html`. Before you use either, however, you should read `http://www.counterpane.com/pptp.html`.

An archive of the old SLIP implementation for BSD with VJ compression is at `ftp://ftp.ee.lbl.gov/cslip-2.7.tar.Z`.

Other important free source sites include `http://www.gnu.org/`, `ftp://ftp.gnu.org/pub/gnu/`, `ftp://ftp.x.org/pub/`, `http://www.netbsd.org/`, `http://www.freebsd.org/`, `http://www.openbsd.org/`, `http://www.linux.org/`, and `http://www.debian.org/`.

Binary-only Software

PPP Implementations

Free implementations for MS-DOS-based PCs are available at `ftp://ftp.simtel.net/pub/simtelnet/msdos/pktdrvr/dosppp05.zip` and `http://mvmpc9.ciw.uni-karlsruhe.de/c:/user/toni/dosppp/`.

Shareware and demonstration drivers for PCs are also available from Klos Technologies at `http://www.klos.com/`.

FreePPP for Macintosh computers based on MacPPP 2.0.3 from Merit is available from Rockstar Studios (which also sells a development kit for PPP experimenters) at `http://www.rockstar.com/ppp.shtml`.

AccessPPP for Macintosh computers based on Merit's MacPPP 2.0.1 is available from `http://www.bekkoame.or.jp/~kkudo/`.

Related Software

A Windows 95 "null modem" driver for using PPP between directly connected machines is available from `http://www.mindspring.com/~kewells/net/`.

A collection of PPP-related software for the HP200LX is at `http://lxtcp.hplx.net/`.

Several different PPP implementations for the Macintosh are available from `http://www.macorchard.com/connect.html`.

Commercial Sources

Klos Technologies, Inc. (12 Jewett Ave, Cortland, NY 13045-2057, USA) makes both PPP drivers for IBM-compatible PCs and PC-based asynchronous and ISDN PPP analyzers, and can license PPP implementations for use in other systems. Phone +1-607-753-0568, fax +1-561-828-6397, e-mail `sales@klos.com`, or visit the Web site at `http://www.klos.com/`.

TechSmith makes the Foray PPP server for MS-DOS-based PCs. Call +1-517-333-2100, fax +1-517-333-1888, e-mail `sales@techsmith.com`, or visit `http://www.techsmith.com/`.

Morningstar PPP, a very well-known commercial implementation of PPP and SLIP for most Unix systems, is available from Progressive Systems. Call +1-614-326-4600 or visit `http://www.progressive-systems.com/`.

Hi/fn licenses STAC and MS-PPC compression algorithms for CCP and makes compression and encryption hardware. Call +1-408-399-3500 or visit `http://www.hifn.com/`.

GN Nettest (the former Azure Technologies) makes the WinPharaoh analyzer. Visit their Web site at `http://www.azure-tech.com/`. Another popular analyzer is the Sniffer TNV from Network Associates; visit `http://www.nai.com/` for more information.

The ANVL test suite from Midnight Networks (now Hammer Technologies) is helpful for doing automated testing of PPP implementations. Visit the Web site at `http://www.midnight.com/`, phone +1-978-694-9959, fax +1-978-988-0148, e-mail `info@midnight.com`, or write 205 Lowell Street, Wilmington, MA 01887-2941, USA.

Other Resources

Several large reference lists exist, including:

`http://people.ne.mediaone.net/carlson/ppp/reference.html`

`http://www.stokely.com/unix.serial.port.resources/ppp.slip.html`

```
http://oh3tr.ele.tut.fi/~oh3fg/ppp/ppp.html

http://www.cs.utk.edu/~shuford/computing_tech.html

http://www.townsley.net/l2tp.html

http://wwwpub.utdallas.edu/~cantrell/ee6345/resources.html

http://www.fdisk.com/doslynx/
```

The "Calgary Corpus" is a body of text files that are standard benchmarks for compression performance. If you are implementing or testing CCP, you will proably want to have these files for reference. They are available from `ftp://ftp.cpsc.ucalgary.ca/pub/projects/text.compression.corpus/`.

The League for Programming Freedom helps protect the rights of individual programmers against the power of corporate software "patenting," "look and feel" copyrights, and other legal issues. For more information, visit `http://lpf.ai.mit.edu/`.

The Free Software Foundation coordinates the production and distribution of GNU and other free software. For more information, visit `http://www.fsf.org/`, e-mail `gnu@prep.ai.mit.edu`, call +1-617-542-5942, or write the Free Software Foundation, Incorporated, 59 Temple Place, Suite 330, Boston, MA 02111-1307, USA.

I am registered with Network Solutions as handle JC6738. My current e-mail and mailing addresses are available by running one of these commands (depending on the whois variant you're using):

```
whois -h whois.networksolutions.com 'handle jc6738'
whois 'handle jc6738'@whois.networksolutions.com
```

Or, if this is not available or doesn't work on your system due to the recent whois server changes, try using the GeekTools interface:

```
http://whois.geektools.com/cgi-bin/proxy.cgi
```

Due to the volume of mail, I regret that not all questions can be answered directly.

Appendix A
Cross-References

(continued)

TABLE A.1   (*cont.*)

Hex Value	Description	RFC	Page
0053	Encryption	1968	196
0055	Link-Level encryption	1968	196
0057	Internet Protocol version 6 (IPv6)	2472	155
0059	PPP Muxing	—	92
0061	IPHC Full Header	2509	130
0063	IPHC Compressed TCP	2509	130
0065	IPHC Compressed non-TCP	2509	130
0067	CRTP Compressed UDP 8	2509	130
0069	CRTP Compressed RTP 8	2509	130
0073	Ascend MP+	1934	227
00C1	Simple Transportation Management Framework (STMF)	—	156
00FB	Link-Level compression	1962	177
00FD	Compression	1962	177
0201	802.1D Hello	1638	148
0203	IBM Source Routing PDU	1638	148
0205	DEC LANBridge 100 Spanning Tree	1638	148
0207	Cisco Discovery Protocol (CDP)	—	—
0281	Multiprotocol Label Switching (MPLS)	—	157
0283	Multiprotocol Label Switching (MPLS) multicast	—	157
2063	IPHC Compressed TCP No Delta	2509	130
2065	CRTP Context State	2509	130
2067	CRTP Compressed UDP 16	2509	130
2069	CRTP Compressed RTP 16	2509	130
4021	STAC LZS	1974	185
8021	Internet Protocol Control Protocol (IPCP)	1332	128
8023	OSI Network Layer Control Protocol (OSINLCP)	1377	134
8025	XNS Control Protocol (XNSCP)	1764	135
8027	DECNet Phase IV Control Protocol (DNCP)	1762	136
8029	AppleTalk Control Protocol (ATCP)	1378	136
802B	IPX Control Protocol (IPXCP)	1552	140
8031	Bridging Control Protocol (BCP)	1638	144
8035	Banyan Vines Control Protocol (BVCP)	1763	149

Hex Value	Description	RFC	Page
803F	NetBIOS Frames Control Protocol (NBFCP)	2097	151
8041	Cisco LAN Extension (LEX)	1841	—
8049	• Serial Data Control Protocol (SDCP)	1963	152
804B	SNA over 802.2 Control Protocol	2043	155
804D	SNA Control Protocol (SNACP)	2043	155
8053	Encryption Control Protocol (ECP)	1968	196
8055	Link-level Encryption Control Protocol	1968	196
8057	IPv6 Control Protocol (IPV6CP)	2472	155
8073	MP+ Control Protocol	1934	227
80C1	STMF Control Protocol (STMFCP)	—	156
80FB	Link-level Compression Control Protocol	1962	177
80FD	Compression Control Protocol (CCP)	1962	177
8207	Cisco Discovery Protocol Control Protocol (CDPCP)	—	—
8281	MPLS Control Protocol (MPLSCP)	—	157
C021	Link Control Protocol (LCP)	1661	72
C023	Password Authentication Protocol (PAP)	1334	96
C025	Link Quality Report (LQR)	1989	77
C027	Shiva Password Authentication Protocol (SPAP)	—	117
C029	Microsoft Callback Control Protocol (CBCP)	—	233
C02B	Bandwidth Allocation Control Protocol (BACP)	2125	228
C02D	Bandwidth Allocation Protocol (BAP)	2125	228
C223	Challenge Handshake Authentication Protocol (CHAP)	1994	101
C227	Extensible Authentication Protocol	2284	115

TABLE A.2   PPP Option Number Cross-Reference
(Allocated but Unused Codes Omitted)

Hex Value	Description	RFC	Page
	LCP Options		
00	Vendor Extensions	2153	72
01	Maximum Receive Unit (MRU)	1661	73
02	Asynchronous Control Character Map (ACCM)	1662	75
03	Authentication Protocol	1661	76

(*continued*)

TABLE A.2   (*cont.*)

Hex Value	Description	RFC	Page
04	Quality Protocol	1661	77
05	Magic Number	1661	78
07	Protocol Field Compression (PFC)	1661	79
08	Address and Control Field Compression (ACFC)	1661	81
09	FCS Alternatives	1570	82
0A	Self-Describing Pad (SDP)	1570	83
0B	Numbered Mode	1663	84
0D	Callback	1570	86
0F	Compound Frames	1570	87
11	Multilink Maximum Reconstructed Receive Unit (MRRU)	1990	211
12	Multilink Short Sequence Number Header Format	1990	212
13	Multilink Endpoint Discriminator (ED)	1990	213
15	DCE Identifier	1976	89
16	Multi-Link-Plus Procedure (MP+)	1934	89
17	Link Discriminator	2125	228
1A	Prefix Elision	2686	91
1B	Multilink Header Format	2686	91
1C	Internationalization	2484	92
1D	Simple Data Link (SDL)	2823	92
1E	PPP Muxing	—	92
IPCP Options			
01	IP Addresses	1172	128
02	IP Compression Protocol	1332	129
03	IP Address	1332	131
04	Mobile IPv4	2290	131
81	Primary DNS Address	1877	132
82	Primary NBNS Address	1877	132
83	Secondary DNS Address	1877	132
84	Secondary NBNS Address	1877	132
OSINLCP Options			
01	Align NPDU	1377	135

Hex Value	Description	RFC	Page
	ATCP Options		
01	AppleTalk Address	1378	137
02	Routing Protocol	1378	138
03	Suppress Broadcast	1378	138
06	Server Information	1378	139
07	Zone Information	1378	140
08	Default Router Address	1378	140
	IPXCP Options		
01	IPX Network Number	1552	141
02	IPX Node Number	1552	142
03	IPX Compression Protocol	1552	142
04	IPX Routing Protocol	1552	143
05	IPX Router Name	1552	143
06	IPX Configuration Complete	1552	144
	BCP Options		
01	Bridge Identification	1638	145
02	Line Identification	1638	145
03	MAC Support	1638	146
04	Tinygram Compression	1638	147
05	LAN Identification	1638	147
06	MAC Address	1638	147
07	Spanning Tree Protocol	1638	148
08	IEEE 802 Tagged Frame	—	149
09	Management Inline	—	149
	BVCP Options		
01	NS RTP Link Type	1763	150
02	Fragmentation (FRP)	1763	150
03	Suppress Routing Updates (RTP)	1763	150
04	Suppress Broadcast	1763	150
	NBFCP Options		
01	Name Projection	2097	151
02	Peer Information	2097	152

(continued)

TABLE A.2   (*cont.*)

Hex Value	Description	RFC	Page
03	Multicast Filtering	2097	152
04	IEEE MAC Address Required	2097	152
	SDCP Options		
01	Packet Format	1963	153
02	Header Type	1963	153
03	Length Field Present	1963	153
04	Multi-Port	1963	154
05	Transport Mode	1963	154
06	Maximum Frame Size	1963	154
07	Allow Odd Frames	1963	154
08	FCS Type	1963	154
09	Flow Expiration Time	1963	155
	IPV6CP Options		
01	Interface Token	2472	156
02	IPv6 Compression Protocol	2509	156

TABLE A.3   PPP RFCs
(In Numeric Order; Obsolete Versions not Listed)

RFC	Title	Page
1332	The PPP Internet Protocol Control Protocol (IPCP)	128
1334	PPP Authentication Protocols	95
1377	The PPP OSI Network Layer Control Protocol (OSINLCP)	134
1378	The PPP AppleTalk Control Protocol (ATCP)	136
1471	The Definitions of Managed Objects for the Link Control Protocol of the Point-to-Point Protocol	35
1472	The Definitions of Managed Objects for the Security Protocols of the Point-to-Point Protocol	35
1473	The Definitions of Managed Objects for the IP Network Control Protocol of the Point-to-Point Protocol	35
1474	The Definitions of Managed Objects for the Bridge Network Control Protocol of the Point-to-Point Protocol	35
1552	The PPP Internetworking Packet Exchange Control Protocol (IPXCP)	140

(continued)

TABLE A.3   *(cont.)*

RFC	Title	Page
1994	PPP Challenge Handshake Authentication Protocol (CHAP)	101
2043	The PPP SNA Control Protocol (SNACP)	155
2097	The PPP NetBIOS Frames Control Protocol (NBFCP)	151
2118	Microsoft Point-To-Point Compression (MPPC) Protocol	188
2125	The PPP Bandwidth Allocation Protocol (BAP)/ The PPP Bandwidth Allocation Control Protocol (BACP)	228
2153	PPP Vendor Extensions	71
2284	PPP Extensible Authentication Protocol (EAP)	115
2341	Cisco Layer Two Forwarding (L2F)	242
2363	PPP Over FUNI	30
2364	PPP Over AAL5	29
2419	The PPP DES Encryption Protocol, Version 2 (DESE-bis)	199
2420	The PPP Triple-DES Encryption Protocol (3DESE)	198
2433	Microsoft PPP CHAP Extensions (MS-CHAPv1)	111
2472	IP Version 6 over PPP	155
2484	PPP LCP Internationalization Configuration Option	92
2509	IP Header Compression over PPP	130
2516	Method for Transmitting PPP Over Ethernet (PPPoE)	245
2615	PPP over SONET/SDH	24
2637	Point-to-Point Tunneling Protocol (PPTP)	243
2661	Layer Two Tunneling Protocol (L2TP)	243
2686	The Multi-Class Extension to Multi-Link PPP	91
2687	PPP in a Real-time Oriented HDLC-like Framing	91
2701	Nortel's Multi-link Multi-node PPP Bundle Discovery	223
2716	PPP EAP TLS Authentication Protocol	115
2759	Microsoft PPP CHAP Extensions (MS-CHAPv2)	113
2823	PPP over Simple Data Link (SDL) using SONET/SDH with ATM-like framing	92

TABLE A.4   PPP RFCs
(Grouped by Function)

RFC	Title	Page
	Basic PPP	
1661	The Point-to-Point Protocol (PPP)	6
1662	PPP in HDLC-like Framing	16
	LCP	
1471	The Definitions of Managed Objects for the Link Control Protocol of the Point-to-Point Protocol	35
1570	PPP LCP Extensions	69
1663	PPP Reliable Transmission	84
1989	PPP Link Quality Monitoring	77
2153	PPP Vendor Extensions	71
2484	PPP LCP Internationalization Configuration Option	92
	Authentication	
1334	PPP Authentication Protocols	95
1472	The Definitions of Managed Objects for the Security Protocols of the Point-to-Point Protocol	35
1994	PPP Challenge Handshake Authentication Protocol (CHAP)	101
2284	PPP Extensible Authentication Protocol (EAP)	115
2433	Microsoft PPP CHAP Extensions (MS-CHAPv1)	111
2716	PPP EAP TLS Authentication Protocol	115
2759	Microsoft PPP CHAP Extensions (MS-CHAPv2)	113
	Network Protocols	
1332	The PPP Internet Protocol Control Protocol (IPCP)	128
1377	The PPP OSI Network Layer Control Protocol (OSINLCP)	134
1378	The PPP AppleTalk Control Protocol (ATCP)	136
1473	The Definitions of Managed Objects for the IP Network Control Protocol of the Point-to-Point Protocol	35
1474	The Definitions of Managed Objects for the Bridge Network Control Protocol of the Point-to-Point Protocol	35
1552	The PPP Internetworking Packet Exchange Control Protocol (IPXCP)	140
1553	Compressing IPX Headers Over WAN Media (CIPX)	142
1634	Novell IPX Over Various WAN Media (IPXWAN)	141

(continued)

TABLE A.4   *(cont.)*

RFC	Title	Page
1638	PPP Bridging Control Protocol (BCP)	144
1762	The PPP DECnet Phase IV Control Protocol (DNCP)	136
1763	The PPP Banyan Vines Control Protocol (BVCP)	149
1764	The PPP XNS IDP Control Protocol (XNSCP)	135
1841	PPP Network Control Protocol for LAN Extension	—
1877	PPP Internet Protocol Control Protocol Extensions for Name Server Addresses	132
1963	PPP Serial Data Transport Protocol (SDTP)	152
2043	The PPP SNA Control Protocol (SNACP)	155
2097	The PPP NetBIOS Frames Control Protocol (NBFCP)	151
2472	IP Version 6 over PPP	155
2509	IP Header Compression over PPP	130
	Special Media	
1598	PPP in X.25	31
1618	PPP over ISDN	24
1973	PPP in Frame Relay	29
2363	PPP Over FUNI	30
2364	PPP Over AAL5	29
2615	PPP over SONET/SDH	24
2823	PPP over Simple Data Link (SDL) using SONET/SDH with ATM-like framing	92
	Compression and Encryption	
1915	Variance for The PPP Connection Control Protocol and The PPP Encryption Control Protocol	170
1962	The PPP Compression Control Protocol (CCP)	177
1967	PPP LZS-DCP Compression Protocol (LZS-DCP)	192
1968	The PPP Encryption Control Protocol (ECP)	196
1969	The PPP DES Encryption Protocol (DESE)	197
1974	PPP Stac LZS Compression Protocol	185
1975	PPP Magnalink Variable Resource Compression	193
1976	PPP for Data Compression in Data Circuit-Terminating Equipment (DCE)	89
1977	PPP BSD Compression Protocol	191

Appendix B
Decimal, Hexadecimal, Octal, and Standard Characters

Dec	Hex	Oct	ANSI C0
0	00	000	NUL
1	01	001	SOH
2	02	002	STX
3	03	003	ETX
4	04	004	EOT
5	05	005	ENQ
6	06	006	ACK
7	07	007	BEL
8	08	010	BS
9	09	011	HT
10	0A	012	LF
11	0B	013	VT
12	0C	014	FF
13	0D	015	CR
14	0E	016	SO
15	0F	017	SI
16	10	020	DLE
17	11	021	DC1
18	12	022	DC2
19	13	023	DC3
20	14	024	DC4
21	15	025	NAK
22	16	026	SYN
23	17	027	ETB

Dec	Hex	Oct	
24	18	030	CAN
25	19	031	EM
26	1A	032	SUB
27	1B	033	ESC
28	1C	034	FS
29	1D	035	GS
30	1E	036	RS
31	1F	037	US

Dec	Hex	Oct	ASCII
32	20	040	SP
33	21	041	!
34	22	042	"
35	23	043	#
36	24	044	$
37	25	045	%
38	26	046	&
39	27	047	'
40	28	050	(
41	29	051	)
42	2A	052	*
43	2B	053	+
44	2C	054	,
45	2D	055	-
46	2E	056	.

Dec	Hex	Oct	
47	2F	057	/
48	30	060	0
49	31	061	1
50	32	062	2
51	33	063	3
52	34	064	4
53	35	065	5
54	36	066	6
55	37	067	7
56	38	070	8
57	39	071	9
58	3A	072	:
59	3B	073	;
60	3C	074	<
61	3D	075	=
62	3E	076	>
63	3F	077	?
64	40	100	@
65	41	101	A
66	42	102	B
67	43	103	C
68	44	104	D
69	45	105	E
70	46	106	F
71	47	107	G
72	48	110	H

Dec	Hex	Oct	Char
73	49	111	I
74	4A	112	J
75	4B	113	K
76	4C	114	L
77	4D	115	M
78	4E	116	N
79	4F	117	O
80	50	120	P
81	51	121	Q
82	52	122	R
83	53	123	S
84	54	124	T
85	55	125	U
86	56	126	V
87	57	127	W
88	58	130	X
89	59	131	Y
90	5A	132	Z
91	5B	133	[
92	5C	134	\
93	5D	135	]
94	5E	136	^
95	5F	137	_
96	60	140	'
97	61	141	a
98	62	142	b
99	63	143	c
100	64	144	d
101	65	145	e
102	66	146	f
103	67	147	g
104	68	150	h
105	69	151	i
106	6A	152	j
107	6B	153	k
108	6C	154	l
109	6D	155	m
110	6E	156	n
111	6F	157	o
112	70	160	p
113	71	161	q
114	72	162	r
115	73	163	s
116	74	164	t
117	75	165	u
118	76	166	v
119	77	167	w
120	78	170	x
121	79	171	y
122	7A	172	z
123	7B	173	{
124	7C	174	|
125	7D	175	}
126	7E	176	~
127	7F	177	DEL

Dec	Hex	Oct	ANSI C1
128	80	200	PAD
129	81	201	HOP
130	82	202	BPH
131	83	203	NBH
132	84	204	IND
133	85	205	NEL
134	86	206	SSA
135	87	207	ESA
136	88	210	HTS
137	89	211	HTJ
138	8A	212	VTS
139	8B	213	PLD
140	8C	214	PLU
141	8D	215	RI
142	8E	216	SS2
143	8F	217	SS3
144	90	220	DCS
145	91	221	PU1
146	92	222	PU2
147	93	223	STS
148	94	224	CCH
149	95	225	MW
150	96	226	SPA
151	97	227	EPA
152	98	230	SOS
153	99	231	SGCI
154	9A	232	SCI
155	9B	233	CSI
156	9C	234	ST
157	9D	235	OSC
158	9E	236	PM
159	9F	237	APC

Dec	Hex	Oct	ISO 8859/1.2
160	A0	240	NBS
161	A1	241	invert !
162	A2	242	cent
163	A3	243	Pound
164	A4	244	currency
165	A5	245	Yen
166	A6	246	vertical bar
167	A7	247	section
168	A8	250	diaeresis
169	A9	251	copyright
170	AA	252	fem. ordinal
171	AB	253	<<
172	AC	254	not
173	AD	255	-
174	AE	256	registered
175	AF	257	macron/overbar
176	B0	260	degree
177	B1	261	+/-
178	B2	262	super 2
179	B3	263	super 3
180	B4	264	acute
181	B5	265	micro
182	B6	266	para./pilcro
183	B7	267	middle dot
184	B8	270	cedilla
185	B9	271	super 1
186	BA	272	masc ordinal
187	BB	273	>>
188	BC	274	1/4
189	BD	275	1/2
190	BE	276	3/4
191	BF	277	invert ?
192	C0	300	A grave
193	C1	301	A acute
194	C2	302	A circum
195	C3	303	A tilde
196	C4	304	A umlaut
197	C5	305	A ring
198	C6	306	AE ligature

199	C7	307	C cedilla	218	DA	332	U acute	237	ED	355	i acute
200	C8	310	E grave	219	DB	333	U circum	238	EE	356	i circum
201	C9	311	E acute	220	DC	334	U umlaut	239	EF	357	i umlaut
202	CA	312	E circum	221	DD	335	Y acute	240	F0	360	eth
203	CB	313	E umlaut	222	DE	336	Thorn	241	F1	361	n tilde
204	CC	314	I grave	223	DF	337	Ess-tzet	242	F2	362	o grave
205	CD	315	I acute	224	E0	340	a grave	243	F3	363	o acute
206	CE	316	I circum	225	E1	341	a acute	244	F4	364	o circum
207	CF	317	I umlaut	226	E2	342	a circum	245	F5	365	o tilde
208	D0	320	Eth	227	E3	343	a tilde	246	F6	366	o umlaut
209	D1	321	N tilde	228	E4	344	a umlaut	247	F7	367	divide
210	D2	322	O grave	229	E5	345	a ring	248	F8	370	o slash
211	D3	323	O acute	230	E6	346	ae ligature	249	F9	371	u grave
212	D4	324	O circum	231	E7	347	c cedilla	250	FA	372	u acute
213	D5	325	O tilde	232	E8	350	e grave	251	FB	373	u circum
214	D6	326	O umlaut	233	E9	351	e acute	252	FC	374	u umlaut
215	D7	327	multiply	234	EA	352	e circum	253	FD	375	y acute
216	D8	330	O slash	235	EB	353	e umlaut	254	FE	376	thorn
217	D9	331	U grave	236	EC	354	i grave				

Index

CD-ROM Warranty

Addison-Wesley warrants the enclosed disc to be free of defects in materials and faulty workmanship under normal use for a period of ninety days after purchase. If a defect is discovered in the disc during this warranty period, a replacement disc can be obtained at no charge by sending the defective disc, postage prepaid, with proof of purchase to:

Editorial Department
Addison-Wesley Professional
Pearson Technology Group
75 Arlington Street, Suite 300
Boston, MA 02116
e-mail: AWPro@awl.com

After the ninety-day period, a replacement disc will be sent upon receipt of the defective disc and a check or money order for $10.00 payable to Addison-Wesley.

Addison-Wesley and James Carlson make no warranty or representation, either expressed or implied, with respect to this software, its quality, performance, merchantability, or fitness for a particular purpose. In no event will James Carlson or Addison-Wesley, its distributors, or dealers be liable for direct, indirect, special, incidental, or consequential damages arising out of the use or inability to use the software. The exclusion of implied warranties is not permitted in some states. Therefore, the above exclusion may not apply to you. This warranty provides you with specific legal rights. There may be other rights that you may have that vary from state to state. The contents of this CD-ROM are intended for personal use only.

More information and updates are available at:

http://www.awl.com/cseng/titles/0-201-70053-0